The Illustrated Life of

JESUS

The Illustrated Life Of
JESUS

HERSCHEL HOBBS

HOLMAN
REFERENCE

Nashville, Tennessee

Executive Editors: David Shepherd, Rick Edwards
Design: Brent Bruce, The Phanco Group

Hobbs, Herschel H.
    The illustrated life of Jesus/by Herschel H. Hobbs and the editors of the Biblical illustrator.
       p. cm.
    ISBN 0-8054-9368-9 (alk. paper)
    1. Jesus Christ--Biography. I. Biblical illustrator. II. Title.

BT 301.2 .H59 2000
232.9'01--dc21
[B]   00-057571

Printed in Korea
1 2 3 4 5 6 04 03 02 01 00
SW

FOREWORD

The Illustrated Life of Jesus is a unique resource, a visual feast that presents the life and teachings of Jesus for the twenty-first century.

The core of the book is a narrative by Herschel Hobbs, one of the leading Christian communicators of the twentieth century. Dr. Hobbs' material appeared originally as *The Life and Times of Jesus* and was published by the Zondervan Corporation in 1966.

Most of the photographs and the in depth articles come from the files of the *Biblical Illustrator*, a quarterly publication that has served Bible teachers and preachers for over 25 years. Every week the *Biblical Illustrator* receives requests for back issues of the magazine.

You can find out a little more about *Biblical Illustrator* at the following web address - *http://www.lifeway.com/bibleinsites/lifework.htm#dirt*. There you will find numerous ways to order the *Biblical Illustrator*.

Unless otherwise noted, Scripture quotations from the Gospels are from the Holman Christian Standard Bible, a contemporary translation of the entire Bible now in progress.

The book contains numerous new maps that Holman Bible Publishers commissioned MapQuest.com to create for the *Holman Bible Atlas* (1999).

May this resource greatly enrich your understanding of and affection for Him, who is the Way, the Truth, and the Life.

Rick Edwards
David R. Shepherd,
Executive Editors

TABLE C

F CONTENTS

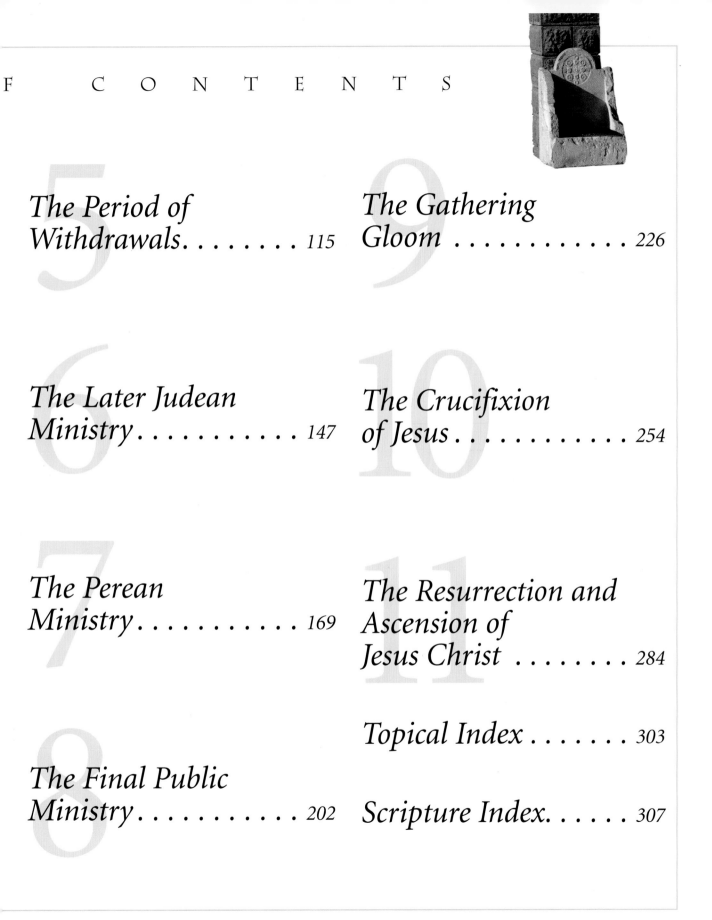

Features of *The Illustrated*

A. A narrative of the life of Jesus by Herschel Hobbs based on A.T. Robertson's *Harmony of the Gospels*.

B. Striking, full color photographs show the places important in Jesus' life.

C. In depth articles from the *Biblical Illustrator* provide historical and cultural information which enhances understanding of the life of Jesus.

A

3. A Question about the Resurrection.

It was the Sadducees' or chief priests' turn again. They did not believe in the resurrection, and so they asked Jesus to solve a problem, probably one of their favorites in their continuing debate with the Pharisees.

Here was their problem. Moses had commanded that if a man died childless his brother should marry his widow and thereby raise up seed unto his brother. Now the Sadducees imagined a case in which there were seven brothers. The first died childless. Then the other six in turn married the widow, each of them also dying without having a child. Finally, the woman herself died. In the resurrection whose wife would she be?

Jesus answered their question by reminding them that they did not even understand their own Scriptures; neither did they know the power of God, for in the resurrection there is no such thing as the institution of marriage. All will be one big family of God.

How did Jesus let them get away with their denial of the resurrection? He cited God's own words, "I am the God of Abraham and the God of Isaac and the God of Jacob" (Matt. 22:32). He did not say, "I was" but "I am." These three patriarchs still lived. So God is not the God of the dead, but of the living.

The Sadducees were silent, but the people were astonished at Jesus' teaching. Naturally the Sadducees were unhappy, but there were some happy people in the crowd. For the scribes (Pharisees) said, "Teacher, You have spoken well" (Luke 20:39). Even if they could not get the better of Jesus, at least He had put the Sadducees in their place, because they did not dare to ask Him any more questions.

4. A Question about Law.

Now the Pharisees must try their hand again. This time they sent one of their experts in the Mosaic Law. He asked Jesus, "Teacher, which commandment in the law is the greatest?" (Matt. 22:36). Or as Mark relates it, "Which commandment is the most important of all?" (12:28). Jesus answered with the words which were dear to every Jewish heart. He quoted the *Shema* (Deut. 6:4–5): "Hear, O Israel! The Lord our God is one Lord. And you shall love the Lord your God with all your heart, with all your soul, with all your mind, and with all your strength. . . . You shall love your neighbor as yourself" (Mark 12:29–31). On these, said Jesus, hang all the law and the prophets.

The lawyer could only compliment Jesus for His answer. In turn Jesus said of the lawyer that he was not far from the kingdom of God. Not far—but not in. It is to be hoped that he did enter the kingdom of God, not through compliments but by faith in Jesus.

B

A seat of judgment possibly from a Jewish synagogue. Jesus said, "The scribes and the Pharisees are seated in the chair of Moses" (Matt. 23:2).

222 *The Illustrated Life of Jesus*

A

word of victory or completion. He wished it to be not the rasping utterance of one who was completely spent. It must be clearly enunciated in order that it might be heard and understood.

There was also a touch of pity in this gruesome scene. A soldier took a sponge and dipped it in the vinegar provided for the Crucifixion detail. Then placing it on a reed, he pressed it to the lips of the Savior.

(6) "It is finished!" (John 19:30).

This was Jesus' word of completion. It means that "it is finished and stands finished." It was a word of full and final completion. Nevermore will Jesus die on a cross. Nevermore will He suffer for the sin of the world. He had made the once-for-all sacrifice. All that was necessary for the Son to do for man's redemption had been accomplished.

The Greek papyri add greatly to the meaning of the word (*tetelestai*). It belongs to a family of words which was used in the legal and commercial life of Jesus' day. One word of this family was used to express the idea of completing a legal deed by dating and signing it. In a very real sense, before the foundation of the world,

---

First-Century Tombs in Judah

Joel F. Drinkard, Jr.

C

The most common type of tomb in Judea in the first century A.D. was the family tomb that could be used by members of an extended family over several generations. Typically, this tomb was a rock-cut, artificial burial cave. Although natural caves were used for burial, and small natural caves may have been enlarged to form some burial caves, the artificial cave cut into rock was more common.

Many of the hillsides near the towns and cities were dotted with these burial caves. The relatively soft limestone common to the region was easily worked with simple cutting tools. Not all burial caves were cut into hillsides. Some were formed by cutting steps down into the bedrock, then cutting a small entrance court, and finally cutting a burial chamber into the vertical wall created by the steps and entrance court. While no general description can cover all the variations of the burial cave, certain

features were common in most of these burial caves.

The burial cave in general was for the wealthier members of society. The poorer people were simply buried in an unmarked pit outside the city. The wealthiest had the largest burial caves, often decorated with a monumental facade cut into the hillside. The burial

B

Tomb of Ben Hazir, a tomb with a monumental facade, a typical first-century tomb of a wealthy family.

Life of Jesus

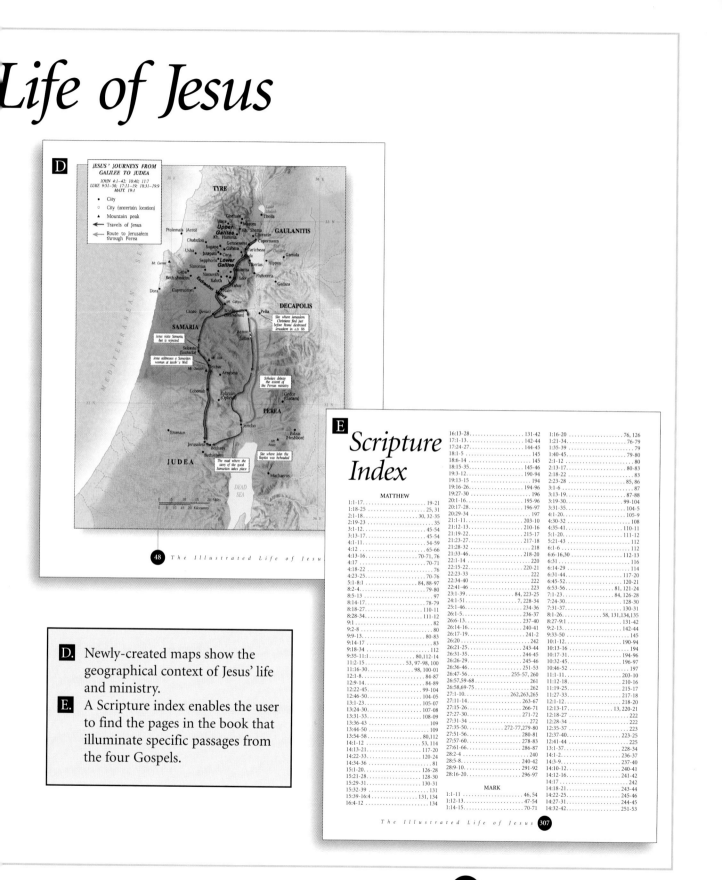

D. Newly-created maps show the geographical context of Jesus' life and ministry.

E. A Scripture index enables the user to find the pages in the book that illuminate specific passages from the four Gospels.

But when the completion of the time came, God sent His Son, born of a woman, born under the law, to redeem those under the law, so that we might receive adoption as sons.

Galatians 4:4-5 (HCSB)

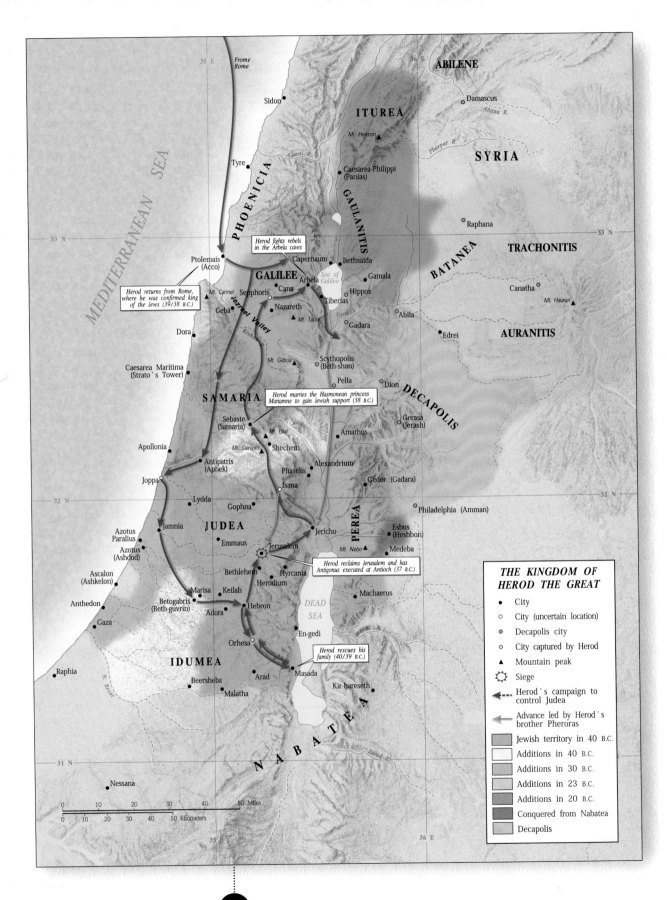

Frome
Rome

ABILENE

Sidon

ITUREA

Damascus

Abana R.

SYRIA

Mt. Hermon ▲

Tyre

Caesarea-Philippi
(Panias)

Pharpar R.

PHOENICIA

Litani R.

Huleh

GAULANITIS

Raphana

TRACHONITIS

35 E

36 E

33 N

33 N

Ptolemais
(Acco)

Herod fights rebels
in the Arbela caves

Capernaum

Bethsaida

BATANEA

Herod returns from Rome,
where he was confirmed king
of the Jews (39/38 B.C.)

GALILEE

Arbela

Gamala

Sea of
Galilee

Canatha

Mt. Hauran ▲

MEDITERRANEAN SEA

Sepphoris

Cana

Mt. Carmel ▲

Jezreel Valley

Nazareth

Hippos

Tiberias

Yarmuk R.

Abila

AURANITIS

Geba

Mt. Tabor ▲

Gadara

Edrei

Dora

Kishon R.

Mt. Gilboa ▲

Scythopolis
(Beth-shan)

Caesarea Maritima
(Strato's Tower)

Pella

Dion

DECAPOLIS

SAMARIA

Herod marries the Hasmonean princess
Mariamne to gain Jewish support (38 B.C.)

Sebaste
(Samaria)

Mt. Ebal ▲

Jordan R.

Amathus

Gerasa
(Jerash)

Apollonia

Mt. Gerizim ▲

Shechem

Antipatris
(Aphek)

Yarkon R.

Phaselis

Alexandrium

Joppa

Isana

Gedor (Gadara)

32 N

32 N

Lydda

Gophna

Philadelphia (Amman)

PEREA

Azotus
Paralius

Jamnia

JUDEA

Jericho

Esbus
(Heshbon)

Azotus
(Ashdod)

Emmaus

Jerusalem

Mt. Nebo ▲

Medeba

Ascalon
(Ashkelon)

Bethlehem

Hyrcania

Herod reclaims Jerusalem and has
Antigonus executed at Antioch (37 B.C.)

Anthedon

Marisa

Keilah

Herodium

Machaerus

Betogabris
(Beth-guvrin)

Hebron

DEAD
SEA

Gaza

Adora

En-gedi

Orhesa

Herod rescues his
family (40/39 B.C.)

IDUMEA

Arad

Masada

Raphia

Beersheba

Malatha

Kir-hareseth

NABATEA

Zered R.

31 N

Nessana

| | 0 | 10 | 20 | 30 | 40 | 50 Miles |
| 0 | 10 | 20 | 30 | 40 | 50 Kilometers |

35

36 E

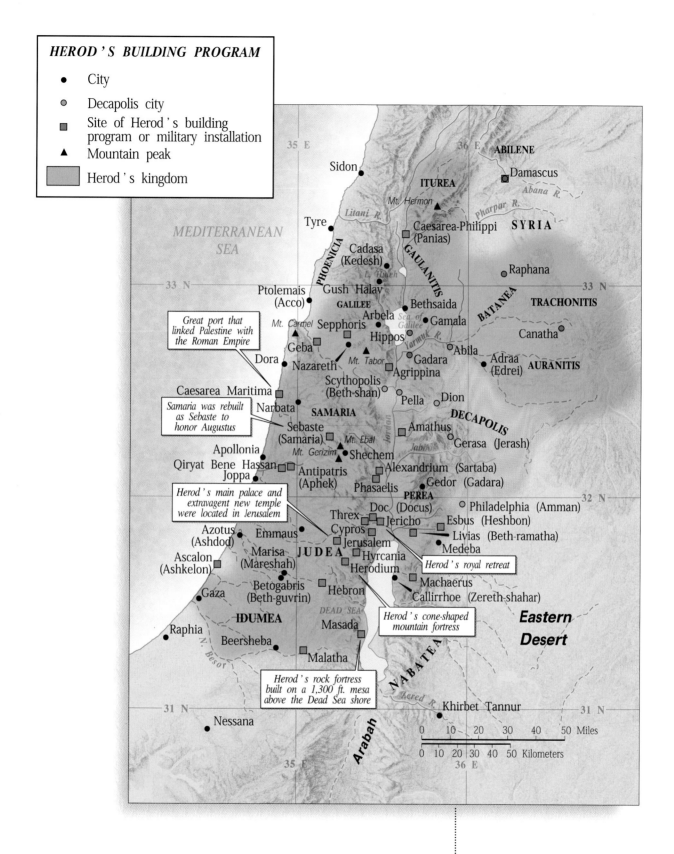

HEROD'S BUILDING PROGRAM

- ● City
- ◉ Decapolis city
- ▪ Site of Herod's building program or military installation
- ▲ Mountain peak
- █ Herod's kingdom

Great port that linked Palestine with the Roman Empire

Samaria was rebuilt as Sebaste to honor Augustus

Herod's main palace and extravagent new temple were located in Jerusalem

Herod's royal retreat

Herod's cone-shaped mountain fortress

Herod's rock fortress built on a 1,300 ft. mesa above the Dead Sea shore

MEDITERRANEAN SEA

ABILENE

Sidon

ITUREA

Damascus

Mt. Hermon

Abana R.

Tyre

Caesarea-Philippi (Panias)

SYRIA

PHOENICIA

GAULANITIS

Pharpar R.

Litani R.

Cadasa (Kedesh)

L. Huleh

Raphana

BATANEA

TRACHONITIS

Ptolemais (Acco)

Gush Halav

GALILEE

Bethsaida

Arbela

Sea of Galilee

Gamala

Canatha

Mt. Carmel

Sepphoris

Hippos

Abila

Adraa (Edrei)

AURANITIS

Geba

Gadara

Dora

Nazareth

Mt. Tabor

Agrippina

Scythopolis (Beth-shan)

Pella

Dion

Yarmuk R.

Caesarea Maritima

Narbata

SAMARIA

Amathus

DECAPOLIS

Sebaste (Samaria)

Mt. Ebal

Gerasa (Jerash)

Apollonia

Mt. Gerizim

Shechem

Jabbok R.

Qiryat Bene Hassan

Antipatris (Aphek)

Alexandrium (Sartaba)

Joppa

Phasaelis

Gedor (Gadara)

PEREA

Philadelphia (Amman)

Doc (Docus)

Threx

Jericho

Esbus (Heshbon)

Azotus (Ashdod)

Emmaus

Cyprus

Livias (Beth-ramatha)

Jerusalem

Medeba

Ascalon (Ashkelon)

Marisa (Mareshah)

JUDEA

Hyrcania

Machaerus

Herodium

Callirrhoe (Zereth-shahar)

Gaza

Betogabris (Beth-guvrin)

Hebron

Jordan

IDUMEA

DEAD SEA

Eastern Desert

Raphia

N. Besor

Masada

NABATEA

Beersheba

Malatha

Zered R.

Khirbet Tannur

Nessana

Arabah

0 10 20 30 40 50 Miles

0 10 20 30 40 50 Kilometers

This study of the life of Jesus is approached with two assumptions: that the four Gospels were written by the men whose names they bear and that these Gospels are trustworthy historical documents. It is not within the scope of this work to deal with technical points of literary or historical criticism but to endeavor to employ the results of both in presenting "the greatest story ever told" about the greatest life ever lived. However, this presentation is made with the conviction that the above-mentioned assumptions are valid in the light of critical analysis.

Each of the four Gospels possesses its own characteristics in keeping with the personality and purpose of the author. And yet when they are combined, they present a well-rounded, Holy Spirit-inspired story of the life of Jesus.

THE HISTORICAL ENVIRONMENT OF THE GOSPELS

In light of the above, it is well to take a brief look at the historical environment of Palestine in the time of Jesus, for His life was not lived in a vacuum. Jesus Christ was a real person who lived in a given period of history, and it is impossible fully to understand the Gospel record without taking this fact into account.

The following two articles about Herod the Great and Augustus will give the setting of Jesus' early life.

Hoard of silver coins, dating from the time of Jesus, was found in the area of Jericho in 1994. These are the same type as those received by Judas Iscariot when he betrayed Jesus. The photo of these coins appeared first in the Biblical Illustrator.

The House of Herod

Larry Gregg

Often a family name evokes identifying images. In American culture the names Kennedy, Vanderbilt, James, and McArthur are synonymous with political ambition, industrial wealth, intellectual genius, and military exploits. For those familiar with late Hellenistic culture and the New Testament Gospels, the name *Herod* evokes images of opportunism, collaboration, intrigue, wanton cruelty, and tragic death. From the second century B.C. until near the end of the first century A.D., the family Herod and the story of classical Judaism and early Christianity were deeply intertwined. Often we think only of Herod (called the Great) and the events surrounding Jesus' birth. This one man was only the most important member of a family that influenced generations of biblical history during the time Rome dominated Israel.

In 168 B.C. the Jews, under the leadership of the legendary Maccabean family,[1] successfully revolted against Antiochus IV, Epiphanes,[2] the Seleucid ruler who sought to force Hellenistic culture on them. The Jewish religious festival of Hanukkah commemorates the relighting of the lamps after the cleansing and rededicating of the temple in Jerusalem in 165 B.C. For approximately one hundred years, the Jews lived as an independent nation ruled over by the Hasmonean dynasty, descendants of the Maccabees. The early part of this period was one of political and religious independence and renewed national vigor.

The adjacent mountain to Lebonah from which Judas Maccabeus stormed down on the Assyrians.

Later the nation succumbed internally to the Hellenism it had fought so hard to resist. At the same time its political leadership declined in ability and fell prey to the opportunism of others.

During the first quarter of the first century B.C. the Hasmonean ruler was Alexander Jannaeus who ruled from 103 to 76 B.C. According to Josephus, Jannaeus appointed one Antipater as his governor of the region of Idumaea, the area on the southwest side of the Dead Sea.[3] This Antipater was followed by his son, also named Antipater (100?–43 B.C.), who became the power behind the Hasmonean throne during the time of John Hyrcanus II. A wily intriguer, Antipater II initially backed Pompey the Great during the Roman civil war between Pompey and Julius Caesar. After Pompey's death, Antipater II cultivated the favor of Caesar and won Roman citizenship for himself and his family in 47 B.C. Antipater II was poisoned in 43 B.C. while raising funds for Cassius following Julius Caesar's assassination on March 15, 44 B.C.[4] Antipater II's political maneuvering set the stage for the emergence of one of his sons, Herod, to be named king of the Jews by the victorious Octavius (the New Testament Caesar Augustus) after Caesar's assassins were defeated.

Herod, the personality from whom the Herodian family takes its name, defies objective analysis.[5] Born in 73 B.C., Herod died in March, 4 B.C., shortly after Jesus' birth. Matthew recorded for us Herod's role in the search of the "wise men from the East" and in the slaughter of the innocent children of Bethlehem.[6]

After Alexander Jannaeus's death in 76 B.C. he was succeeded by his wife Alexandra Salome who ruled from 76 to 67 B.C. During this time and particularly after her death, a major rivalry developed between Alexander Jannaeus's two sons Hyrcanus II and Aristobulus II. This rivalry was exploited by Antipater II until the death of Aristobulus II in 63 B.C. From that time forward Antipater II effectively controlled the nation through Hyrcanus II. Proving himself to be as ethically flexible and politically opportunistic as his father, Herod took Antipater's place as chief advisor to John Hyrcanus II. Herod ingratiated himself to the Hasmonean dynasty by betrothing himself to (ca. 42–40 B.C.) and later marrying (37 B.C.) Mariamme, the granddaughter of both Aristobulus II and Hyrcanus II.

This dynastic intrigue within the Hasmonean family took place in the larger context of a struggle for world domination. The Parthian Empire sought to expand westward at the same time Rome was asserting its domination over the Middle East. In 40 B.C. the Parthians captured Jerusalem and took John Hyrcanus II prisoner. Herod fled to Rome and

View of buildings in the model of first-century Jerusalem, showing the first wall (left) and the tower of Marianne (extreme right). Herod the Great built the Tower of Mariamne along with other buildings in Jerusalem. This tower was built in honor of one of his wives whom he later killed because he suspected she was plotting to dethrone him.

placed himself under the protection and sponsorship of his good friend Mark Antony. Josephus related that Mark Antony suggested to Octavian that Herod be appointed king.[7] Herod, ethnically an Idumaean and not a Jew, was appointed king of the Jews in 40 B.C. Returning to Palestine, Herod proceeded to conquer the geography associated with his title: Judea, Galilee, Perea, and Idumaea. His reign effectively began in 37 B.C. when his forces captured Jerusalem. Later he added additional territory to his

Harbor at Caesarea Maritima, one of Herod the Great's most famous building projects.

kingdom so that during its greatest extent it approximated the area controlled by David and Solomon.

The alliance between Octavian (later Augustus) and Mark Antony did not long survive the destruction of Caesar's assassins. In the rivalry that developed between Octavian and Antony, Herod initially supported Mark Antony. Amazingly, after the defeat of the forces of Antony and Cleopatra at the naval battle of Actium in 31 B.C., Herod met with Octavian at Rhodes where he was pardoned by Octavian and reconfirmed as king of the Jews. One assumes that Octavian's generosity was prompted by the need for a strong personality to create a buffer between his own empire and that of the Parthians while he stabilized the political and social turmoil that had convulsed the Roman Empire for decades.

Herod married five wives (Doris, Mariamme I, Mariamme II, Malthace, and Cleopatra of Jerusalem) and also had several concubines. These relationships produced a brood of offspring, descendants, and relatives by marriage whose names are scattered throughout the New Testament.

Those who come to power by treason, intrigue, and violence have every reason to assume that their security is

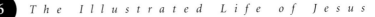

An inscription mentioning Herod the Great, Rufus, and Gratus. Annius Rufus and Valerius Gratus were governors before Pontius Pilate.

threatened by the treason, intrigue, and violence of others. Such was the case of Herod the Great. The first decade (37–27 B.C.) of Herod's 33-year reign was devoted to securing control over the kingdom. From 27 to 13 B.C. Herod made use of his close alliance with Rome to develop the commercial and political importance of his kingdom while engaging in extensive building projects to fortify the nation and strengthen its domestic economy. His last years, from 13 to 4 B.C., were marked by domestic turmoil; his children's, chief advisors', and other family members' intrigues; his own declining health; and megalomanic paranoia. All our sources are replete with stories of Herod's execution of his sons whom he perceived as rivals and even of his favorite wife, Mariamme. The fear that drove him to destroy those most dear to him led to the often-quoted phrase of Augustus Caesar that "it would be safer to be one of Herod's pigs than one of his sons." His confusion as to who should be his successor led to the revision of his will seven times. And he ordered the execution of his son, Antipater, only five days before his own death. Herod ordered that dozens of the leading citizens of the kingdom be executed upon his death so there would be mourning in the land.[8] The order was not carried out, but it illustrates the madness that beset Herod the Great's last days.

Undoubtedly the most enduring of Herod the Great's achievements was his massive building program. While much can be said in criticism of him, one cannot deny that he was an architectural genius. He built new cities such as Caesarea Maritima and Sebaste (Samaria); fortresses and palaces including the Antonia in Jerusalem, Masada, Machaerus, and Herodium. Herod extended his political influence by building monuments and public buildings in Phoenicia, Syria, Asia Minor, and Greece. He built theaters, amphitheaters, baths, gymnasia, hippodromes, and pagan temples. Finally, his most important project was the expansion and reconstruction of the temple in Jerusalem. While still incomplete during Jesus' ministry, it remained so majestic in appearance that it evoked the disciples' grudging admiration (Matt. 24:1; Luke 21:5).

Peter Richardson described the Herod family as "truly remarkable—the best-known family of antiquity for the longest period of time."[9] Such a conclusion is neither inaccurate nor understated; it was a truly remarkable family indeed.

[1]The family name arose from the nickname Maccabeus (the Hammer), associated with its most famous military leader, Judas Maccabeus.
[2]Many biblical scholars associate the "abomination that makes desolate" of Daniel 11:31 and 12:11 with Antiochus's forced sacrifice of a swine on the altar of the Jerusalem temple.
[3]Flavius Josephus, *Antiquities*, 14:80–84.
[4]Ibid. 14.280 and following.
[5]The best attempt at an objective scholarly analysis of this personality to date is that of Peter Richardson, *Herod: King of the Jews and Friend of the Romans* (Columbia, S.C.: University of South Carolina Press, 1996).
[6]Incidentally the association of the birth of Jesus and the death of Herod the Great point out an ancient error in calculation of the year of the birth of Jesus. If Herod was alive in the weeks following Jesus' birth and we can definitively date Herod's death in March, 4 B.C., then Jesus had to have been born earlier in the year 4 B.C.
[7]Flavius Josephus, *Antiquities*, 14.382; *Wars*, 1.282.
[8]Flavius Josephus, *Antiquities*, 17.168-323.
[9]Peter Richardson, 314.

Larry Gregg is a freelance writer in Rutherfordton, North Carolina.

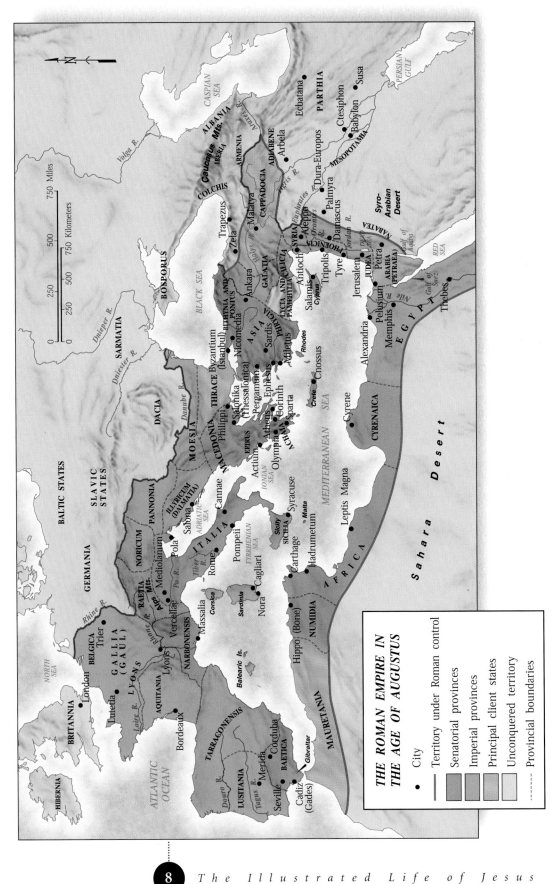

THE ROMAN EMPIRE IN THE AGE OF AUGUSTUS

- City
- Territory under Roman control
- Senatorial provinces
- Imperial provinces
- Principal client states
- Unconquered territory
- Provincial boundaries

In those days a decree went out from Caesar Augustus that the whole empire should be registered. This first registration took place while Quirinius was governing Syria. So everyone went to be registered, each to his own town.

Luke 2:1-3 (HCSB)

Harold S. Songer

An inscription celebrating Augustus' birthday 63 B.C. reads: "The birthday of the god was for the world the beginning of tidings of joy which have been proclaimed for his sake."[1] The god was Augustus. The word translated "glad tidings" is translated "gospel" in our New Testament (compare Mark 1:1). Thus, the term *gospel* in the first century meant news about an event that could change every person's life for the better. This claim is precisely how Augustus was seen. His presence and leadership inaugurated the Pax Romana—an age of peace and prosperity beyond what persons had thought possible.[2] Indeed, Augustus was admired and respected by Romans of every class for bringing peace and economic prosperity to the Empire.

Augustus from Veii, colossal head of Augustus.

Augustus, the title by which Gaius Octavianus (GAY-yuhs ahk-TAY-vih-AY-nuhs) is usually known, reigned from 27 B.C. to A.D. 14. This article will focus on how he emerged victorious in the civil war that marked the transition from the Republic to the Empire and what were the major dimensions of the Empire's prosperity.

To understand the Roman attitude toward the reign of Augustus as the ushering in of a new age, one must realize how deplorable conditions in Roman life had become in the last years of the Republic. Specific changes in the conditions of various areas of life—military, economic, and social—will be discussed later, but all of the problems Augustus wrestled with were aggravated by the civil war that devastated huge sections of the Roman domain from 44 to 27 B.C.

The assassination of Julius Caesar in 44 B.C. was planned by members of the Roman Senate who felt that Caesar's exercise of power was dictatorial. These men dreamed that his murder would free the Senate to solve the social, economic, and military problems of Rome. Unfortunately, the murderers underestimated the impact of their action and how it would shock the populace, and they overestimated the ability of the Senate to act with wisdom and speed.

Two days after the murder, certain realities began to emerge. The streets of Rome alternated between periods of eerie silence and periods of frenzy as alternately a fearful population hid in their homes and then protested Caesar's death and sought his murderers. The Senate, in weakness, could only ratify the decisions Caesar had made and proposed. Leading senators added to the confusion by contending for positions of power.

Antonius (an-TOH-nih-us, commonly known as Mark Antony) used the funeral of Caesar to gain popular support for himself and stirred the populace so deeply that the murderers fled from Rome. At the same time Gaius Octavianus (Augustus), who was named as Caesar's successor in his will, decided to assume leadership. This decision focused the conflict between Antony and Octavianus because Antony had seized the property of Julius Caesar that had been left to the future Augustus.[3]

Temple of Augustus in Rome.

quickly resumed. After several political skirmishes in which the rivalry between the two clearly emerged, Antony's entrenchment in Egypt with Cleopatra set the stage for Augustus's victory. Egypt was a wealthy country and supplied grain that Rome needed. Antony's marriage to Cleopatra and his reigning like a Hellenistic king caused the people of Rome to view him as an enemy. When he tried to return to Rome with military force, his fate as the enemy of Rome was sealed. The decisive battle occurred near Actium (ACK-tee-uhm) in 31 B.C. Antony's army surrendered and Cleopatra and Antony fled to Egypt. Augustus moved on Egypt from both east and west. His two arch opponents—Antony and Cleopatra—committed suicide. The confiscated treasures of Egypt paid for the war, and Augustus returned to Rome in triumph. On January 16, 27 B.C., the Senate gave him the honorific title by which he is yet known—Augustus.

The struggle for power between these two aspiring leaders had to be postponed, however. A common threat forced them into an unstable alliance. Brutus (BROO-tuhs) and Cassius (KAS-ih-uhs)—the two major conspirators against Caesar—had seized power in the eastern half of the Empire and had assembled such menacing forces that response was necessary. Antony and Augustus, along with Lepidus (LEHP-ih-duhs) who arranged the alliance, formed a triumvirate (rule by three); and they were at first confirmed in power for five years.

The decisive battle between the two forces occurred at Philippi in 42 B.C. with Antony heroically guiding the armies while Augustus stayed in his tent. Brutus and Cassius were defeated, and both died. Antony then went to Egypt to consolidate the now subjugated Eastern Empire, and Augustus returned to Rome to face the massive economic difficulties precipitated in Italy by the wars.

But the postponed struggle between Antony and Augustus

The resolution of the civil strife left the Roman Empire with serious internal problems to solve. The frontiers were not clearly defined, and some provinces were only partially subjugated. The economy of the provinces and of Italy needed both reform and renewal. The social problems created by the slave population and the attitudes toward marriage cried out for attention. Augustus gave concerted attention to all these areas of Roman life with such success that a sense of peace and progress—the Pax Romana—began to permeate Roman society.

To the average Roman, Augustus's major accomplishment was to achieve peace. This peace included suppressing the civil war and stabilizing the

Senate building in Roman forum.

Altar of Peace in honor of Augustus.

national frontiers in the Empire so as to render invasion by plunderers unlikely. In some instances, as in the provinces of Spain and North Africa, the issue was to maintain control of an area rather than to establish a boundary. The Spanish population was split into many small groups to make united opposition practically impossible, but this fragmentation resulted in groups pillaging and plundering one another. The inhabitants of the Cantabrian Mountains along the northern coast of Spain are a prime example. They were fiercely independent and preyed on the agricultural population to the south, eroding Roman reserves and supplies. Augustus himself directed the first campaign against the Cantabrians in 26 B.C., and subsequent campaigns ended in 19 B.C. with Spain consolidated as a province.

Only fierce and unrelenting suppression of such tribes could secure the frontier in many areas. Although Augustus noted that "he preferred not to wipe out utterly such tribes as could safely be spared,"[4] harsh suppression was also necessary in the Alps, Balkans, Taurus Mountains, and North Africa.

The northern provinces of Germany and Gaul posed different problems because a clear border had to be established. Augustus moved the frontier northwestward from the Rhine to the Elbe (EL-buh) and authorized the force needed to make the provinces secure.

The eastern frontier—Palestine, Egypt, and Syria—ringed the Mediterranean shore and provided crucial linkage for the roads needed by the Roman military machine. The most troubled area was Palestine, where Herod the Great (37–4 B.C.) established firm order and enjoyed high favor with Augustus. The will of Herod, who died in 4 B.C., requested that his kingdom be divided among his three sons: Philip, Antipas (AN-tih-pas), and Archelaus (AHR-kuh-LAY-uhs). While all three sons presented their petitions in Rome, a Jewish delegation also came to Augustus to ask him to abolish the Herodian monarchy and establish a theocracy under Roman protection.

Augustus decided to place the three sons of Herod over roughly the territories Herod had desired, but none was named as king. The failure of the Jewish embassy fanned the fires of resentment in Judea, and Archelaus was deposed in A.D. 6. Judea was assigned to the jurisdiction of Roman procurators, of whom the most famous was Pontius Pilate (A.D. 26–36).

All of these massive military operations to secure the Roman frontiers and swiftly suppress rebellion made one matter clear: Augustus had the power and the resolve to guarantee peace in the Empire. In addition, the road system necessary to sustain the vigorous military enforcement of the Pax Romana allowed merchants, goods, mail, and news to flow rapidly. People in the Empire both experienced and articulated an increasing sense of corporate well-being, security, and confidence.

Augustus turned his attention also to the economy. As early as the third century B.C., the Roman economy was marked by an increasing capitalistic spirit as Italian merchants fanned out into provinces and newly acquired territory. But in the closing years of the Republic, the economic situation deteriorated as both production and trade were choked by the disturbances on the frontiers and by the general unrest of the population. With the outbreak of civil war in 44 B.C., the economy was further debilitated by the devastating effects of conflict and the massive seizures of both goods and property by the military forces as they sought to sustain themselves.

With the coming of the Pax Romana in 27 B.C., interference in ownership of property ceased, law and order were established, and a mood of grateful optimism grew rapidly. Augustus reversed the tendency of the state to control the economy and—except for the grain trade from Egypt—actively fostered private enterprise in the Empire.

Whether the balance of trade between Italy and the other sections of the Empire was favorable or not is difficult to tell, but whatever differences there may have been did not slow down the Italian economy. Exports from the rich natural resources of Italy

Portrait bust of Livia, second wife of Augustus.

flowed to all parts of the Empire: wine, foodstuffs, and products of amber, gold, silver, cloth, copper, bronze, glass, pottery, and iron. Imports poured into Italy: wheat, papyrus, glass, and precious stones from Egypt; asphalt, figs, linen, silk, spices, and olives from Syria; and window mica from Cappadocia.

Business also was enhanced by the Augustan financial reforms. Under the Republic the Senate assumed responsibility for financial management, but Augustus shouldered this responsibility. He reduced the number of taxes, public officials, bureaucratic systems, and powers of provincial governors to exploit provincials.[5] In addition, the currency was stabilized through monetary reforms that established an imperial mint and ensured equal value to correlated coins of precious metal. This action could hardly be better illustrated than by the account in Mark (12:13–17, RSV) of Jesus asking Jewish representatives, "Whose likeness and inscription is this?" and their response, "Caesar's." The record is clear evidence of standardized Roman currency in Palestine where the tradition of not having images on coins was strong.

Social reforms also received attention. Although the civil war that began in the Roman Republic in 44 B.C. divided persons in the Roman dominion into various camps, the divisions did not represent a real fragmentation of a unified people. Thus, the military victory of Augustus in 27 B.C. only made possible the creation of a sense of solidarity in the Roman Empire, a

RES°GESTAE°DIVI° AVGVSTI at the Augustin Altar of Peace in Rome. Reproduction of Augustus' accomplishments.

task to which Augustus consciously gave himself. The strategy Augustus chose was to emphasize the traditions of the Romans, to create a proud consciousness of belonging to the Empire, and to stress the responsibility persons had as Romans to succeeding generations.

A large slave population, particularly in Italy, was a major obstacle to this strategy. This cheap labor force resulted in an increasingly small market for the employment of freedmen, with the result that the birthrate among lower-economic-level, non-slave families decreased sharply. The threat was clear. If Romans (Italians) did not have children, the population could be maintained only by immigration and the manumission (freeing) of salves. The creation of Roman national solidarity was practically impossible under those circumstances. The problem was further aggravated by the legal situation that allowed formal or informal manumission. The former was

expensive and conferred full citizenship, but the latter was easily conferred by any slave owner and left the freed slave in an ambiguous position—legally a slave, functionally free. One of the many injustices of such informal manumission was that the children of such freed slaves could not pass their quasi-freedom to their own children.

Augustus moved to rectify this spectrum of injustices by a measure—Lex Junia—which conferred stability and rights to those informally manumitted and specified their right to hold and sell property. This privilege—which did not include inheritance—clarified and strengthened the class structure of Roman society. The major boon was, however, to the next generation, since the children were considered to be legally freeborn Latins and thus well on their way to full citizenship.

Another social reform related to the widespread practice of freeing slaves indiscriminately through formal manumission, thus swelling the ranks of persons who held Roman citizenship but who had neither the resources nor the understanding to utilize the privilege. In addition to cheapening citizenship, this indiscriminate freeing of slaves made them responsible to care for themselves and burdened the Roman society with the care of aged persons who were citizens without resources.

To counter this injustice, Augustus developed laws to restrict the number of slaves who could be freed. The laws specified what fractions of an owner's total number of slaves could be freed. Thus, the laws sharply reduced the number of formal manumissions. Another measure placed restrictions on which slaves were eligible for freedom and forbade the freeing of slaves who had been involved in certain crimes.

Within Roman society itself, a need for moral reform also existed, particularly in the area of marriage. The basic problem Augustus had to deal with was economic. The two practices in need of reform were the husband's right to deprive his wife and family of inheritance and the wife's right to deprive the husband of access to her dowry. The result of these practices was the lack of a secure economic base to marriage, which eroded the value of marriage itself, made family life unstable, and blurred the line between marriage and mere cohabitation. Augustus developed specific measures to correct these abuses of marriage, but then he went much further. He deeply felt that the moral decay associated with a low view of marriage threatened the future of Roman society. He took a stern position for moral legislation by paying a high personal cost. He banished his daughter Julia for her sexual adventures, tried to legislate against marriages between widely differing classes, decreed that every Roman of the upper classes between twenty-five and sixty-five years of age should be married, and gave preference in appointments to public offices to persons married and with children.

Augustus made long-lasting contributions to the Romans whom he served by his military exploits, economic leadership, and social reforms. But his greatest contribution to the world was one he never planned to make. By creating the Pax Romana, he developed a social and historical matrix in which Christianity could both better be planted and survive. Ironically, the best-known passage in the New Testament referring to him is associated with the birth of Jesus: "In those days a decree went out from Caesar Augustus that the whole empire should be registered" (Luke 2:1).

[1]Werner George Kummel, *Introduction to the New Testament* (Nashville: Abingdon Press, 1975), 35.
[2]S.A. Cook, F.E. Adcock, M.P. Charlesworth, eds., *The Cambridge Ancient History* (Cambridge: University Press, 1971), 10:384–85.
[3]Martin P. Nilsson, *Imperial Rome* (New York: Schocken Books, 1962), 4–5
[4]Cook et al, *Cambridge Ancient History*, 345.
[5]Ibid., 191–93.

Harold S. Songer is retired professor of New Testament interpretation and assistant provost, The Southern Baptist Theological Seminary, Louisville, Kentucky.

*In the beginning was the Word,
and the Word was with God,
and the Word was God. …*

*The Word became flesh
and took up residence among us.
We observed His glory, the glory as
the only Son from the Father,
full of grace and truth.*

JOHN 1:1,14 (HCSB)

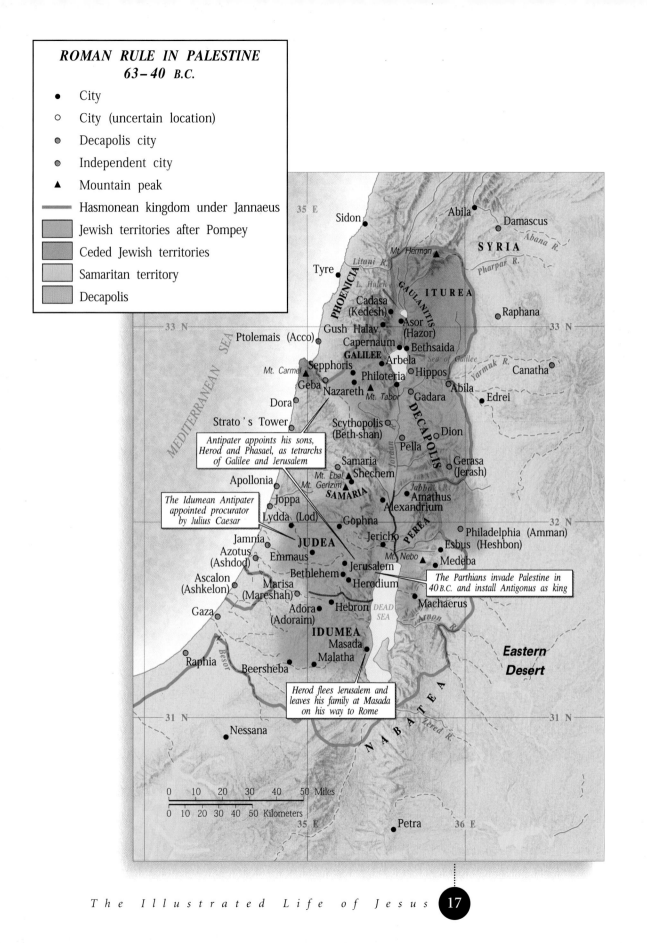

ROMAN RULE IN PALESTINE
63–40 B.C.

- ● City
- ○ City (uncertain location)
- ◉ Decapolis city
- ● Independent city
- ▲ Mountain peak
- ━━ Hasmonean kingdom under Jannaeus
- Jewish territories after Pompey
- Ceded Jewish territories
- Samaritan territory
- Decapolis

35 E

Sidon

Abila

Damascus

Abana R.

Mt. Hermon

SYRIA

Pharpar R.

Tyre

PHOENICIA

Litani R.

L. Huleh

GAULANITIS

ITUREA

Raphana

33 N

33 N

Ptolemais (Acco)

Cadasa (Kedesh)

Gush Halav

Asor (Hazor)

Capernaum

Bethsaida

Sea of Galilee

GALILEE

Arbela

Hippos

Canatha

Sepphoris

Mt. Carmel

Philoteria

Yarmuk R.

Geba

Nazareth

Mt. Tabor

Gadara

Abila

Edrei

Dora

DECAPOLIS

Strato's Tower

Scythopolis (Beth-shan)

Dion

> *Antipater appoints his sons, Herod and Phasael, as tetrarchs of Galilee and Jerusalem*

Pella

Gerasa (Jerash)

Samaria

Mt. Ebal

Shechem

Apollonia

Mt. Gerizim

SAMARIA

Jabbok R.

Amathus

Joppa

Alexandrium

> *The Idumean Antipater appointed procurator by Julius Caesar*

Lydda (Lod)

Gophna

32 N

Jericho

PEREA

Philadelphia (Amman)

Jamnia

JUDEA

Esbus (Heshbon)

Azotus (Ashdod)

Emmaus

Mt. Nebo

Medeba

Ascalon (Ashkelon)

Bethlehem

Jerusalem

> *The Parthians invade Palestine in 40 B.C. and install Antigonus as king*

Marisa (Mareshah)

Herodium

Gaza

Adora (Adoraim)

Hebron

DEAD SEA

Machaerus

Arnon R.

IDUMEA

Masada

Malatha

MEDITERRANEAN SEA

Raphia

Beersheba

Besor

> *Herod flees Jerusalem and leaves his family at Masada on his way to Rome*

N A B A T E A

Eastern Desert

31 N

31 N

Nessana

Zered R.

0 10 20 30 40 50 Miles

0 10 20 30 40 50 Kilometers

35 E

Petra

36 E

The Period of Preparation

The Preexistence of Christ

The story of the life of Jesus Christ did not begin in Nazareth or Bethlehem but in eternity. It is true that Jesus of Nazareth was God; it is even more correct to say that God became Jesus of Nazareth. "In the beginning was the Word, and the Word was with God, and the Word was God" Himself (John 1:1).

The "Word" or Logos was commonly used for reason or speech. Ancient writers employed it in various ways. To Heraclitus it was the principle which controlled the universe. The Stoic philosophers used it to express the soul of the world, and Marcus Aurelius by it connoted the generative principle in nature. Philo, the Jewish-Alexandrian philosopher-theologian, employed it as a substitute for the Hebrew word *Memra* (Word) and used it almost in a personal sense. But the Apostle John personalized it and used it as a name for the Messiah, along with the Son of God, Son of Man, and other personal names for deity.

This eternal Christ was the Creator of the universe from atoms to suns. Apart from Him not even one thing came into being which did come into being. Furthermore, He was and is the source of all life, a life which is the light of men. Through the centuries the darkness of evil had sought to snuff out this light but without success. And in God's own time this Light, this Logos, entered into the arena of history that He might destroy the works of darkness.

No greater words were ever penned than "The Word became flesh and took up residence among us. We observed His glory, the glory as the only Son from the Father, full of grace and truth" (John 1:14). Yes, the eternal Christ who is God Himself became a flesh-and-blood man. He pitched His tent of flesh and dwelt for a little while among men. He was God as though He were not man. Yet He became man in every sense of the word, apart from sin, that He might both identify Himself with man and fully reveal the Father to men. When God revealed His law, He did so through Moses, but when He revealed His grace and truth He did so through Jesus Christ.

For "God, who at sundry times and in divers manners spake in time past unto the fathers by the prophets, Hath in these last days spoken unto us by his Son, whom he hath appointed heir of all things, by whom also he made the worlds; Who being the brightness of his glory, and the express image of his person, and upholding all things by the word of his power, when he had by himself purged our sins, sat down on the right hand of the Majesty on high" (Heb. 1:1–3).

The fruit of the pomegranate was juicy and its flower a beautiful scarlet. Pomegranate bushes were often grown in gardens and beside houses. Moses was instructed to embroider pomegranate fruits on the hem of the priests' robes and their form ornamented the columns of Solomon's Temple in Jerusalem. The pomegranate symbolizes royalty and its beauty reflects the glory of Jesus. This photo was taken in Sabaste, a city that Herod the Great built.

THE GENEALOGY OF JESUS CHRIST

When Christ entered bodily into the arena of history, He did so as a Jew. This was in keeping with God's eternal purpose, for in a world filled with paganism the Jews had clung to the idea of the one true God, Jehovah.

The Jews placed great value upon lineage. The Old Testament testifies to this fact. Josephus introduced his own autobiography by giving his genealogy, which he says he found in the public records. These records were kept by the Sanhedrin. Herod the Great was a half-breed, and for that reason, along with many others, was despised by the pure-blooded Jews. Out of spite he destroyed all the genealogical records so that he could say that no one could prove a better pedigree than he could.

Therefore, to the Jewish mind the record of the life of Jesus would be incomplete without His genealogy, and the Gospel accounts include two such records. Luke is said to have listed Jesus' genealogy according to the line of Mary His mother. He began with "was thought to be the son of Joseph," and ends with "son of Adam, son of God" (Luke 3:23–38). Matthew, on the other hand, traces His lineage, through Joseph, the foster-father, as was required by Jewish law. In a genealogy it was not required that every name be listed but only that the line be established.

Matthew began his record with the simple yet profound statement, "The historical record of Jesus Christ, the Son of David, the Son of Abraham" (1:1). He divided the genealogy into three sections of fourteen generations each: Abraham to David; David to the Babylonian captivity; the captivity to the birth of Jesus. Through Abraham God's covenant of grace was given. The Hebrew nation reached its greatest glory under David whose throne became a symbol of the everlasting kingdom of the Son of David. During and following the Babylonian captivity the Messianic hopes of the Jews burned the brightest. So "Jesus Christ, the Son of David, the Son of Abraham" was the Messiah, the Desire of all nations.

Certain other matters of interest emerge from an analysis of Jesus' genealogy. For instance, certain notorious sinners are included in His line. Judah and David were adulterers. Solomon, Manasseh, and Amon were worshipers of pagan gods. Furthermore, contrary to Jewish custom, the genealogy included the names of women. Tamar had sinned with Judah.

Rahab is called a harlot of Jericho. The Hebrew word translated "harlot" means "public woman." She may not have been a harlot but simply a public woman or innkeeper. She was a Canaanite. Ruth was a Moabitess. Neither of these last two women were Hebrews. Of interest also is the fact that Jesus' lineage includes some who had lived in political bondage.

Therefore, Jesus' genealogy is more than a mere recitation of names. It shows that He was the son of Abraham, the son of David, and the fulfillment of prophecy. Also it becomes the gospel in miniature. Jesus came not to call the righteous but sinners to repentance. In His lineage He is identified with sinners, and in Christ "there is no . . . male or female; for you are all one in Christ Jesus. And if you are Christ's, then you are Abraham's seed, heirs according to the promise" (Gal. 3:28–29).

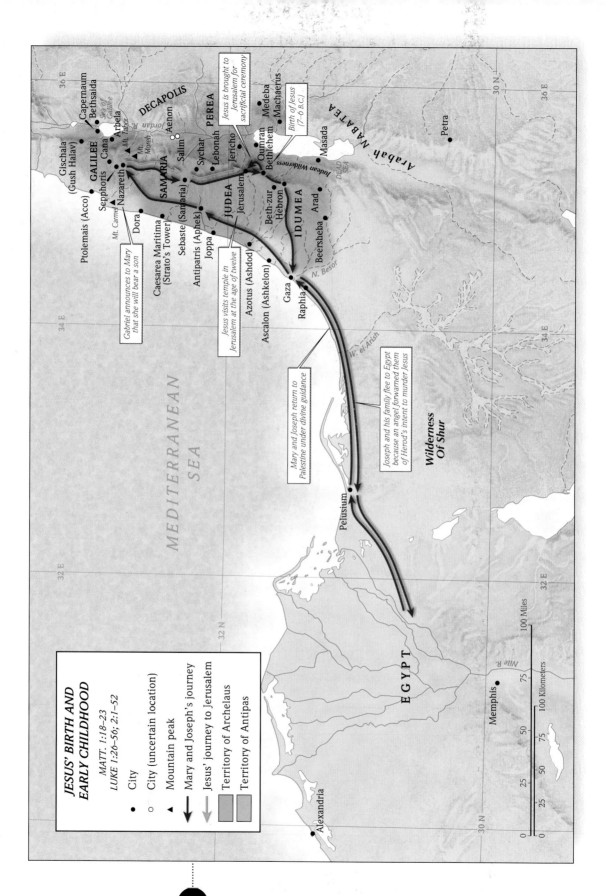

JESUS' BIRTH AND
EARLY CHILDHOOD

MATT. 1:18–23
LUKE 1:26–56; 2:1–52

- • City
- ○ City (uncertain location)
- ▲ Mountain peak
- → Mary and Joseph's journey
- → Jesus' journey to Jerusalem
- ▮ Territory of Archelaus
- ▮ Territory of Antipas

Gabriel announces to Mary that she will bear a son

Jesus visits temple in Jerusalem at the age of twelve

Jesus is brought to Jerusalem for sacrificial ceremony

Birth of Jesus (7–6 B.C.)

Joseph and his family flee to Egypt because an angel forwarned them of Herod's intent to murder Jesus

Mary and Joseph return to Palestine under divine guidance

MEDITERRANEAN SEA

DECAPOLIS

PEREA

GALILEE

SAMARIA

JUDEA

IDUMEA

Arabah NABATEA

EGYPT

Wilderness Of Shur

Capernaum
Bethsaida
Sea of Galilee
Arbela
Aenon
Medeba
Machaerus
Petra
Gischala (Gush Halav)
Cana
Mt. Tabor
Salim
Sepphoris
Arbela
Mt. Moreh
Sychar
Lebonah
Qumran
Masada
Nazareth
Jericho
Bethlehem
Ptolemais (Acco)
Mt. Carmel
Sebaste (Samaria)
Jerusalem
Dora
Caesarea Maritima (Strato's Tower)
Beth-zur
Hebron
Antipatris (Aphek)
Joppa
Arad
Azotus (Ashdod)
Beersheba
Ascalon (Ashkelon)
N. Besor
Gaza
Raphia
Pelusium
Nile R.
Memphis
Alexandria
Jordan R.
Judean Wilderness
DEAD SEA

0   25   50   75   100 Miles
0 25 50 75 100 Kilometers

"Now, Master, You can dismiss Your slave in peace, according to Your word. For my eyes have seen Your salvation, which You have prepared in the presence of all peoples; a light for revelation to the Gentiles and glory to Your people Israel."

THE AGED SIMEON
LUKE 2:29-32 (HCSB)

The Birth and Childhood of Jesus

Bethlehem, the village where Jesus was born, viewed from Tekoa, home of the Old Testament prophet Amos.

The Annunciation to the Virgin Mary

It was three months before the birth of John the Baptist. If strange things were happening to Elizabeth, an even stranger experience awaited her cousin, Mary, who lived many miles to the north in Nazareth of Galilee. Mary was a virgin maiden betrothed to a village carpenter, Joseph by name, and probably many years her elder. In Jewish life the betrothal was more than an engagement and less than marriage in the present-day sense. It usually lasted for one year, during which time unfaithfulness on the part of the woman was punishable by death.

There is every evidence from both her words and deeds that Mary was a chaste and pious young woman. Nevertheless she was naturally startled when one day the angel Gabriel suddenly appeared to her. He was on another mission of glad tidings from heaven to earth, for he told Mary that she was highly favored of God in that she was to become the mother of the virgin-born Son of God. Quite naturally this raised a biological problem, and Mary herself became the first person to utter a question as to the possibility of the virgin birth: "How can this be, since I have not been intimate with a man?" (Luke 1:34).

But Gabriel brushed aside biological problems by telling Mary that this was to be a divine birth. Like begets like. Men and women beget sons and daughters, and God in the Virgin Mary would beget the Son of God. As proof of God's power to perform His word Gabriel cited the conception of the aged Elizabeth, which to say the least was a supernatural act on God's part.

Mary gave consent of her will to the will of God. It was not as simple as the saying of it, for hers was a secret which she could share with no one in Nazareth, not even with Joseph. Most certainly it would bring down upon her the scorn of her neighbors. It might mean the loss of her betrothed, and it could mean death by stoning. But God had spoken, and she obeyed.

Shortly thereafter Mary hastened to Judea to visit her cousin. Maybe it was to verify the angel's words. More likely it was to seek comfort and courage from the one person who would understand, and when Mary had greeted Elizabeth, John the Baptist, whose voice one day as the forerunner of the Messiah would echo throughout the wilderness of Judea, leaped in his mother's womb at the presence of his Lord who now reposed in the virgin womb of His mother. In response to the twofold blessing of Elizabeth on Mary and her unborn child, the virgin mother uttered words of poetic beauty. They were words fraught with the knowledge of the Hebrew Scriptures. By them one is reminded of the song of Hannah when God answered her prayers in the birth of Samuel (1 Sam. 1:9–18).

The curtain of silence is reverently drawn about the three months which followed, but they must have been days of prayer and rejoicing by two kindred spirits in whom the Lord had wrought wondrously. Just before the Baptist was born, Mary returned to Nazareth.

Mary's secret could be hidden no longer, and when Joseph knew her condition, he was greatly troubled. As far as he knew, she had been unfaithful to him, and in that state of mind two courses were open to him. Either he could expose her as a public example which probably would mean her death, or else he could put her away privately. His love for her triumphed over his injured sense of justice, and he chose to follow the latter course. But before he could do so, God, in a dream, let him in on His and Mary's secret, and never does Joseph appear greater than in his choice to protect Mary and the Babe with his name. He shared her shame before men and her glory before God.

Long-haired sheep grazing near a village on the rocky slopes of the Judean hills in Israel. The shepherds were watching a flock like this when suddenly an angel of the Lord appeared to them and announced the birth of Jesus in Bethlehem.

The door to the traditional place of Jesus' birth in Bethlehem.

Below: Shepherd fields in Bethlehem

In faraway Rome Augustus Caesar ruled his vast empire with an iron hand. True to Roman fashion he was primarily concerned that his subjects should keep the peace and pay their taxes. In 8 B.C. he had inaugurated a periodical census every fourteen years in order to enroll his people for taxation. According to Tacitus even the regna, the dependent kingdoms, were included in this census.

Probably two years later this census was carried out in Palestine. Herod, the vassal king, would not think of disobeying Augustus. Yet, knowing the Jew's aversion to paying taxes to Rome, he delayed it as long as he dared. Even then he sought to placate the Jews by adhering to their customs in dealing with them along tribal lines. So when the order for enrollment was finally given, it called for every Jew to be enrolled at the place where the tribal register was kept.

Thus Joseph and Mary journeyed from Nazareth to Bethlehem, for they

Bethlehem

Gary Hardin

Phillips Brooks visited Israel in 1865 at the age of thirty-six. On Christmas Eve, Brooks and several friends rode on horseback from Jerusalem to Bethlehem. Excitement filled Brooks' heart as he walked the streets of Bethlehem and meditated on the night when Christ was born. Three years after this Bethlehem tour, he wrote the four stanzas of the Christmas carol, "O Little Town of Bethlehem."

Although Bethlehem is most familiar as the birthplace of Jesus, the city's heritage reaches beyond the nativity. The city lies six miles southwest of Jerusalem. Jews, Christians, and Moslems venerate Bethlehem and consider it to be one of the authentic sites in the Holy Land.

Positioned twenty-three hundred feet above sea level, the area surrounding Bethlehem contains soil suitable for fruit trees and vines. Toward the west, in the distant background, lies rugged wilderness. The Dead Sea lies fifteen miles to the east. South of Bethlehem, rain diminishes, and the land becomes barren. However, it may have been more fertile in the past, a possibility supported by the success of reforestation. The wilderness area to the east contains chasms and hidden caverns that served as a refuge for rebels and hermits. In recent years, these caves have yielded many ancient scrolls and manuscripts.

In Bible times Bethlehem's location gave the city a position of strength and desirability. A garrison of Philistines occupied the city in David's time (2 Sam. 23:14). Rehoboam fortified the town as a defense against the threats of Philistia, Egypt, and Edom (2 Chron. 11:6).

The name of the town means "house of bread." In the Bible the town sometimes is referred to as Bethlehem-judah (Judg. 17:7), Ephrath (Gen. 35:19), Ephratah (Ruth 4:11), and Caleb-ephratah (1 Chron. 2:24). The Ephrath and Ephratah designations may refer to a city or area originally independent of Bethlehem. Since David is noted as an Ephrathite (1 Sam. 17:12), the two cities of Ephratah and Bethlehem evidently were not identical, but Ephratah was an older settlement which became absorbed into Bethlehem. These various designations for the town of Bethlehem also served to distinguish it from another Bethlehem in Zebulun that is mentioned in Judges 12:8,10.

Archeological digs in Bethlehem in the 1940s and 1950s uncovered fossilized bones and flints that date to

were descendents of David and members of the tribe of Judah. Though they were peasants, royal blood flowed in their veins. By this time Mary was great with child, and this journey of approximately one hundred miles worked a great hardship on her. Nevertheless Caesar's decree must be obeyed.

However, she and Joseph moved under a greater word than that of the Roman emperor, for God had said that His Son, the Messiah, should be born in Bethlehem. Augustus knew nothing of this prophecy and cared less. But unknowingly he was an instrument in God's hands, as his decree like an invisible cord drew the virgin mother toward her destiny.

After several days of travel, late in the afternoon these weary travelers climbed the last rocky, steep ascent leading into Bethlehem. The streets were crowded with hundreds of other men and women bent on the same mission. Clouds of dust boiled up from the stirring of the hundreds of feet of men and animals. A bedlam of noise characteristic of such a scene filled the ears of the weary couple from Nazareth as laboriously they made their way to the village inn. But it was already filled to overflowing.

So because there was no lodging to be had, Joseph bedded his wife down in the area provided for the animals. Here Mary "gave birth to her firstborn Son, and she wrapped Him snugly in cloth and laid Him in a manger" (Luke 2:7).

Thus was the Son of God born. Not in a king's palace nor in the home of the wealthy or mighty, but to a peasant mother whose delivery room was a stable. No physician stood by to assist. Only the gnarled hands of a village carpenter came to her aid, but they were hands made tender by a conquering love and a devotion to God. As the newborn Babe slept through the night, He was under the watchful eyes of His mother and foster father, but most of all He was secure under the never-failing gaze of His Heavenly Father.

The next morning Bethlehem roused from her sleep. It was business as usual as the bazaars rang with the noise of

View overlooking Bethlehem with Herodium in the background. Herodium was a fortress-palace built by Herod the Great near Bethlehem. The Jewish historian, Josephus, tells us that this is the site where Herod the Great was buried.

Area thought to be the manger where Jesus was laid in the cave that is under the Church of the Nativity in Bethlehem.

five miles from Bethlehem.

Shortly after the conquest, each of the twelve Israelite tribes received a portion of Canaan as an inheritance. The tribe of Judah received a parcel of land that included Bethlehem. Judah enlisted the help of the tribe of Simeon in driving out the Canaanites who already were settled in the territories near Bethlehem (Judg. 1:3-19). Caleb gained full possession of Hebron by driving out the three sons of Anak (Judg. 1:20).

Bethlehem's prominence in the Old Testament rests largely on its association with David. It was a walled town as early as David's time. David was born in Bethlehem (1 Sam. 17:12), and he shepherded his father's sheep there (1 Sam. 17:15). Elhanan, one of David's mighty men, was born in Bethlehem (2 Sam. 23:24), while Asahel, David's nephew (1 Chron. 2:15–61), was buried there (2 Sam. 2:32). The Philistines then held control of the areas (1 Chron. 11:15–19).

Bethlehem never enjoyed prominence in the Old Testament; in fact, Judah did not find its real identity until the time of David. Various heterogeneous elements formed the tribe: Calebites, Kenizzites, and Jerahmeelites. David prepared the way for these various elements to be

Neolithic times. This evidence points to the presence of man in the area of Bethlehem during times when crude stone tools were used. The information from the Amarna Letters verifies Bethlehem's existence from the fourteenth century B.C. The Amarna Letters contain a reference in which Abdi-Heba, the prince of Jerusalem, complains that Bit-Lahmi (Bethlehem) has gone over to the 'Apiru. The 'Apiru (Hapiru, Habiru) are believed by some scholars to have been connected with the Hebrew patriarchs.

At the time of the conquest, Bethlehem was situated in the southern territory of the land of Canaan. Joshua 10 recounts the conquest of this area by Joshua and the Israelites. Canaanite forces from five important cities in the southern territory of Canaan—Jerusalem, Hebron, Lachish, Jarmuth, and Eglon—united to battle against the Israelites but were defeated. None of them were more than twenty-

Bethlehem's Manger Square and the Church of the Nativity.

Countryside between Jerusalem and Bethlehem. The olive trees of a small orchard can be seen. When Joseph and Mary took Jesus from Bethlehem to *Jerusalem to present Him to the Lord at the Temple, they may have passsed through this countryside.*

merged by conquering their common enemy, the Amalekites (1 Sam. 30:17–18).

Although Bethlehem enjoyed prominence during David's monarchy, the king did not settle in Bethlehem but rather in the more important Hebron, the Calebite town. It was at Hebron that David was acknowledged as king over the house of Judah (2 Sam. 2:1–4).

After David's lifetime the town of Bethlehem declined in its importance with Old Testament historical events. Both Ezra and Nehemiah (Ezra 2:21; Neh. 7:26) mention that citizens of Bethlehem returned to the city from the Babylonian Exile (about 538 B.C.). At this time in history the city was sparsely populated.

Micah 5:2 greatly influenced the town's later history because of the relationship between Bethlehem and David's family. Matthew 2:2–6 and John 7:42 acknowledge Micah's words to be a prophecy of the birth of the Messiah. From the town of King David, the prophet Micah saw a greater King coming, the Christ. Micah's prophecy lifted Bethlehem from obscurity to fame (Matt. 2:6).

In the New Testament Bethlehem received notoriety as the birthplace of Jesus (Luke 2:4, 15). Mary and Joseph went there to be enrolled in the census. An early tradition dating back to Justin Martyr holds that a cave-stable was the place of the nativity.

Herod (Matt. 2:1) built one of his forts, "The herodium," near Bethlehem. He won an important victory over the last Maccabean king there.

The Roman emperor, Hadrian, leveled the city and desecrated the site of the nativity in A.D. 132 because Bethlehem was fast becoming a Christian shrine. The town remained almost nonexistent until Constantine I, the converted Roman emperor, revived the town as a sacred place. Under Constantine's rule, Christian festivals and pilgrimages flourished. Constantine's mother,

Helena, made a pilgrimage to the Holy Land in A.D. 326–327 which made a great impression on her life. Under her influence the emperor constructed three imperial churches in Palestine, one of which was the Church of the Nativity in Bethlehem, in A.D. 326. This church was built over the traditional cave-stable believed to have been Jesus' birthplace. The church still stands today, though it was enlarged by Justinian and modified thereafter. It is the oldest church in continuous use in the world.

By the end of the fourth century, Jerome and a group of monks settled in Bethlehem. There Jerome directed pilgrimages, founded convents for women, and established a monastery. While living in Bethlehem, the great scholar began his revision of the Old Latin New Testament, which eventually led to the composition of the Vulgate.

Gary Hardin is pastor, Packard Road Baptist Church, Ann Arbor, Michigan.

commerce. The enrollment was finished, and the crowds moved out to return to their homes. Caesar's bidding had been done, and the village of David returned to normal. Only a few simple folks knew that on that night in this little village there had transpired the greatest event in the history of the world.

In infinite proportion it was much like the little community near Hodgensville, Kentucky. Early one morning a man was returning from a trip to Elizabethtown some miles away. He met a neighbor who was eager to learn what was happening in the outside world. After telling him of wars in Europe and events in Washington, the man asked, "What has happened here while I was away?" The neighbor replied, "Nothing. Oh, I believe that Mrs. Lincoln did give birth to a baby boy last night. I hear that they named him Abraham. But nothing important ever happens around here." Nothing important. If he had only known!

"And you, Bethlehem, in the land of Judah, are by no means least among the leaders of Judah: because out of you will come a Leader who will shepherd My people Israel" (Matt. 2:6).

THE HOMAGE TO THE INFANT

Jesus' birth was largely unnoticed by the world. Outside of the Bible no ancient historian took note of the event. They were so bent on recording the affairs of men and nations that they failed to recognize God's history within history, whereby in the person of His Son He had entered into the arena of time to answer the universal cry of men's hearts. But it did not occur without recognition by those whose hearts were prepared to receive it.

Heaven itself rejoiced over the glorious event. For the angelic hosts burst asunder the barrier of invisibility to proclaim the Savior's birth and to sing the first Christian anthem dedicated to His praise.

For their audience they had a handful of lowly shepherds, the simple folk who counted for little in the tides of history which ever beat upon the shores of time. But their hearts were firmly fixed in God's promises upon which they meditated in the quiet hours of the night. In Bethlehem's fields where Ruth had gleaned in the fields of Boaz, later to become his bride and the Moabitish ancestress of the Savior; where David had tended his sheep, all the while contemplating on God's glory and on Him who was to be born; there the shepherds first heard the glad tidings that unto them had been born a Savior, Christ the Lord.

The shepherds hastened to Bethlehem to find it as the angels had said. They found Mary and Joseph and the Babe lying in a manger. God in a cradle! Upon hearing from the shepherds about the heavenly declaration, Mary placed this event alongside the message of Gabriel, pondering them in her heart. And she knew that God had fulfilled His promise. The shepherds returned to their work, carrying back into their mundane sphere the memory of an experience which would forever cast an aura of glory about them and about all others who in humble trust come to Him who fills the universe with His presence, yet who for a little while was contained in a baby's crib.

When Jesus was eight days old, He was circumcised according to Hebrew law. At this time also He was formally given the name of Jesus. This is the Greek form of the Hebrew Word *Joshua* or *Yeshua*, meaning "Jehovah is salvation." Thus was obeyed the Word of God through Gabriel who said, "You are to name Him Jesus, because He will save His people from their sins" (Matt. 1:21).

The second group to pay homage to the Christ Child were two aged saints in the temple in Jerusalem. Again in keeping with Hebrew law forty days after Jesus' birth, Mary and Joseph took Him to the temple to make the prescribed sacrifice for the purification of the mother and the dedication of the Child. These peasant people received scant notice as they offered the sacrifices of the poor, two doves and two young pigeons. The priests were too busy with their sacrifices and teaching of the Scriptures to notice Him who was Lord of the temple. But two saints in Israel did take note of Him.

One was the aged Simeon. He had been promised by the Holy Spirit, probably in answer to his prayers, that he should not die until he had seen the Lord's Christ. When he looked upon the infant Jesus, the Holy Spirit told him that this was He. So taking Him into his arms, he blessed God, and in words of poetic beauty declared Jesus to be "a light for revelation to the Gentiles and glory to your people Israel" (Luke 2:32). Then he added words of an ominous note as to Mary he spoke of the sword which should pierce through her soul. Mary would realize the full import of these words when one day she would see her Son hanging on a cross. Truly her soul must have been a study of mingled lights and shadows as she heard Simeon's prophetic utterance.

Simeon's words aroused the soul of Anna, an aged prophetess who dwelt in the temple day and night as she was absorbed in prayer and wor-

Entry plaza of the Church of the Nativity.

ship. She also approached the infant, praising God and speaking of the Christ to all who were looking for the redemption of Jerusalem and Israel.

And the One bringing salvation was made evident to those whose hearts dwelt in the Lord and feasted upon the promises of His Word. So it was then; so it is now and always.

Mary and Joseph marveled at these things as they returned to Bethlehem. Apparently they decided not to return to Nazareth, for the next time they are mentioned in the Gospel narrative (Matt.), they are dwelling in a house in Bethlehem.

Probably some days or even months later a strange caravan arrived before the palace of Herod the king in Jerusalem. Wise men or Magi from the east came inquiring, "Where is He who has been born King of the Jews? For we saw His star in the east and have come to worship Him" (Matt. 2:2).

The exterior of the Church of the Annunciation in Nazareth. This is the traditional site of the angel's annunciation to Mary of Jesus' coming birth.

Who were these Magi? Tradition numbers them as three, stemming from the gifts which they presented before the Babe. Furthermore, it identifies them as coming from Europe, Asia, and Africa respectively. But these are traditions unsupported by the Gospel record.

In all likelihood they came from a land east of Palestine, probably from the Mesopotamian valley. Herodotus tells of such a people as being a former Median tribe. They had attempted an unsuccessful rebellion against the Persians. Therefore, they became a priestly tribe very much like the Levites among the Israelites. They were skilled in philosophy, medicine, and natural science. Especially were they students of astrology, the forerunner of modern astronomy. According to the ancients a man was believed to be affected by the star under which he was born. Any unusual phenomenon in the heavens was said to herald some special intervention of God into the natural order.

Recall that at this particular time an air of expectancy hovered over the ancient world. Wherever the Jews went, they carried their Scriptures which told of the promised Messiah. It is not surprising, therefore, to read from Tacitus, in the first century B.C., "that at this very time the East was to grow powerful, and rulers coming from Judaea were to acquire universal empire." Later both Suetonius and Josephus echoed the same thought. There was an almost universal expectancy regarding a Savior. Ancient inscriptions reveal this title as being ascribed to many rulers, including Augustus Caesar himself.

One can hardly question but that the Magi were aware of this expectancy. Probably they had received it from the Jews themselves who were in

Euphrates River near Deir Ezzor. This is one area that is thought to be the home of the Magi. This river forms the Mesopotamian Valley along with the Tigris River. The Magi may have originated somewhere in the Mesopotamian Valley.

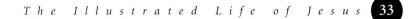

their land in abundance. They may even have been students of the Hebrew Scriptures. So when in the East they discovered an unusual star in the heavens they interpreted it as signifying a great divine event, as the birth of some unusual person. Therefore, they journeyed to Judea, the land in which this expectancy centered.

Many attempts have been made to identify this star with known astronomical phenomena, but no such explanation meets the requirements of the biblical language which describes it. The Gospel record calls it "His star," pointing to a special star for a special event. If one accepts the position that God created the universe, there is no reason He could not have created this star for the purpose of heralding the greatest event in history, namely, the Incarnation of God in human form.

Nevertheless, when the Magi inquired of Herod as to the whereabouts of the one "born King of the Jews," he summoned the chief priests and scribes. From them he learned that the Scriptures taught that He should be born in Bethlehem. Learning this the Magi departed. They rejoiced when once again the "star" appeared in the night sky. Following it they were led to the house where the young Child was, and falling down before Him they worshiped Him, presenting unto Him gifts: gold, frankincense, and myrrh.

These gifts are not without significance. Gold, the gift for a king; frankincense, suggestive of worship and sacrifice, the gift for a priest; myrrh, used to embalm the dead, the gift for one who is to die. Thus there was prophecy in these gifts. Jesus was born to rule in the hearts of men. As their High Priest He opened the way of man to God, and He did so in His atoning death.

Their mission accomplished the Magi prepared to return to their home, but being warned of God that evil stalked the land, they gave Jerusalem and Herod a wide berth in so doing. In their coming to Bethlehem, they had

A wide shot of the entire tell atop Herodium. Herodium was one of Herod's most famous palace-fortresses. Possibly the fortress from which the troops were sent to kill the babies.

blazed the path over which many who are wise would come to kneel before Him who is Truth.

The words of the Magi, "He who has been born King of the Jews," struck a note of terror in Herod's heart. Though he was in the twilight of his years, still he held tenaciously to his throne. To hold on to it, he had killed too often to let any impending threat go without notice. He had even killed members of his family. So feigning a desire to pay homage to this Child, he asked the Magi to bring him tidings as to the Child's whereabouts. Homage indeed! At the hand of a sword!

Bas relief of carpenter tools from the Roman period. These are the kinds of tools that Joseph and Jesus may have used in their work.

Therefore, when he learned that the Magi had avoided him, he sent troops to dispatch the infant King. To ensure that they did so, they were to slay every child up to two years of age in the area about Bethlehem. But his satanic plot was thwarted. Having been warned of God, Joseph already had taken Mary and the Babe to Egypt. However, the "innocents" died in Herod's futile effort. How many? No one knows. One may wonder why no record of this murderous deed is found outside the Bible, but such a foul deed by this despot whose hands dripped with the blood of royalty hardly merited notice in the chronicles of time.

These groups gathered about the Christ Child in His birth hour are not without a broader significance than the event of the moment. For while they were real people in actual experiences, they are suggestive of others of their kind through the succeeding ages. The humble, simple folk find in Jesus the answer to their deepest needs. The devout ever gather about Him in worship and praise. Wise men find in Him the answer to the intimate questions of life as they lay the fruits of their labors at His feet, and worldly systems ever oppose Him as they see in Him One who ultimately will bring to naught all of their schemes. But to all who come to Him in faith, He is ever God's Son born to be King.

THE SILENT YEARS

How long the little family remained in Egypt is a matter of speculation. It could have been for only one year. But at Herod's death God told Joseph that they should return to Palestine. Upon learning that Archelaus, Herod's son, reigned in Judea, Joseph followed God's guidance to return to their former home in Nazareth, and with this the curtain of silence fell upon the life of Jesus for more than twenty-five years. Only once is the curtain parted to give one brief glimpse of the young lad Jesus.

Human curiosity is such that it yearns for more detail as to these early years. In the years following Jesus' life, there arose many apocryphal gospels purporting to reveal His childhood. They tell many ridiculous stories about Him. According to them He made birds of clay, pitched them in the air, and they flew away. When

The interior of the Church of Annunciation in Nazareth. The place at the center in the background is the site, according to tradition, where the Annunciation took place.

His playmates angered Him, in a fit of anger He turned them into little goats. Instead of Jesus being subject to His parents, He is pictured as being a problem to them and to the neighbors. One has but to compare these stories with the dignified, beautiful account of Luke to understand that man's fanciful imagination can become a dangerous thing. The one clear statement in the canonical gospels covering approximately eleven years of Jesus' childhood is that "the boy grew up and became strong, filled with wisdom, and God's grace was on Him" (Luke 2:40).

But even though the Scriptures are largely silent, there are many things which may be learned about this period. His home was that of a peasant carpenter, but Joseph was tender, wise, and a godly man. Every Jewish lad was required to learn a trade. Under Joseph's wise guidance Jesus learned the trade of carpentry. However, in all likelihood His mother exerted the greater influence upon Him. From the Gospels it is clear that she was a woman pure and sensitive of soul. She possessed a great knowledge of the Hebrew Scriptures. God makes no mistakes. And He entrusted His Son to a mother full of grace and to a foster father who nobly stood beside her in the stewardship which God had placed upon them.

Jesus grew up in a normal home. After His birth there were other children born to Joseph and Mary. His half brothers were named James, Judas (Jude), Joseph, and Simon. There were at least two half sisters whose names are not given. In later life they did not accept Jesus as the Christ until after His Resurrection. Thereafter James and Jude became leaders in the Early Church; each wrote an epistle which bears his name.

There is strong evidence that Jesus' brothers and sisters did not understand Him. From this it may be inferred that they were never close to Him. Therefore, Jesus must have spent much of His time in the company of His mother or else alone.

As a normal Jewish lad Jesus received His education, first, in the home, and, later, in the synagogue under the tutelage of a scribe. Quite naturally this centered largely in the Scriptures, but His eager mind thirsted after knowledge, and He was "filled with wisdom" gained in the school of God.

Evidently Jesus spoke at least three languages. He quoted the Scriptures from the original Hebrew and not from the Greek translations. On more than one occasion He spoke in Aramaic, the current tongue among the Jews. And likely He was conversant in the Greek language, since it was commonly spoken in Palestine at that time.

Jesus' teachings reveal His tremendous understanding of both nature and human nature, and Nazareth and its environs were an ideal place in which to learn both. Nazareth is located in a beautiful valley surrounded by the hills of Zebulon and joined on the west by the Plain of Esdraelon. In the springtime beautiful flowers abounded. As Jesus wandered these hills, He learned about nature. He knew the habits of birds and animals. Farmers sowing and reaping were a common sight to Him.

In the closely knitted life of a village, He had a perfect laboratory in which to study human nature at its best and worst. Nazareth was a notoriously wicked town, and by observing it the boy Jesus learned the sordid nature of sin and its degrading effect upon men. But He saw the better side of life also. His mother was busy at the ordinary chores of the home: kneading dough, baking bread, patching worn garments, sweeping the floor, or searching for a lost coin. And then there was contact with the neighbors. Even today one may see the well which until recent years was the

A colonnaded street in Sepphoris.

only source of water for the village. How often Jesus must have gone with His mother to draw water and to listen as the women exchanged morsels of news! All of these things bore fruit in His later life as He drew upon the ordinary things of daily life to impart eternal truth.

Then there was the larger scope of learning. For One who never set foot out of Palestine, except as an infant, Jesus possessed great knowledge of the world in which He lived. How as a lad He must have dreamed as from a nearby hill He gazed upon the blue waters of the Mediterranean whose waves lapped the shores of the ancient world! The caravan route brought a constant stream of travelers through Nazareth. With wide-eyed wonder Jesus must have listened as He drank in the many stories of distant lands. All of these things, plus the liberal Greek atmosphere of Galilee, served to develop in Jesus a cosmopolitan view which enabled Him to overcome any temptation toward a narrow Jewish nationalism. His heart went out to all nations and to all men, and the simplicity of His surroundings made Jesus unusually sensitive against the stale and sophisticated emptiness of the teachings of the religious leaders of His day.

During all of these years Joseph and Mary made annual visits to Jerusalem for the Passover. Whether they took Jesus with them is not known, but when He reached the age of twelve, He became a "son of the Law" and began to observe the ordinances of Jewish worship. So at twelve years of age, He did accompany His parents to this great feast. While there He spent much time in the temple. The parents evidently traveled in a caravan, so that when they left Jerusalem to return to Nazareth they went a full day's journey before discovering that Jesus was not with them. Returning to Jerusalem, they finally found Him in the temple among the teachers both listening and asking questions. His hungry mind was feasting upon this intellectual and spiritual experience, and the learning of His years is evidenced in the astonishment of all as to His comprehension of the things of God.

The natural relation which Jesus bore to His mother and Joseph is seen in her mild rebuke that He had caused them such anxiety. But He replied, "Why were you searching for Me? . . . Didn't you know that I must be involved in my Father's interests?" (Luke 2:49).

This statement definitely reveals Jesus' consciousness of His unique relation with His Heavenly Father. Was it just now dawning upon Him? Or had He known it all along? To say dogmatically either way is mere speculation, but in all likelihood there had never been a moment in His conscious life when this awareness was not present with Him.

However He was still subject to His parents. With them He returned to Nazareth. There He continued to advance or to cut His way forward "in wisdom and stature, and in favor with God and with people" (Luke 2:52). Yes, Jesus learned. It was in keeping with His complete identity with man, apart from sin, that He learned as must any other child. But He learned His lesson well.

From this point on Joseph is not mentioned as being alive. Tradition says that he died when Jesus was a youth, maybe sixteen years old. Thereafter, Jesus assumed the duties of a man. He became the carpenter of Nazareth and the breadwinner in the family. Doubtless Mary more and more turned to Him for strength and succour. This within itself may not have improved the attitude of the brothers and sisters toward Him.

Nevertheless, the Savior of men was a hard-working artisan among His neighbors, until one day God whispered in His heart that the time of His public ministry had arrived.

An overview of modern Nazareth from the northeast looking southwest.

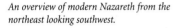

Richard Vinson

An overview of modern Nazareth from the southwest.

NAZARETH IS about fifteen miles from the Sea of Galilee and about twenty miles from the Mediterranean Sea. It lies just north of the plain of Esdraelon that separates the central hill country from the northern regions. Hills surround Nazareth except to the south, so that the high plains terminate in Nazareth. Nazareth is thirteen hundred feet above sea level. It gets an adequate rainfall, and since it is in a basin, it gets the runoff from the hills around. There is, however, only one spring in the town, thus, in ancient times the town's size was limited.[1]

Nazareth is never mentioned in the Hebrew Bible. More surprisingly, the Jewish historian Josephus never wrote about it even though he wrote about towns and cities all around it. Sepphoris was an

> *Then He went down with them and came to Nazareth, and was obedient to them. His mother kept all these things in her heart. And Jesus increased in wisdom and stature and in favor with God and with people.*
>
> Luke 2:51-52 (HCSB)

important walled city just three miles north. In 4 B.C., when Herod the Great died, a revolutionary named Judas raided the arsenal at Sepphoris and briefly took over the city. He hoped to free southern Galilee from Roman rule. The Romans defeated Judas' forces, burned Sepphoris, and sold the inhabitants into slavery. Josephus gave no word about Nazareth or its citizens' possible role in the revolt.[2]

The lack of notice is not because Nazareth was not there. Excavations have uncovered some burial caves that prove there was a small village early in the Middle Bronze Age (about 2200–2000 B.C.). Other caves show occupation later through the period of the monarchy, the Hellenistic period, and the Roman period.[3] The number of artifacts found from periods before the Maccabees (around 165 to

Sepphoris as seen from Nazareth. Some scholars suggest that Jesus may have worked on building projects in Sepphoris as a young man.

that after the destruction of the temple in A.D. 70, one of the twenty-four priestly "courses" was based in Nazareth.[8]

The Torah said that priests could not own farmland and were to be supported, at least in part, by the contributions of the people. Priests ate from the sacrifices offered at the temple, from first-fruit offerings, and from the tithes. After the fall of the temple, there was no central collection agency, and it made more sense to resettle the priests, distributing the "courses," or the different branches of the priestly clan, throughout Palestine so that they were not an economic drain on just one area.[9]

That a branch of the priestly family was based in Nazareth means that there were enough Jews there to take care of them and that the agriculture of the area produced a surplus. Some scholars think that the priests' presence meant that the population of Nazareth was exclusively Jewish.[10] Having the priests to feed meant that the farmers in the area needed to harvest the crops carefully, separating the priests' portion of the grain, olives, and wine, so that it could be guaranteed "clean" according to the stricter standards of priests' food. However, a branch of the priestly family was settled in Sepphoris. Sepphoris was populated by both Jews and Gentiles, so we should be cautious in assuming anything about the ethnic makeup of Nazareth.[11]

Nazareth has sometimes been described as being a secluded farming village in Jesus' day.[12] The "farming village" description is confirmed by archaeology. Digs have unearthed grain silos, cisterns, wine, and olive presses. Such finds are evidence that most of the residents were small-scale farmers. The plains to the south were among the most fertile in all Israel. Good farmland was close at hand. We can assume that the farmers of Nazareth grew the usual grain crops (wheat, barley, spelt), vegetables (beans, lentils, peas, onions, cucumbers), olives, grapes, and figs.[13] Farmers planted crops on a staggered schedule beginning when the early rains came around October. They prayed for good rains during the winter months and in the early spring and hoped to bring in a good harvest around April or May. Since little or no rain falls in the summer, the Feast of Weeks, coming seven weeks after the spring equinox, marked the virtual end of the growing season.

That Nazareth was secluded, however, ought to

63 B.C.) is much smaller than the number from the Maccabean period. Nazareth probably had been there all along but was so small and rural that it was not mentioned when people wrote accounts of important events in Israel.[4] Also the population possibly increased during the second century B.C., when the Maccabees were trying to make Galilee a more Jewish area than it had been previously.[5]

There have been few controlled archaeological digs at Nazareth. Thus, evidence about life there in the first century is slim. The evidence we have shows that in Jesus' day, Nazareth was a small community with a significantly Jewish population.[6] Based on the location of the tombs, archaeologists can estimate the size of the ancient village (because Jewish tombs were always beyond the borders of the living space) and thus estimate its population. One estimate suggests sixteen hundred to two thousand people lived there.[7] We have to say "significantly Jewish" because, not having any census data, we never can be certain how many inhabitants were Gentiles. Galilee had a mixed population, and that could have been true of Nazareth. Some scholars believe that this seems unlikely, however, because an inscription from Caesarea shows

be reconsidered. As noted earlier, Sepphoris was just three miles north. It sat on a hill visible from the top of the ridge overlooking Nazareth. The afternoon sun shining on the city walls and rooftops would have made it impossible to ignore. Farmers would have regularly gone to Sepphoris to sell goods in its two large markets.[14] Sepphoris was also the site for governmental services for the whole area. Villagers from Nazareth who needed to buy licenses or pay taxes would have done so in the town. Sepphoris also had a bank, and some scholars believe that evidence exists to show that the bankers sent lenders to the villages on a regular basis.[15]

Archaeologists, studying the pottery found in Sepphoris, have concluded that it was actually made in a few of the small villages nearby. Rural craftsmen and craftswomen made the eating and cooking dishes, brought them into Sepphoris, and sold them to the city folk.[16] Perhaps the people of Nazareth excelled in one such craft. Joseph and Jesus, we recall, were named tekton [TEK-tone] in the Gospels (Matt. 13:55; Mark 6:3). Tekton means some sort of skilled builder. Perhaps they were carpenters, but they could as easily have been stonemasons. They may have worked in Sepphoris. Herod Antipas, son of Herod the Great, made the city his capital and rebuilt it from the Romans' devastation. He built a magnificent palace, a theater seating four to five thousand people, impressive city walls, and a fortress.[17] All this construction is dated during Jesus' life. Perhaps He and other builders from Nazareth found most of their employment in Sepphoris.

Housing in an average rural first-century village would have depended on the family income and size. Houses had two to four rooms with a flat roof and sometimes a second story. Animals often were kept in one of the rooms or in a side room separated by a wall. Sometimes homes were built around a central courtyard where cooking could be done, thus keeping the house itself cooler and freer of smoke. The nuclear family in Judea averaged between four and five persons, and about half of the households were extended or multiple families, averaging five to fifteen members.[18]

Although Sepphoris probably controlled many governmental functions, the male heads of household in Nazareth likely continued to manage local affairs. These "elders" solved legal disputes, assigned punishments for all but the most serious offenses, and made certain that the faith of Israel was upheld. One scholar, basing his estimates on descriptions in Josephus, states that the average size of a village council of elders was seven.[19] The priests who lived there also would have had leadership roles because of their education and their traditional status.

[1] D. C. Pellett, "Nazareth," *Interpreters Dictionary of the Bible*, vol. 3 (Nashville: Abingdon Press, 1962), 525.
[2] Josephus, *Jewish War*, 2.68.
[3] Ayala Sussmann, ed., *Excavations and Surveys In Israel 1982*, vol. 1 (Jerusalem: Israel Department of Antiquities, 1984), 78.
[4] Jack Finegan, *The Archaeology of the New Testament* (Princeton: Princeton University Press, 1969), 27.
[5] Eric M. Meyers and James F. Strange, *Archaeology, The Rabbis, and Early Christianity* (Nashville: Abingdon Press, 1981), 57; E. Mary Smallwood, *The Jews under Roman Rule* (Leiden: E. J. Brill, 1976), 14.
[6] Finegan, 29.
[7] Meyers and Strange, 56.
[8] Finegan, 29.
[9] E. P. Sanders, *Jewish Law from Jesus to the Mishnah* (Philadelphia: Trinity Press, 1990), 25–26.
[10] Meyers and Strange, 57.
[11] Thomas R. W. Longstaff, "Nazareth and Sepphoris: Insights into Christian Origins," *Anglican Theological Review Supplement* 11 (March 1990): 12–13.
[12] Pellett, 525.
[13] Mark W. Gregory, "Agriculture/Farming," *Mercer Dictionary of the Bible* (Macon, Georgia: Mercer University Press, 1990), 15.
[14] Longstaff, 11.
[15] David Adan-Bayewitz and Isadore Perlman, "The Local Trade of Sepphoris in the Roman Period," *Israel Exploration Journal* 40 (1990): 153–172.
[16] Ibid.
[17] Longstaff, 11.
[18] Douglas A. Knight, "Family," *Mercer Dictionary of the Bible*, 294.
[19] Sanders, 17–18.

Richard B. Vinson is professor of New Testament, Averett College, Danville, Virginia.

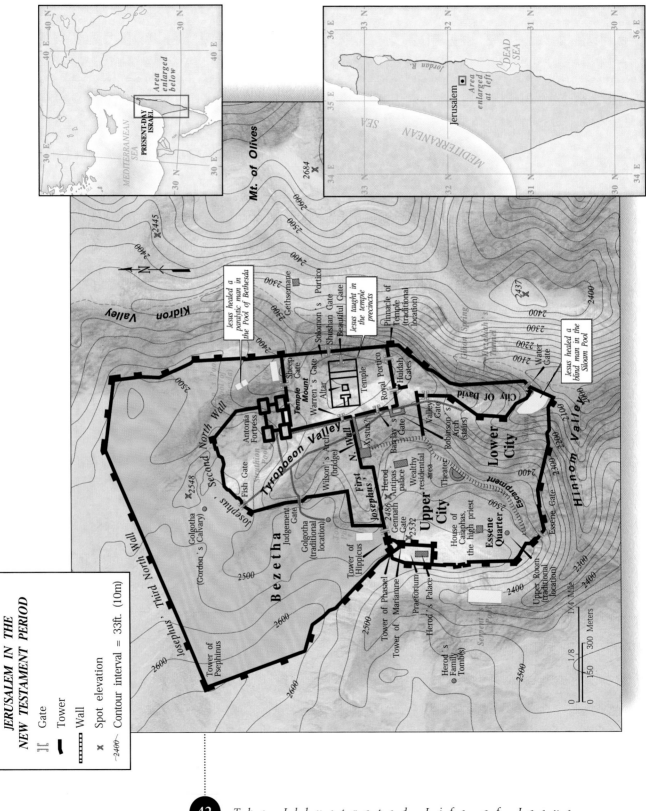

JERUSALEM IN THE
NEW TESTAMENT PERIOD

][Gate
— Tower
▪▪▪ Wall
✕ Spot elevation
~2400~ Contour interval = 33ft. (10m)

PRESENT-DAY ISRAEL

Area enlarged below

Area enlarged at left

DEAD SEA

MEDITERRANEAN SEA

Jerusalem

Jordan R.

Mt. of Olives

2684 ✕

Kidron Valley

✕2445

2400

2500

2600

Jesus healed a paralytic man in the Pool of Bethesda

Gethsemane

Jesus taught in the temple precincts

Solomon's Portico

Shushan Gate
Beautiful Gate

Pinnacle of Temple
(traditional location)

Sheep Gate

Temple Mount

Warren's Gate
Altar

Temple

Huldah Gates

Royal Portico

Jesus healed a blind man in the Siloam Pool

Water Gate

City of David

Antonia Fortress

Second North Wall

Fish Gate

Tyropoeon Valley

Wilson's Arch (bridge)

Xystus

N. Wall

Barclay's Gate

First Josephus

Valley Gate

Robinson's Arch (stairs)

Lower City

Hinnom Valley

✕2548

Bezetha

Judgement Gate

Colgotha
(traditional location)

Josephus'

2486 ✕
Gennath Gate

Herod Antipas' palace

Wealthy residential area

Theater

Escarpment

2500

2400

2300

2200

2100

Golgotha
(Gordon's Calvary)

Tower of Hippicus

✕2532

Upper City

House of Caiaphas, the high priest

Essene Quarter

Essene Gate

Third North Wall

Josephus'

Tower of Phasael

Tower of Mariamne

Praetorium

Herod's Palace

Upper Room
(traditional location)

Tower of Psephinus

2500

2600

2500

2400

2300

Herod's Family Tomb(s)

2400

2500

1/4 Mile

1/8

0   150   300 Meters

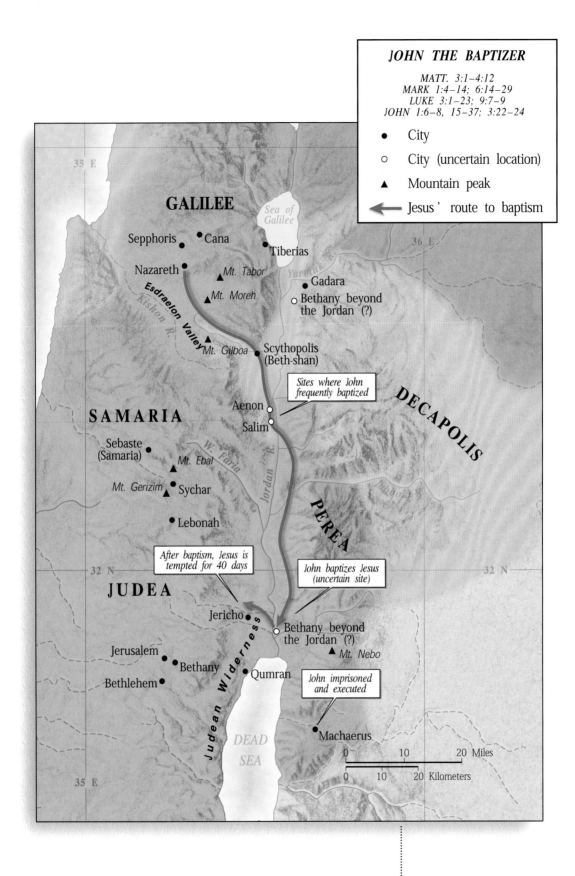

JOHN THE BAPTIZER

MATT. 3:1–4:12
MARK 1:4–14; 6:14–29
LUKE 3:1–23; 9:7–9
JOHN 1:6–8, 15–37; 3:22–24

• City
○ City (uncertain location)
▲ Mountain peak
← Jesus' route to baptism

GALILEE

Sea of Galilee

Sepphoris • Cana
• Tiberias

Nazareth
▲ Mt. Tabor
▲ Mt. Moreh

Esdraelon Valley

Kishon R.

Yarmuk R.

Gadara
○ Bethany beyond the Jordan (?)

▲ Mt. Gilboa
Scythopolis (Beth-shan)

DECAPOLIS

Sites where John frequently baptized

Aenon ○
Salim ○

SAMARIA

Sebaste (Samaria)
▲ Mt. Ebal
Mt. Gerizim ▲ • Sychar

W. Fari'a

Jordan R.

PEREA

• Lebonah

After baptism, Jesus is tempted for 40 days

JUDEA

John baptizes Jesus (uncertain site)

Jericho ••

Jerusalem •
• Bethany

Bethlehem •

Judean Wilderness

• Qumran

○ Bethany beyond the Jordan (?)
▲ Mt. Nebo

John imprisoned and executed

DEAD SEA

• Machaerus

0   10   20 Miles
0   10   20 Kilometers

In the fifteenth year of the reign of Tiberius Caesar, while Pontius Pilate was governor of Judea,…God's word came to John the son of Zachariah in the wilderness.

LUKE 3:1-2 (HCSB)

The Time of The Beginning

It had been four hundred years since a prophet of God had appeared among His people. Since the days of Malachi, there had been a famine of prophetic preaching in Israel. During this interval the temple ritual had continued, but even this had largely lost itself in the dry desert sands of a meaningless rote. Still there remained hungry hearts which waited and prayed for the coming of the Messianic age. And then came John the Baptist. It was probably late in A.D. 25 or the early spring of A.D. 26. John was of the priestly line. A priest began his

The Ministry of John the Baptist

A coin of Herod Antipas. This coin has the following inscription in Greek: "Of Herod the Tetrarch, year 33." It has on it a palm branch. As the Herods minted coins, they were sensitive to the Jewish concern with graven images. As a result, the Herods avoided producing coins with human likenesses.

ministry at the age of thirty, so John was probably that age when he appeared in the mission for which he had been prepared.

With the sense of a true historian, and following the custom of the ancients, Luke dated this event according to the rulers of the day. "In the fifteenth year of the reign of Tiberius Caesar, while Pontius Pilate was governor of Judea, Herod was tetrarch of Galilee, his brother Philip tetrarch of the region of Ituraea and Trachonitis, and Lysanias tetrarch of Abilene, during the high priesthood of Annas and Caiaphas, God's word came to John the son of Zachariah in the wilderness" (Luke 3:1–2).

Of him Alexander Maclaren said, "John leapt, as it were, into the arena full-grown and full-armed." His message was not his own but that of God, as in the wilderness of Judea he declared, "Repent because the kingdom of heaven has come near" (Matt. 3:2). Like some new Elijah dressed in rugged clothes made of camel's hair and bound about him with a leather girdle, he strode suddenly into the arena of history to herald the approaching King. His body fed upon the frugal fare of locusts and wild honey, but the soul of this son of the desert

John The Baptist

James Carter

ON MANY OCCASIONS an "advance man" is sent into a community to prepare for the coming of someone of importance. Perhaps the purpose of the advance man is to prepare the way for a political figure, an entertainment event, or an evangelistic crusade. The major responsibility of this individual is to see that all the groundwork has been done, that the details are all covered, and that the person or event is properly introduced to the community.

In many ways, John the Baptist could be considered an advance man for Jesus Christ's coming into the world. He was the forerunner of Jesus. He was the herald voice preparing the way for the Lord.

John descended from a priestly family. His mother, Elizabeth, who was a relative of Mary the mother of Jesus, was from a priestly family. She was described as one of the daughters of Aaron (Luke 1:5). Zechariah, his father, was a priest in the course of Abijah (Luke 1:5). John was born about six months before Jesus in a city in the hill country of Judea. His ministry was in southern Judea in the wilderness area and in the Jordan valley. Two places are mentioned in John's Gospel as the scene of his ministry, neither of which can be positively iden-

tified: Bethany or Bethabara (John 1:28) and Aenon near Salim. He grew up in the desert area (Luke 1:80).

Baptism was such an important part of John's ministry that it gave him his title: John the Baptizer or John the Baptist. Baptism also described his message because he was characterized as "baptizing in the wilderness and preaching a baptism of repentance for the forgiveness of sins" (Mark 1:4).

Baptism was not unknown prior to the ministry of John the Baptist. The Levitical law prescribed some washings in connection with cleansing (Lev. 14:8–9,19–20; 15). The prophets had anticipated that God would open in Israel a fountain for cleansing (Zech. 13:1). Proselytes, those persons converting to Judaism, were baptized as a means of the ceremonial cleansing for their uncleanness as Gentiles.[1]

The baptism administered by John was different, however. "Baptism of repentance"

Sandals of the first century A.D.

was nourished by a revelation from God which fell upon him as manna from heaven.

No wonder the multitudes left their homes, cities, and villages to hear him, for his preaching echoed the voice of God. Both his message and his mission bristled with the words of the Old Testament prophets. A steady stream of repentant sinners was being baptized in the Jordan River as evidence of their readiness to participate in the coming kingdom.

But not all who came did so with such willingness, for when word reached Jerusalem about this revival meeting, some Pharisees and Sadducees came to investigate it. Seeing this delegation, the Baptist boldly charged them: "Brood of vipers! Who warned you to flee from the coming wrath?" (Matt. 3:7). He saw them as a brood of snakes fleeing for safety before a desert fire. It was a shocking figure but one readily understood by them. Challenging them to repent, he reminded them that they could no longer smugly claim that as descendents of Abraham they were already in God's kingdom. Looking about at the multitude of desert stones, he said that God could of them raise up such children to Abraham. But the relationship which He demanded was a spiritual one. If they expected to participate in His kingdom, they must not only repent but show evidence of it in their works, for the axe of God's judgment was already laid at the roots of the trees. Any tree failing to yield such fruit would be cut down and cast into the fire.

Hearing these scorching words, the crowds asked, "What then should we do?" (Luke 3:10). And fitting his words to the need in each case, John told them, not how to be saved, but how to prove the genuineness of their repentance (Luke 3:11–14).

However, John's message was not solely one of judgment, for it sounded the note of hope also. The people were in a state of eager expectation. In reply to their question if he were the Christ, John said that there came One after him who was infinitely greater than he was. He was not even worthy to unloose the shoes of the One whom he heralded. Instead of baptizing them with water, as he had done, this One would baptize them in the Holy Spirit and the power of fire. He would come for both salvation and judgment. Drawing upon a common scene in Palestine, then as now, he pictured this One as one winnowing grain. As both wheat and chaff were thrown upward, they were separated by the wind. The grain was gathered and stored; the chaff was used for fuel. So would the One coming after John separate the true from the false. Salvation for the one; condemnation for the other! Such was the gospel which John preached in the wilderness of Judea.

Tiberius was the Emperor of Rome when Jesus began his public ministry.

meant a repentance for the past life and a cleansing of sin as symbolized by the baptism. This baptism also implied a loyalty to the kingdom of God. This rite of baptism was complete within itself. And when people expressed repentance and requested baptism, John demanded evidence of their repentance (Matt. 3:4–12).

The Synoptic Gospels (Matthew, Mark, and Luke) give a description of John the Baptist's ministry. They also record Jesus' baptism by John the Baptist. The Gospel of John gives John's testimony to Jesus (John 1:19–36). While the Synoptic Gospels present John as the forerunner of the Messiah, as a preacher of repentance, as an ethical teacher, and as the baptizer of a new remnant community, John's Gospel concentrates on the task of John the Baptist as a witness to Jesus.[2] The witness of John the Baptist to Jesus is presented in John 1:19–36 as occurring in a three-day period.

The first portion of this three-day period is found in John 1:19–28. The first witness of John to Jesus was negative in that John denied being several persons. Through that witness he declared that he was not the Christ, the promised Messiah of God. His task

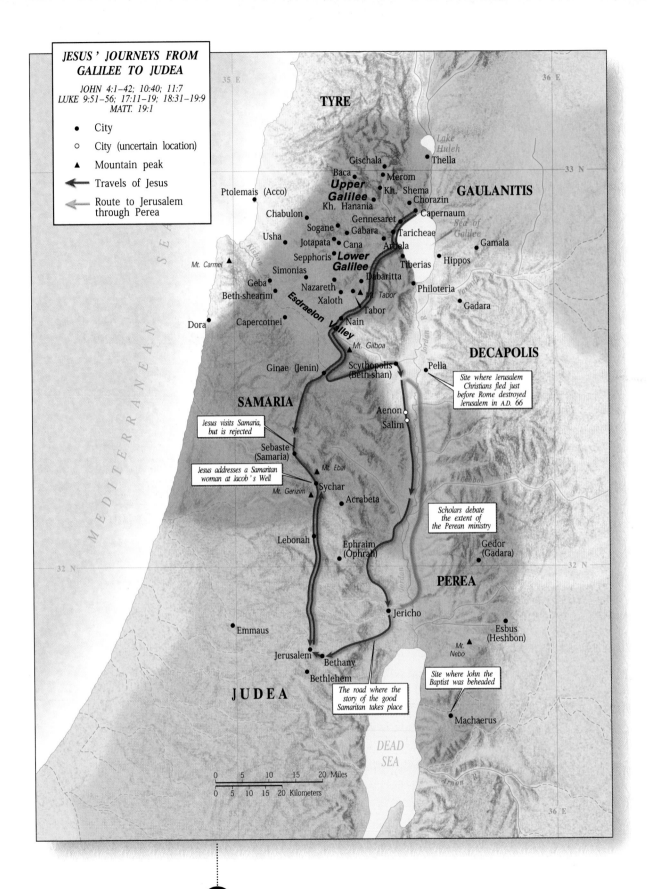

JESUS' JOURNEYS FROM GALILEE TO JUDEA

JOHN 4:1–42; 10:40; 11:7
LUKE 9:51–56; 17:11–19; 18:31–19:9
MATT. 19:1

- • City
- ○ City (uncertain location)
- ▲ Mountain peak
- ← Travels of Jesus
- ← Route to Jerusalem through Perea

TYRE

Lake Huleh

Gischala
Thella
Baca
Merom
Upper Galilee
Kh. Shema
GAULANITIS
Ptolemais (Acco)
Chorazin
Kh. Hanania
Capernaum
Chabulon
Gennesaret
Sea of Galilee
Sogane
Gabara
Taricheae
Usha
Gamala
Jotapata
Cana
Arbela
Sepphoris
Lower Galilee
Tiberias
Hippos
Mt. Carmel
Simonias
Dabaritta
Geba
Nazareth
Mt. Tabor
Philoteria
Beth-shearim
Xaloth
Gadara
Tabor
Dora
Capercotnei
Nain
Esdraelon Valley
Mt. Gilboa

DECAPOLIS

Ginae (Jenin)
Scythopolis (Beth-shan)
Pella

Site where Jerusalem Christians fled just before Rome destroyed Jerusalem in A.D. 66

SAMARIA

Aenon
Salim

Jesus visits Samaria, but is rejected

Sebaste (Samaria)

Jesus addresses a Samaritan woman at Jacob's Well

Mt. Ebal
Sychar
Mt. Gerizim
Acrabeta

Scholars debate the extent of the Perean ministry

Lebonah
Ephraim (Ophrah)
Gedor (Gadara)

PEREA

Jericho
Esbus (Heshbon)
Emmaus
Mt. Nebo

Jerusalem
Bethany
Bethlehem

Site where John the Baptist was beheaded

JUDEA

The road where the story of the good Samaritan takes place

Machaerus

DEAD SEA

| 0 | 5 | 10 | 15 | 20 Miles |
| 0 | 5 | 10 | 15 | 20 Kilometers |

MEDITERRANEAN SEA

35 E
36 E
33 N
32 N

"I baptize you with water for repentance. But the One who is coming after me is more powerful than I; I am not worthy to take off His sandals. He Himself will baptize you with the Holy Spirit and fire. With a winnowing shovel in His hand, He will clear His threshing floor and gather His wheat into the barn, but the chaff He will burn up with fire that never goes out."

Matthew 3:11-12 (HCSB)

Columns of Herod's palace at Machaerus. Archaeologists have recently discovered a large subterranean structure. Some believe this is the dungeon where John the Baptist was held. Josephus says Machaerus is the site where John was imprisoned and executed.

John the Baptist was six months older than Jesus, so evidently his ministry had covered that period of time when it took a most unique turn. Luke notes that at this time Jesus was about thirty years of age (3:23). Even though He was not of a priestly line, still He was to serve as the priest. Thus He began His public ministry when He reached His thirtieth birthday.

The news of John's ministry spread like wildfire throughout Palestine. Finally it reached the village of Nazareth, and hearing it, Jesus knew that His time had come. So closing His carpenter's shop, He went forth to meet His destiny.

Suddenly the Forerunner stood face-to-face with his Christ. Whether they had met before is not certain. Since they were related, it is possible that they had done so as children, but the probability seems to have been otherwise. In all likelihood John's parents had died when he was very young. Thereafter, he became a child of the desert; possibly he was reared by some desert group such as the Essenes. At any rate it would appear that he and Jesus for the first time stood face-to-face on the banks of the Jordan.

was to be the forerunner; he was to announce the coming of the Christ (John 1:23).

A committee of Jews from Jerusalem came to visit John. The committee was composed of priests, Levites, and Pharisees (John 1:19,24). Apparently the Pharisees were a part of that official delegation and not a separate group of people questioning John. The priest and the Levites would be the authorities on ritual activities. The Pharisees were interested in keeping the law. While the Pharisees did not normally ally with the priests and the Levites, this time they would make sure things were in order. They had one question for John: Who was he? (John 1:19).

John answered them with a threefold denial that he was the Christ. Each denial was more emphatic than the next. He was not the Christ (John 1:20). He was not Elijah, who had been taken directly to heaven, and thus

Wilderness of Judea where John the Baptist preached.

The River Jordan near where Jesus was baptized by John the Baptist.

Sunset over Herod's palace at Machaerus where John the Baptist was killed. Machaerus was a palace-fortress located about fifteen miles southeast of the mouth of the Jordan on a site rising 3,600 feet above the sea.

many thought would appear prior to the coming of the Messiah (John 1:21). And he was not that prophet that was predicted in Deuteronomy 18:5 to precede the Messiah (John 1:22).

If John were not any of those three, who was he? John answered them in the words of Isaiah 40:3. He was a voice that cried in the wilderness, the voice of a herald that would announce the coming of a king. His purpose was to prepare a straight and smooth roadway for the passage of the Lord as one would prepare a smooth road for a king in his travels. That was his task.

As John had given a threefold denial of his identity as the Christ, he also downplayed his work in three ways. He was not the Word, but a voice; he baptized with water, not the Holy Spirit; and he was not worthy to do the work of a slave of the promised Messiah.[3]

The scene of this exchange was identified as Bethany (HCSB) or Bethabara (KJV). The exact identity of this place on the other side of the Jordan River from Jerusalem is not known. The meaning of "Bethany"—house of depression or misery—is not significant for John's ministry. The meaning of "Bethabara" is interesting. It means "the place of crossing over" and is sometimes identified to tourists as the same spot for both Joshua's crossing the Jordan River and Jesus' baptism. That would lend itself to the observation that just as Joshua led the people across the Jordan River into the Promised Land, so Jesus was to cross over into the Promised Land at the head of the new people of God. That derivation is speculative.[4]

On the second day of his witness to Jesus, John gave a positive witness (John 1:29–34). This witness, too, was threefold. Through this witness John gave an understanding of the nature of the Christ. The baptism of Jesus by John the Baptist is not mentioned in the Gospel of John.

And yet John seems instinctively to have recognized Jesus as the Christ. A divinely given sign by which he would know the Christ had not yet been fulfilled (John 1:33–34). Without question John had baptized those who expressed their repentance, but when Jesus stood before him, he hesitated, stating that he should be baptized by Jesus rather than Jesus be baptized by him. Jesus brushed aside his hesitation, saying, "'Allow it for now, because this is the way for us to fulfill all righteousness.' Then he allowed Him to be baptisced" (Matt. 3:15).

So John and Jesus went down into the waters of the Jordan. Following Jesus' baptism a most remarkable thing happened. The heavens were opened, and John saw the Spirit of God descending as a dove upon Jesus. Then he heard a voice out of heaven saying, "This is My beloved Son. I take delight in Him!" (Matt. 3:17). John had his sign. He knew that Jesus was the Christ, and this fact had been authenticated by the presence of the triune God. In all probability only John and Jesus saw the "dove" and heard the "voice." It was a dual sign given only to them and not to the multitude. The revelation of God is given only to those who are prepared to receive it.

What is the significance of this divine manifestation? The dove is symbolic of gentleness, innocence, and meekness. Furthermore, the Levitical law prescribed one dove, along with a lamb, or two doves only for the poor, as a sacrificial offering. So the anointing of Jesus by the Spirit in the form of a dove foretold His ministry as a sacrifice for sin, and the Father's approval of the Son further attested His sinless purity as a fit offering for sin. Jesus had lived as a man for thirty years. So completely was He one in the will of God that He was well pleasing to God. Elsewhere throughout His ministry the Father will repeat this approval, but it came first as Jesus stood in the flowing waters of the Jordan.

Why was Jesus baptized? The baptism of John symbolized repentance from sin and a willingness to participate in the coming kingdom. But that Jesus' baptism involved more than these is evidenced by John's hesitancy to baptize Him, for Jesus had committed no sin from which He should repent.

Jordan River Valley near where John the Baptist ministered.

(And He was Himself the King of the kingdom.) It is quite true that in His baptism Jesus authenticated the mission of John, but His own words express an even greater purpose—"to fulfill all righteousness" (Matt. 3:15). It was to perfect the righteousness which Jesus came to establish, the righteousness of God in Christ Jesus.

And how was this made possible? Through the death, burial, and Resurrection of Jesus. It was thus that He identified Himself with the sins of men and gave them victory over them. Therefore, He submitted to baptism at the hands of John, but in so doing He portrayed that which He would do in order to redeem man from sin. He died for man's sin; He was buried; He rose from the grave in triumph over sin and death. So His baptism at once looked both backward and forward. Backward to the fact of man's sin and Jesus' identity with sinful man.

Close-up of wilderness terrain on the east face of the Mount of Temptation.

But this witness must have taken place after the baptism.

The first element of John's testimony is an announcement. He announced that Jesus was the Lamb of God who would take away the sin of the world (John 1:29). In the Old Testament the lamb, or another animal such as a goat, was used as a sacrifice in the daily burnt offering, the victim that bore the sins of the people on the Day of Atonement. The meat that was ritually slain, roasted, and then eaten at the Passover was the symbol of the servant who suffered in silence as he bore the people's grief and sin. But John's identification of Jesus went beyond all these. "He was the Servant who suffered as a lamb (Acts 8:32–35), the true Passover sacrifice (1 Cor. 5:7), the unblemished offering (1 Pet. 1:19), and the slain but conquering leader of the flock (Rev. 5:6,12; 7:14,17; 17:14; 22:1,3)."[5]

John also gave testimony to Jesus' preexistence. John identified Jesus as the One who actually was before him both by preexistence and by purpose (John 1:30). While it could mean that John had not previously met Jesus, he probably meant that he had not known Jesus as the Christ until his baptism.[6]

John's third testimony related Jesus to the Holy Spirit. He had witnessed the Holy Spirit descend from heaven as a dove and rest upon Jesus. That was God's sign that the One on whom the dove rested would minister with the Holy Spirit rather than with water (John 1:34). John baptized only with water. Jesus would immerse people in the power of the Holy Spirit of God. John's concluding testimony was that Jesus was the Son of God (John 1:34).

John the Baptist was arrested by Herod because of John's denouncement of Herod's marriage to Herodias, his sister-in-law. Imprisoned at Machaerus, Herod had John beheaded at the request of Herodias' daughter, who was prompted by her mother (Matt. 14:3–12). Of John the Baptist Jesus said, "Among those born of women no one greater than John the Baptist has appeared" (Matt. 11:11).

[1]Floyd V. Filson, "John the Baptist," *The International Standard Bible Encyclopedia*, rev. ed., 4 vols. (Grand Rapids: William B. Eerdmans Publishing Co., 1982), 2:1109.
[2]William E. Hull, "John," *The Broadman Bible Commentary*, vol. 9 (Nashville: Broadman Press, 1970), 221.
[3]Ibid., 222.
[4]Raymond E. Brown, *The Gospel According to John I-XII*, The Anchor Bible (Garden City, N.Y.: Doubleday and Co., 1966), 44–45.
[5]Hull, 223.
[6]James E. Carter, "John," *Layman's Bible Book Commentary* (Nashville: Broadman Press, 1984), 25.

James E. Carter is retired director of church/minister relations, Louisiana Baptist Convention, Alexandria, Louisiana.

Forward to His redeeming act as the sacrifice for the sins of the world. Thus at the outset of His ministry, Jesus symbolized that which all believers through the subsequent centuries have portrayed when they in an act of obedience follow Him in baptism.

THE TEMPTATIONS OF JESUS

Immediately following His baptism, Jesus retired into the wilderness of Judea. This He did under the leading or driving (Mark 1:12) of the Holy Spirit. The purpose of this retirement was that He might be tempted by Satan.

The traditional Mount of Temptation is a wild, barren mountain just west and north of Jericho. From the time of the Crusades, it has been called Quarantania, a name derived from the forty days of fasting. One can still stand on the mound of ancient Jericho and view it as it rises sharply and forebodingly out of the desert. Here for forty days Jesus was alone with no companions but the wild beasts of the desert. These days He spent in fasting, not as a

The "Wilderness" in Jesus' Temptation

Mike Fuhrman

Matthew (3:1; 4:1), Mark (1:4,12), and Luke (4:1–2) locate John the Baptist's ministry and Jesus' temptation in the "wilderness," which some English translations render "desert." This suggests a neat but misleading equation of the various "wilderness" regions mentioned in the Bible with such well-known desert regions as the Sonoran Desert of the southwestern United States. The wilderness areas of the biblical lands generally designate rocky areas rather than landscapes covered by sand dunes and cacti. When thinking of the meaning of "wilderness" in the Scriptures, we might think in terms of the badlands of South Dakota or the rangelands of the American West rather than in terms of the Mojave Desert. The Greek text of the New Testament uses only the word *eremos* to denote the wilderness. However, the Hebrew text of the Old Testament employs several different terms that can be translated "wilderness," each conveying a different nuance of meaning. Some in fact can denote a desert region, but this is not always the case.

Eastern slope of the Mount of Temptation from the Jordan River Valley.

The Bible uses "wilderness" to refer to several different geographical areas of ancient Palestine and adjacent regions. Generally speaking, these wilderness areas lay south, southwest, and east of the inhabited land of Israel, corresponding to the regions of the Sinai Peninsula, the Negeb, and the Transjordan. The wilderness area that was the apparent locale for the temptation of Jesus is yet another area situated on the eastern slopes of the Judean mountains, which was often called Jeshimon, "the desolation."

The Greek word *eremos*, translated "wilderness" in the New Testament, conveys the basic sense of "abandoned." This could denote abandoning a person, such as one's father or wife, abandoning a cause, or abandoning a locality. When referring to a locality, *eremos* does not necessarily denote a desert. It may only suggest a place that is "empty" or "without inhabitants," such as an "abandoned city" or

Wasteland of the northern Negev.

a "thinly populated district."[1] In Luke 15:4, where the shepherd leaves the ninety-nine sheep in order to search for the one that is lost, *eremos* denotes what in the western United States would be called the "range," or in the British Isles, a lonely "heath."

Popular thought in biblical times associated the wilderness with snakes, scorpions, and beasts of prey—a place of danger. Jewish tradition viewed the wilderness as a favorite haunt of demons (Luke 8:29) and monsters such as Lilith, the night hag (Isa. 34:14). Such associations indicate a place still in a state of primeval chaos, a place of darkness (Jer. 2:6,31) cut off from life (Lev. 16:22).

In the Old Testament several Hebrew terms, the most prominent of which is *midhbar*, refer to arid or semiarid lands not suited for permanent settlement but which could be used as grazing grounds for flocks and herds. The Book of Numbers in the Hebrew Old Testament is literally called *bemidbar*, "in the wilderness," or "in the desert." These arid and semiarid regions experience enough precipitation, though infrequent, and possess enough wells and oases to make some nomadic or seminomadic life possible. For this reason they have sometimes been called "tame" deserts. Indeed, *midhbar*, which occurs 269 times in the Old Testament to refer to the wilderness, apparently comes from a root word that means "to bring the flock to pasture" and hence serves as a technical

The Mount of Temptation as seen from the top of Old Testament Jericho.

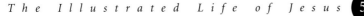

term in the Old Testament for pasture areas adjoining a semi-permanent shepherd encampment.

The historical significance of the term *wilderness* derives from its association with the experience of the Hebrew children during the Exodus. The Exodus experience depicts the wilderness in terms of both divine grace, when God performs special signs and wonders for His people, as well as in terms of the disobedience of God's people. In the wilderness of the Sinai Peninsula, the Israelites experienced God's miraculous provision of quail, manna, and water from the rock, as well as God's leader-

Mount of Temptation rising up to the west of the tel Jericho.

ritual but in preoccupation with the will of God. He had embarked upon His ministry. What kind of ministry would it be? He was the King of the kingdom. What would be the nature of His kingship? These were the questions which so occupied His mind that He lost all sense of hunger. Finally He became aware of His physical needs, and then Satan made his attack upon the Son of God.

Why should Jesus be tempted of Satan at this time? It has been noted that Jesus came into the wilderness "to be tempted of the devil" (Matt. 4:1). "To be tempted" is an infinitive of purpose meaning to "test, to prove, either in the good or evil sense." God would permit Jesus to be tested to prove the good; Satan would test Jesus in an effort to prove Him evil. It is in this latter sense that the experience may be called temptation.

At this point the question naturally arises as to whether Jesus could yield to temptation. Of course He did not possess a sinful nature. Nor was He guilty of antecedent sins which made Him liable to yielding to the overtures of Satan. But it must be admitted that He had the power to yield, or else the temptations were not real, and if they were not real, then He merely pretended to be tempted. Such would make Him guilty of hypocrisy, the sin which Jesus assailed more than any other. It must be remembered that Jesus had completely identified Himself with man, apart from sin, and He was tempted in His humanity, not in His deity. As such He had the power to sin, but a more glorious truth is that He also had the power not to sin. And so He "was in all points tempted like as we are, yet without sin" (Heb. 4:15).

Another question presents itself. Were these temptations merely psychological experiences, or did they involve a bodily confrontation between Jesus and Satan? Some hold to the former position, but there is no reason the latter could not be true. As

God was manifested in bodily form, in like fashion Satan, the adversary, appeared to Jesus in bodily form. The struggle which raged on Quarantania and in Jerusalem was but a visible phase of the conflict which ever goes on in the spiritual realm. The "devil" means "slanderer," and Satan ever slanders God to man (Gen. 3:4) and man to God (Job 1:9–11). Such was the struggle which raged in the temptations of Jesus.

Before examining the three temptations themselves, it is well to note that in resisting them Jesus did so in the realm of His humanity, not His deity. For his purpose Satan assumed that Jesus was the Son of God, but Jesus did not call upon His divine power to resist the evil one. Indeed, the first two temptations were designed to lead Him to do so, yet He did not separate Himself from man in this struggle. Apart from His sinless nature and life, Jesus called upon no power that is not available to any man as he faces temptation. His only weapon was the Scripture, the Sword of the Spirit, and He wielded it within the center of the will of God.

In order to understand the temptations of Jesus in the wilderness, two things must be kept in mind. They must be cast against the backdrop of current Jewish expectations concerning the Messiah. The Jews thought of Him as the ruler of an earthly kingdom, doing great wonders and providing them with an abundance of material prosperity, and Jesus was aware of these things which were so evident in the three proposals of Satan. Furthermore, these temptations were aimed at the three areas of man's being in which he may be tempted: physical appetites, aesthetic nature, and spiritual ambition. These areas are evident in Satan's temptation of Eve: "And when the woman saw that the tree was good for food [physical appetite], and that it was pleasant to the eyes [aesthetic nature], and a tree to be desired to make one wise [spiritual ambition, cf. Genesis 3:5] . . ." (Gen. 3:6).

The first temptation was directed at physical appetite: "tell these stones to become bread" (Matt. 4:3). This involved Jesus' use of His divine power for selfish purposes. It expressed distrust in God's benevolence and power to care for His own, but more it suggested that He should be a bread Messiah, ministering only to the physical needs of men. Every age has produced such, as power-mad rulers have enslaved their subjects under the guise of giving them prosperity in material things.

In reply Jesus quoted from Deuteronomy: (Note also the other two temptations.) "Man must not live on bread alone, but on every word that comes from the mouth of God" (Matt. 4:4; Deut. 8:3). Man must have bread, but he needs far more than bread. Jesus refused to call upon His divine power to provide for His own human needs. He had identified Himself with man and would trust in His Father to provide His every need. He came to give men more than bread for their bodies, it was the living Bread for their souls.

The second temptation was aimed at Jesus' aesthetic nature. Transporting Jesus into the temple area in Jerusalem, Satan caused Him to look from its highest point into the valley far below. He preyed upon the natural tendency

ship by the pillar of cloud by day and a pillar of fire by night. Unfortunately, in the wilderness the Israelites also murmured repeatedly against Moses and rebelled against the Lord. In the wilderness the Israelites received the evil report brought back by ten of the twelve spies sent to spy out Canaan, and in the wilderness God disciplined Israel by condemning an entire generation to die there.

Theologically, beginning with the Old Testament prophets and continuing on through the intertestamental period into the New Testament era, the wilderness began to assume a deep and rich symbolic significance for the Jewish people as the place where God delivers His people. During the several hundred years between the Exodus and the Old Testament prophetic era, the more painful memories of the wilderness experience during the Exodus faded. The classical Hebrew prophets began to associate Canaan and its idolatry with the root of the Israelite troubles. At the same time the gracious, saving aspects of Israel's experience in the wilderness nurtured in Judaism a tendency to remember the wilderness in great and glorious terms. Its special features, for example, the miraculous provision of manna, came to be associated with the blessings of the Messianic Age. The

of dizziness: "throw yourself down." Put God to the test. And then Satan also quoted from Scripture: "For it is written, 'He will give His angels orders concerning you, and, in their hands they will lift you up, so you will not strike your foot against a stone'" (Matt. 4:6).

But note that whereas Jesus quoted from the Law, Satan quoted from the Psalms (Ps. 91:11–12). He quoted poetry as though it were prose. Also Satan omitted one vital phrase: "For he shall give his angels charge over thee, to keep thee in all thy ways" (Ps. 91:11). Satan sought to divert Jesus from His way to Satan's way. The Jews thought of the Messiah as suddenly coming to His temple, perhaps floating down from its pinnacle amid the acclaim of the multitudes.

But Jesus again refused Satan's proposal: "You must not tempt the Lord your God" (Matt. 4:7; Deut. 6:16). He did not come to found a kingdom upon outward spectacular deeds but upon truth in the inward parts. He would not do so by daring God but by trusting Him.

The third temptation was based upon spiritual ambition. In His mission Jesus challenged Satan's falsely assumed sovereignty over the earth. He would assert His own sovereignty as seen in His kingdom, and this assertion involved His death for the sins of men.

But from an exceeding high mountain, Satan caused the kingdoms of the world and their glory to pass in review before Jesus. And then his proposal: "I will give You all these things if You will fall down and worship me" (Matt. 4:9). He offered Jesus a shortcut to world supremacy.

In the first place, this was not Satan's to give. In the second place, it would have been an empty sovereignty. In the third place, had Jesus succumbed to this temptation, the very moral structure of the universe would have collapsed. God would have been defeated, and Satan would have been sovereign indeed.

view thus arose that at some future time God would again take the Israelites back into the wilderness (Hos. 2:14–15) to be renewed there in a new exodus (Isa. 40:3–5; Ezek. 20:30–38). The belief thus arose in the Judaism of the New Testament era that the end-time salvation would begin in the wilderness and that the Messiah would first appear there. For this reason, several first-century messianic pretenders, particularly those belonging to the party of the Zealots, would gather a following in the wilderness and revolt against Rome (see Acts 21:38). Biblical interpreters often refer to this theological meaning of the wilderness as "the wilderness tradition."

Mark made references throughout his Gospel to wilderness themes. For example, just as God fed the children of Israel manna in the wilderness, Jesus fed the multitude in a wilderness place east of the Sea of Galilee (Mark 8:1–9). The wilderness setting for John the Baptist's ministry and for Jesus' temptations would certainly call to mind for any first-century Jew or Jewish Christian an entire construct of theological ideas associated with the wilderness, with the theme of a new exodus, the theme of the wilderness as the place where God renews and delivers His people, and especially the theme of the wilderness as the locus of the end-time salvation.

[1]*Theological Dictionary of the New Testament*, vol. 2, ed. Gerhard Kittel, ed. and trans. Geoffrey W. Bromiley (Grand Rapids: Wm. B. Eerdmans Pub. Co., 1964), 657.

Michael Fuhrman is associate professor of Christian studies and director of in-service training, Southwest Baptist University, Bolivar, Missouri.

But Jesus again wielded the Sword of the Spirit: "Go away, Satan! For it is written: 'You must worship the Lord your God, and you must serve Him only.'" (Matt. 4:10; Deut. 6:13). Jesus chose to follow God's way, even though it led Him to a cross. It was the longer, harder way, but it was the only true way.

Satan left Jesus for a season, but he would return again and again, even as he has come to men and nations through the ages. Unhappily they have ever fallen victims to his wiles. But the Son of God came forth from the wilderness in triumph to walk ever in the ways of His Father, and He calls all men everywhere to follow in His train.

THE FIRST DISCIPLES

In the meantime John the Baptist continued to preach along the banks of the Jordan. When once again he saw Jesus in his midst, he clearly identified Him as the Christ, setting forth the divine fulfillment of the sign by which he would recognize Him. In one sentence he foretold the nature of His mission as he said, "Here is the Lamb of God, who takes away the sin of the world" (John 1:29). As the result of this proclamation, two of John's disciples left him to follow after Jesus. These were Andrew and, probably, John, the beloved disciple. Andrew brought his brother, Simon, later to be called Peter, to Jesus. By implication it may be inferred that John did the same for his brother James.

The next day Jesus left the Jordan valley to return to Galilee. Along the way He called Philip to follow Him, and Philip led Nathanael to become a disciple of Jesus. All of these men had been drawn to John the Baptist, but both by his preaching and the power of Jesus' personality, they left the "forerunner" to follow the Christ. Later, as Jesus' ministry broadened, this very fact engendered jealousy among those who still clung to John the Baptist. But ever true to his mission, he declared, "He must increase, but I must decrease" (John 3:30). So John, with his mission accomplished, waned before Jesus as the moon does with the rising of the sun.

THE FIRST MIRACLE

Three days after His return to Galilee, Jesus, His mother, and His disciples were guests at a marriage feast in Cana, a village located only a few miles from Nazareth. When the supply of wine was exhausted, Mary called the emergency to the attention of her Son. Mildly rebuking His mother for her implied request that He do something about it, Jesus proceeded to turn water into wine, a wine which the steward of the feast declared to be better than the first.

Four lessons may be drawn from this incident. First, Jesus avowed that, in contrast to John the Baptist's ascetic nature, He would render His ministry as a social being. Second, He respectfully reminded His mother that no longer would He be merely her Son but her Lord. Third, by calling attention to the steward's response, John, the author of the fourth Gospel, mystically suggests that the revelation of God in Jesus is better or more complete than that found in the Old Testament. Fourth, by this miracle the disciples were led to believe fully in Jesus as the Christ. It was the "beginning of his signs" (John 2:11, ASV) which would show forth His deity.

From Cana Jesus and His company paid a brief visit to Capernaum, the city which later would serve as His headquarters for the Galilean ministry. From here He probably returned to His home in Nazareth where He remained in seclusion for some time.

THE FIRST CLEANSING OF THE TEMPLE

Several months had elapsed since Jesus' baptism which probably took place in the late summer of A.D. 26. It was now the spring of A.D. 27, just prior to the Passover, which comes during the week before Easter Sunday. This was the greatest of all the feasts of the Jews, memorializing Israel's deliverance out of the bondage of Egypt. So Jesus and His disciples journeyed from Galilee to be present for this feast. The synoptic Gospels (Matt., Mark, and Luke) record only one visit of Jesus to Jerusalem, but John, in keeping with his purpose to report portions of His ministry omitted by the others, includes several visits prior to His final one at the close of His ministry.

Apart from a Jew's natural desire to be in Jerusalem for the Passover, Jesus' present journey seems to indicate a greater purpose. A. T. Robertson calls the first year following Jesus' baptism "The Year of Obscurity." It is recorded only in John's Gospel. The synoptic Gospels plunge Jesus immediately into His Galilean ministry. Why this period of "obscurity"? For some unknown reason the Lord delayed what may more likely be

called His public ministry. But what more appropriate time could He have chosen to inaugurate it than the Passover, and that in Jerusalem itself? It was the feast of deliverance, and Jerusalem was the capital city of the Jewish religion. So He began by challenging the center of Judaism, and at the time of year when the Jews were most expectant concerning their Messiah.

He threw out His challenge in the temple itself, the center of Jewish worship. This He did by cleansing the temple. This act was not only a protest against the emptiness of the Jewish religion, but it was directed immediately against merchandising in the temple itself. What had begun as a service to the worshipers had degenerated into a system of defrauding them. This constituted what was commonly called "The Bazaars of annas," for it was under the control of the former high priest and his sons.

Pilgrims came from great distances to sacrifice in the temple. Therefore oxen, sheep, and doves were kept in the Court of the Gentiles to be sold at exorbitant prices to the worshipers. Furthermore, each adult male Jew was required to pay annually the half shekel temple tax. Since it must be paid in Jewish coins, money changers were set up to exchange foreign coins for this Jewish money. A fee was charged to make this exchange. One has but to visit a modern bazaar in the Near East to grasp something of the bedlam which existed in this "House of Prayer." Not only were the Jews exploited, but it was a scandal to the Gentiles who were permitted in this part of the temple area.

So in righteous indignation Jesus made a scourge of cords and drove the animals out of the temple. He overthrew the tables of the money changers and told those who sold doves to take them away. "Stop turning my Father's house

Cana in the Asochis Valley, the site of Jesus' first miracle as recorded in John's Gospel.

into a marketplace!" or an emporium (John 2:16). Note the sense of divine Sonship once again expressed by Jesus.

Upon learning of Jesus' action, the Jewish religious leaders came to Him with a challenge as to the authority by which He did this. They demanded a "sign" to justify such action. According to their own belief, they were justified in making this demand. For to them only a prophet or the Messiah Himself could exercise authority beyond their own over the temple, and since Jesus did not claim to be a prophet, His act could have but one meaning. It signified that He claimed Messianic authority. The Jewish leaders comprehended the significance of Jesus' deed.

Since Jesus was not yet ready to proclaim His Messiahship openly, He replied with a veiled "sign" which was yet in the future. "Destroy this sanctuary, and I will raise it up in three days" (John 2:19). He may have pointed to His body as He spoke of His death and Resurrection, but the Jews were in no position at this time to grasp His meaning. They thought only of the material temple. Herod the Great began to build the temple in 20–19 B.C. It was now in its forty-sixth

The Origin of Passover

Jerry W. Lee

As a rule people resent being passed over. The concept seems so totally unfair. Yet when Israel was passed over, the event became the basis for the observance of a commemorative feast. They called it Passover. The word sounds like a verb, but the term is a noun. The celebration still continues to be observed annually, making it the world's oldest religious festival.

The verb (*pasah*) from which we get the word Passover (*pesah*) has two primary meanings. The word may mean to "pass" or "leap over." A second meaning is to "be lame, limp."[1] Some scholars accept this latter meaning in that God skipped over the Hebrews. The word was used to refer to the dancing antics of Baal's priests on Mount Carmel in Elijah's day (1 Kings 18:26). The most likely meaning, however, is the first one: to pass or leap over.

The Passover had its origin in Egypt. Prior to Israel's

Ceramic vase with jumping deer, symbol of Rhodes. The verb Hebrew verb pasah *may mean to leap over.*

birth as a nation, they had gone to Egypt as an honored and privileged family. In time, however, they became a despised and feared people. Consequently, they were reduced to slavery for several centuries. They needed deliverance.

God called Moses to be Israel's deliverer. The ten plagues were visited upon Egypt to vindicate Yahweh's sovereignty as Israel's God. The conflict was between Yahweh and the gods of Egypt. The Passover event was associated with the tenth and final plague that broke the pharaoh's resolve and determination to hold Israel in slavery. God had affirmed repeatedly that they shall "know that I am Yahweh." That phrase meant that the Egyptians would be convinced that nothing could prevent God's sovereign will from being realized.

The Pharaoh's obstinate refusal to submit to God's commands brought divine wrath and judgment on Egypt. Because of his rebellion in hardening his heart, he

Freshly slaughtered beef and lamb hanging in the open air of a meat shop in the old section of Jerusalem.

lamb or a goat on the tenth of Abib. The lamb was to be without blemish and not more than one year old. The animal was to be shut up for four days. On the fourteenth of Abib the entire family was to be gathered in the dwelling for the celebration.

Through Moses God had proclaimed that on that night throughout Egypt the firstborn male would die. A provision for escape was made for His people in God's plan of a Passover sacrifice.

The celebration was first and foremost a family celebration. All family members were to be gathered along with any sojourners (*ger*) and servants who had been circumcised. By that act they chose to identify themselves with the covenant people.

The head of the household, the father, served in the place of a priest. At twilight, or literally, "between the two evenings," he was to kill the animal and catch the blood. The time was probably between the time of sunset and the approaching darkness. By the New Testament time the sacrifice was performed in the temple by the priests about 3:00 P.M.

In Egypt, with the family and any guests gathered inside, the father took a branch of hyssop (Ex. 12:22) and applied the blood to the two doorposts and the lintel. That served as an effective barrier to the entrance of the destroyer or death angel that would visit the land of Egypt that night.

The meal consisted of three basic items: meat, bread, and salad. The meat was to be the lamb or goat roasted in an unusual way: whole, without any broken bones, and with the entrails. It was not permitted to be boiled or eaten raw. Apparently they would eat the choice parts.

In addition the Israelites had unleavened bread. Leaven was a symbol of impurity. Furthermore, the use of leaven required time for the dough to rise; but on this occasion they did not have time for such an occurrence. The meal was to convey a sense of haste.

brought death and ruin upon his own family and Egypt.

Passover occurs within the first month of the Hebrew calendar. That calendar was influenced by their agricultural economy. The first month, Abib, would correspond to our March/April. The word *Abib* means "newly ripened corn." Thus Passover was a spring festival associated with the new year and the beginning of the barley harvest. (Only later was the Babylonian calendar adopted and the name Nisan used to designate the month.)

The observance began with the selection of a sacrificial

The green salad consisted of "bitter herbs." This was comprised of ingredients such as a wild or bitter lettuce, dandelion, endive, and chicory.[2] The flavor was to represent the harsh and bitter slavery to which they had been subjected.

Nothing was to be saved for the next day. It was not merely to be discarded. Instead, it served as a sacrifice in that it was to be burned in a fire before morning.

The meal was not intended to be eaten leisurely. Everything about it was to convey the expectancy of an immediate journey. Not only were they to

Tel-El-Yehuda/possibly Goshen, where the people of Israel lived in Egyptian captivity. This is one of the areas in Egypt where Israel was settled and flourished.

year of building and was not finished until A.D. 64—six years before it was destroyed by the Romans. So Jesus' words seemed preposterous to the Jews. They showed their scorn of this Galilean peasant when they asked literally, "And will You raise it up in three days?" (John 2:20). Therefore the Jewish leaders as a group scornfully rejected this first challenge of Jesus.

However, many of the people did believe on Him as they witnessed the many miracles which He performed. Still Jesus did not commit Himself to them since He knew their innermost thoughts. The time had not yet come for Him to do so.

THE VISIT OF NICODEMUS

But there was one Jewish leader who did not reject Jesus. This was Nicodemus, a Pharisee and a member of the Sanhedrin, the ruling body or Supreme Court among the Jews. He was a man of position, power, wealth, and righteous character. Some suggest that his use of the word *we* indicates that he came to Jesus as the representative of a group of interested inquirers.

At any rate Nicodemus sought out Jesus under the cover of night. It is quite natural that this teacher among the Jews would come to this unknown, unaccredited teacher thusly. He wished to escape the criticism of his colleagues who had rejected Jesus as being of no consequence. In spite of that fact, Nicodemus was convinced by Jesus' signs that He was a teacher come from God.

However, when Nicodemus so stated this, Jesus brushed his compliments aside as He went to the very heart of the matter: "Except a man be born again, he cannot see the kingdom of God" (John 3:3). As a good Jew Nicodemus thought that he was already in that kingdom. Furthermore, his mind could go no further than the physical birth. Did Jesus mean that he should

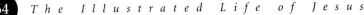

experience another such birth? But Jesus told him that he must be born both naturally and spiritually. By his natural birth ("of water") he entered into certain natural relationships. By his spiritual birth ("of . . . the Spirit") he would enter into certain spiritual relationships. Thus Jesus clearly declared the nature of His kingdom as spiritual.

That this experience involved a mystery beyond man's natural comprehension Jesus recognized as He compared it to the mystery of the wind. Both must be accepted by faith based upon the evident results of each.

Nicodemus still did not understand. So Jesus led him to more familiar ground, that of the Scriptures of which he was a master. Citing the incident of Moses lifting up the brazen serpent in the wilderness (Num. 21:8–9) Jesus said, "So the Son of Man must be lifted up, so that everyone who believes in Him will have eternal life" (John 3:14–15). Then there follows John 3:16, the "Little Gospel," and other words of infinite depth and meaning. Some hold these words (John 3:16–21) to be comments made by John, but there is no reason they could not have been spoken by Jesus Himself. Words of such matchless beauty and profundity fall naturally from the lips of the Teacher.

Did Nicodemus at this time believe in Jesus as his Savior? The answer to this question is not given. But, if not then, certainly prior to Jesus' death Nicodemus did make such a committal.

JESUS' DEPARTURE FOR GALILEE

Following the interview with Nicodemus, Jesus enjoyed a brief but fruitful ministry in Judea. John the Baptist's ministry was on the decline. More and more people were coming to Jesus, who soon was making and baptizing more disciples than the Baptist. John's Gospel points out, however, that Jesus baptized no one, leaving this work to be done by His disciples. Nevertheless reports of Jesus' successful ministry came to the Pharisees, and this increased their hostility toward Him. Furthermore, at this time word came to Jesus that John the Baptist had been imprisoned by Herod Antipas, the puppet king of Galilee and

be fully clothed, but their loins also were to be girded. This was not a relaxing style of dress. Instead, the bottom hem of the robe was pulled from the back up between the legs. Then it was tucked snugly into the front waist band effectively making a pair of walking trousers. Whereas normally they may have eaten barefooted, on this occasion they were to wear sandals. They also were to hold a staff in their hands.

The meal was to be eaten in haste. The normal response would be for the mother to instruct her children to "Slow down," "Don't eat so fast," "Chew your food," or "You may choke." But not on that night! She may have said, "Don't take so long," "Eat quickly," or "Hurry, hurry." They were expecting to make a journey to freedom! Deliverance was at hand. The Passover was occurring at that moment. Throughout Egypt the death of the firstborn was occurring in every home except those whose doorways were covered by the blood of the Passover animal.

The Passover meal was to be a teaching device. In successive generations one was designated to ask, "What does this ceremony mean to you?" (Ex. 12:26). The answer focused on the covenant relationship and that God had

Forum columns from Samaria.

honored His covenant promises in sparing Israel. Divine judgment against those who rebelled against God was evident in the death of the firstborn. Divine love was evident in the passing over of those who observed the Passover.

Israel traced its national origin to this event. The Israelites had entered Egypt as a special family; they emerged from Egypt as a potential nation. God had acted in their behalf. Such a memorable event must never be forgotten. Thus the celebration of Passover continues to celebrate the freedom and new life given by God to His people.

¹Brown, Driver, and Briggs, *A Hebrew and English Lexicon* (Oxford: Oxford University Press, 1962), 820.
²Geoffrey W. Bromiley, gen. ed., *International Standard Bible Encyclopedia* (revised) (Grand Rapids: Eerdmans, 1988), 1:520.

Jerry W. Lee is professor of Old Testament, Florida Baptist Theological College, Graceville, Florida.

Perea, a region east of the Jordan. John was probably imprisoned at Machaerus, a strongly fortified castle east of the Dead Sea. This would indicate that Herod Antipas also may have been there at this time.

Therefore, because of the rising hostility of the Pharisees in Jerusalem and Herod's show of opposition to John the Baptist, Jesus felt that it was wise to go to the more favorable atmosphere of Galilee. He was not running from opposition, but He would pick His time and place to meet it.

JESUS AND THE WOMAN OF SAMARIA

"He had to travel through Samaria" (John 4:4). What did the fourth evangelist mean by these words?

The Samaritans were a hybrid race produced by a union of Israelites and other people sent into the Northern Kingdom following its conquest by Assyria. Following the Babylonian captivity of the Jews, they had opposed efforts to rebuild Jerusalem. These things, plus the long enmity which existed between the kingdoms of Israel and Judah, resulted in a strong antagonism between the Jews and Samaritans in Jesus' time.

Partly out of fear of the Samaritans and also their resentment toward them, the Jews avoided their land whenever possible. Therefore, for Jews traveling between Judea and Galilee, it was customary to cross the Jordan River and journey north or south on its eastern side. On occasion Jesus followed this route, though for different reasons. He also traveled through Samaria more than once, as He did on the occasion at hand.

Why was it that "He had to travel through Samaria"? Certainly this need was neither physical nor geographical. This was probably one of those times where John wrote words containing a mystical or spiritual meaning. The need, therefore, was a spiritual compulsion, for Jesus knew the experience which awaited Him there.

The Samaritan village of Sychar was about

twenty-five miles from Jerusalem. Nearby was Jacob's well. It was/is a flowing spring about one hundred feet deep. One may still visit this well and drink its cool water. It is perhaps the most certain spot in modern Palestine insofar as its connection with Jesus is concerned.

When Jesus and His disciples arrived at this well, the disciples went into the nearby village to purchase food, leaving Jesus to rest. It was the sixth hour, about noon, the hottest time of the day. Usually the women came to draw water in the cool of the evening. A lone Samaritan woman came to draw water. She was a woman who lived a sordid life and could not associate with the decent women of the town. And Jesus proposed to lead her to receive Him and the life which He could give. Shortly before, Jesus had dealt with a man of the upper stratum of Jewish life. Now He is confronted with a woman of the lower stratum of Samaritan society, and His manner of dealing with her provides the classic example in soul-winning.

Jesus began the conversation by establishing a common bond of need. The woman had come to draw water, and Jesus was thirsty, so He said, "Give Me a drink" (John 4:7). She responded by raising the wall of prejudice which to her was so evident between a Jewish man and a Samaritan woman. Not only did Jews have no dealings with the Samaritans, but Jewish men, and especially rabbis, which Jesus appeared to her to be, had little dealings with women. One of their daily prayers was to thank God that He had not made them a Gentile, a Samaritan, or a woman.

Jesus ignored these prejudices of race and sex. Instead He contrasted the natural water in Jacob's well with the spiritual water which He longed to give her. To drink from Jacob's well was to thirst again, but His water quenched thirst completely and permanently. Furthermore, it would become in her an ever-flowing spring of eternal life. Her only interest in such water was that she no longer would have to make the long walk daily to draw water from Jacob's well. She showed no evidence of a sense of spiritual need.

To reveal her need to her, Jesus probed into her personal, sinful life by telling her to call her husband. When she denied having a husband, Jesus revealed to her His knowledge of her five previous husbands. Also He reminded her that

Samaria countryside through which Jesus passed as He traveled from Judea to Galilee. Here in this region, Jesus encountered the woman of Sychar at Jacob's Well.

even then she was living with a man outside of marriage. It was then that her flippancy and hostility gave way to admiration as she admitted that Jesus was a prophet.

However, she used this admission only to turn the conversation from her shady personal life toward a theological controversy. Towering high above them was Mt. Gerizim where the Samaritans had their place of worship as over against the Jewish worship in Jerusalem. She sought refuge in this age-old dispute, but again Jesus drew her back to the main question by pointing out that God is a Spirit whose true worship depends not upon a place but upon one's spirit in worship.

Headed off again the woman made one last effort to escape. She brought up the question of the Messiah, who when He should come would resolve all questions. And for the first time Jesus clearly declared His Messiahship by saying, "'I am He,' . . . 'the One speaking to you'" (John 4:26).

It was at this point that the disciples returned, and the woman used this interruption to return to the village, leaving her waterpot behind. But Jesus' words had done their work. For when she came into the village, she said to the men, "Come, see a man, which told me all things that ever I did: is not this the Christ?" (John 4:29). Her question was a veiled admission that He was. Subsequently the men also believed on Him as "the Saviour of the world" (John 4:42). Not of the Jews only, but of the whole world! And for two days they enjoyed the supreme privilege of having Jesus in their village.

From Sychar Jesus went on into Galilee, and there He began His great Galilean ministry.

But after John was arrested, Jesus went to Galilee, preaching the good news of God: "The time is fulfilled, and the kingdom of God has come near. Repent and believe in the good news!"

MARK 1:14-15 (HCSB)

The Great Galilean Ministry

Cana of Galilee as viewed from Sepphoris. Cana is where Jesus turned water into wine and where a nobleman met Jesus and asked Him to heal his son in Capernaum. Cana was the home of Nathanael, one of the Twelve.

The Opening Events

Following the first year of comparative obscurity, Jesus launched His more public ministry in Galilee. This period lasted for approximately eighteen months, from the fall of A.D. 27 until the spring of A.D. 29. Jerusalem and Judea had clearly demonstrated their hostility to Him, and so it was natural that He would return to the more favorable intellectual and spiritual climate of His own section of Palestine. On one occasion during this period Jesus made a visit to Jerusalem.

Jesus returned to Galilee to find that the fame of His miracles and teachings had spread throughout the region. Wherever He went, He echoed the message which John the Baptist had preached: "Repent, because the kingdom of heaven has come near" (Matt. 4:17).

On His way back to Nazareth, He passed through Cana. In Capernaum the son of an official of Herod Antipas was ill. His father, hearing that Jesus was back in Galilee, sought Him out and found Him in Cana. In response to his request that Jesus come to Capernaum to heal his son, Jesus told him to return home, that his son was well. The father did so, and found that his son had been healed the hour Jesus had spoken His words to him.

A lintel from the fourth century A.D. synagogue in Capernaum with a replica of the Torah Ark carved on it.

First-Century Galilee

Thomas V. Brisco

Follow Me, . . . and I will make you fishers of men!" (Matt. 4:19, NASB). These words spoken to Galilean fishermen by Jesus began His great Galilean ministry. Galilee played a major role in Jesus' life and ministry. He called His first disciples from the working class of the region. His parables are laced with the images of His native land. Jesus' mighty works and remarkable teachings attracted crowds from Galilean villages. What do we know of first-century Galilee?

Our knowledge of first-century Galilee comes from a variety of literary sources including the Gospels, the writings of first-century Jewish historian Flavius Josephus who commanded Jewish troops in Galilee during the first Jewish revolt

Sea of Galilee from the Church of the Beatitudes.

against Rome (A.D. 66–70), and later rabbinic writings (the Mishnah and Tosephta). Recently, archaeology has enriched our knowledge of Galilee in the time of Jesus.

To understand Galilee and its people, we must grasp something of the geography and history of the region. The term *Galilee* refers to the mountainous region of northern Palestine.[1] The name *Galilee* comes from a Hebrew word meaning "ring" or "cylinder," an allusion to the fact that this mountainous land was "encircled" by lower elevations often populated by Gentiles of mixed origins (compare Isa. 9:1, "Galilee of the Gentiles"). The coastal plain and the two major cities Acco/Ptolemais and Tyre bordered Galilee to the west. Western Galilee was a natural agricultural hinterland for the coastal cities. The fertile Jezreel Valley

Gadara, and Scythopolis.

Historically the Israelite tribes of Naphtali, Zebulun, Issachar, and Asher settled Galilee. However, Galilee came under Gentile control during the Assyrian invasion in 733 B.C. and remained outside of Jewish control for six centuries down to the eras of the Maccabean Revolt and Hasmonean Dynasty (167–63 B.C.). The Maccabean brothers Jonathan (160–142 B.C.) and Simeon (142–135 B.C.) assisted Jews in Galilee and campaigned against Seleucid troops in the region (I Macc. 5:14–23; 11:63; 12:46–49). The Hasmonean rulers John Hyrcanus (135–104 B.C.) and Aristobulus (104–103 B.C.) solidified Jewish control over Galilee, the latter forcing circumcision upon Itureans who lived in the area. Galilee was fully integrated into the Jewish state ruled by Alexander Jannaeus (103–76 B.C.).

By the late second century B.C. Galilee came under Jewish control. But who were the Galileans? Some scholars think they were descendants of the old Galilean Israelite tribes who remained culturally intact through the centuries. Others believe Galileans were converted Itureans. Yet others say Galilee was "rejudaized" during the Maccabean and Hasmonean periods by the establishment of Jewish fortresses in Galilee and Jewish immigration.[2] The last alternative seems most plausible, but undoubtedly all three suggestions contain elements of truth. In any case, Galilee was essentially Jewish and under Jewish control by the late second century B.C.

The Romans acknowledged the Jewish character of Galilee by their administrative policies. The Roman general Pompey, who conquered Palestine in 63 B.C., placed all of western Palestine including Galilee under the authority of the Jewish high priest and ethnarch ("ruler of a people") Hyrcanus II. Politically Hyrcanus depended on the Idumean strongman Antipater, a man

Part of the market area of first-century Tiberias, on the western shore of the Sea of Galilee.

Roman arch, Sepphoris, located near Nazareth, was the capital of Galilee during most of Jesus' lifetime.

Olive tree roots spread widely to gain nourishment on rocky hillsides, hence the trees are often well spaced. Olive trees flower at about ten years but don't yield fruit until they are 40 or 50 years old.

to the south isolated Galilee from the more politically dominant parts of Palestine, Judea, and Samaria. The steep descent of the Jordan Rift Valley formed Galilee's eastern boundary from Lake Huleh through the Sea of Galilee to Scythopolis. Though technically a part of the Rift Valley, the Sea of Galilee played an important role in Galilee's economy. Galilee extended north almost to the Litani River. By the first century Galilee was surrounded by Hellenized cities and regions including Tyre, Ptolemais, and the Decapolis cities Hippos,

Shortly after Jesus' return to Nazareth, as was His custom, He went into the synagogue on the Sabbath day. It was customary at times, when some notable person was present, for the ruler of the synagogue to request him to read the Scriptures and to comment on them. On this occasion this privilege was accorded to the hometown Boy who was receiving so much notice. Jesus chose to read from the roll of Isaiah (61:1–2). As was customary He stood up to read and then sat down to speak. The people were astonished to hear Jesus say, "Today this Scripture has been fulfilled in your hearing" (Luke 4:21).

And then the congregation began to buzz. "Isn't this Joseph's son?" (Luke 4:22). In response Jesus reminded them that a prophet is not accepted in his hometown. He drove this lesson home by citing examples from their own history in which foreigners had enjoyed blessings from God rather than His own people, because they had rejected God's messengers. The people caught the point, and their wonder gave place to rage. They seized Jesus and rushed out to the edge of the town intent upon casting Him to His death over a cliff (tourists today are shown what is said to be this cliff), but in the confusion Jesus slipped away from them. Had He not done this, Nazareth might have robbed Jerusalem of its infamy as the place where the Son of God was slain. Jesus never actually lived in Nazareth after He left there for His "rendezvous with destiny" in the Jordan valley.

Following this rejection by Nazareth, Jesus established His base of operations in Capernaum, a city on the northwestern shore of the Sea of Galilee. While He

trusted by the Romans, who appointed his son Herod governor of Galilee. In 40 B.C. the Romans selected Herod as a client-king and gave him responsibility for all Palestine. Herod the Great ruled the Jews until his death in 4 B.C.

Augustus divided Herod's kingdom among three of Herod's surviving sons. Herod Antipas received Galilee and Perea along with the title *tetrarch*—"ruler of a fourth." Herod Antipas ruled Galilee from 4 B.C. until he

Modern Nazareth and the Basilica of Annunciation.

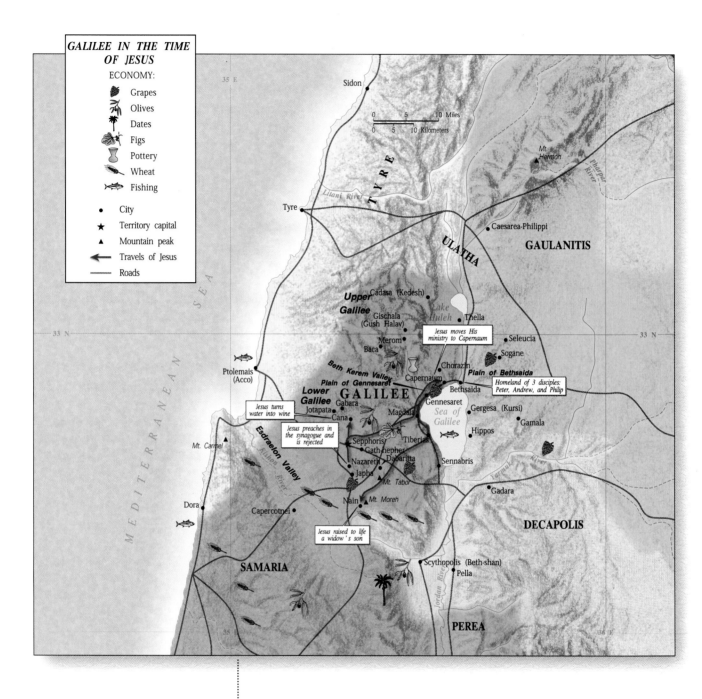

GALILEE IN THE TIME OF JESUS

ECONOMY:

- Grapes
- Olives
- Dates
- Figs
- Pottery
- Wheat
- Fishing

- • City
- ★ Territory capital
- ▲ Mountain peak
- ← Travels of Jesus
- — Roads

35 E

Sidon

0   5   10 Miles
0   5   10 Kilometers

Litani River

TYRE

Tyre

Mt. Hermon

Pharpar River

36 E

Caesarea-Philippi

ULATHA

GAULANITIS

33 N

Upper Galilee

Cadasa (Kedesh)

Lake Huleh

Thella

Gischala (Gush Halav)

Jesus moves His ministry to Capernaum

Seleucia

Merom

Baca

Sogane

Chorazin

Plain of Bethsaida

33 N

Beth Kerem Valley

Capernaum

Plain of Gennesaret

Bethsaida

Homeland of 3 disciples: Peter, Andrew, and Philip

Ptolemais (Acco)

Lower Galilee

GALILEE

Gennesaret

Gergesa (Kursi)

Jesus turns water into wine

Gabara

Jotapata

Magdala

Sea of Galilee

Hippos

Gamala

Cana

Jesus preaches in the synagogue and is rejected

Sepphoris

Gath-hepher

Tiberias

MEDITERRANEAN SEA

Mt. Carmel

Esdraelon Valley

Kishon River

Nazareth

Dabaritta

Japha

Sennabris

Mt. Tabor

Dora

Capercotnei

Nain

Mt. Moreh

Yarmuk River

Gadara

DECAPOLIS

Jesus raised to life a widow's son

SAMARIA

Jordan River

Scythopolis (Beth-shan)

Pella

35

PEREA

36 E

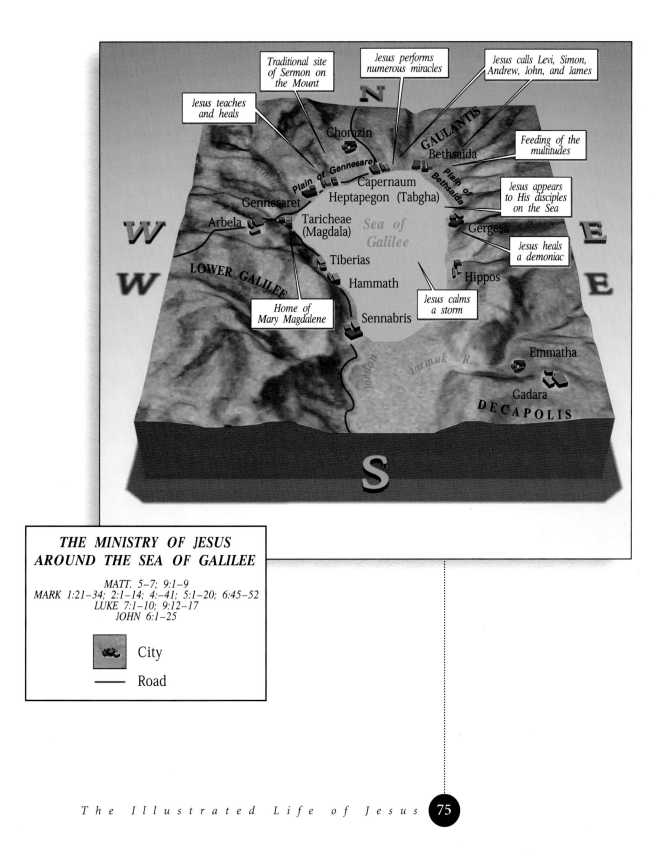

Traditional site of Sermon on the Mount

Jesus performs numerous miracles

Jesus calls Levi, Simon, Andrew, John, and James

Jesus teaches and heals

Chorazin

GAULANTIS

Bethsaida

Plain of Gennesaret

Plain of Bethsaida

Feeding of the multitudes

Capernaum

Heptapegon (Tabgha)

Jesus appears to His disciples on the Sea

Gennesaret

N

W

W

W

E

E

E

S

Arbela

Taricheae (Magdala)

Sea of Galilee

Gergesa

Jesus heals a demoniac

Tiberias

Hippos

LOWER GALILEE

Hammath

Jesus calms a storm

Home of Mary Magdalene

Sennabris

Jordan

Yarmuk R.

Emmatha

Gadara

DECAPOLIS

THE MINISTRY OF JESUS AROUND THE SEA OF GALILEE

MATT. 5–7; 9:1–9
MARK 1:21–34; 2:1–14; 4:–41; 5:1–20; 6:45–52
LUKE 7:1–10; 9:12–17
JOHN 6:1–25

City

——— Road

was deposed by the Romans in A.D. 39, a time span that included Jesus and John the Baptist's ministries.

Josephus divided Galilee into two parts, Upper and Lower Galilee. Topographically and culturally the two regions were distinct.[3] The Beth-Hakerem Valley ("Valley of the Vineyards") sharply divides the two Galilees. Sheer cliffs rising 2,000 feet on the north side of the valley mark the southern border of Upper Galilee where elevations reach 3,963 feet at Mount Meron. Upper Galilee is a maze of jagged peaks and uplifted plateaus torn by frequent fault lines. Travel is difficult, especially north to south. Although fertile

Capernaum Synagogue.

spent very little time here, He always returned to Capernaum after various journeys throughout Galilee. Some of the most vital events in the Galilean ministry did take place in this populous and prosperous city, however.

Having established His headquarters for the Galilean campaign, Jesus was now ready to gather about Him certain disciples who would figure prominently in this effort. Already there were those who had received Him as the Messiah, but upon their return to Galilee, they had resumed their occupations. Among these were Peter, Andrew, James, and John. These two pairs of brothers were fishermen, along with Zebedee, the father of the latter pair. Fishing was one of the principal occupations about the Sea of Galilee, since fish was a major item on the diet of the people.

Early one day Jesus was walking along the seashore. He saw these men fishing and later washing their nets. The Lord called to these four brothers to leave their occupation and to accompany Him on His mission. From fishers of fish He would make them fishers of men. Apparently they had had a fruitless night at fishing. Simon protested when Jesus, a landlubber, told them to try again; but when they let down their nets, they brought up a multitude of fish. This so impressed them that the four brothers responded to Jesus' call to follow Him.

This little company returned to Capernaum, and on the Sabbath Jesus taught in the synagogue. This synagogue was to be the scene of some of His greatest work. Unlike the people of Nazareth those of Capernaum responded favorably to His teachings, noting that He taught with an authority and freshness so different from the rote repetitions of the Jewish scribes.

On this occasion there was present a man possessed by an unclean spirit

Housing area in front of the synagogue in Capernaum.

or a demon. Demon possession is a mystery which has plagued interpreters through the ages. Some would explain it as the superstitions of an ignorant, ancient age, but Jesus accepted it as a reality. It is untenable with His very person to say that He either did not know better or else that He merely went along with their superstitions. Modern man knows far too little about the spirit world to deny arbitrarily the reality of this phenomenon. As with Satan in the wilderness, it is reasonable to say that evil spirits entered into men even as God was incarnated in Jesus of Nazareth. Furthermore, who can deny that some men today are demon possessed, only it is referred to in terminology adapted to modern modes of thought? This fact certainly would explain the actions of many which are a moral and spiritual puzzle otherwise.

and well watered, the region's natural isolation impeded urban development. The scattered villages of the region, however, participated in a lively trade with Tyre and the Golan. The Gospels do not mention any of the villages or towns (for example, Gischala, Baca) in connection with Jesus' ministry but do recount a visit by Jesus to the "area of Tyre and Sidon" where He healed the daughter of a Syro-Phoenician woman (Matt. 15:21–28).

Lower Galilee, Jesus' home and the scene of His earliest ministry, is a land of gentle ridges running east to west where elevations never exceed 2,000 feet. Four valleys—the Beth-Hakerem, Saknini, Beth-Netofah, and Tiran Valleys—bisect the mountains, facilitating travel. Villages cling to the slopes at the ridges whose slopes were suited to vineyards and orchards; the valleys pro-

vided for grain crops like wheat and barley. Nazareth, however, sits on top of the ridge overlooking the fertile Jezreel Valley to the south. The main trade route crossed the Jezreel with one segment entering Lower Galilee near Mount Tabor continuing on to the western shore of the Sea of Galilee. Another important route connected Ptolemais with Tiberias via Sepphoris, one of the principal cities of Galilee located only three and a half miles north of Nazareth. Merchants and caravans were a common site in and around Lower Galilee.

Josephus's well-known description of Galilee praises the agricultural fertility of the land.[4] Land was the measure of social and economic status. Many Galileans were peasant farmers who owned or leased a small plot of land. Typical farms included a vineyard, an olive grove,

A first-century boat found in the mud of the Lake of Galilee. This boat is typical of the fishing boats Peter, Andrew, James, and John would have used on the Sea of Galilee.

At any rate the Scriptures treat demon possession as a reality. On this occasion the demon even talked to Jesus, probably through the person indwelt by it. But Jesus cast it out of him, and the people were amazed that even demons were subject to Him. It is no wonder His fame continued to spread abroad.

Going from the synagogue Jesus and His company went to Simon Peter's home, which was probably nearby. Finding Simon's wife's mother ill of a fever, which no doubt was common in this semitropical area, Jesus healed her. The miraculous element in this healing is evident in the fact that immediately she was strong enough to prepare a meal for them.

Since it was a Sabbath day, the Jews were forbidden even to bear their sick to Jesus, but at sunset, the end of the Sabbath day, they did bring them to Him. It was a beautiful ending to an eventful day—Jesus moving among this multitude of sick and demon-possessed people in His healing ministry. Truly they would be reminded of Isaiah 53:4: "He Himself took our weaknesses and carried our diseases" (Matt. 8:17).

and a small piece of land for growing wheat and vegetables. Galilee was renown for its olive oil and produced enough oil, wine, and wheat to export. Larger estates existed in the region similar to the Herodian royal estates in the Jezreel Valley. A few may have been owned by wealthy absentee landlords. The parables of Jesus mention such landlords (Matt. 21:33–41) and the stewards of larger estates (Luke 16:1–8) as well as tenants who leased the land (Luke 20:9). The small-scale farmer also appeared in Jesus' parables, a situation perhaps more typical of Galilee in the first century (Matt. 21:28–32). However, not all Galileans were so fortunate; families could lose their land by crop failure resulting in unmanageable debt, unpaid taxes, and confiscation of property. Jesus also spoke of the day laborers who waited in the village center hoping for a chance to work in the fields (Matt. 20:1–16).

Recent studies indicate that although Galilee was largely rural and agrarian, the cultural ethos was more complex. Like his father, Herod Antipas embarked on a building program, only on a smaller scale. In Galilee Herod rebuilt Sepphoris in the heart of Lower Galilee after its destruction in 4 B.C. He founded Tiberias on the western shore of the Sea of Galilee, dedicating the new city to his patron Tiberius Caesar in A.D. 19 or 20. Both cities served as administrative centers for Galilee, Sepphoris until about A.D. 20 and Tiberias thereafter. The effects of these two urban centers on Galilee and

The Sepphoris (Zippori) theater.

Hoard of 336 silver coins. As a tax collector, Matthew collected many coins in his work prior to his following Jesus.

A GROWING POPULARITY

The Galilean ministry was characterized by Jesus' growing popularity. Not that He deliberately courted it. The contrary was true, but He found a ready response among these people who were so far removed from Jerusalem. At the same time Jesus experienced the increasing hostility of the Pharisees both in Jerusalem and in Galilee. It was His popularity among the people that inspired the Phraisees' opposition, for they feared that their hold on the multitudes would be broken.

Having chosen His first four disciples, Jesus took them on a tour of Galilee. Wherever He went the people flocked to Him to hear His preaching and to behold His healing miracles. Jesus' message on the kingdom excited their imagination, even though their concept of a political kingdom was far removed from the spiritual kingdom which He envisioned. Nevertheless the people came from Galilee, Decapolis, Jerusalem, Judea, and Perea to hear and to see.

During His first tour of Galilee, Jesus greatly excited the people by healing a leper. Leprosy was the most dreaded of all diseases in ancient Palestine, and lepers were forbidden to live among other people. They were not even supposed to come nearer than one hundred feet from those who were free of leprosy. If someone approached them, they were required to give the warning cry, "Unclean!" One rabbi boasted of having driven one leper from him with stones.

So when this leper came to Jesus, people might suppose Him to shrink from him. Instead He touched him, saying, "Be made clean," and immediately his leprosy was healed. It was obviously a miracle, but even though Jesus ignored the taboos of the Jews, He did not evade divine law. Therefore, He told the leper to go to the priest, make certain sacrifices required by the Mosaic Law, and thus be pronounced clean. And despite Jesus' stern admonition that the man not tell of this healing, he did so wherever he went, so much so that the crowds were greater than ever. For some time, because of the rising enthusiasm, it was necessary that Jesus avoid cities. Then the people flocked to Him in the country.

After some days Jesus returned to Capernaum. As the news spread, the people ran to the house where He was staying. Among those gathered there were Pharisees and teachers of the Law (scribes), not only the Mosaic Law, but the

Jesus' ministry have been much discussed. Both cities injected a strong urban factor in an otherwise rural society and brought elements of Roman culture closer to the traditional Galilean culture. Excavations at Sepphoris have revealed a Roman theater seating over three thousand, possibly built by Herod Antipas. Josephus described Herod's palace at Tiberias decorated with animal figures offensive to Jews.[5] Sources also mention a hippodrome at Magdala, just north of Tiberias.

What effect these cities had on Galilean society is debatable. Some scholars speak of an "urban overlay" that impacted rural Galilee or suggest a cosmopolitanism that penetrated Galilean society through these centers of Roman/Herodian administration.[6] Others cite the unwelcome tax burden placed by Herod's building program on Galilean peasants.

The proximity of Sepphoris to Nazareth invites the notion that Jesus visited the nearby city often, perhaps even finding work alongside his father in the rebuilding of Sepphoris. All this remains speculative, as is the idea that Jesus was deeply influenced by a purported Hellenistic/Roman culture at Sepphoris; but the excavations at Sepphoris demonstrate that Jesus grew up in a more varied social environment than previously thought. Yet the Gospels never mention a visit by Jesus to either Sepphoris or Tiberias; He seems to have been most at home in the villages and small towns of Galilee (Luke 4:14–15; Matt. 9:35–38).

Jesus' earliest ministry took place in Lower Galilee, although the Gospels mention very few specific sites. Jesus initially proclaimed the message of good news in a synagogue in Nazareth, but His hometown rejected him (Luke 4:16–31). The Gospels record another visit to Nazareth with discouraging results (Matt. 13:54–58). Jesus performed His first miracle at a wedding feast at Cana, a village nine miles north of Nazareth identified with the abandoned ruins of Khirbet Kana (John 2:1–11). Nathaniel, one of the disciples, was a native of Cana (John 21:2). On another occasion Jesus resuscitated the son of a widow at Nain, a village located on the edge of the Hill of Moreh (Luke 7:11–17).

Most of Jesus' Galilean ministry centered on the Sea of Galilee. Lower Galilee was closely linked with the Sea of Galilee and the associated plain of Gennesaret on the northwestern edge of the lake. A freshwater lake 13 miles long and 7 miles wide, the Sea of

multitude of rules of conduct which were prescribed as being related to the Mosaic Code.

As Jesus was teaching, four men approached, bearing a paralytic on a pallet. When they could not get into the house because of the crowd, they carried the man to the roof by way of an outside stairs. After tearing a hole in the roof, they lowered him into the presence of Jesus, but Jesus did not at once heal the man. Instead He said, "Friend, your sins are forgiven you" (Luke 5:20). This was the first record of Jesus having spoken such words. The scribes were horrified, for according to them only God could forgive sin. In their hearts they accused Jesus of blasphemy, but perceiving their thoughts, Jesus challenged them. "Which is easier: to say, 'Your sins are forgiven you,' or to say, 'Get up and walk'? But so you may know that the Son of Man has authority on earth to forgive sins"—He told the paralyzed man, "I tell you: get up, pick up your stretcher, and go home" (Luke 5:23–24). The religious scholars were mute as the man did as he was bidden, but the people glorified God.

The order of Jesus' words is significant. He forgave the man's sins before He healed his body. Four reasons may have prompted this. First, Jesus' primary mission was related to man's sin. Second, this man's physical condition may have been due to his spiritual need. Third, Jesus posed a situation by which to prove His authority to forgive sin. Fourth, by the scribes' claim that only God had such authority, the indirect result was their own unwilling testimony to the deity of Jesus. So the people were amazed, and the Pharisees were confounded.

THE CALL OF MATTHEW (LEVI)

Capernaum was one of the most important cities of Galilee. In a sense it was at the crossroads of the ancient world, for the international highway from Egypt to Damascus passed through it. This alone would make it a great center of tax collections. All of the merchandise which passed over this segment of the road would have to pay duty as it entered the territory of Herod Antipas.

The Roman system of tax collecting was most unusual according to modern standards. The Roman government auctioned off to the highest bidder the privilege of collecting taxes in a given area. This person, in turn, must so levy taxes as to make a profit. Under him would be lesser officials who did his bidding. These collectors as a class were called "publicans," a word derived from the Latin word *publicanus*, one who did public duty. But in this case the duty was for private gain, a fact which gave rise to much graft and extortion. Quite naturally the publicans were a hated class among the Jews, not only for their evil practices but also because they were regarded as traitors to their people. The term *publican* carried the same stench as the modern word *traitor*. For personal gain they sold themselves to the Jews' captors as instruments of oppression. No wonder, then, a common phrase was "publicans and sinners."

Matthew, or Levi as he is sometimes called, was a publican. He was one of the underling collectors, either under a commercial tax collector or under

Herod Antipas himself. At any rate Jesus passed by his "receipt of custom" or place of toll. Seeing Matthew, He simply said, "Follow Me." Matthew, like the two sets of brothers, may have known Jesus previously. Certainly he had heard of Him, so he left his tax table to serve the table of the Lord.

It was quite an occasion in Matthew's life, so to celebrate it, he gave a feast in honor of Jesus and His disciples. To it he invited his publican friends and others. Customarily those other than guests stood about and watched the festivities, and among this group were the ever-present Pharisees and their scribes. They were horrified that Jesus would eat with such a motley crowd: publicans and sinners, indeed! To the Pharisees this was an immoral act. When Jesus heard their criticism, He said to them, "Those who are well don't need a doctor, but the sick do" (Matt. 9:12). Jesus came not "to call the righteous, but sinners to repentance" (Matt. 9:13).

By their own standards the Pharisees were righteous and needed no repentance as did these publicans and sinners. So taking them at their own word, Jesus turned the tables on them. They felt no need of His spiritual healing.

Galilee lies 690 feet below sea level; an abundance of water combined with a subtropical climate created ideal agricultural conditions. Josephus praised the fertility of the plain of Gennesaret (Ginnosar), mentioning figs, olives, walnuts, palm trees, and grapes native to the plain. The major valleys of western Lower Galilee converge on the plain. Jesus often taught the multitudes and healed the sick who gathered from the villages of Galilee on the plain of Gennesaret (Matt. 14:34–36; Mark 6:53–56).

The Sea of Galilee supported a major fishing industry, as the remains of numerous harbors and anchorages around the lake testify. Small fishing fleets from Capernaum, Tiberias, Magdala, and Bethsaida-Julius plied the lake seeking daily catches of fish. Magdala (Greek Taricheae meaning "salted fish") prepared and exported salted sardines. Remains of a first-century boat

Sunrise over Sea of Galilee.

Where else would the physician be but among those who need His ministry?

In this scene one sees the added opposition to Jesus on the part of the Pharisees. First, they accused Him of blasphemy. Now they charged Him with immorality. And so the story ever went.

However, the matter did not end there. For among the onlookers was a group of the disciples of John the Baptist, and while the Pharisees licked their wounds, they took up the charge against Jesus: "Why do we and the Pharisees fast often, but Your disciples do not fast?" (Matt. 9:14).

At least two things may have prompted this question. First, they were perhaps critical because, while their teacher was in prison, Jesus and His disciples were attending a banquet. The Baptist would not have done so under any circumstance. And then there was the matter of fasting itself. The Jews placed a great emphasis upon this practice. Jesus Himself fasted on occasion, but He did so out of preoccupation for His spiritual concern, not as a rote performance as did the Pharisees. In reply to their question, Jesus reminded John's disciples that as long as He was with His disciples they had no reason to fast. There

---

retrieved from the lake allows us to reconstruct a typical fishing boat of Jesus' day. The boat, made of wood, was 27 feet long and 7.5 feet wide. A crew of four or five manned the boat that was equipped with oars and a sail. Several other adults could be accommodated for travel across the sea.

Other industries included a textile trade based on locally grown flax and possibly a leather industry. Later rabbinic sources mention tanners at Tiberias.

Two cities along the northern edge of the lake were particularly important to Jesus' ministry. Capernaum became the center of Jesus' ministry around the lake; Matthew referred to Capernaum as "his own town" (Matt. 9:1). The 13-acre site of Capernaum may have supported a population of ten to fifteen hundred. Capernaum was a customs town as well as home to a fishing industry. The border between the tetrarchy of Herod Antipas and his brother Philip was the Jordan River only a few miles east of the city. Jesus called the tax collector Matthew from his post near Capernaum (Matt. 9:9).

Jesus performed numerous miracles in Capernaum. The beautiful limestone synagogue crowning Capernaum today dates from a later period but may have been built on the site of the one mentioned in the Gospels. The remains of several modest houses dating from the first century made of basalt built around common courtyards have been found. Later Christians

identified one of the houses with Simon Peter, eventually erecting an octagonal church around the structure.

Opposite Capernaum across the Jordan River was Bethsaida-Julius. Herod Philip expanded the city and named it Julius in honor of Augustus's daughter. Bethsaida has been identified with et-Tell, a large mound about one and a half miles north of the Sea of Galilee. Three of Jesus' disciples—Philip, Andrew, and Peter—were from Bethsaida (John 1:44; 12:21). One of the feeding of the multitudes occurred near Bethsaida (Luke 9:10–17).

[1]For a discussion of the geography of Galilee, see Sean Freyne, *Galilee from Alexander the Great to Hadrian 323 B.C.E. to 135 C.E.* (Notre Dame, Ind.: University of Notre Dame Press, 1980), 1–15.

[2]For discussion compare Richard A. Horsley, *Archaeology, History, and Society in Galilee: the Social Context of Jesus and the Rabbis* (Valley Forge, Penn.: Trinity Press International, 1996): 15–42 and Sean V. Freyne, "Archeology and the Historical Jesus," in *Archaeology and Biblical Interpretation*, John R. Bartlett, ed. (London: Routledge, 1997), 132–38.

[3]See Eric M. Meyers, "Galilean Regionalism: A Reappraisal," in *Studies in Judaism and Its Greco-Roman Context*, ed. William Scott (Atlanta: Scholars Press, 1985).

[4]Josephus, *Jewish War*, 3:3:1–3.

[5]Josephus, *Vita*, 64–65.

[6]James F. Strange, "Some Implications of Archaeology for New Testament Studies," in *What Has Archaeology to Do with Faith?* eds. James H. Charlesworth and Walter P. Weaver, (Philadelphia: Trinity Press International, 1992), 23–49.

Thomas V. Brisco is professor of biblical backgrounds and archaeology, Southwestern Baptist Theological Seminary, Fort Worth, Texas.

would be a real occasion for them to do so after He was taken from them. Thus He made an indirect reference to His death and return to heaven.

Then Jesus went to the heart of the matter by speaking two parables, those of new cloth on old garments and new wine in old wineskins. If an old garment were patched with new cloth, the new cloth would shrink, and the hole in the old garment would be torn larger. In essence, Jesus did not come to patch up the old garment of Judaism but to weave a new garment altogether. Furthermore, if new wine were placed in old brittle wineskins, as the new wine worked, it would expand or generate gases which would burst the old skins, thus losing the new wine. In effect, the old forms of Judaism could not contain the new revelation which Jesus brought. It must be contained in new wineskins or expressions. To try to pour the Christian revelation into Old Testament forms is to destroy both.

A GROWING OPPOSITION

Probably in the spring of A.D. 28. Jesus and His disciples left Galilee to attend the Passover in Jerusalem. While there Jesus walked by the pool of Bethesda, meaning "the house of mercy." In Jesus' day this pool was fed by an underground spring which flowed intermittently. Jewish belief held that the water was stirred by an angel and that the first one to step into the pool at such times would be healed of his disease. Therefore, its five porches were filled with those hoping to be healed. Among these was a man who had had an infirmity for thirty-eight years.

Seeing him, Jesus asked if he wished to be healed. The man replied that he did but that others beat him into the water each time it was troubled. So Jesus simply told him to arise and to take up his bed and walk. The man proceeded to do so. It was on the Sabbath, and Jewish law forbade one to bear a burden on this day.

The Pool of Bethesda in Jerusalem, where Jesus healed a man who had been ill for thirty-eight years.

Jesus and the Sabbath Laws

Don Stewart

The doctrinal conflict between the religious leaders called Pharisees and Jesus was inevitable. The Pharisees were responsible for directing the national, cultural, political, and spiritual lives of the people of Israel at the grassroots level. They were the spiritual teachers in the local synagogues all over the country. The other primary leadership group, the Sadducees, administered the rituals at the temple in Jerusalem and had contact with the people primarily on three major holy days each year. They seem not to have thought that Jesus posed a challenge for traditional Judaism until He drove the money changers out of the temple late in His ministry (see Matt. 21:12; Mark 11:15). Consequently, the conflict between Jesus and religious leaders for nearly all of His ministry was between Jesus and the Pharisees.

Jesus refused to abide by the Pharisaic misinterpretation of God's laws. There was an interesting contrast between Jesus and the religious establishment of His day, Judaism. The conflict between Jesus and the Pharisaic leaders over Sabbath practices paints a vivid picture of the theological and methodological differences between them.

Talmudic Law was the basis of the Jews' Sabbath practices. Space will not allow a recounting of the process by which oral interpretations of God's Law (the Torah) became the Jewish Talmud. Suffice it to say that the

Gergesa grainfield. This is the kind of grainfield that Jesus and His disciples passed through on the Sabbath.

interpretations of the Tannaim, the teachers, who explained the oral traditions that grew from the Law and the repeating of those explanations by the Amoraim, the speakers, who simply parroted the words of the teachers of the Law, became more important than the Torah itself.[1] The teachers' commentary and the speakers' repetitions of that commentary were being taught as though they were God's laws when they were not (compare Matt. 15:9; Mark 7:7–8).

Jesus rebuked the Pharisees for keeping the "letter of the Law" while violating its spirit. Jesus charged them with burdening people with rules impossible to keep. He condemned the Pharisees also for failing to instruct the people adequately in keeping those rules while holding them responsible for their keeping. By this practice, in Jesus' words, the Pharisees were refusing to "lift a finger to move" (Matt. 23:4) from the people's shoulders the heavy ritual loads they placed there without the blessings of the Lord (Matt. 23:4; Luke 11:46).

Other than in His claim to be the Messiah, there was no arena of life in which Jesus came into such sharp conflict with the Pharisaic leaders as in the matter of keeping the Sabbath. He set Himself squarely against many of the Sabbath restrictions enforced by the Pharisees. Jesus taught that those Pharisaic rules were contrary to the purposes for which God had given the Sabbath in the first place.[2]

Synagogue (partially reconstructed) at Qasrin. The interior structure is similar to those of first century synagogues. The benches on either side are where the men sat during the service.

This fact brought down the wrath of the Jewish leaders upon the man and upon Jesus, for when they challenged the man for breaking the Sabbath, he related what Jesus had done. Thereafter, the Jews persecuted Jesus. He received no thanks for healing the man, only criticism for doing it on the Sabbath. In reply Jesus said, "My Father is still working, and I also am working" (John 5:17). By this time the Jews were worked into a murderous rage, for to them Jesus not only broke the Sabbath; He also claimed equality with God. Sabbath breaking and blasphemy! So they said.

Then followed one of Jesus' marvelous discourses as recorded in John (5:19–47). He reiterated His relation to the Father, stating that God had accorded Him the right of judgment and made Him worthy of all honor. He challenged these Jews in one of the Pharisees' most precious beliefs, the resurrection of the dead, by saying that at His word the dead would rise. He charged them with refusing to hear John the Baptist, and now they were rejecting Him. Even the Scriptures, of which they claimed to be experts, revealed Him, but they refused Him. He called upon even Moses, whose teachings were their law, to witness against them, because Moses wrote of Him. Then He flung the sharpest javelin of all. They did not even believe Moses, so how could they believe Him of whom Moses wrote?

This opposition to Jesus did not hinge primarily upon His person as much as it did upon the institution of the Sabbath. His person was incidental only in that He claimed authority over the Sabbath and it was at this point that the Jewish leaders hounded Jesus the most.

Judaism was based upon three things: the Law, the temple, and the Sabbath, and in each of these the Jewish leaders found themselves at odds with Jesus. However, to the Jews the Sabbath was the most sacred of all. Other religions had

The disagreement over the use of the Sabbath occurred frequently between the Pharisees and Jesus because the Pharisees overlooked God's basic Old Testament principle of Sabbath in the Torah. Jesus reminded the Pharisaic leaders often that the Sabbath was made for man, not man for the Sabbath (Mark 2:27).

The Pharisees in Jesus' day seemed to think that the Sabbath was an end in itself. They made it an institution before which the pious Israelite had to renounce his personal interests. In other words, the Pharisees taught that man was made to glorify the Sabbath.[3] The Pharisees, following the traditions of the Tannaim and the Amoraim, neglected God's real laws.[4] This writer agrees with Matthew Henry who wrote that the Sabbath was treated by the Pharisees as a sacred and divine institution but went on to declare that it was given by God as a privilege and benefit, not a task and a drudgery.[5]

God did not intend for the Sabbath to be a burden to man. Consequently, for the Pharisaic teachers to make it so was a grievous sin. People were not made for the

Wildflowers above the Sea of Galilee in northern Israel.

their scriptures and temples, but only Judaism had its Sabbath. So it was the Sabbath which particularly made Judaism distinct from all other religions. One can well understand why the Jews would be so sensitive at this point. While Jesus had disregarded their meticulous laws concerning the Sabbath prior to this time, this instance was pivotal, because it happened in Jerusalem itself.

Once again Jerusalem had rejected Jesus, so He and His disciples returned to Galilee. Apparently some Pharisees dogged their steps even then. It was the time of the approaching grain harvest, so on a Sabbath day they walked along a path provided for travel through the grainfields. Being hungry, the disciples followed a time-honored and permitted custom. They plucked some heads of grain, rubbed the grain free from the chaff, and ate it (Luke 6:1). A simple matter, to be sure, but to the Pharisees this constituted harvesting and threshing. And this violated the Sabbath day.

Jesus asserted His authority over the most unique institution in Judaism. Already He had demonstrated His authority over the temple, and now this. Soon He will do the same with regard to the Law (Matt. 5:17ff.). However, in no instance did Jesus discount these institutions; rather He placed them in their proper perspective. All of this was lost on the Pharisees, however, for He was destroying their playhouse, and for this they never forgave Him.

View of Jordan Valley just South of Sea of Galilee.

Shortly after the above instance, Jesus, in the presence of the Pharisees, on another Sabbath, healed a man with a withered hand (Mark 3:1–6). In so doing He pointed out the inconsistencies of their teachings regarding healing on the Sabbath day. Immediately thereafter the Pharisees took counsel with the Herodians as to how they might destroy Jesus. This within itself shows the extent of the Pharisees' hatred toward Jesus. They were arch political enemies of the Herodians. The former were bent on restoring the ancient kingdom of Israel. The latter were dedicated to the restoration of the kingdom of Herod, a bitter foe of the Pharisees. Yet in their common enmity toward Jesus these two groups became strange bedfellows.

THE CALLING OF THE TWELVE APOSTLES

At this point Jesus' public ministry was at approximately the halfway mark (perhaps A.D. 28), and it seems at this time to take a somewhat new turn. Henceforth Jesus will place a greater emphasis on teaching as He gradually reveals His person

Sabbath, as if the act of keeping it would be a service to God and buy one God's favor. Neither did God expect worshipers to keep the Sabbath's outward observances to their own hurt.

The Sabbath rules of men were found in the second of the six orders of the Talmud, the Moed. In that document, there were hundreds of Sabbath rules, most of which were unknown to the average Jew. One of the understood rules, however, was that a healing could not occur on the Sabbath unless the person in need would die probably before the next day. The restoration of a withered hand (see Mark 3:1-6) was the healing of an infirmity that was not life threatening. Consequently, by Pharisaic standards Jesus should have waited on the man's healing until the day after the Sabbath.

Nevertheless, knowing what the reactions of the Pharisees would be to His public challenge, Jesus performed the miracle in the synagogue on the Sabbath where religious leaders and laity alike were gathered for public worship. This act was a conscious challenge of the human rules for Sabbath observance found in the

Side room in the synagogue at Capernaum. The synagogue dates from the 4th cent. A.D. This view looks toward the place some believe to be the location of Simon Peter's house.

Talmud. This public breach of a traditional Sabbath restriction emphasized the primary and secondary teachings of the text: Jesus was and is the Lord of the Sabbath; and the Sabbath is made for the benefit of man, not man to glorify the Sabbath (Mark 2:27–28).

Religious scholars long have agreed that the Sabbath was instituted by God for humanity at the time of creation. Its purpose was intended to be of permanent and universal benefit, both theologically and practically. The physical nature of humankind requires a regular Sabbath (a designated weekly time of rest). In the opinion of students of religion, sociology, psychology, and physiology, human beings are constituted in such a way that their mental, physical, emotional, and spiritual welfare needs at least one day in seven for physical and mental rest, as well as time for spiritual refreshment.[6]

Jesus cast a demon out of a man on the Sabbath. The confrontation generated by Jesus' lack of respect for Pharisaic restrictions on Sabbath practices was later intensified by His unusual popularity. Jesus was loved by the Jewish public because of the compassion that motivated His healing ministry. His miraculous power inevitably

and purpose. It is as though He is beginning to prepare for the climax which awaits Him at the cross.

In this light it is significant that in a special way He chose twelve men who were to bear a particular relationship to Him. These men were called Apostles or "the ones sent forth." Mark gave three reasons for this action: "that they might be with him and that He might send them out to preach and to have authority to drive out demons" (3:14–15). These men were Simon Peter, James, John, Andrew, Philip, Bartholemew (Nathanael), Matthew, Thomas, James the son of Alphaesus, Thaddaeus, Simon the Canaanite (or Zealot), and Judas Iscariot. Previous mention has been made of the first seven; but the last five are mentioned for the first time. Perhaps Jesus had won them in much the same manner as He had the others. For some time certainly some of them had accompanied Jesus in His ministry. From this point on all of them would enjoy the special advantage of His association and teaching. Jesus proceeded to train them for the day when the Bridegroom would be taken from them.

What a strange and motley group they were! As far as is known, they were selected from the common run of people. In this group were at least four fishermen, a publican, and a former member of the fanatical revolutionary party called the Zealots, who were bent upon the overthrow of Roman rule in Palestine. This group finally brought on the Jewish War against the Romans (A.D. 66–70) which resulted in the destruction of Jerusalem and the Jewish nation. And one of the Twelve was to betray Jesus in the end.

One naturally asks why Jesus chose these particular men. Certainly He did so carefully, for the selection was made after a night spent in prayer. Perhaps as good an answer as any is that in each of these men Jesus saw certain qualities, which if dedicated to Him, would make them valuable servants in the work which He was launching: For instance, the enthusiasm of Peter; the depth of spirit in John; the patient plodding of Andrew; the record-keeping ability of Matthew; the heroic devotion of Thomas; the business ability of Judas Iscariot. They were diamonds in the rough, and only one, Judas Iscariot, failed to respond to the Master's confidence in and compassion for them. Still Jesus chose him, knowing that he was a bad one from the beginning. At the proper time in this account, certain things will be pointed out about him, but, even so, he will forever remain a mystery.

THE CONSTITUTION OF THE KINGDOM

After Jesus had chosen the twelve Apostles, He took them up into a mountain. However, the multitudes followed Him, so finding a level place in the mountain where they might be seated in comfort, Jesus also sat down and taught them. When a rabbi taught officially, he was always seated.

The place of this teaching is in dispute. Some hold that it was Mount Tabor, but since it was a fortified place inhabited by many people, it is an unlikely site for the sermon. At the time Jesus was in search for solitude. A more likely place would be the Horns of Hattin, a double-topped mountain between Capernaum and Nazareth. It more nearly fits the description of the topography given in the Gospels. Since it is designated as "the mountain" (RSV), it evidently was a well-known landmark.

Sea of Galilee from Capernaum. Another view of the location for the Sermon on the Mount.

Various titles have been given to this sermon. Coming as it did immediately after the selection of the Apostles, it has been called "The Ordination Address to the Twelve." Other titles are "The Manifesto of the King" and "The Magna Charta of the Kingdom." Perhaps as good a designation as any is "The Constitution of the Kingdom," for in it the King declared those qualities and practices which should characterize the Kingdom-citizen. Even though the multitudes heard it, the sermon was given primarily to the disciples of Jesus.

1. The Characteristics of the Kingdom Citizen

Jesus began the Sermon by setting forth the characteristics of those who are in the kingdom of God. Primarily they are described as "blessed" or "happy." These characteristics are called "The Beatitudes." In the Greek version these "blessed's" are used without the verb "to be." Therefore, they may be called absolutes. They set forth the nature of the kingdom citizen.

The Greek word is *makarios,* and its meaning can be determined by noting

provided a ministry dimension beyond the reach of the Pharisaic leadership (see Mark 1:27,37,39,45).

Jesus' defense for His overt challenge to the Pharisees' authority was that He was Lord of the Sabbath and had the right to determine what was acceptably good in keeping the Sabbath. A healing on the Sabbath, for instance, was equally as acceptable as David's eating of the bread reserved for the priests in the Old Testament to meet the need represented by human hunger.

When Jesus, in the presence of "some of the scribes" (Mark 2:5–7,), again challenged the religious leadership in Capernaum (see Mark 2:1), the account in the text is clear. He forgave the sins of the paralytic first. He knew that His public claim to divine privilege and power would capture the theological interest of the teachers and arouse their opposition. Jesus used that miraculous event as a certification of His divine position. In fact, Jesus' clear claim was that indeed He was, is, and always will be no less than God. He is interested in strengthening relationships between Himself and His disciples, between His disciples and His Father. He is interested in religious institutions and/or rituals, including the Sabbath, only as they assist in accomplishing better relationships.

[1] I. Epstein, "Talmud" in *The Interpreter's Dictionary of the Bible* (Nashville: Abingdon Press, 1962), 4:512.
[2] John Richard Sampey, "Sabbath" in *The International Standard Bible Encyclopedia* (Grand Rapids: Wm. B. Eerdmans Publishing Co., 1939), 4:2631.
[3] Ibid.
[4] Epstein, 4:512.
[5] Matthew Henry, "Mark" in *Commentary on the Whole Bible. Condensed Version* (Grand Rapids: Zondervan Publishing House, 1960), NT 167.
[6] G. Easton, *Easton's Bible Dictionary,* 3rd ed. (Nashville: Thomas Nelson Publishers, 1897), 1015–16.

Don Stewart is professor of New Testament and Greek, New Orleans Baptist Theological Seminary, New Orleans, Louisiana.

that it is the word used to denote Cyprus as the *makaria*, the Happy Isle. This island was said to be so blessed with minerals, fertility, water, and climate as to produce everything which was necessary for the perfectly happy life. So, in effect, by using this word to describe the kingdom citizen, Jesus said that He possesses within Himself everything that is necessary to live the full, rich life.

Now what is it that makes possible such a life? In eight terse statements Jesus answered this question (Matt. 5:3–12). The "poor in spirit" are those who recognize that they are sinners, who possess nothing which merits their approach to God. Therefore, they "mourn" as for the dead because of their sins and the sins of others. The "gentle" are the teachable ones who submit themselves to God as those who need to be forgiven and to be instructed of God. In this state they are never satisfied with their achievements but constantly "hunger and thirst" after the true righteousness. Having obtained mercy they are "merciful." This word means to get inside another's skin so as to see his needs as one's own, and as they show this mercy to others, they receive it in turn. Such are the "pure in heart." They are clean, sincere, and without alloy with nothing between the soul and the Savior; and because of this, they have constant access to God's presence. In Oriental courts the king lived in seclusion for protection from some evil designing enemy. They communicated with their subjects through some trusted, single-hearted, loyal official who was always admitted to the presence of the king. The Christian is such a person in relation to God, and such persons will be "peacemakers" between God and man and between man and man. Since God is a God of peace, those who make such peace will be recognized as being "sons of God" or like Him. They will, by the world, "be persecuted for righteousness," but they are to rejoice in it, knowing that in Christ they are sufficient within themselves and will be greatly rewarded in heaven for their faithfulness and patient endurance.

Looking back over these "Beatitudes," one sees a progression: conviction for sin, repentance for sin, committal to Christ, progressive development in righteousness, mercy toward others, sincerity of heart in constant fellowship with God, evangels of the gospel of peace between God and man and between man and man, and patient endurance and joy as one

Dry wadi bed along the road to Jericho. Here is illustrated the contrast Jesus drew between building on the sand and building on a rock (Matt 7:24-27).

Olive trees were the source of oil for lamps. A lamp is small but it gives light to an entire room.

Wayne Dehoney

Along the northwestern shore of the Sea of Galilee, the rocky, semidesert hillside sweeps upward in an arc to form a natural amphitheater. At the eastern edge on the brow of a hill stands a beautiful marble church, the Chapel of the Beatitudes. It was erected by the Order of St. Francis in 1938 on the traditional site where it is believed that Jesus delivered the Sermon on the Mount (Matt. 5–7).

We read that Jesus came preaching, teaching, and healing throughout the regions of Judea and Galilee. Great crowds followed Him. Seeing the multitudes, Jesus went up to a mountaintop, perhaps to this very site where the chapel is located today. Here He sat down and began to teach His followers about the kingdom of God.

By using our imagination in this geographical setting, many dimensions of the Sermon on the Mount may come alive for us.

Jesus may have sat facing the sea. His disciples would then have gathered below Him, sitting on the rocks and the ground and looking up at Him. Let us sit down in their midst as Jesus speaks.

We soon discover that the Master Teacher is lacing His sermon of abstract spiritual principles with vivid concrete illustrations drawn from the immediate surroundings.

Directly below, on the seashore, fishermen are cleaning the night's catch and salting it down to preserve the fish for market and for storage. "You are the salt of the earth," Jesus says. "Your purpose in the world is to preserve society and prevent it from decay."

"But what if the salt has lost its taste?" Jesus asks. The salt had come

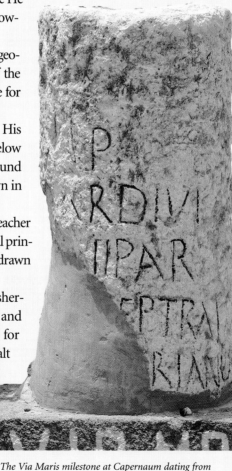

The Via Maris milestone at Capernaum dating from the second century A.D. This is the kind of milestone Jesus likely pointed to when he told His disciples to go the second mile (Matt. 5:41).

from the Dead Sea to the south and contained a high degree of insoluble minerals. When exposed to the weather, the salt would leach out. The residue, while still looking like salt, would fail to preserve the fish, and they would spoil. This residue was more than just useless. It was a hazardous waste that would contaminate good soil. The only safe place of disposal was "to be thrown out and trampled on by men." What a vivid description of the disciple who looses his spirituality. Instead of being a redemptive influence in society, such a disciple becomes not only useless but possibly harmful.

"You are to make your presence known in the world," Jesus said, "like that city." As He talked, He pointed to the northwest over His shoulder at the city of Meron (called Safed today) that is dramatically outlined against the skyline. "A city set on a hill cannot be hid."

Stretching out His left hand toward a cluster of windowless rock houses on the outskirts of Capernaum, Jesus said, "You are the light of the world. You do not cover the oil lamp in your house with a basket. You set the lamp on a pillar so it will light the whole house. So let your life be as a light to all the world around you."

Pointing farther to the east at the city of Capernaum, He singled out the largest building, the synagogue. "Concerning prayer, do not pray as those hypocrites there, praying at the street corners to be seen and heard of men. Or do not pray as some Gentiles do, simply reciting vain repetitions." Opening His hands to us, Jesus said, "But when you pray, come to God in private saying, 'Our Father in heaven . . .'"

Just north of Capernaum was a branch of the famous Via Maris, the "Way of the Sea." This famous highway began at the marker in the forum in Rome and ran across Asia Minor, down through Palestine into Egypt. Mileposts were set along the way measuring the distance to the capital. (One such milepost is on display today in the excavations at Capernaum.)

Roman law provided that a soldier could conscript any citizen of an occupied land and press that person into service for a mile. Jesus points to a milepost on the nearby road. "If a soldier forces you to go a mile, instead of showing sullen and exacting obedience to the law, joyfully render voluntary service for a second mile also." Jesus then gave other examples of the "second mile" principle that distinguishes the character of the Christian: "love your enemies," and "do good to them who wrong you." "If you do only as the law requires, how are you any different from the publicans and the people of the world?"

"And be not wrought with

A scroll of the law from the 16th century A.D.

experiences the enmity of the world.

It is understandable, therefore, that Jesus said that such are to be "salt" and "light." They are to cleanse, season, and preserve society; they are to be the means of giving God's revelation, illumination, and healing to a lost world. This light is not to be hidden from men but shared with them. Thus Jesus commanded His followers to shine before men, that they by the Christian's good works will be brought to glorify their Father in heaven.

Possibly in this tone of teaching, the Apostles already were beginning to see the contrast between the principles of the kingdom and the burdensome legality of Judaism. So Jesus warned them, "Stop thinking or do not begin to think that I came to destroy, or render inactive, the law or the prophets. I came to fill them full of meaning." The kingdom citizen will not be gauged by outward conformity to the letter of the Law. He will be measured or weighed by his spiritual understanding of and obedience to the deeper meaning of God's teachings. In truth more will be expected of him than the demands placed upon him by the scribes and Pharisees. Such is the nature of kingdom citizenship.

2. *The Letter and the Spirit of the Law*

Jesus then proceeded to illustrate the superiority of His ethical demands over those of the scribes in their teaching of the Old Testament and of their oral law by which they sought to explain and apply the Old Testament Scriptures. In so doing He chose six examples: murder, adultery, divorce, oaths, retaliation, and love for one's enemies. In each of these Jesus went beyond the overt act to the inner spirit. Already He had claimed authority with respect to the Temple and the Sabbath. Now He does the same with regard to the Law. "It was said . . . But I tell you" has the finality of divine authority. It is of interest to note that in each case the "I" is written out in the Greek text, which gives it an emphatic meaning. No matter what the scribes have been saying. The One having authority is now speaking.

T h e   I l l u s t r a t e d   L i f e   o f   J e s u s

The law against murder Jesus extended beyond the overt act to include the entire realm of attitudes toward another person. Anger against a fellowman makes one liable ("in danger of") to the local court of twenty-three people. Contempt for one's intelligence ("Fool") makes the offender liable before the Sanhedrin, the council of seventy in Jerusalem. And slander against one's character ("You moron") makes one liable to being thrown into the Gehenna of fire, the garbage dump outside the city of Jerusalem. "Gehenna of fire" was a figure used by Jesus, and only by Him, to depict the horrors of hell. Into this garbage dump were thrown the unclaimed bodies of executed criminals, and this is probably the meaning of Jesus' words here, although the thought of eternal punishment is also involved.

Murder is in one's heart before it is in his hand. It is a progressive attitude which, if not curbed, will eventually express itself in the overt act. Even if it does not erupt into violence, it is a destructive attitude nevertheless, both to its subject as well as to its object. Wrong attitudes toward others even make true worship of God impossible. It is far better to guard the attitudes of one's heart than to regret the bloody acts of one's hands.

The same is true with respect to the law forbidding adultery. The scribes forbade the overt act, but Jesus warned against lust in the heart. Temptation becomes sin at the point of the consent of one's will. If one is held back from the overt act only by a lack of opportunity or from fear of the consequences, he is already guilty of adultery in his heart. The proper safeguard is a correct respect for human personality, both of one's own and that of another.

Jesus' teaching concerning divorce should be considered in the light of the prevailing practice. According to the school of Hillel, a man might divorce his wife for any cause, but Jesus said that it is to be permitted only for "a case of sexual immorality" (Matt. 5:32). Some interpreters question the genuineness of these words, but there is strong manuscript evidence for accepting them. Near the close of His ministry, Jesus will enlarge upon this teaching (Matt. 19:3ff.).

The practice of taking oaths was a much abused one among the Jews. So unreliable were they in their dealings with one another that they swore by all sorts of things; their heads, hair; the Temple, its altar and sacrifices; by heaven, and by the throne of God. Jesus said that the Christian should be so trustworthy that his word would be his bond. When he says "yes" or "no," that should end the matter. But this is not to mean a prohibition against testifying under oath, for Jesus Himself did that (Matt. 26:63–64).

"An eye for an eye, and a tooth for a tooth," said the Law. But Jesus taught that the Christian should suffer wrong rather than to live by the law of retaliation. Furthermore, his love should not stop with his neighbor. He should love his enemies also. What credit is there in the Christian loving only those who love him? Even Gentiles and

anxiety over what you will wear." With a wide sweep of a hand, Jesus said, "Look at the flowers of the field!" It is springtime, and the anemones and poppies blanket the hillsides in a riot of color. "They do not toil or spin, yet even Solomon in all his glory could not be dressed in such beauty. If God so cares for the flowers of the fields and the birds of the air, how much more shall He care about you, His children."

Picking up a round stone at His feet and examining it, He asked, "If your son asks for bread, will you give him a stone?" Tossing it aside, He took a stick and began to probe in the crevice of a large rock and continued, "Or if your son is hungry and crying for a fish, would you go out into the rocks searching for a poisonous snake to give him?"

"If you as an earthly father

Theater mask from Philippi. Hypocrite is based on the Greek word hypokrisis, *which among other things, meant actor. Greek actors wore masks of the kind seen in this structure from Philippi.*

know how to do good things for your children, how much more so does your Heavenly Father desire to do good for His children? Just ask, seek, and knock, and He will respond."

Jesus continued, "The way of the kingdom is not easy." He pointed to a high pinnacle, a promontory six miles away, rising vertically one thousand feet above the eastern shore of the Sea of Galilee. Hippos, the walled city of the Decapolis, was built on the flat top of this natural fortress. A zigzagging, narrow, hazardous road led from the shore side up to the barricaded city gate. "Like that path, difficult and narrow is the upward way to life in the kingdom of God, and few there are who will pay the price to attain it."

Jesus then pointed directly to Tiberias, a city built by Herod Antipas at the location of some ancient baths and hot mineral springs, to be the new capital of Galilee. The sprawling city of Tiberias was built along the shore on the flat lands, without walls and gates and with broad open streets. Tiberias was an anathema to the devout Jew because it was built on the site of a cemetery. The city symbolized uncleanliness, wickedness, and worldliness. Jesus said, "On the other hand, broad is the street and easy is the way that leads to destruction!"

publicans did this. The goal of the Christian should be to emulate the character of his Heavenly Father. In Him alone does one find perfection or completeness.

3. The Practice of True Righteousness

There is no area in the Christian's life which is so sacred but that Satan will not endeavor to pervert it to his own evil ends. So Jesus warned against such a danger. Three of the most religious acts of the Jews were giving alms, prayer, and fasting. Jesus did not condemn these as such, but He did condemn the wrong attitude in doing them.

Those who did their righteous deeds "to be seen" of men Jesus called "hypocrites" or play actors. "To be seen" renders a word from which comes the word "theater." So these people were merely putting on a theatrical performance before an audience. They did so for the plaudits of the crowd, and receiving these plaudits they had their reward. They were paid in full, and, therefore, should expect to receive no reward from God.

The Christian, on the other hand, should do his righteousnesses out of a pure heart as unto God and not unto men. Alms should be given out of a heart of compassion. Prayer should be uttered out of a heart of hunger after fellowship with God. Fasting should result from a preoccupation with God's will. Giving no thought to reward, yet such will surely be rewarded of God.

Since prayer occupies so vital a place in the Christian's life, Jesus dwelt upon this subject. He did not condemn public praying any more than He did public almsgiving and fasting, but the motive which prompts it must be an inner one. Prayer should not be mere empty repetition, which is so common in pagan prayers. Instead it should be the outreach and upreach of a hungry soul toward God. In this connection Jesus gave what is called "The Lord's Prayer." It may more correctly be labeled "The Model Prayer," for in giving it Jesus was not praying but teaching. An analysis of this prayer reveals that it contains in embryo everything for which a Christian should pray. It is also a model for guiding the Christian in prayer because it presupposes a right relationship between God and man, that of Father and child.

Jesus' warning concerning the three deeds of righteousness flows naturally into His teaching concerning kingdom values. "Don't collect for yourselves treasures on earth. . . . But collect for yourselves treasures in heaven" (Matt. 6:19–20). The "hypocrites" regarded religion in terms of earthly values and rewards. The Christian should place the emphasis on heavenly values and rewards. The Christian who has a "single" eye, or one in proper focus, will be full of heavenly light, but those whose eyes are "evil," or out of focus, will be full of darkness. The "evil," eye depicts one who is cockeyed. One eye is trained on earthly values, while the other is pointed toward heaven and its values. The result is a split personality which is torn between heaven and earth. Jesus said that it is impossible to be a slave to two owners, God and money. Each demands absolute loyalty—and it is impossible to give this to both. The Christian is not to be unmindful of his physical needs, but his primary concern should be to seek to bring in the rule of God and the practice of the true right-

Outside the Hellenistic ruins of Bethsaida with the Sea of Galilee in the background. Jesus proclaimed woe to both Bethsaida and Chorazin because of their unbelief in spite of the many miracles they had seen (Matt. 11:21-22).

the Roman authorities probably lived.

"Hear my words and do them!" Jesus said. "Only a foolish man would build an expensive mansion on the silt and sand beside the river. For when the rains come and the Jordan floods, the foundation will be washed away and the house will be destroyed. The wise man builds his house on the table rock of the hillside, where the house will withstand the storms and is above the floods."

Jesus brought to an end the Sermon on the Mount with the admonition, "So is the life of the one who hears these teachings of mine and doeth them. That person builds on a rock, and that life will withstand the floods and the storms of time."

And the people were astonished at what Jesus said, for He taught with great authority. Yet all who heard Him could understand.

Then Jesus declared, "By their fruits you can identify the true citizens of the kingdom of God!" The rocky parts of the hillside were infested with thistles and thornbushes. Jesus asks, "Do you gather grapes off these thistles or figs off these thorn trees?"

Jesus concluded His sermon on the kingdom of God by pointing to the city of Bethsaida four miles to the east. This was the hometown of Simon Peter. The city was nestled in a valley on the banks of the Jordan River east of the point where it enters the Sea of Galilee.

Bethsaida was a two-level city. The lower part was made up of fishermen's shacks and houses built in the flood plain along the riverbanks. The upper part was on the hillside, where the people of wealth and

Wayne Dehoney is retired senior professor of preaching/evangelism, Southern Baptist Theological Seminary, Louisville, Kentucky.

Houses at Chorazin north of the Sea of Galilee.

eousness of God. This is enough to employ all of his daily energies without being torn apart by the cares of tomorrow, for "Each day has enough trouble of its own" (Matt. 6:34).

4. The Problem of Judgment

In kingdom relationships one Christian should not set himself up as the judge of others, for judgment belongs to God alone. This does not mean that the Christian should not exercise discrimination. The very opposite is true, as Jesus had shown in the preceding part of this sermon, but he is not to be a self-appointed judge of others.

In vivid Oriental fashion Jesus drove home this point—a man with a log in his eye cannot remove a splinter or a speck of dust from another's eye. Does not this suggest that the spiritual sin of censorious criticism outweighs the physical sin of the one being judged? If one Christian brother would help another with his problem, he must come to him in love and not in condemnation.

Nor should the Christian become embroiled in the controversies of non-Christians (Matt. 7:6). "Dogs" and "swine" lack the capacity to appreciate kingdom ethics. The Christian would be far wiser to endeavor to lead them to Christ, else he will himself be destroyed by them rather than lead them to appreciate and practice that which they do not understand. In reality this exhortation climaxed Jesus' teaching about kingdom righteousness and values. The kingdom of God will not be brought in through external reformation but through the experience of inner regeneration. The message of Jesus was ever "Ye must be born again."

5. The Source of Power

How shall the Christian find the power to live up to the high standards set forth by Jesus in this Sermon? He said, "Keep asking, and it will be given to you. Keep searching, and you will find. Keep knocking, and the door will be opened to you" (Matt. 7:7). Note the progression: ask, search, knock. This implies the earnest and continuing effort of the Christian to obtain the power to rise to the standard of righteous living which Jesus set forth, and God will surely give it to the one asking, seeking, and knocking.

Within one's own heart what shall be the determining factor? This Jesus stated in "The Golden Rule" (Matt. 7:12). Other teachers had uttered words which are outwardly similar. For instance, Hillel said, "What is hateful to yourself, do to no other." Confucius said, "What you do not want done to yourself, do not do to others." Similar? They miss by the distance between the poles what Jesus said. Their rules are silver. Jesus' rule is golden. Theirs are negative; His is positive. Selfishness alone would enable a pagan to keep theirs. Only a regenerated nature is capable of keeping that of Jesus. Hillel's rule reflects the nature of Judaism. Refrain from doing to others the evil that you do not wish them to do to you. Jesus' rule is the fruit of kingdom righteousness. Think of something good that you would like for someone to do for you, then go and do it for another. Jesus pointed out that this is not merely a new ethic for a new kingdom, it is the very essence of the Law and the Prophets if one reads them with spiritual discernment. Thus He did not come to destroy them or to render them inactive. He came to fill them full of meaning, and that is the essence of the Sermon on the Mount.

6. The Conclusion of the Sermon

Jesus concluded His sermon by driving home its truths in three parables: two gates, two trees, and two foundations. Two gates are open before every man,

An exterior view of a basalt house door. Jesus said, "Keep knocking, and the door will be opened to you" (Matt. 7:7).

the broad and the narrow. The former leads to destruction; the latter leads to life. Two trees offer their fruits to every man, the corrupt tree and the good tree. The good tree, or the ministry of Jesus, yields good fruit. The corrupt tree, the false prophets of outward conformity, brings forth evil fruit. The one brings life; the other brings death.

The climax of the Sermon pictures two foundations. The one is the man who hears and does the words of Jesus. The other is the man who does neither. Outwardly the structures of the two houses or lives appear the same. The test comes with the storm, and the difference is in the foundations. The life founded upon Christ stands; the other falls.

No wonder the people marveled at these authoritative words of Jesus. Nor is it amazing that when He came down out of the mountain they continued to follow after Him.

AN INQUIRY AND A EULOGY

Jesus and the Twelve returned to Capernaum where, from a distance and by His authoritative word, He healed the servant of a Roman centurion, a commander of one hundred soldiers. Later, perhaps the next day, they visited the village of Nain, and there Jesus raised from the dead the son of a widow. Quite naturally news of these incidents spread throughout Galilee, reaching even into Judea.

John the Baptist was still in prison at Machaerus. One day his disciples brought him word of Jesus' mighty works. Evidently they were still resentful of His rising popularity while their teacher sat in a dungeon. It is possible that they even questioned whether Jesus was the Messiah, and this could have caused John to become confused in his thoughts.

At any rate he sent his disciples to Jesus with an inquiry: "Are You the Coming One, or should we expect someone else?" (Matt. 11:3). Literally, "Are you the Coming One, or do we look for another Messiah of a different kind?" "The Coming One" was a term used for the Messiah in the Minor Prophets, whose major picture of Him was one of judgment. The Major Prophets presented him more as a gentle, suffering Servant. Both of these elements were

The Sea of Galilee.

present in John's preaching in the Jordan valley, although its burden emphasized the former. It is in this light that John's question takes on meaning.

In contrast to his emphasis on the judgment aspects of the Messiah's work, John heard that Jesus was a gentle Teacher and Healer. So actually John asked Jesus if there were to be two Messiahs. That Jesus was fulfilling the Major Prophet role was quite clear. Would there be another Messiah of a different kind who would fulfil the Minor Prophet role.

Jesus replied by pointing out the work that He was doing—healing and preaching. "Go and tell John these things," was His answer. In a sense these were some of the things which John himself had said that the Messiah would do (John 1:29–34). To the modern reader this may appear to be an inadequate answer, but John would see and understand. The day of opportunity must precede the day of judgment. The former was central at this time; the latter would come in due time to those who rejected the opportunity. But even then Jesus' ministry was one of mingled mercy and judgment, as is seen in the woes which He pronounced upon the Galilean cities which were even then rejecting Him (Matt. 11:20–24). They were being judged within the context of history. So the mission of the Messiah was one—a mingling of mercy and judgment. In His redemptive work Jesus fulfilled the former. In the final judgment the latter will find full expression. But, even so, every man, yes, every nation, stands in a moment of crisis as he/it faces the question as to what reaction to give to Christ.

Possibly after John's disciples departed, some of those about Jesus criticized him for his question about the Messiah. But no criticism fell from the lips of Jesus. Instead He delivered a eulogy concerning John. Did anyone think of John the Baptist as a fragile reed shaken by the wind? Or as a lounge lizard enjoying the gratuities of a king? Quite the contrary was true concerning him. It was not his faith but his understanding that had faltered. His present predicament was due to his courage in daring to challenge the king and his conduct. Should he be regarded as a prophet? Yea, more than a prophet. He was the forerunner of the Messiah. There was none born of a woman who was greater than John. Yet even the least one in the kingdom of heaven is greater than John. Not greater in stature but in privilege. John was the acme of the old revelation, but everyone in the kingdom who comes after him stands on his shoulders.

Alabaster aryballos (small Greek flask with flattened lip).

Beelzebub: Background and Meaning

Douglas A. Diehl

Interest in demons is at a peak today. A quick look through the weekly *TV Guide* or the local listings of motion pictures can demonstrate that fact. For some people, this interest in the subject of demons is only for the sake of curiosity or "a good scare." They give no serious thought to the possible existence of demons. For others, however, "evil" is not, as our scientific age would suggest, just a way of describing behaviors or events that produce painful results. For these people, "evil" has a personal dimension, sometimes even a name.

Basalt column capital from the Temple Baal Shemin in Sia, Syria.

Throughout history, evil personified has been given many names such as Belial, Sammael, Satan, Mastema, and Azazel.[1] "Beelzebub" is one such name used in the New Testament to refer to a being who was believed to be a part of the demonic forces at work in Jesus' time. This article will examine the background and meaning of the name *Beelzebub* as it relates to the event in Jesus' life recorded in Matthew 12:22–29.

The exact spelling of the name of this "ruler of the demons" has been the source of some debate. Three main spellings of this demon's name are found in the various Greek manuscripts of the New Testament. In English these would be rendered "Beelzebub," "Beezebul," and "Beelzebul." Today a majority of scholars believe that the last of these spellings, "Beelzebul," is the spelling that appeared in the original manuscripts of the Gospels. I will use the name *Beelzebub* in this article (even though "Beelzebul" is probably the form in the original manuscripts of the New Testament) because "Beelzebub" is the most familiar form, having been utilized by the King James Version and the New International Version. All three forms of the name may have been used interchangeably in first-century Jewish conversation to emphasize various meanings associated with the demon's name.

The exact meaning of the name *Beelzebub* is difficult to determine. The name likely is related to the Philistine god, "Baal-Zebub," whose main sanctuary was at Ekron. Often in the history of religion, the gods of one nation became the demons of their enemies.[2] The name *Baal* (root of the "Beel" in the name considered here) was the generic name for the various gods of the Canaanites and may be translated "lord." In the name "Beelzebul," the "zebul" may be related to the Hebrew verb "to inhabit" or the noun "dwelling place" (1 Kings 8:13). In this case,

Basalt altar for sacrifices.

And then as though turning upon the Pharisees and lawyers who were in the group, Jesus turned from praising John to a censure of those who by violent means tried to force the kingdom of heaven into their own preconceived molds. While publicans and common people were being baptized by John, they held themselves aloof from him. And they were doing the same thing with respect to Jesus. The Lord likened them to children playing in the marketplace, some of which may have been in evidence at the time. It was certainly a com-

the name *Beelzebul* may have meant "lord of habitation," that is, the one who dwells in the possessed.[3] If "zebub" was an alternate ending of the demon name, the "zebub" may be related to the Hebrew verb "to flit about" or the noun "fly." Thus, if or when the name *Beelzebub* was used, it could have meant "lord of flies"; that is, the lord of the places of pagan sacrifice where filth attracts flies,[4] or the lord of the demons who take the form of flies. All of these meanings may have been included as a part of the nature of this most odious, demonic character in popular, first-century Judaism.

The possibility that the name *Beelzebub* may have meant "lord of flies" is particularly interesting given what

we are coming to know of the popular beliefs about demons in the days of Jesus. Flies held a significant place in Jewish demonology. Douglas Penney and Michael Wise have recently pieced together a fragmentary text from the Dead Sea Scrolls (numbered 4Q560). The text appears to include an exorcism formula and to begin with the name *Beelzebub* (though the word is partially destroyed, making certain identification impossible). If so, the subject of this exorcism incantation—childbirth—is especially interesting. A demon would typically enter the room of a pregnant woman, disguised as a fly, to disrupt the birth of a child.[5] Possibly, the name "lord of flies" was a designation given to the chief among demons since some believed that demons assumed the form of a nearly undetectable fly.

Whatever the exact meaning of the name *Beelzebub*,

Capernaum Synagogue.

mon sight then as it is now. Some said to their fellows, "We played the flute for you, but you didn't dance; we sang a lament, but you didn't weep!" (Luke 7:32). They would neither dance nor play funeral. The trouble was that they just did not want to play.

Applying this truth, Jesus said that John came as an ascetic, and the Pharisees called him insane. Jesus came as a social being, and they labeled Him a glutton, a drunkard, and a friend of publicans and sinners. They simply did not want to play. Nevertheless, "wisdom is vindicated by her deeds" (Matt. 11:19). The fruits of the labors of both John and Jesus would prove the reality of their missions.

Children playing a sidewalk game in a street in Jerusalem. Jesus likened the religious leaders of His time to children playing in the street (Luke 7:32).

A STUDY IN CONTRASTS

As if in answer to Jesus' charge concerning the Pharisees' attitude toward Him as a social being, Simon, a Pharisee, invited Jesus to a meal. When they sat down or reclined on couches to eat, a notoriously sinful woman came and performed what seems to present-day people to be a strange act. She stood behind Jesus weeping so that her tears fell on His feet. Then she wiped His feet with her hair as she kissed them profusely. She ended by pouring ointment on His feet. A similar thing was done by Mary of Bethany shortly before the crucifixion. Some would make these two events identical, but the contrast of circumstances and personalities makes this most unlikely.

In the event at hand the Pharisee in his mind criticized Jesus for allowing this sinful woman to do as she did. To him it was proof that Jesus was not a prophet.

Knowing his thoughts, Jesus used the occasion to teach a great lesson in forgiveness and love. A certain lender forgave the debts of two men, one of which owed ten times as much as the other. When asked which of the two would love the benefactor the more, Simon gave the obvious answer. The one who was forgiven the more.

Then Jesus applied the lesson. It was evident that the woman loved Jesus more than Simon did because she was to be forgiven the more. The difference between the sinful woman and the self-righteous Pharisee who felt no need for forgiveness was one of compassionate love as over against cold courtesy. Then fitting His deeds to His words, Jesus said to the woman, "Your sins are forgiven" (Luke 7:48). The crowd buzzed within themselves that He should claim to forgive sins, but Jesus ignored them as He said to the woman, "Your faith has saved you. Go in peace" (Luke 7:50).

Shortly after this incident Jesus and the Twelve made a second preaching tour of Galilee. They were accompanied by certain women who had been healed of evil spirits and diseases. One of these was Mary Magdalene out of whom Jesus had cast seven demons. It is usually held that this indicates that she had been a very sinful woman, but this is not necessarily true. This extreme case of demon

Winged demon (at left) is from Sakcegozu, Aramean style with Assyrian and Hittite elements (730-700 B.C.).

many extrabiblical materials and the New Testament itself make clear that Jews in the first century believed in the widespread existence of demons and were frightened by their power. Penney and Wise state:

"The era of the Second Temple was a magical time. A wealth of indirect evidence proves that, on the popular level, magic was often of greater practical significance than were many aspects of the Law of Moses. The intensity of the unseen spiritual battle to which the common man might easily fall victim appears in Rabbi Huna's well-known exegesis of Ps 91:7, 'Everyone among us has a thousand demons on his left hand and ten thousand at his right.' Against these invisible legions of demons, magic offered a tangible, material defense whose potential benefits a prudent individual could not afford to ignore."[6]

A grainfield in the Asochis Valley. In the foreground are thistles which Jesus referred to in his Parable of the Sower.

possession could have been something else entirely, and probably was. Nevertheless, these women, like the one in Simon's house, showed their great love for Jesus by ministering to Him and the Twelve out of their material substance. This little band of women is symbolic of that innumerable caravan of women who have done likewise through the ages. If any group should love Jesus, it is womanhood for whom Jesus did and does so much! And, incidentally, this event suggests the source of livelihood for Jesus and His little band.

THE MINISTRY OF THE PARABLE

The following events all occurred in a single day which A. T. Robertson called "The Busy Day." Doubtless it was one of many such days in the life of Jesus. The happenings of this day took place near and on the Sea of Galilee.

1. A Blasphemous Accusation

The day began in a house. The crowds which awaited Jesus' ministry were so great that He could not find time even to eat. Such dedication to His work was interpreted by His friends as a form of insanity.

In the course of this morning, Jesus healed a blind and mute demoniac. Seeing this, the people asked, "Perhaps this is the Son of David!" (Matt. 12:23). Jesus avoided this term because to the Jews it carried a highly political Messianic connotation. Such a declaration apparently drove the Pharisees to desperation, for they responded, "The man drives out demons only by Beelzebul, the ruler of the demons" (Matt. 12:24). This statement evidently was made to the people and not to Jesus directly. "Beelzebul" was a title of contempt which the Jews applied to Satan.

Knowing their evil thoughts, Jesus called the Pharisees to Him, and in four points He answered their charge. First, if by the power of Satan He cast out

demons, then Satan is casting out Satan. How then shall his kingdom of evil stand? Second, the Pharisees' disciples claimed, though falsely, to cast out demons. Did they also work by Satan's power? Let them decide the issue. Naturally they would say that it was by God's power. Third, if Jesus cast out demons by the power of God, then why did not the Pharisees accept Him? Fourth, the very fact that He was casting out Satan proved that Jesus' power was superior to Satan's power. Thus the Pharisees were without a logical answer to Jesus' arguments.

Then Jesus pronounced upon them what is called the "unpardonable sin," or the sin against the Holy Spirit (Matt. 12:31–32). This was not a sin of impulse. It was the climax of a deliberate hardening of their hearts against Jesus. Neither was it a sin of ignorance. The Pharisees committed it in the full knowledge of Jesus' miraculous deed. Others saw it and glorified God. The Pharisees saw it and blasphemed or spoke insultingly of the Holy Spirit. They witnessed an obviously good work of God's Spirit, yet they attributed it to Satan's evil spirit. They had lost the power to discern between good and evil. To them good was evil, and evil was good. Like Milton's Satan in *Paradise Lost,* they said, "Evil, be thou my good." So like John the Baptist, Jesus called them a "generation of vipers" or a brood of snakes. Terrible words! But they came from Him who is infinite Mercy to all who will receive it.

As if to prove their spiritual emptiness, the Pharisees sought to counter Jesus' words by asking that He show them a sign of His deity. They ignored completely the "sign" which He had just given in casting out the demon. The only sign Jesus promised them was the sign of Jonah which in effect was His resurrection from the dead (Matt. 12:39–40). Because His contemporary generation, of which the Pharisees were a sample, rejected Him, the Ninevites and the queen of Sheba would witness or be evidence against them in the final judg-

An octagonal church built in the 5th century A.D. *over St. Peter's house, which was 1st century* A.D.

ment. For the former responded to the preaching of Jonah, and the latter came from afar to hear the wisdom of Solomon. But a greater than either Jonah or Solomon was among that generation, and they were rejecting Him.

Jesus closed this interview by condemning the entire Pharisaical system. So empty were their teachings that those to whom they sought to minister were left in a worse condition than when they found them. It is a sad picture of the spiritual poverty of those who claimed to be religious teachers. No wonder, therefore, theirs was a generation of spiritual dearth.

2. A New Relationship

During all this time Jesus was still in a house. Just at this point someone came to him with word that His mother and brethren were outside wishing to see Him. Why they had come is not stated. It is generally held that, fearing that He was beside Himself, they wished to take Him home. But this is mere supposition. Their coming could have been for any legitimate reason.

At any rate when Jesus heard it, He replied that no longer should they presume upon a family relationship, and then looking about at His disciples, He said, "Here are My mother and My brothers! Whoever does the will of God is My brother and sister and mother" (Mark 3:34–35). There is every reason to believe that Jesus' mother fell within this category, but His half brothers did not believe on Him until after His Resurrection. The point of Jesus' words is that the true relationship with Him is spiritual and not genetical.

3. Jesus Teaching in Parables

At this juncture, probably about noon, Jesus left the house and went out to the seaside. The crowds were so great that He got into a boat and pulled away from the shore to enable all to see and hear, and then He began to teach them in parables.

The beliefs held by first-century Jews about demons play an important role in understanding the meaning of Matthew 12:22–29.

The accusation in Matthew 12 that Jesus was in league with Beelzebub perhaps was not in response to the miraculous healing itself. Instead, the accusation that Jesus was demon possessed was in response to Jesus' tendency to heal on the Sabbath. The healing of the mute man apparently took place on the Sabbath—the same day on which other Sabbath controversies had occurred (see Matt. 12:1,10). When Jesus healed on the Sabbath and taught that it was lawful to do so, the scribes and Pharisees believed He was acting and teaching in direct contradiction to Moses' law. They thought He was exhibiting the third manifestation of demon possession listed above—teaching heresy. At this point Matthew's Gospel is consistent with what we know

from John's Gospel. In John, Jesus was accused of being demon possessed on three occasions (John 7:20; 8:48; and 10:20). Each time, His teachings, not His actions, precipitated the accusation.

[1] Jeffrey Burton Russell, *The Devil: Perceptions of Evil from Antiquity to Primitive Christianity* (Ithaca, N.Y.: Cornell University Press, 1977), 211.
[2] Werner Foerster, "beezebouvl," *Theological Dictionary of the New Testament*, (Grand Rapids: Wm. B. Eerdmans Publishing Company, 1964), 1:605–06.
[3] T. Rees, "Beelzebub" in *The International Standard Bible Encyclopaedia*, vol. 1, ed. James Orr (Grand Rapids: W. B. Eerdmans Pub. Co., 1939), 423.
[4] Foerster, 1:606.
[5] Ibid.
[6] Douglas L. Penney and Michael O. Wise, "By the Power of Beelzebub: An Aramaic Incantation Formula from Qumran" (4Q560), *Journal of Biblical Literature* 113.4 (1994), 631–34.

Douglas A. Diehl is pastor, Crossroads Baptist Church, San Antonio, Texas.

Previously from time to time Jesus had employed this method of teaching, but here He used it altogether. And this is significant. The Pharisees had definitely shown that they were not disposed to heed His teachings but were using His words as a basis of criticism. The people as a whole were so enchanted by the Pharisees' dream of a kingdom of earthly grandeur that they were, for the most part, incapable of understanding the spiritual nature of Christ's kingdom. So Jesus with good reason adopted the parabolic method of teaching by which He might impart truths to His disciples. It was not a deliberate attempt to hide truth but was an effort to depict it in vivid imagery to those who were capable of receiving it.

The parable was a favorite method of teaching among the Orientals. By it they took one central truth and so adorned it in familiar dress that it might be viewed from many angles. The parables of Jesus have been called earthly stories with heavenly meanings. They were handles by which His listeners might pick up truth and take it home with them.

For convenience the parables under consideration may be divided into two groups: those spoken to the larger audience by the seaside and those delivered to the disciples in a house. Each of them depicts some aspect of the kingdom of God.

1. By the Seaside

The first parable is called the Parable of the Sower, but more correctly it is the Parable of the Soils, for one sower sowed the same kind of seed in different types of soil with varying results.

To understand it one must recall the situation. A grainfield usually has a hard path running through it over which people might travel. Palestine is underlaid by a hard pan of limestone rock. In many places the topsoil is very thin. In a given field there would be deeper, richer soil infested with thorn-

The slope of the hill from Gergesa into the Sea of Galilee where Jesus cast the demons into the pigs.

bushes or other wild growth. Then there was good soil which was free from such. So the scene is fixed.

A sower broadcasts the field with seed. Some falls on the hard path where the ever-present birds eat it. Other seed falls on the thin soil and takes root. The warmth of the limestone rock causes it to grow quickly in the early springtime, but because it has no firm rootage, it soon withers under the hot sun. Yet other falls on the rich soil infested with thorns. While it grows, it bears no fruit because the thorns choke it out, depriving it of needed nutrition. But that which falls on the good, clean soil bears an abundant harvest.

Privately the Twelve asked Jesus to interpret this parable. The sower may be anyone who scatters abroad the Gospel of the kingdom. He is not responsible for the results but for the sowing. Some gospel seed will fall on hard hearts which do not receive it, and Satan immediately takes it away. Other seeds are received enthusiastically but without comprehension of the true meaning of the gospel. Under tribulation those receiving it soon show their true colors as they wilt away. They were never really in the kingdom. Other seeds fall into lives which genuinely receive them, but they are so cluttered up with the cares of the world that, while the plants live, they bear no fruit. However those who are completely dedicated to the Lord bear an abundant harvest in the kingdom.

The same gospel sown in different soils with such varied results!

An analysis reveals that these results were and are obtained both among those who heard Jesus and who hear His evangels today. It is no wonder that Jesus said, "Therefore, take care how you listen" (Luke 8:18).

Another parable deals with the nature of the growth of the kingdom. The seed is sown, and the sower leaves it there. It grows and bears fruit without his knowledge of the process. It is a gradual growth: the blade, the head, and then the ripened grain. Then he knows that the harvest is ready, and he reaps.

In like fashion God places His kingdom upon the earth. It does not grow by outward force or adornment. The growth is secret, inward, and gradual. When in His wisdom, not man's, the harvest is ripe, He will reap.

At first sight the Parable of the Tares may resemble that of the soils, but it teaches a different truth altogether. In the Parable of the Soils, there was one sower, one type of seed, but different soils. In that of the tares there were two sowers, two types of seed, and one kind of soil.

Again it is necessary to note certain conditions in order to understand this parable. "Tares" or "darnel" and wheat were similar plants until the grain formed in the head. Then darnel formed black, inedible grains. It was a common practice for one's enemy to oversow his sown field with darnel.

Jesus drew upon this phenomenon to teach the nature of the kingdom of God. A man's field was oversown with darnel. Later when this was discovered, the owner's servants asked if they should pull up the darnel, but he wisely told them that to do this would injure the wheat. So he left them to grow together until harvest. Then the darnel was burned and the wheat stored in his barn.

Later in the house Jesus interpreted this parable to His disciples. Here the sower of the good seed, or sons of the kingdom, is the Son of man. The enemy is the devil, and his seed are the sons of the evil one. The harvest is the end of the world, and the reapers are the angels. The point is that as Jesus is sowing down

Looking west over Israeli Valley seen in distance, near North Ashuna, just south of Sea of Galilee.

the world with sons of the kingdom, Satan is oversowing the world with his sons. To man's outward judgment they may appear similar, but the harvest time will reveal the difference, and the Son of man knows His own. Men are not to endeavor to remove the sons of Satan lest they injure the wheat. Then the sons of the kingdom will be gathered unto the Son of man, and the sons of the evil one will be cast into hell. "Anyone who has ears should listen!" (Matt. 13:43).

The Parables of the Mustard Seed and the Leaven teach similar truths but with different emphases. Like the very small mustard seed which grows into a large plant, so from a small beginning the kingdom of God will grow—to unbelievable proportions. And as a small piece of leaven placed in dough silently works until it leavens the whole lump, so will the kingdom spread until it fills the earth. Some see "leaven" as a universal symbol of evil. Thus to them this parable means that evil will permeate the kingdom while it is on earth, but this is an unwarranted position. Leaven was to be put in a certain bread sacrifice prescribed by the Law of Moses (Lev. 23:17). Is this also evil? No! Jesus was simply drawing upon a common custom to teach a spiritual truth.

The disciples in keeping with their contemporaries were expecting the kingdom to spring forth full-grown in a day. Jesus said that its growth will be gradual and without outward ostentation. This is a comforting thought after two thousand years. The growth of the kingdom seems to be slow and ineffective, but silently, inwardly it continues to increase, and its leaven permeates even those elements which oppose it.

Distant view of Machaerus, a fortress built by Herod the Great and the place Josephus says John the Baptist was imprisoned and executed. This site is near the locations where John preached and baptized.

2. In the House

Having finished His teaching by the seaside, Jesus retired into a house. It may have been Simon Peter's house in Capernaum, and there, after explaining the Parable of the Tares, Jesus spoke four additional parables to the Twelve.

In the Parables of the Hidden Treasure and the Pearl of Great Price, Jesus teaches the price which He will pay for the kingdom. Some regard it as the price which one must pay to get into the kingdom, but man does not buy his way into it. Jesus, and Jesus alone, purchased the kingdom!

In ancient times it was a common practice for one to bury his treasure. It might be a robber, or it might be the rightful owner. At any rate someone buried a treasure, went away, and never returned. Perhaps he died without revealing its location. In due time the land belonged to another who was unaware of the treasure. Someone found it, hid it, and purchased the field, selling all that he had in order to do so.

Some see a moral difficulty here, but it was not so regarded in that day. However, one must not press every point in a parable. The one truth is that finding the treasure the man "for joy" sold all that he had and bought the field. Likewise Jesus sold all that He had, His life, in order to purchase the kingdom. This is suggestive of Hebrews 12:2: "Who for the joy that was set before him endured the cross, despising the shame . . ."

The Parable of the Pearl relates the same truth. A traveling pearl merchant found a pearl of superlative value. To purchase it he sold all that he had. Jesus, likewise, gave His all, even His life, in order to purchase the kingdom.

The Parable of the Net reiterates with a different figure the truth set forth in the Parable of the Tares. It was a common sight around the Sea of Galilee to see fishermen letting down their nets. In them they caught all manner of fish. The good they kept, but the bad they threw away. Even so, in the net of the kingdom age there will be found true and false confessors, but in the consummation of the age the true will be saved and the false or bad will be cast into hell.

With this Jesus finished this particular body of His teaching about the kingdom. But one thought remained. Jesus is, in truth, a scribe teaching about the kingdom. He is also teaching the Twelve to become scribes in the kingdom. As such they are to bring out of their treasures of knowledge things "new and old." Like Jesus, they are to teach the old truths, the Old Testament, but they are also to declare the new revelation which is in Jesus Christ. They are not yet ready to do so, but their time will come.

3. A Visit to Gerasa

It was probably the middle of the afternoon of "The Busy Day." The crowds still followed Jesus. So for a brief respite He and the Twelve took a boat to go to the eastern shore of the Sea of Galilee. Jesus was tired after a strenuous day, so He lay down to sleep on a cushion in the back of the boat. The valleys on the eastern shore empty into the sea so as to form wind funnels. Sometimes

A pot and hoard of silver coins dating from the 1st century A.D. In Jesus' time, people often buried their treasure.

without warning the wind rushes down suddenly turning a placid lake into a seething cauldron. This phenomenon occurred at this time, possibly as the result of an afternoon thunderstorm. The sea rocked as if it were an earthquake. The waves were beating into the boat so that it was in danger of sinking. In their jeopardy the disciples called to Jesus, "Lord, save us! We're going to die!" (Matt. 8:25). Some of the Twelve were men of the sea, and most likely had done their best to weather the storm, but when all of their skills failed them, they called on Jesus. Fishermen calling to a landlubber for help! This shows their conviction as to the supernatural power of Jesus.

But despite their faith in Jesus, He still rebuked them for their lack of faith. This suggests that they lacked enough faith to believe that God would preserve His Son even in a storm such as this one was.

Then Jesus rebuked the winds and the sea. Here was the Master of nature bidding these elements to behave: "And there was a great calm" (Matt. 8:26).

According to the language this was not a gradual subsiding of the storm's force as would be true in a natural phenomenon. It was a sudden calm, denoting the miraculous

Gergesa and the Sea of Galilee. The only place on the east side of the Sea of Galilee where a hill comes down to the shore.

element. No wonder the Twelve wondered that even the natural elements were subject to Jesus. Literally, "the men began to marvel . . . and the sea kept on obeying him" (Matt. 8:27).

Probably late in the afternoon Jesus arrived on the eastern shore of the Sea of Galilee. He was in the region of the Decapolis which was largely Gentile territory. This particular locality was called the country of the Gadarenes or the Gerasenes. There He was confronted by two demon-possessed or insane men who dwelt among the tombs. They were a scourge to the entire area. Efforts had been made to bind them in fetters and chains, but they broke them in pieces. Night and day they wandered among the tombs and in the mountains, crying out and cutting themselves with stones. Passersby gave them a wide berth.

But when these demoniacs saw Jesus they ran and knelt before Him crying out that He would not torment them, for Jesus had commanded the demons to come out of the men. The demons themselves were speaking through their victims. They recognized Jesus as the "Son of the most high God," but when they were commanded to come out of the men, they implored Jesus to permit them to enter into a herd of swine which was feeding nearby. They did not want to be disembodied. When their petition was granted the swine were crazed so that they ran into the sea and were drowned.

Word soon reached the owners of the swine. So they, along with the entire city, came to find the demoniacs clothed and in their right minds. One would think that they would be delighted to find them so, but instead they asked Jesus to leave their land. Was it simply that they preferred swine over souls? Perhaps. But Luke says that they were terrified over the entire matter, and this may suggest another reason for their request. This was pagan territory, and pagans were fearful of their gods. The entire affair, including the confession of Jesus' deity by the demons, suggested to them that a god was among them. So out of fear they asked Jesus to leave.

The Lord granted their request, but He did not leave Himself without a witness among them. For in reply to one healed man's request to be allowed to accompany Jesus, He said, "Go back home to your own people, and report to them how much the Lord has done for you and how He has had mercy on you" (Mark 5:19). This man became an evangel throughout the Decapolis. This within itself brought a happy ending to "The Busy Day."

A FINAL VISIT TO NAZARETH

The next day Jesus and the Twelve returned to Capernaum. There He healed a woman who had been suffering from an issue of blood for twelve years, raised the daughter of Jairus from the dead, and healed two blind men and a mute demoniac. Then He paid a last visit to Nazareth. His home village had failed her first test—so Jesus gave her another.

Again on the Sabbath day Jesus taught in the synagogue. This time there was no violence. They met His words with cold unbelief. True He spoke wonderful words, and they knew by hearsay of His mighty works, but their familiarity bred contempt. Was not this the former village carpenter, the son of Mary and Joseph? And His half brothers and half sisters were still their neighbors. So since they knew Him so well, He could not be the Messiah. Apparently they shared with Nathanael the belief that nothing good could come from their town.

Therefore, in the light of their cynicism Jesus spoke words of universal import: "A prophet is not without honor, except in his hometown among his relatives, and in his household" (Mark 6:4). Not only His fellow-Nazarenes, but His own family, except Mary, rejected Him. So wondering as to their unbelief, Jesus left Nazareth never to return.

A THIRD TOUR OF GALILEE

However, even if Nazareth would not receive Jesus, the harvest was plenteous elsewhere. So one day he called the Twelve to Him that He might send them on a preaching tour of Galilee. The time had arrived when they should attempt to use what they had been taught. Furthermore, to empower them for their work, He endued them with authority to cast out demons and to heal diseases.

Also Jesus gave them instructions, not only for their immediate journey but for all who would come after them in the preaching of the Gospel. Dr. W. Hersey Davis divides these instructions according to three periods in the gospel age: to the time of the crucifixion (Matt. 10:6–15); from Pentecost to the fall of Jerusalem (Matt. 10:16–23); from the fall of Jerusalem to the end of the age (Matt. 10:24–42).

1. To the Time of the Crucifixion

In this period the apostles are sent to the Jews only, even excluding the Samaritans. In the Commission following the Resurrection they are sent into the whole world, with a specific mention of Samaria. But now they are to proclaim to the Jews that the kingdom of heaven is at hand. Their work will be authenticated by miraculous works. During this time, haste is essential. Therefore, they are to travel without provisions as men on an urgent mission, but they are not to go as beggar-prophets. Those to whom they minister will provide for their needs. Wherever they are welcomed they are to speak words of peace and blessing, but when they are rejected they are to shake off from their feet the dust of that house or city as a judgment against them. This was a typical Oriental gesture, and in the final judgment it will be more tolerable for Sodom and Gomorrah than for such cities.

2. From Pentecost to the Fall of Jerusalem

Here a sudden change of atmosphere is seen. The apostles now are sent forth as sheep among wolves. They will be persecuted by both Jews and Gentiles. It was only during this period that the Christians were persecuted by both of these groups. They will be scourged in the synagogues, and Dr. Davis notes that such has not happened since the fall of the Jewish state in A.D. 70.

During such a time they were not to worry about their defense before governors and kings. The Holy Spirit would give them the words to say. This was because they had not yet had time or opportunity to hammer out the terms of faith.

This period in Christian history was characterized by bitter family strife as Jews became Christians. The most intimate of family relationships were broken as the members betrayed other members to the persecutors, even unto death.

Jesus told His apostles that they were not to tarry in one city under persecution. If one place would not hear them they were to go to another, and He said that they would not have gone through "the towns of Israel before the Son of Man comes" (Matt. 10:23). After the fall of Jerusalem there were no "towns of Israel." The coming of the Son of Man does not necessarily refer to the end of the age. It could also be any cataclysmic event in history. This coming of the Son of Man was the destruction of Jerusalem under Titus in A.D. 70.

3. From the Fall of Jerusalem to the End of the Age

This period marks the identification of the Christians with Christ. As the world had persecuted and blasphemed Christ, so would it do to His people (Matt. 10:24–25). But they are not to fear their persecutors. Rather they are to be fearful of failing to do the will of God. They can be certain that God's care will ever be about them. They are going forth to declare the gospel. There will be varied responses to it, but men must make a choice between Jesus and even the unbelieving members of their families.

Death may await those who proclaim the gospel, so they should be prepared to die in the cause. But in so doing they will have fulfilled the purpose of their being, and that will be life indeed.

4. The Mission of the Twelve

Therefore, the Twelve went forth to begin their first phase of this agelong mission, and it was a successful mission indeed. It was a glorious experience of preaching, casting out devils, and healing the sick. The power which Jesus had given to them really worked!

THE DEATH OF JOHN THE BAPTIST

When Herod killed John the Baptist, the disciples of John claimed his body and buried it. Then they brought the sad news to Jesus. Evidently at this stage in Jesus' ministry, John had been dead for some time. The thing that made a change in the present ministry of Jesus was the fact that the superstitious Herod, when he heard of Jesus' works, said that He was John the Baptist come to life again. This fact posed a threat to Jesus Himself, and since His hour had not yet come, He decided to leave Herod's territory. This among other matters caused Jesus to bring to a close His Galilean ministry. From this time on His ministry took a different turn and was focused on a different purpose. It was ever working toward the accomplishment of God's redemptive will and purpose, for He causes even the wrath of men to praise Him.

"If anyone wants to be My follower, he must deny himself, take up his cross, and follow Me. For whoever wants to save his life will lose it, but whoever loses his life because of Me and the gospel will save it."

MARK 8:34-35 (HCSB)

The Period of Withdrawals 5

Mountains of the Hermon range in nothern Israel. This was one of the areas where Jesus withdrew with His disciples.

It was one year before the crucifixion of Jesus. This means that it was just prior to the Passover in A.D. 29. Shortly after Jesus learned that Herod Antipas had cast his designing and superstitious eyes upon Him, the Twelve returned with exciting reports of their successful tour of Galilee. Doubtless they were physically tired and emotionally exhausted. So Jesus said to them, "Come away by yourselves to a remote place and rest a little" (Mark 6:31).

Thus there began a period of four withdrawals from Galilee which was to last for approximately six months, from the Passover until abut the time of the Feast of the Tabernacles. This encompassed a period from spring until autumn.

Five reasons may be given for these withdrawals. Jesus withdrew from the jealous superstition of Herod Antipas. He wanted to escape the rising fanaticism of the Galilean crowds. The hostility of the Jewish rulers was deepening. The season of extreme heat around the Sea of Galilee was approaching, so Jesus went to the seashore and the mountains to rest. And He wanted privacy in which to instruct the Twelve. The end was rapidly approaching, and they must be prepared for it. Two things are worthy of note. In each of these withdrawals, Jesus avoided the territory of Herod Antipas and those areas which were under the direct influence of the Jewish rulers. After each withdrawal He returned to Galilee but only for brief periods, and the teaching of this period centered upon the King of the Kingdom or the Person of Christ. It was one of the most important segments of Jesus' ministry.

THE WITHDRAWAL INTO BETHSAIDA JULIAS

1. The Feeding of the Five Thousand

Even though it was the time of the Passover, Jesus did not go to Jerusalem for its observance. Instead He and the Twelve took a boat and rowed to the northeastern side of the Sea of Galilee. They landed in the region connected with the city of Bethsaida Julias, so named to distinguish it from the western Bethsaida near Capernaum. It was in the tetrarchy of Philip. Although this was a heavily populated section, the spot chosen by Jesus was a "desert place," not necessarily a desert but a deserted area which promised privacy.

House ruins at Bethsaida with Hellenistic villas in the background. The region of the Feeding of the Five Thousand.

A First-Century Fishing Boat

George W. Knight

The adventure began when two brothers, Moshe and Yuval Lufan, left their kibbutz home of Nof Ginnosar to search for any treasure recently revealed by the rapidly receding waters of the Sea of Galilee. The lack of rainfall in 1985 and into 1986 had caused heavy demand on the lake for water for irrigating crops—thus, the water level was the lowest in memory. Only a few hundred yards from their kibbutz, the tractor wheel spun in the mud and scattered several ancient coins. When they examined the area, several iron nails were discovered. Then they observed the shape of a boat buried in the mud. Only the outline could be seen, but it was obviously a boat. It must have been old because it was completely buried in the mud and silt.

Shelley Wachsmann, the excavator, recounts in his recent book about the project an incredible story of many people from many walks of life contributing to the discovery, recovery, and preservation of this fascinating artifact. He recalls the scribbled note on his desk, which read, "Shelley, a boat, possibly ancient, has been found in the Sea of Galilee. Please investigate...."[1] The next day, February 5, the Lufan brothers pointed to the outline of the craft. Kneeling in a light rain, Wachsmann scratched away the mud to reveal the mortise-and-tenon construction, a sure sign of antiquity. At this moment a rainbow appeared over the Sea of Galilee, and they pondered how this boat sank in this spot and what the discovery might mean.

Model of Kinneret boat at Nof Ginnosar on the Sea of Galilee.

Such a momentous discovery was difficult—no, impossible —to keep secret, and by the weekend newspapers were already issuing stories about the discovery of a boat in Galilee from the time of Jesus. Immediately speculation ran rampant about the significance of the find. Some accounts suggested it was somehow connected with Jesus, and others told of a great hoard of gold coins. The Ministry of Tourism encouraged the excitement for its own purposes. It became immediately clear to the discoverers that guarding the site against treasure hunters as well as the curious would be impossible. So the excavation of the

However, it was not so to be, for the people, discerning Jesus' destination, ran around the northern edge of the sea. When the little company arrived, they were met by the multitudes; and even though Jesus had come there to rest, His compassion was such that He taught them and healed their sick.

The people had been without food all day. Therefore, late in the afternoon the Twelve came to Jesus with the suggestion that He should send the crowds away into the nearby villages that they might buy food. But Jesus astounded them by saying, "You give them something to eat" (Mark 6:37). The disciples had compassion on the people; they recognized their hunger, but it never occurred to them that they should or could do anything about it. They failed to recognize the resources that were at their disposal. How like modern Christians they were! Hungry people must be fed, but let them do it themselves, or else let the civic authorities assume the responsibility. Herod Antipas could have said as much, but Jesus still says, "You give them something to eat."

Thrown back upon their own resources, the Twelve began to count the cost or to reckon their ability only in monetary terms. They estimated that it would require "two hundred pennyworth," or about thirty-four dollars, of bread to feed the crowd, but Jesus told them to search among the people to see what food was available. Finally, Andrew reported that he had found a lad who had five barley cakes and two dried fishes. This was the food of the poor. Perhaps it was a lunch which the lad's mother had fixed for him. Someone remarked that the greatest miracle that day was not Jesus' multiplying the loaves and fishes but that this growing lad had not eaten his lunch so late in the day. Evidently he was quite absorbed in the events which he was witnessing.

At any rate Jesus told the people to sit down in groups of hundreds and fifties. Note Jesus' use of organization to ensure that all would be fed. It was a beautiful sight. At this time of year the grass was green. As the groups clothed in their varicolored robes sat on the green grass, it made a colorful display.

site planned for a later time after the lake had covered again was revised to an immediate attempt to recover the boat.

The months and years of planning, recruiting the experts and workers, and raising funds normally required for an archaeological excavation were telescoped to three days. The plans were approved by the director of the Department of Antiquities, and the team began to arrive for the beginning of the project on February 16, 1986. The boat was to be excavated and then moved to the Yigal Allon Center at Ginnosar where it would be treated and preserved. The seemingly difficult task began to take on more complications. The winter rains caused the level of the lake to rise toward more nor-

Floor mosaic from the church at Tabgha in Galilee, Israel, showing the bread and fish.

mal levels, a great event for all purposes except the pending excavation. The morning the excavation was to begin, a nearby community sent an armed band to lay claim to the boat. One-half of the day was lost to diplomatic and police negotiations to settle the claim.

The problem of the rising water was addressed by the Kinneret Authority. Even though it was suggested that the level of the lake should be lowered to save the excavation of the boat, the answer was to build a dike around the excavation site. This was done on the second day of work when the Authority workers brought materials and constructed the protective dike of dirt and sandbags.

The excavation process offered several challenges for which creative solutions had to be found. For example, tools usually used in excavation threatened to damage the fragile wooden hull of the boat. The answer was to excavate with their hands. The urgency of the project at first led to around-the-clock work. It was feared that important items might be overlooked or discarded in the mud and dark. So all of the mud removed from inside and alongside the boat was put into plastic boxes that were identified with their location and stored for later examination.

Then Jesus blessed the food, began to break it, giving it to His disciples, who in turn distributed it among the people. It was an awesome occasion, for the supply seemed to be inexhaustible. As the Lord of the harvest had produced the food by the gradual working of His natural laws, so in accelerated fashion He reproduced it by supernatural laws. The result was that five thousand men, to say nothing about the women and children, were fed. Judging by a modern congregation there could have been fifteen or twenty thousand people involved! When all had been fed, Jesus ordered that the fragments of food be gathered. He wasted nothing which He had made. The remainder filled twelve baskets. This type of basket was a cophinus, a small hand basket used to carry food.

Various efforts have been made to explain this event by natural means. One suggests that the disciples discovered a cache of food stored in a cave as military supplies. A more likely theory holds that Jesus and the Twelve shared their own meager lunch, and this set off a wave of generosity as others shared their food with others. But there is no reason to reject the miraculous element if one believes Jesus to be the Son of God. If God could produce the food in the first place, there is no reason He could not, by laws unknown to man, reproduce it in this fashion.

Behind this event is a great spiritual truth. The supplier of the loaves and fishes was only a lad. He did not have very much, but what he had he gave to Jesus; and Jesus blessed it, enlarged it, and with it fed a multitude. What He did with this lad's food He can do with anyone's life.

2. A Revolutionary Effort Rejected

The miracle electrified the multitude, and that which Jesus feared began to take shape. The people were on the verge of trying to acclaim Him their political king. Had they succeeded in doing so, it would have meant rebellion against Rome, and like all such sporadic rebellions, it would have brought the wrath of Rome down upon Jesus and upon the people. The result would be the destruction of the purpose for which Jesus came into the world.

The people were ripe for such a revolution. For it to flame into reality called only for a leader, and in Jesus they thought that they had found one. They had either witnessed or heard of His many past miracles, and now this. With Him as their military leader, they would need no medical corps. He could heal them of their wounds. There would be no need for further recruitment. If a soldier were killed, Jesus could restore him to life, and they would have a ready source of military supplies. With a handful of food Jesus could feed an army.

But there was an even greater cause for their proposed action. One of their favorite messianic prophecies was Deuteronomy 18:15. Moses had said, "The Lord thy God will raise up unto thee a Prophet from the midst of thee, of thy brethren, like unto me; unto him ye shall hearken." Certainly Jesus' miracles attested to the fact that God had raised Him up. Most certainly He was a Prophet. He was a Jew, one of their "brethren," and He was a Galilean, one from their very midst. And He was like unto Moses. Moses had furnished manna and quail in the wilderness, and Jesus had miraculously fed them with loaves and fishes in "a desert place." So they were ready to "hearken" unto Him.

Note Jesus' actions in the light of this situation. First, He forced the disciples to embark. Second, He dismissed the multitude. Did He send the disciples away or get them out of this revolutionary atmosphere? Or were they the actual source of it? It is entirely possible that the latter was true. So Jesus had to send the Twelve away before He could quiet the multitude. And, third, He went into the mountain to pray. The recent situation was Satan's temptation all over again. Jesus needed this communion with His Father, not only for Himself, but also for the Twelve, that they might come to understand fully His Person and purpose.

It was just one year before the crucifixion, and they were still captivated by the Jewish dream of a political kingdom and a political messiah. They had so much to learn before they could go forth as heralds of the kingdom of heaven. Old obsessions die hard, but although He had dull students, Jesus was the Teacher and was possessed of infinite patience.

3. Jesus Walks on the Water

In the meantime the disciples were rowing their way back to Galilee. At this

As the project progressed, the problem of just reaching the places to excavate without doing irreparable damage became very serious. The solution was to build metal frames above the boat and suspend wooden platforms by ropes from the frames. The workers would lie on the platforms as they removed the mud. The mud that had hidden the boat

Anchor Weight from Galilee.

had also protected it. When the wooden structure began to be exposed, new difficulties presented themselves. The cell structure of the waterlogged wood had actually been replaced with water, and as the wood began to dry it would warp and crack and disintegrate. This was addressed by various methods of covering the wood, keeping it wet, and shading it from the sun.

Photographing the dark hull and distinguishing the important features was another challenge. The individual planks were outlined with white plastic string, with great care given to distinguishing each plank and not the cracks. That was done by identifying the mortise-and-tenon joints holding the boards together and marking the pegs. Nails were circled with white string to mark them. The timbers were identified with red plastic tags. Each part was numbered and identified as to location. Now the boat was excavated and photographed; and then the issue became, How do we move it to the place of preservation?

The conservator proposed to frame the inside and outside of the boat with fiberglass and polyester molded in the shape of the hull. First, the frames were fitted inside the boat and covered with plastic sheeting. Polyurethane foam was sprayed over the plastic that soon hardened in the shape of the craft. The outside was more difficult because tunnels had to be dug under the boat so the fiberglass frames could be put in place. Then the tunnels

point it is about six miles across the sea. Evidently the sea was running heavy because of a great wind, for by the fourth watch of the night, sometime between three and six A.M., they were only halfway across. Suddenly they saw what appeared to them to be a phantom walking on the water. It was Jesus coming to them. Failing to recognize Him in the darkness, the disciples cried out in fear. However, their hearts were gladdened to hear Him say, "It is I; be not afraid" or "stop being afraid" (John 6:20).

Peter went from fear to joy, as no doubt did all the others, but true to his nature Peter went further. He asked Jesus if he might come to Him on the water. Some may consider this a rash request, but Jesus did not. He told him to do so, and Peter did as Jesus bade him do. It was a miracle to be sure, even as it was for Jesus to walk on the waves,

First-century lamp and pot.

were filled with the polyurethane that held the boat up when the rest of the mud under the hull was removed. The remainder of the outside was fitted with the fiberglass frames molded to the shape of the boat. The spaces between were filled with the foam, and wooden beams were placed under the entire unit to give it additional support. The remaining uncovered areas were sprayed with the polyurethane foam. The finished project looked like "an overgrown, melted marshmallow"[2] or as the excavator later described it, "a weird and huge many-legged caterpillar wearing suspenders."[3]

The boat was stabilized in its cocoon of orange foam, but it was still sitting in the mud more than 1,600 feet from the building where it was to be preserved. Options

considered for moving the artifact to the museum were helicopter or truck and trailer. Both were discarded as too likely to cause damage. The final solution, and the most obvious, was to sail the old craft to its final resting place. The pit was flooded, the dike was breached, and the Galilee boat set sail for the first time in 2,000 years, buoyed by the foam and supported by its fiberglass frame. The whole assembly was lifted to shore by a crane. Within ten days the concrete and tile tank was finished, and the boat placed in it. The foam and fiberglass covering was removed, and the tank filled with water to cover the boat. The conservation then consisted of adding a synthetic wax, called polyethylene glycol, in slowly

Sea of Galilee at Nof Ginnosar. Area where the first-century boat was found.

but when one reckons it in the light of Jesus' word and power, there is no reason to question it. This was a picturesque moment as, with his eyes upon Jesus, Peter walked toward Him. But when he shifted his attention to the hurricane-like wind, he became afraid and began to sink. "Lord, save me," he cried, and Jesus did so, reaching forth His hand to him. Presently they were in the boat, and the wind ceased immediately. When a storm abated naturally, it did so gradually, leaving the sea rough for a time. This immediate ceasing was a miracle just as much as walking on the water. Evidently the disciples had not been properly impressed by the multiplying of the loaves and fishes, though it is strange that their hearts were so hardened. But they were deeply moved by the spectacular events on the sea, and it is this fact which suggests why Jesus did the latter.

The miracle of the loaves and fishes had served only to fan the disciples' enthusiasm for their mistaken idea concerning the kingdom, and Jesus had soon cooled their ardor in this regard. Perhaps resentment was in their hearts because they had been so rebuked, but the miracles on the sea reconfirmed their faith that Jesus was the Messiah, although He refused to fill their own expected role. Indeed, their confusion may explain why Jesus permitted Peter to come to Him on the water. It was to teach all of the disciples a lesson. As long as they kept their faith centered in Jesus they were safe. It was only when they became engulfed in the contrary winds of current Messianic expectations that they were in danger of losing their sense of equilibrium and direction. Apparently for the moment the Twelve learned the lesson, for in the boat they worshiped Jesus, saying, "Truly You are the Son of God" (Matt. 14:33).

It was a fitting end to a turbulent day. Jesus was in the midst of His small worshiping congregation, and their cathedral was a little boat whose vaulting ceiling was a star-studded night sky. Perhaps as they disembarked, the eastern

First-century boat found in mud at Nof Ginnosar. A different view at an advanced stage of preservation.

increasing concentrations to the water while gently increasing the temperature of the solution. The process was designed to let the chemical gradually penetrate the cell structure of the wood and replace the water. When finished, the boat could be studied and displayed in the dry.

The Galilee boat is 26.5 feet long, 7.5 feet wide, and 4.5 feet high. It apparently had a deck at both the front and rear. The mast was missing, but the place where it was attached was plainly visible. Not only

Sea of Galilee from Capernaum

could the boat be powered by wind, but it had places for four oars. The crew would be as many as five persons, one for each of the oars and one for the rudder.[4] The capacity of the boat was proposed on the basis of some passages in Josephus where he described himself, some friends, and some soldiers being on a boat. With the crew the total may have been 15 people.[5] Again, he told of ten men of Tiberias traveling in a fishing boat. With the crew the number of people in the boat would have been fifteen.[6]

Archaeological dating can be done by many means, and several were appropriate to the boat. Carbon 14 is a test that is applied to many organic materials. The wood in the boat tested 40 B.C. plus or minus eighty years. That is, the trees out of which the boat was built were cut between 120 B.C. and A.D. 40. The pottery found in the immediate proximity dated from about 50 B.C. to the Jewish-Roman War, ending in A.D. 70. This was affirmed by the lamp, which was placed between 50 B.C. and A.D. 50. The coins found were not of much value for dating because they had no definable archaeological context. A final aid to dating was the construction techniques. The expert on ancient ship construction suggested that the style and techniques were like those on the Mediterranean between the first

sky was growing light, heralding the dawn of a new day.

4. *The Collapse of the Galilean Campaign*

While Jesus and the Twelve were crossing the lake, the crowd was doing the same; and upon their arrival in Capernaum, they found Jesus in the synagogue. Seeking to make conversation, they asked Him when He had returned to Capernaum; but knowing their hearts, Jesus replied, "You are looking for me, not because you saw the signs, but because you ate the loaves and were filled" (John 6:26). It was breakfast time, and they were hungry again. The words "were filled" render a word which may be translated "were gorged." One classical Greek writer used it of a cow eating its food and gorging its stomach but never saying "thanks" or asking whence came the food or for what purpose it was given. These people had missed the point of the miracle altogether. They sought Jesus now only because they were hungry again. In the wilderness temptation Jesus had refused to be a bread messiah, the very kind of messiah which they now wanted Him to be. In effect, the people were saying that if Jesus would not claim their loyalty by leading them in a revolution, at least He might do so by feeding them. But Jesus would do neither.

Instead, in the discourse which followed He sought to lead them to a spiritual understanding of His person and purpose (John 6:27–65). Rather than to labor for physical bread which soon perishes, He challenged them to seek after spiritual bread which results in eternal life. In turn they asked what they should do to work the works of God. They were still thinking on a physical level. Jesus said that they should believe on Him whom God had sent. That He spoke of Himself they realized. Ignoring the sign of the day before, they asked Him for a sign in order that they might believe on Him. Then speaking specifically they cited Moses' sign of giving their forefathers manna in the wilderness. The day before, on the basis of the miracles of the loaves and fishes, they had identified Jesus as the Prophet who would be like Moses, but Moses had given new manna each day. Was this not their subtle way of asking Jesus for more loaves and fishes for this new day? If Jesus wanted them to believe on Him, let Him feed them again.

But Jesus sidestepped their ruse by reminding them that it was God, not Moses, who gave the manna. Furthermore, their forefathers ate it and died, but the bread of God which He offered them would give to them eternal life. Like the woman of Samaria was with water, they were ready for that kind of bread. Or were they? Nevertheless, still thinking of their stomachs, they said, "Sir, give us this bread always!" (John 6:34).

So they wanted bread! Very well, Jesus would offer it to them. But it was hardly the bread which they expected, for He said, "I am the bread of life . . . No one who comes to Me will ever be hungry, and no one who believes in Me will ever be thirsty again" (John 6:35). He is both meat and drink, the two primary necessities of life. This multitude stood in the presence of Life but would not accept Him. Jesus "came down from heaven," in keeping with the Father's will, to give them life; but they would not receive it.

The mention of heaven gave the dialogue a different turn. The previous day the crowd was ready to make Jesus a political Messiah because He was one of their brethren, out of their very midst. But now "the Jews," probably Jewish rulers, used that fact to dispute His claim. Said they, "Isn't this Jesus the son of Joseph, whose father and mother we know? How can He now say 'I have come down from heaven'?" (John 6:42). But Jesus pressed His point. "I am the living bread that came down from heaven. If anyone eats of this bread he will live forever. The bread that I will give for the life of the world is My flesh" (John 6:51). "How," asked the Jewish rulers, "can this man give us His flesh to eat?" (John 6:52). Failing to rise above the physical level, they saw Jesus' teaching as cannibalism.

The murmuring of the Jewish rulers infected the crowd, so finally they said, "This teaching is hard. Who can accept it?" (John 6:60). Despite the fact that Jesus insisted that He spoke not in physical terms but in words of "spirit" and "life," the multitudes forsook Him. Never thereafter would Jesus' popularity with the people of Galilee be the same. When He made clear that He would not accede to their own concept of the messiah, they left Him. They were more concerned about their stomachs than about their souls.

Evidently the departure of the crowd made the Twelve themselves uneasy. Were they about to follow the people in forsaking Jesus? So Jesus asked, "Will you also go away?" And Simon Peter, as usual speaking for the group, replied, "Lord, to whom should we go? You have the words of eternal life. And we have come to believe and know that You are the Holy One of God!" (John 6:68–69). They had been disappointed the day before. They did not fully understand Jesus' words now, but they were convinced that He was the true Messiah of God. They did not yet fully comprehend the Person and purpose of Jesus, but they were learning, and anchored as they were by their faith in Christ, they would go on growing in the grace and in the knowledge of the Lord.

The events of these past twenty-four hours had clearly demonstrated Jesus' wisdom. The kingdom of God would not come through mass movements but through decisions of faith and commitment within the individual heart. So Jesus continued to focus His efforts on this little group. Yet even among them was one who did not share their faith and commitment, for Judas was a devil. Therefore, it is evident that one year before the dastardly deed Jesus knew His

Mikvah (ritual bath) at Qumran. Pools such as this were used by the Jews for ritual washings.

betrayer by name. Only twelve left out of this multitude, and one of them a devil. Still Jesus ever pressed His way forward.

5. An Unhappy Interlude

Even though the Galilean campaign had collapsed, Jesus remained there for a short period before departing on the second withdrawal. During this interval Pharisees and scribes from Jerusalem, the Jewish rulers, accosted Him with a question: "Why do Your disciples break the tradition of the elders? For they don't wash their hands when they eat!" (Matt. 15:2). Apparently they had noted that the Twelve ignored this custom, which to Jewish rulers was a sin equal to sexual immorality. The elders taught that before eating a Jew should rinse his hands and arms up to his elbows.

Now this had nothing whatever to do with physical hygiene. It was a matter of ceremonial purity. In a sense it was due to superstition, for it was believed that demons rested on one's hands. Therefore, to eat with unrinsed hands was to permit them to enter into the body. But the primary purpose in this tradition was related to racial and social prejudice. A Jew in the marketplace might inadvertently touch the garments of a Gentile or publican. He was then con-

---

century B.C. and the second century A.D. But there were no other examples from the Sea of Galilee with which to compare it. Taking all of the various evidences into consideration, the excavator proposed a date for the boat between 100 B.C. and A.D. 67.[7]

One other bit of circumstantial evidence has intrigued this writer. A mosaic from the first century was discovered in a house in Migdal only about 1.5 miles from the location of the Galilee boat. The mosaic depicts a boat that appears to be of the same class and type with a sail, four oars, and a rudder. Since it is from the same area, the same time period, and shows the same kind of vessel, this depiction may well reflect the appearance of the ancient boat during its productive days.

Does this recent discovery add anything to our understanding of the Gospels? Yes! It puts us in touch with a real ship of the period of Jesus and the apostles. The size was adequate for the Lord and twelve apostles to safely cross the sea regularly, as described in Matthew 14. The suggested crew of five may be indicated by the call of James and John, who had been fishing with Zebedee and hired servants (Mark 1:16–20). The ancient mosaic of Migdal pic-

tures such a craft at sea fulfilling its intended purpose. Yes, the Galilee boat does by its physical presence and our contemplation on it take us back to that ancient sea shore and the ministry of Jesus of Nazareth, who there fed the hungry, taught the crowds, and healed the sick.

[1]Shelley Wachsmann, *The Sea of Galilee Boat: An Extraordinary 2000 Year Old Discovery* (New York: Plenum Press, 1995), 4.
[2]Shelley Wachsmann, "The Galilee Boat—2,000-Year-Old Hull Recovered Intact," *Biblical Archaeology Review* 14 (September/October 1988): 29.
[3]Wachsmann, *The Sea of Galilee Boat*, 216.
[4]Josephus, *The Wars of the Jews*, 2.21.8 described four sailors, and *The Life of Flavius Josephus*, 32, added a helmsman to the crew.
[5]Josephus, *The Life of Flavius Josephus*, 32.
[6]Josephus, *The Wars of the Jews*, 2.21.9.
[7]Wachsmann, *The Sea of Galilee Boat*, 349.

George W. Knight is Cook-Derrick Professor of New Testament and Greek, Hardin-Simmons University, Abilene, Texas.

sidered as defiled; hence the rinsing before eating. Even one's eating utensils might have been touched last by the hands or lips of such. So they also must be rinsed.

It is difficult even among present-day racial and social tensions to understand the vicious nature of the ancient Jews in this regard. Even when a faithful Jew crossed from Gentile territory into a Jewish land, in contempt he stamped the dust of the former from his feet. So this pride of race held the Jews aloof from the rest of men as being cursed of God. Naturally this prevented them from reaching non-Jews for God, which was their divinely given mission. Why should they bother with the rest of the world? For according to them salvation was for the Jews only.

Of course Jesus held no such attitude. He never disobeyed a law of God nor taught that men should do so, but the empty traditions of the elders were another matter. The Jewish leaders, on the other hand, might have ignored disregard for their traditions on the part of the despised "people of the land" or common herd, but to them it was unthinkable that the disciples of a reputed rabbi should do so. Thus their critical question.

In this light one may understand Jesus' reply. He accused the Pharisees of breaking God's commandments in order to keep their traditions, and then He cited one example. God through Moses had commanded men to honor their parents and that anyone who spoke evil of them should be put to death (Ex. 20:12; 21:17). Yet in the face of this the Jews had a tradition known as Corban. This word was applied to that which had been consecrated to God or to the temple. The treasury of the temple was called by this name (Matt. 27:6). On the surface this might appear to be a noble practice, but in actuality it was a vicious thing. By it the son of aged parents might escape responsibility for their care simply by saying that all of his possessions were Corban. This meant that they were dedicated to God and the temple. The man might maintain control over them until his death. Or he might even break the pact of dedication. But as long as it was in force, he was free from the responsibility of caring for his parents. Thus Jesus accused the Pharisees and scribes of setting aside the authority of God's commandments and instead pressing the authority of their own traditions.

Then He turned to the multitude that had been listening. This was probably made up of many who so recently had chosen to follow the Jewish leaders rather than Him. He challenged them to hear and to understand what He was about to say: "It's not what goes into the mouth that defiles a man, but what comes out of the mouth, this defiles a man" (Matt. 15:11). The word rendered "defiles" means to make common or to desecrate. In the ceremonial sense it meant to defile or to pollute. The Pharisees were concerned about ceremonial defilement. Jesus was concerned about the dignity and worth of the whole man.

This pronouncement of Jesus cut across the entire system of the clean and unclean which was so great a part of the Jewish teachings and practices. This involved not only their religious forms but also their attitude toward other people. Jesus had already asserted His authority with respect to the Sabbath, the temple, and the Law. Now to this list He added the matter of the teachings of God versus the traditions of men. So the breach between Him and the Jewish leaders was evidenced even more.

With Jesus' words still ringing in the ears of the people, He went from them to enter a house. The Twelve came to Him to remind Him that He had offended the Pharisees. Though Jesus had broken with the Jewish teachers, the disciples were not fully severed from them in their minds. Jesus reminded them that this system of teaching was not of God, and, therefore, should be refuted. They were blind guides leading blind people. The end was the destruction of such leaders and those who insisted upon following them.

The tremendous import of Jesus' words about that which defiles a man is seen in Peter's request for more light on the subject. It was to him a revolutionary thought. So Jesus used a well-known physiological fact to show that what a man eats later passes from the body. Therefore, it is not what goes into a man's stomach that desecrates him. It is that which comes from his heart which does so. Those who were so careful to escape ceremonial pollution were unknowingly being polluted in their hearts and souls. This was a much needed lesson then even as it is now.

THE WITHDRAWAL INTO SYROPHOENICIA

This encounter with the Pharisees prompted Jesus to depart from Galilee on a second withdrawal, and it may even have helped in determining the place of retirement. Of course, at that time of year the cool breezes of the seacoast would prove inviting, but a deeper meaning than that is involved in the Gospel accounts.

Jesus and the Twelve journeyed to the region of Tyre and Sidon, an area on the Mediterranean coast south of modern Beirut, Lebanon. It was Syrophoenician territory and so outside the borders of Israel. Therefore, in going to this Gentile territory, it seems that Jesus did so as a direct challenge to the vicious attitude of the Pharisees. This becomes even more apparent as the story develops.

Shortly after arriving in this area, Jesus was confronted by a woman whose daughter was possessed of an unclean spirit. Over and over she cried out to Him for help. Now this woman was not only a Gentile, or non-Jewish, but she was also a Canaanite, a descendant of the despised pagans who had inhabited the land before the Israelite invasion. There could hardly have been one who would be more despised by the Jews and by them to be considered beyond the scope of God's love and mercy. In all likelihood Jesus' foreknowledge that He would meet her had led Him to this region.

This woman had heard of the wonderful powers of Jesus. People from this area had been among the crowds which followed him in Galilee, and possibly because of their reports, she believed Jesus to be the Jewish Messiah. At any rate she kept on calling to Jesus, "Have mercy on me, Lord, Son of David! My daughter is cruelly tormented by a demon" (Matt. 15:22). But Jesus ignored her cries. The disciples were embarrassed by her and asked Jesus to send her away, but He answered them, "I was sent only to the lost sheep of the house of Israel" (Matt. 15:24).

Why did Jesus ignore the woman? And why did He answer the disciples thusly? Some say that He was testing the woman's faith. Others even accuse Jesus of sharing Jewish prejudice, which was later broken down by the woman's persistence, and this in spite of His words to the Pharisees about their traditions. Still others insist that Jesus was not yet ready to enlarge His ministry to include non-Jews, even though He had already done so on occasion.

When all elements of this incident are considered, it seems most likely that Jesus acted as He did in order to teach the Twelve a lesson. What He had taught them by word He now demonstrated by His actions. In effect this woman was symbolic of the entire Gentile world. It is quite evident that the Twelve still shared the prejudices of the Jews toward non-Jews. It is so easy to be enslaved by a vicious system toward others en masse, but it is quite another thing to see that system in operation against one individual. Therefore, in this event Jesus held up a mirror before His disciples in order that they might clearly see themselves and the entire Jewish attitude toward other people. In effect, He acted that part as an object lesson to them.

Finally, when Jesus continued to ignore the woman, she came and knelt before Him. In reply to her agonizing plea, "Lord, help me!" Jesus said,

Amrit—Ancient Marathos Phoenician settlement which was conquered by Alexander the Great in 333 B.C. This is the region of Syrophoenicia, one of the places Jesus withdrew with His disciples.

The Mediterranean Sea on the coast of Israel near the border with Lebanon. Just south of Tyre.

Dog statue found at Pella.

"It isn't right to take the children's bread and throw it to their dogs" (Matt. 15:26). The Jews regarded themselves as the children of God. To them the Gentiles were dogs or wild beasts. Even though Jesus softened this attitude by using the diminutive "little dogs" or household pets, the disciples would catch the point. And the woman seized upon Jesus' choice of words by replying, "Yes, Lord . . . yet even the dogs eat the crumbs that fall from their masters' table!" (Matt. 15:27). Let the Jews have the full meal. All that she was asking was for a few morsels which fell from the table. True, she was not a Jew, but she was a personality created by God, and as such she was capable of responding to God's love and grace.

The lesson was over. Therefore Jesus said, "Woman, your faith is great. Let it be done for you as you want" (Matt. 15:28). And her daughter was healed from that hour. Not because she was a Jew, which she was not. Nor because she was a non-Jewish Canaanite. But because she had faith. If so unlikely a prospect, according to Jewish standards, could believe and share in the grace of God, there was no reason to withhold the gospel of the kingdom from anyone. This was Jesus' way of saying to the Twelve what the Lord later said to Peter alone: "What God hath cleansed, that call not thou common [unclean]" (Acts 10:15). The Twelve had seen an acted parable, but had they yet learned its meaning? Truly, racial prejudice does not die an easy death.

THE WITHDRAWAL INTO THE DECAPOLIS

From Syrophoenicia Jesus and His little band traveled north and east until they came to the region of the Decapolis on the eastern shores of the Sea of Galilee, (notice how He avoided the Jewish area and the territory of Herod

Antipas), but even here He could not avoid the crowds. They brought their sick to be healed by Jesus, and when He healed them, "they gave glory to the God of Israel" (Matt. 15:31).

This is a significant statement. The title "God of Israel" suggests that these people were not Jews but Gentiles. Decapolis was a Gentile or Greek area. So the crowds which now followed Jesus were most likely Gentile in nature.

At this juncture Jesus performed His second miracle of feeding the multitude, this time about four thousand men, besides women and children. The general pattern of the two feedings was similar, but the details were different. Some interpreters see the account of this latter feeding as a repetition of the former, but the fact that Jesus later referred to both as separate events clearly identifies them (Mark 8:19–20).

Following the feeding of the four thousand, Jesus made a brief visit to Galilee in the area of Magadan (Dalmanutha). No sooner did He arrive back in Jewish territory than He was attacked by the Jewish leaders. But this time something new was added, for along with the Pharisees Jesus was also attacked by the

Caesarea Philippi

John C. H. Laughlin

The site of ancient Caesarea Philippi is located about twenty-four miles north of the Sea of Galilee. Lying at the southwestern base of the Mount Hermon range, it is very close to the modern borders of Lebanon and Syria. From this site comes one of the three sources of the River Jordan. The original name of the place was "Panion," which refers to the cave sanctuary located here that was dedicated to the Greek god Pan. This sanctuary is believed to have been established at least as early as the beginning of the second century B.C. Nearly two thousand years ago, Josephus, the first-century Jewish historian, gave a graphic description of this cave.

Cave and temple at Banias.

In the mountains here there is a beautiful cave, and below it the earth slopes steeply to a precipitous and inaccessible depth, which is filled with still water, while above it there is a very high mountain. Below the cave rise the sources of the river Jordan.[1]

Later sources refer to the site as "Paneas," "Panias," and "Panium." "Banias," the site's modern name, is the Arabic version of the Greek name.

Agrippa II, around the middle of the first century A.D., named the city "Neronias," in honor of the Roman

When Jesus came to the region of Caesarea Philippi, He asked His disciples, "Who do people say that the Son of Man is?" And they said, "Some say John the Baptist; others, Elijah; still others, Jeremiah or one of the prophets." "But you," He asked them, "who do you say that I am?" Simon Peter answered, "You are the Messiah, the Son of the living God!" And Jesus responded, "Blessed are you, Simon son of Jonah, because flesh and blood did not reveal this to you, but My Father in heaven. And I also say to you that you are Peter, and on this rock I will build My church, and the forces of Hades will not overpower it. I will give you the keys of the kingdom of heaven, and whatever you bind on earth will have been bound in heaven, and whatever you loose on earth will have been loosed in heaven." And He gave the disciples orders to tell no one that He was the Messiah. From then on Jesus began to point out to His disciples that He must go to Jerusalem and suffer many things from the elders, chief priests, and scribes, be killed, and be raised the third day. Then Peter took Him aside and began to rebuke Him, "Oh no, Lord! This will never happen to You!" But He turned and told Peter, "Get behind Me, Satan! You are an offense to Me, because you're not thinking about God's concerns, but man's."

MATTHEW 16:13-23 (HCSB)

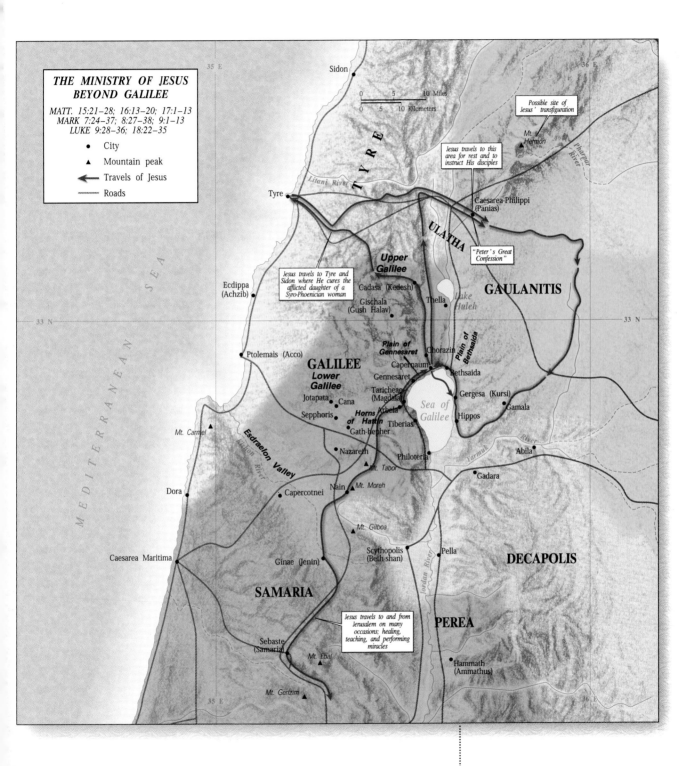

THE MINISTRY OF JESUS
BEYOND GALILEE

MATT. 15:21–28; 16:13–20; 17:1–13
MARK 7:24–37; 8:27–38; 9:1–13
LUKE 9:28–36; 18:22–35

- • City
- ▲ Mountain peak
- ← Travels of Jesus
- —— Roads

Possible site of Jesus' transfiguration

Jesus travels to this area for rest and to instruct His disciples

"Peter's Great Confession"

Jesus travels to Tyre and Sidon where He cures the afflicted daughter of a Syro-Phoenician woman

Jesus travels to and from Jerusalem on many occasions; healing, teaching, and performing miracles

Sidon
Tyre
Ecdippa (Achzib)
Ptolemais (Acco)
Caesarea-Philippi (Panias)
Mt. Hermon
ULATHA
GAULANITIS
Lake Huleh
Cadasa (Kedesh)
Gischala (Gush Halav)
Thella
Upper Galilee
Plain of Gennesaret
Chorazin
Plain of Bethsaida
Capernaum
Bethsaida
GALILEE
Lower Galilee
Gennesaret
Taricheae (Magdala)
Gergesa (Kursi)
Jotapata
Cana
Arbela
Gamala
Sepphoris
Horns of Hattin
Tiberias
Hippos
Sea of Galilee
Gath-hepher
Nazareth
Philoteria
Abila
Mt. Tabor
Mt. Carmel
Gadara
Dora
Nain
Mt. Moreh
Capercotnei
Mt. Gilboa
Caesarea Maritima
Scythopolis (Beth-shan)
Pella
DECAPOLIS
Ginae (Jenin)
SAMARIA
PEREA
Sebaste (Samaria)
Mt. Ebal
Hammath (Ammathus)
Mt. Gerizim

MEDITERRANEAN SEA
Litani River
Pharpar River
Jordan River
Yarmuk River
Kishon River
Esdraelon Valley

35 E
36 E
33 N

0   5   10 Miles
0   5   10 Kilometers

Excavations at Banias showing part of the government complex.

emperor Nero.[2] However, this name never seems to have caught on. The city built here in 3 B.C. by Herod Philip, the son of Herod the Great, was called "Caesarea Philippi."[3] It is this name by which the site is known in the New Testament (see Matt. 16:13; Mark 8:27). Also, according to Josephus, Herod the Great built a temple of white marble here in honor of Augustus sometime after 20 B.C.[4]

Prior to the establishment of the cult of Pan, it is not clear what activities, if any, took place on the site. Some scholars have suggested that cultic practices associated with the names "Baal-gad" (see Josh. 11:17; 12:7; 13:5) and "Baal-hermon" (see Judg. 3:3; 1 Chron. 5:23) may have occurred here.[5] However, the establishment of the cults devoted to Pan and other deities prevailed here during the Hellenistic and Roman periods. According to literary, inscriptional, and numismatic sources, the Pan cult was still thriving in the first century of our era when Banias became a large Roman city. This city existed in

Jesus' time and is now beginning to come to light, thanks to recent archaeological excavations.

Even though this site has long been known to biblical historians and geographers, systematic excavations did not begin until the mid 1980s. Two separate excavations were begun. One has centered on the Pan sanctuary both inside and outside the cave. This work has been

Underground access tunnel to the government complex at Banias.

Sadducees. Evidently word had reached Jerusalem that the Pharisees were not doing very well in opposing Him. So reinforcements were dispatched in the form of the rationalistic, realistic Sadducees. This suggests the desperation of Jesus' opposition, for nothing short of that would have produced this coalition of two groups which so bitterly opposed each other. Like the Pharisees and Herodians earlier, so now these widely diverse groups found a common cause in their enmity toward Jesus.

They came to Jesus challenging His messiahship by demanding that He show them

Overview of Banias center.

"a sign from heaven." Earlier the scribes and Pharisees had demanded a "sign" (Matt. 12:38). Now the sign must be from "heaven." Quite naturally this additional demand shows the hand of the Sadducees, for they did not believe in signs and especially "a sign from heaven." However the Pharisees had a hand in this also. "Signs" on earth were one thing. They believed in them, but "a sign from heaven," perhaps some cosmic disturbance, would be even greater. In neither case did this coalition believe that Jesus could produce such a "sign." Even if the Pharisees believed that He was capable of doing so, since He had refused to work signs on demand, they probably figured that He would not comply this time. In any case their demand would serve to discredit Jesus.

Again the Lord refused to be lured into their trap. Instead, by referring to well-known meteorological facts, He said that they were capable of predicting the weather by reading sings in the heavens but that they were incapable of discerning "the signs of the times." A spiritual revolution was transpiring all about them, but they did not see it.

So once again He gave them only the sign of Jonah, or the sign of His resurrection from the dead. That would be "a sign from heaven" par excellence, but when it came, they did not accept it. Such is ever the reaction of unreasoning prejudice. With these words Jesus left them and departed on His fourth withdrawal.

THE WITHDRAWAL INTO CAESAREA PHILIPPI

This time Jesus took a boat across the Sea of Galilee, landing at Bethsaida Julias. He was passing through the general area of the first retirement on His

under the direction of the district archaeologist of the Golan who works for the Israel Antiquities Authority. The other excavation is centered in the city itself and is being carried out by a consortium of American colleges and universities under the direction of Dr. Vassilios Tzaferis, also of the Israel Antiquities Authority.[6] I have had the good fortune of being associated with this latter excavation since 1989.

The ancient Roman city of Caesarea Philippi covered many acres; and while much has been discovered during the previous seasons, much still remains to be found. Our major problem here, as on

Scythopolis, a Decapolis city beside Beth Shean.

many antiquity sites, is that much of the ancient remains have been robbed out, reused and/or otherwise destroyed or lost. Thus caution is in order in trying to reconstruct the archaeological history of the site. Also modern roads have been built on the site, thus limiting in some cases what we can do. However, enough has been found to allow us to conclude that during the early Roman period (basically the first century A.D.) Banias was a large city containing many magnificently built monumental buildings.

While the Gospels do not claim that Jesus and his disciples actually entered the city of Caesarea Philippi, what way to the region of Caesarea Philippi. On the way across the sea, He warned the Twelve against the teachings of the Pharisees and Sadducees and the way of life represented by Herod Antipas. At last Jesus expected some privacy in which to teach the Twelve concerning the King and the kingdom. He would not be an earthly king like Herod, nor would His kingdom fit into the erroneous ideas of the Pharisees and Sadducees. So He prepared for His forthcoming teaching by seeking to negate those contrary systems of life and thought.

1. The Region of Caesarea Philippi

Several reasons probably led Jesus to select this area for His fourth retirement which probably involved several months of this period. It was now evidently summertime, and the area about the Sea of Galilee is unbearably hot at that time of year. So Jesus led the Twelve into the cool of the mountains. Furthermore this was Gentile territory far removed from the Galilean multitudes which had cast their lot with His enemies. It was outside the domain of Herod Antipas and in that of Herod Philip who had shown no apparent interest in Jesus. It was an area into which Jesus had not gone heretofore. This, plus the comparatively sparse population, promised relief from the crowds and an unbroken opportunity to teach the Twelve. Time was now of the essence.

2. The Testing of the Twelve

For almost three years Jesus had been gradually unveiling Himself as the Christ, the Son of God. Since the calling of the Twelve, He had concentrated more and more on teaching them this truth, and this amid the cross currents of the erroneous concepts of the Jews. How well had the disciples learned their lesson? Examination time had arrived.

Immediately preceding the examination, Jesus had withdrawn from the

would they have seen if they had done so? While we cannot answer this question in its totality, we now have enough archaeological data to allow some speculation.

They most likely would have come into the city by way of its main street, the "cardo," part of which was discovered in 1994. This street ran in a north-south direction and was lined with large columns, parts of which were found reused in later walls. Entering the city from the south, they would have passed through its center or "forum."

One building that would surely have caught their eye contained twelve large, connected, vaulted rooms that extended more than the length of a football field! These arched rooms were constructed entirely of "dry stone" (that is, without any kind of cement or binding material). Each room is approximately twenty-five feet high, thirty feet long, and twenty feet wide. On the back wall near the top of each room is a large window. Jesus and his disciples would have seen this building as it actually was and would no doubt have

Pan niches at Banias.

understood its function(s), which unfortunately we do not. They would not have seen what subsequently happened to it: some of the rooms on either end of this building collapsed in later years and were rebuilt, probably during the Crusader period in the twelfth century.

Also they might not have seen one of the most magnificent buildings yet dis-

Overview of Banias complex (east side).

Citadel or palace walls at Banias.

covered. In 1993, several yards west of the building with the vaulted rooms, the remains of another large building began to be exposed. The date of this structure has tentatively been placed in the middle of the second century, thus dating later than our imagined visitors. This building was constructed of large, dressed limestone blocks that fit together so well that they will not allow a thin modern knife blade to go between them. This was an extremely large building consisting of a network of underground passageways. Associated with this building were upper rooms with marble floors as well as public baths. The building is thought to have been a governmental palace complex.

On the other hand, Vespasian and Titus, both Roman generals, along with their troops might well have seen and used it. Vespasian was invited by Agrippa himself to visit the city.[7] Titus is said to have stayed there "a considerable time, exhibiting all kinds of spectacles. Here many of the prisoners perished, some being thrown to wild beasts, others

Twelve to pray. While this was a period of great stress for Him, to the disciples it was vacation time. The region about Caesarea Philippi contained many items of historical interest. It requires little imagination to visualize the Twelve in holiday mood looking at these things and seeking to identify them with certain historical persons. It was probably in such an atmosphere that Jesus came to them with the question, "Who do people say that the Son of Man is?" (Matt. 16:13). Possibly without turning from their present interest, they replied, "Some say John the Baptist; others, Elijah; still others, Jeremiah or one of the prophets" (Matt. 16:14). These were the current opinions among the multitudes, but note that they did not mention some of the less flattering opinions.

Then Jesus shocked them into alert attention with the question, "Who do you say that I am?" (Matt. 16:15). That was quite another matter. The answer was of utmost importance for both them and Jesus. Were they merely a part of the multitudes? Or had they been able to discern the self-revelation of Jesus? Perhaps the disciples for a moment looked at one another in stunned silence, and then their spokesman replied. Simon Peter said, "You are the Messiah, the Son of the living God!" (Matt. 16:16). So in the atmosphere of these dead gods, Simon rose to the occasion, and by their silent assent the others passed the examination with him.

No wonder, Jesus exclaimed with joy; "Blessed are you, Simon son of Jonah, because flesh and blood did not reveal this to you, but My Father in heaven" (Matt. 16:17). Here is that word "blessed" again. So with that faith in Jesus, Simon and the others had within them all that is necessary to live a full and abundant life, and they had not received this faith through the leaven of the Pharisees, Sadducees, or Herod. Neither had it come by man's reason. It was God's revelation which had broken through this miasma of opinions to enable them to see God's glory in the face of Jesus Christ. Furthermore, Simon had fulfilled Jesus' prophecy concerning Him. He had indeed become Cephas, a stone (John 1:42). Cephas is the Aramaic equivalent of the Greek word *petros*. So Simon was now Simon Peter.

With this Jesus made one of the greatest pronouncements of the ages. The Father had revealed one truth. Now Jesus ("and I say") revealed another: "And I also say to you, that you are Peter, and on this rock I will build My church, and the forces of Hades will not overpower it. I will give you the keys of the kingdom of heaven, and whatever you bind on earth will have been bound in heaven, and whatever you loose on earth will have been loosed in heaven" (Matt. 16:18–19).

These have become some of the most debated words as to meaning that Jesus ever uttered. Were they spoken to Peter alone or to the Twelve? What did He mean by "Peter" and "rock"? What is the nature of the "church"? And what did Jesus mean by the "keys of the kingdom . . . bind . . . and loose"? Quite obviously they cannot be bypassed without some discussion.

There are those, principally the Roman Catholics, who insist that Jesus spoke to Peter alone. This position is based upon His use of the singular pronouns *thou* and *thee*. However, it should be recalled that Peter, a person, replied to Jesus' question as the representative of the Twelve. Therefore, it may be inferred that, in turn, Jesus replied to the Twelve through Peter, a person. This position is supported by the fact that later Jesus spoke the words about binding and loosing to the entire group where He used the plural pronoun *ye* (Matt. 18:18). Indeed, in this latter passage the words were spoken with reference to the action of a local congregation. This within itself enlarges immeasurably the meaning of Jesus' words spoken to Peter.

Furthermore, those who insist that Jesus spoke to Peter alone equate *Peter* and *rock*. Thus they hold that the church was founded upon Peter as the first pope and that to him and his successors in that office are entrusted "the keys of the kingdom" or the power to forgive or not to forgive sins. Let it be said, however, that there is no evidence in the New Testament to support the supremacy of Peter. Nor does early Christian history lend aid to the idea that he was ever a pope, an office which developed much later. The fact that Peter's name always appears first in the list of the Twelve should not so be construed. At best he was first among equals, by virtue of his self-appointed position as the spokesman for the group. To be sure he played a prominent part, along with others, in first-century Christianity, but his contemporaries certainly did not accord to him any place of superiority (cf. Acts 11:1ff.; Gal. 2:11ff.). Peter himself regarded his position not as an elder above other elders but as one among them (1 Pet. 5:1).

An examination of Jesus' words substantiates these positions. Take, for instance, the words *Peter* and *rock*. The former is the masculine *petros*, a small stone. The latter is the feminine *petra*, a ledge rock or foundation rock. So a *petros* is a small stone broken off of a *petra* and partaking of its nature. Perhaps when Jesus uttered these words, He was looking at the large ledge rock which was the foundation upon which the city of Caesarea Philippi was built. At least that thought could well have been in the picture. Some insist that Jesus spoke in Aramaic which made no such distinction in the word *rock*. Even if this be true, it must be admitted that when he wrote in Greek Matthew had made the distinction which evidently portrays Jesus' meaning.

Even in the word *petros* Peter did not regard himself as a rock different from other Christians or the foundation itself. For in 1 Peter 2:5–6 he pictures Jesus Christ as the foundation and believers in Him as living stones (*lithoi*) used in the building of "a spiritual house," the Church.

Now if the "rock" does not refer to Peter, to whom or what does it refer! It is held by some as referring to the faith of the apostles that Jesus is the Christ, the Son of the living God, but this would mean that the Church is built upon the faith of persons. This would be in conflict with the words in 1 Peter 2:5–6 where Christ is the foundation and believers are living stones out of which the "spiritual house" house is built. It is more in keeping with other scriptural teachings to say that Jesus as "the Christ, the Son of the living God" is the *petra* or ledge rock upon which the Church is built. This would explain why Jesus

Coins of Herod Philip and Agrippa I, both minted at Banias.

compelled in opposing masses to engage one another in combat."[8] In all, Josephus claimed that more than twenty-five hundred Jews were killed at Banias. Even allowing for some exaggeration, these references to large numbers of people visiting Banias for extended periods of time and entertaining themselves with "all kinds of spectacles" imply facilities large enough to accommodate such activities. Did the sound of Roman feet echo off the walls of the underground chambers recently discovered? Did the Roman generals and their troops relax and joke in the bathhouses? Did they cheer and applaud in some Roman arena or theater yet undiscovered as many Jews met their grisly deaths? Perhaps in some future season we will be able to find more of the missing pieces.

Continuing north along the cardo, Jesus and his group would soon have arrived at part of the city devoted to public buildings of a different sort. The remains that have been found here include large column drums measuring over four feet in diameter, large heart-shaped column bases and other large bases, intricately decorated friezes and mosaic floors, elaborate water-pipe systems, as well as pieces of different colored frescos. All of these fragments point to a monumental Roman city. Some of these buildings would have functioned as temples; another one, perhaps a nymphaeum; and still others as public gathering places of different kinds. Due to subsequent building, both ancient and modern, the full extent of this part of the city may never be known. But its elaborateness is well attested archaeologically, indicating that Philip spared no expense in its spacious construction.

Now, if our first-century "tourists" looked straight north, they would have seen the large cave sanctuary of Pan. In front of it might have stood the marble temple built by Herod in honor of Augustus, and, no doubt, other structures would have been here as well. We can only wonder what Jesus and his disciples might have said about all of this.

By the end of the first century, however, the city that our early first-century visitors would have seen and known existed no more. Major changes took place that indi-

had waited until such a moment to make this pronouncement. Until He was accepted as such by His followers, there was no true basis upon which to found the Church. In a very real sense the Church existed the moment a group of believers received Jesus as Christ, the Son of the living God. But when such a group clearly avowed that faith, as here, Jesus formally pronounced that out of such believers He would build His Church with Himself as its foundation.

However, strange to say, theologians have dwelt so long and ardently upon the identity of the *petra* that the heart of Jesus' statement has been largely lost, for He said, "On this rock I will build My church." In the Greek text "My" is in the emphatic position. Why this emphasis? It is because of the nature of the Church.

The word for "church" was not a new addition to man's vocabulary. It was a much used word, *ekklesia*, meaning "the called out ones" or "assembly." In the political sense it was used of the assembly of the citizens of certain Greek cities which was granted the privilege of self-rule by the Roman Empire. It was a local democratic assembly acting within the framework of the laws of the empire. This usage is found in the New Testament (Acts 19:39). Furthermore, in the Greek translation of the Old Testament, it is used to refer to the nation of Israel assembled before God (Deut. 31:30), and it is so used in the New Testament (Acts 7:38, Heb. 2:12). In this sense the word *ekklesia* speaks of a theocratic assembly or one ruled directly by God. Both of these uses of the word were familiar to the Twelve.

So, in effect, Jesus said, "The Greeks have their assembly and the Jews have their assembly. Now I will build my assembly." In the New Testament, in the Christian sense, "church" is used largely to speak of a local church operating through democratic processes under the lordship of Jesus Christ. But it is also used in the general theocratic sense to refer to all of the redeemed people of God through the ages assembled before Him and under His rule. Comparing Matthew 18:17 with Matthew 16:18, it is evident that Jesus used the word *church* in both senses. So when He spoke of the Church, He referred to that "spiritual house" built out of "lively stones" with Him as the foundation. Quite obviously only those who believe in Him as "the Christ, the Son of the living God" can in truth be a part of it in either the local or general sense.

Jesus also spoke of the enduring nature of His Church. "The forces of Hades will not overpower it" (Matt. 16:18). The best manuscripts read "the gates of Hades." Hades was the abode of the dead. The word *prevail* means "to have strength against." Gates are to keep one either out or in. Those inside the abode of the dead are trying to get out, and Jesus promised that "the gates of Hades" shall not have strength against His Church (redeemed ones) to keep it in the abode of the dead. It is true that in Christ the Church shall triumph over the powers of evil, but here the Lord's promise is with respect to the resurrection out of the abode of the dead.

Now what did Jesus mean by "the keys of the kingdom of heaven"? The answer is found in a literal translation of the words which follow: "And whatsoever thou shalt bind on earth *shall have been bound* in heaven; and whatsoever thou shalt loose on earth *shall have been loosed* in heaven" (author's italics) (Matt. 16:19, KJV). Thus it seems that heaven has decreed that when certain things are done on earth they shall have been done in heaven. Now this obviously cannot refer to the power of forgiving or not forgiving sins being conferred upon any person or group of persons, for the Bible clearly teaches that only God can do this. Even He forgives sin on the basis of the gospel of grace through the redemptive work of Christ. In this light, therefore, may it not be said that the gospel is "the keys of the kingdom"? Keys are for either locking or unlocking doors.

Therefore, evidently Jesus was saying that He was entrusting to His Church the gospel of Christ. If the Church binds the gospel on earth by not proclaiming it, heaven has already decreed that it is bound in heaven. On the other hand, if the Church looses the gospel on earth, heaven has already decreed that it is loosed in heaven. Or to put it another way, heaven has already decreed that men can be saved only by believing the gospel. If it is bound, there is no other way by which men can be saved; but if it is loosed, men will believe it, and those who do will be saved. Thus Jesus bestowed upon His Church not only a great privilege but a greater responsibility.

Nevertheless, in spite of the foregoing events, Jesus enjoined the Twelve not to tell any man that He was the Christ. Though they believed Him to be "the Christ, the Son of the living God," they did not yet comprehend the full meaning of these words. They must first learn the true nature of the Christ and of His kingdom before they were ready to use "the keys of the kingdom."

3. The Crucifixion and Resurrection Foretold

In the above light one can understand why Jesus chose this particular time to begin plainly to teach the Twelve about His death and Resurrection. For it was through this redemptive work that God would be able to forgive sins or to deal with man on the basis of grace rather than on the basis of law.

This was no new note in Jesus' teaching, for He had alluded to it in a veiled fashion many times. Now He began to speak of it plainly. Only six months remained before His death. Therefore, "From then on Jesus began to point out to His disciples that He must go unto Jerusalem and suffer many things from the elders, chief priests, and scribes, be killed, and be raised the third day" (Matt. 16:21). The fact that He "began" implies that He continued to do so.

That this instruction was needed is seen in the reaction of Simon Peter. He "began" to rebuke Jesus for so speaking, insisting that such should never happen to Him. Truly they were not ready to tell any man that He was the Christ. A conquering and reigning Christ, yes! But one who would die, never! They were still wedded to the messianic ideals of their age. Evidently Peter's mind went blank with the words "be killed." He seems never even to have heard Jesus say, "And be raised again the third day."

In response Jesus turned suddenly upon Peter, saying, "Get behind Me, Satan!" (Matt. 16:23). He was a stumbling block across Jesus' path to the cross.

cate the buildings of the earlier city were already in disuse. One such bit of evidence is a water channel that cut through the yellow floor that belonged to the building that may have functioned as a nymphaeum. All indications point to a decline in both the quality and quantity of the city.

Like many ancient sites in this part of the world, Banias witnessed many centuries of struggle for existence. The names of many gods and goddesses were no doubt invoked here. Perhaps, then, it is most fitting that tradition has located in this vicinity the great confession of Peter: "You are the Messiah!" (Mark 8:29).

[1] Josephus, *Antiquities*, 15.10.3.
[2] Ibid., 20.9.4.
[3] Ibid., 18.2.1.
[4] Josephus, *Jewish Wars*, 1.21.3.
[5] John Kutsko, "Caesarea Philippi" in *The Anchor Bible Dictionary*, vol. 1 (New York: Doubleday, 1992), 803.
[6] Vassilios Tzaferis, "Cults and Deities Worshipped at Caesarea Philippi–Banias" in *Priests, Prophets, and Scribes: Essays on the Formation and Heritage of Second Temple Judaism in Honour of Joseph Blenkinsopp*, JSOT Supplement Series 149, ed. Eugene Ulrich, et al. (Sheffield: Sheffield Press, 1992), 190–201. For a helpful background study on the cult of Pan, see Philippe Borgeard, *The Cult of Pan in Ancient Greece*, trans. Kathleen Atlass and James Redfield (Chicago: University of Chicago Press, 1988).
[7] Josephus, *Jewish Wars*, 3.9.7.
[8] Ibid., 7.2.1.

John C. H. Laughlin is chair and professor, Department of Religion, Averett College, Danville, Virginia.

A silver Tyrian half shekel dating from the first century A.D. This was the official coin for the Temple Tax.

He who had so recently spoken a revelation from God was now the very voice of Satan. He recoiled at the thought of Jesus' dying, but Jesus told him that anyone who proposed to follow Him must be prepared to die also. Any man who sought to save his life by taking the easy way would lose it. Only those who were willing to lose their lives for Jesus' sake would find the true meaning of life.

The disciples were not yet free from the Jewish concept of the Messiah and His kingdom, but that system would soon pass away. Jesus said, "There be some standing here, which shall not taste of death, till they see the Son of man coming in his kingdom" (Matt. 16:28). Here He looked even beyond His Resurrection, for all of the Eleven lived beyond that point. Obviously Jesus was not speaking of the end of the age, for none of those present lived until then. In Jewish apocalyptic thought any great intervention of God in history was regarded as a "coming." The only such event which some, not all, of the Twelve lived to see was the destruction of Jerusalem in A.D. 70, so evidently it was to this that Jesus referred. It marked the fall of the Jewish nation and of the Jewish system of religion, which was so powerful in Jesus' lifetime. Thereafter Christianity was completely divorced from Judaism, and by the world was regarded as a religion in its own right. It was in this sense that they saw "the Son of man coming in his kingdom."

So the old system is passing away, and the full revelation of God in Christ is rapidly coming to its full fruition. These things Jesus declared in the vicinity of Caesarea Philippi.

4. The Transfiguration of Jesus

One week later Jesus took Peter, James, and John and went up into the slopes of Mount Hermon. It had probably been a week of strained relations between Him and the Twelve. While they regarded Him as the Christ, they still did not understand His nature as such. It is possible that during this week the conversation with Peter about the cross had been repeated many times, for the fact that Jesus "began" to teach and Peter "began" to rebuke Jesus suggests repeated action in this regard.

At any rate in the mountain Jesus "was praying" (Luke 9:29). For what He was praying is not stated. Perhaps He was praying that somehow God would give to the three disciples such a demonstration as to His person that it would clear their minds of any mistaken ideas about Him. If so, His prayer was soon answered, for suddenly He "was transformed in front of them" (Matt. 17:2). In that moment His garments became glistening white, and His face shone as the sun.

Why was He transformed? Some hold that it was to encourage Jesus to go on to the cross in spite of men's thoughts to the contrary. However, there is no evidence that He had ever entertained any idea of avoiding the cross. Therefore, was the Transfiguration for Jesus' benefit or for that of His disciples? The answer may be found in the words "*in front of them*". It is possible that in His night vigils as He prayed alone, in perfect communion with the Father, this had happened before with no human being to see. But now He "was transformed *in front of them*" (author's italics).

And they saw Him in His glory. This was no light shining upon Jesus from without. It was His deity shining forth from within. Here Jesus is seen in His perfect humanity-deity. It was as if a wick which had been turned down low were suddenly turned up to full strength. The deity which had been present in Jesus all the while was suddenly turned up to white heat. Had there been one flaw in His character, this outrushing of deity would have killed Him, even as sudden heat shatters a lamp chimney which possesses a flaw in the glass.

In this moment Moses and Elijah appeared talking with Jesus. Why these two Old Testament "worthies"? Because in a very real sense they were representative of the Old Testament revelation. "Moses and the prophets" was a common Jewish designation for their Scriptures: Moses symbolized law and Elijah symbolized prophecy. And of what did they speak? The Greek text says that they "spoke of his exodus which he was about to accomplish in Jerusalem" (Luke 9:31). His "exodus" involved both His death and Resurrection, the very things of which He had spoken to Peter.

Even though the three disciples were drowsy at the outset, this supernatural phenomenon must have shocked them into a full awareness, and they most likely listened to this conversation. They heard these representatives of the Old Testament talking with Jesus about the thing which they had been unable to comprehend. In effect they had a preview in real life of Jesus' words spoken to His disciples after the event. "These are My words that I spoke to you while I

Sunset over the Sea of Galilee.

was still with you, that everything written about Me in the law of Moses, the Prophets, and the Psalms must be fulfilled. . . . This is what is written: the Messiah would suffer and rise from the dead the third day" (Luke 24:44,46).

However, Peter was so enraptured by the scene that he missed the point of it. For he said, "Lord, it's good for us to be here! If You wish, I will make three tabernacles here: one for You, one for Moses, and one for Elijah" (Matt. 17:4). The Feast of Tabernacles or Booths was approaching, and Peter may have been suggesting that they remain there to celebrate it. During this feast it was customary for faithful Jews to dwell under booths or small brush arbors. This was to commemorate the dwelling in booths of their fathers in their wilderness wanderings.

Even as Peter spoke, a luminous cloud overshadowed them. It was the Shekinah glory of God's presence, for out of the cloud came a voice saying, "This is My beloved Son. I take delight in Him. Listen to Him!" (Matt. 17:5). As at His baptism, so here, the Son is still well pleasing to the Father. It was His approval of all that Jesus was saying, and they were to hear and heed Him.

But was not this approval of the Son also a rebuke for the disciples? For they were still wedded to the current views of the Christ derived from an erroneous interpretation of their Scriptures. Furthermore, instead of holding Jesus distinct and apart from all others, Peter's suggestion about the tabernacles had proposed that Jesus be but one among three. His proposal placed Jesus alongside Moses and Elijah, not superior to them. He was but another teacher come from God, rather than the Teacher who fully revealed both the Old Testament Scriptures and the Father's will. So the Father said that no longer were they to "hear" Moses and Elijah. They were to "hear" Jesus alone as He unfolded the true meaning of the Law and the Prophets.

In stark terror at the voice out of the cloud, the disciples had fallen on their faces. Meanwhile the scene had disappeared, and when at Jesus' touch and reassurance they looked up, "they saw no one, except Jesus Himself" (Matt. 17:8). Moses and Elijah had vanished from view—only Jesus remained. This was the lesson of the Transfiguration. The Old Revelation merged into the New with its fulfillment in Jesus. There would still be times when the disciples would have difficulty in this matter, but they never forgot this experience (2 Pet. 1:17–18: 1 John 1:1–3). Not until after the Resurrection of Jesus from the dead would it become clear, and for that reason Jesus commanded that until then they were not to reveal this experience to any man.

5. The Return to Galilee

Shortly thereafter Jesus and the Twelve returned to Galilee. On the way back the Lord continued to teach about His rapidly approaching death and resurrection. Hopefully Peter, James, and John now understood better the meaning of His words. The other disciples who knew nothing of what happened on Mount Hermon certainly did not comprehend them. None of the group dared to question Jesus further about the matter. At least, this time there was no protest from Peter, but they all "were deeply distressed" (Matt. 17:23) at the prospect.

Back in Capernaum Peter was confronted by those who were supposed to collect the half-shekel temple tax. It was to be paid by every male adult Jew at the time of the Passover. Since Jesus and the Twelve had been out of Galilee since that time, they had not paid it. The collectors asked Peter whether his teacher paid this tax, and he answered in the affirmative. Even though Jesus was the Lord of the temple, He did not ignore this obligation. Therefore, He told Peter to catch a fish in whose mouth he would find a shekel with which to pay the tax for both of them. This was the nearest Jesus ever came to working a miracle for His own benefit, but even this was primarily for the sake of Peter and the collectors, lest He offend the latter.

Throughout the past six months Jesus had focused His teaching upon the King and the kingdom. Therefore during this brief sojourn in Capernaum the disciples reasoned among themselves about which one should be the greatest in the kingdom of heaven. Using a little child as an object lesson, Jesus taught them that humility, not selfish ambition, was the kingdom criterion of greatness. Possibly their reasoning had erupted into harsh words and hurt feelings, so Jesus taught the Twelve how Christians should settle their differences. The injured party should take the initiative in a personal confrontation with the offender. Rather than to air his grievance to others, he should tell it to the offender alone. Failing there, he was to take one or two other Christians with him. If this failed, the matter should be brought before the local congregation. If the guilty one refused to hear the church, he was to be regarded as a Gentile and a publican. Such an unrelenting spirit would indicate that he was not himself a Christian in the first place. This power of discipline Jesus deposited in the church, and when it acted in His spirit, He assured the body that He would be present with them in the action.

This teaching brought the inevitable question from Peter. "Lord, how many

Mount Hermon is part of the Hermon range which is approximately 28 miles in length and reaches a width of 15 miles. Hermon is 9,100 feet above sea level and is the highest mountain in Syria. Its peak is covered with snow two-thirds of the year. Water from its melting snow flows into the rivers of the Hauran and provides the principal source for the Jordan River. Some scholars believe the transfiguration of Jesus occurred on Hermon.

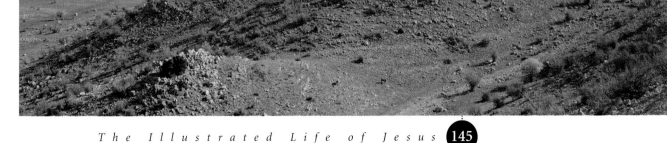

times could my brother sin against me and I forgive him? As many as seven times?" (Matt. 18:21). The rabbis taught that one should forgive three times, so Peter thought that he was being generous. But Jesus punctured his ego by saying, "Seventy times seven" (Matt. 18:22). It is hardly conceivable that one would offend another so many times, so, in effect, Jesus taught unlimited forgiveness. Forgiveness should not be measured by a mathematical formula but by one's spirit.

The Feast of Tabernacles was drawing near, so Jesus' brethren, His half brothers suggested that He should go to Jerusalem. Any man who wanted public recognition in Palestine should not confine His wondrous works to Galilee. In their unbelieving state they were either unaware of or else chose to ignore the fact that Jesus had already performed many miracles in Jerusalem with little appreciable results.

For the time Jesus chose to remain in Galilee. His brothers proposed to tell Him how to do His work, but His time to challenge Jerusalem fully had not come. However, after His brothers had departed from Jerusalem, probably in a caravan, Jesus also went to the feast in secret or traveled only with the Twelve.

So approximately six months before the Crucifixion, Jesus ended His ministry in Galilee and its environs. Henceforth, possibly with one brief interval, He concentrated on Judea, Perea, and Jerusalem. The opposition to Him which had been growing from the beginning finally would rise to a mighty crescendo of hate. The hour of the power of darkness was drawing ever nearer, and when it finally arrived, Jesus' hour would have come.

"If you continue in My word, you really are My disciples. You will know the truth, and the truth will set you free."

JOHN 8:31-32 (HSCB)

The Later Judean
Ministry

A Roman street in the city of Jerusalem.

This phase of Jesus' ministry covered about three months, from the Feast of Tabernacles until the Feast of Dedication. The time was the fall and early winter of A.D. 29. This period began in Jerusalem and continued in Judea. At one point Jesus visited Bethany, and then at the close of this ministry He returned to Jerusalem for the latter feast. It was a period marked by a growing and sharper conflict between Jesus and the Jewish rulers.

The Feast of Tabernacles was the most popular of all the Jewish feasts. As Pentecost, held fifty days after the Passover, was the feast of the firstfruits and marked the beginning of the wheat harvest, Tabernacles was the feast of the general harvest marking the end of the harvest season. It was held early in October and was a time of great rejoicing, something akin to an American Thanksgiving. This feast was also called the Feast of Booths. It commemorated the wanderings of Israel in the wilderness and God's care for His people. The feast lasted for eight days, the first and last days being days of holy convocations.

JESUS COMES TO THE FEAST

At the beginning of the feast, Jerusalem was buzzing with excitement. Jesus had not yet made an appearance, but it was generally expected that He would do so. It had been about eighteen months since He had visited Jerusalem. The

Jerusalem

Thomas D. Lea

Model of the city of David in Jerusalem.

Because of its importance to Christianity, Judaism, and Islam, Jerusalem is the world's most significant religious city. For Christians the area around Jerusalem is important because it was the location of Christ's Crucifixion and Resurrection. It also will be linked with His glorious return (Zech. 14:4–5).

Early texts mention the name of the city as *Urusalim*; the earliest Hebrew pronunciation was *Yerushalem*. The city had been known by additional names during the centuries such as Salem (Gen. 14:18), Jebus (1 Chron. 11:4), Zion (2 Sam. 5:7), and the City of David (2 Sam. 5:9). The word originally may have meant "foundation of (the god) Shalem." This name reflected the pagan background of the original inhabitants. The usage of the term in Genesis 14:18 is interpreted by the writer of the Hebrews as an indication that the name of the city also signifies "peace" or "foundation of peace" (Heb. 7:2).

Topographically, Jerusalem consists of a complex of several hills composed of hard limestone. A short distance from the western and southern limits of the city lies the L-shaped valley of Hinnom (Josh. 15:8). On the eastern side is the deep gorge of the Kidron Valley (2 Sam. 15:23). The brook Kidron flows through the gorge. In ancient times there was a third valley which ran from north to south and intersected the Kidron just north of its junction with the Hinnom. It was known as the Tyropoeon (also "cheesemakers") Valley, but many destructions of the city have filled in much of the former course of this valley.

East of the Tyropoeon Valley was a smaller hill with a crest of only twenty-two hundred feet. It has sharp, easily defensible cliffs and was the original Zion or "City of David." Just north of this and slightly higher is the hill of Moriah. Here Abraham went to offer Isaac (Gen. 22), and Solomon built the first temple (2 Chron. 3:1). West of the Tyropoeon were other hills which were not included in David's Jerusalem. As the city grew over the centuries, these western hills gradually were incorporated into the city walls. The gates to modern Jerusalem date from the mid-sixteenth century when the Turks controlled the city. The modern walled city excludes most of David's city and extends westward toward the Hinnom Valley.

Two springs have provided water for the city over the centuries. The Gihon Spring (1 Kings 1:33) begins in the Kidron Valley and has been the most consistent supplier of water. The En-rogel (Josh. 15:7) lies farther south, below the junction of the Kidron and the Hinnom.

Ancient remains add to our knowledge of the Holy City. Herod glorified the city with his many building projects, including the Tower of Phasael, built in 29 B.C. and named after the king's brother. Among the discoveries of Dame Kathleen Kenyon is a Jebusite wall. Across the Kidron is the Mount of Olives, the site of many important biblical events.

Serious archeological exploration of Jerusalem was late in developing because of the continuous inhabitation of the site. Notable excavations of the city still are underway and are yielding much additional information about the history of this important site.

The earliest inhabitants of the Jerusalem area lived on the small hill just south of the temple mount. The hill was protected by steep slopes on three sides made from the valleys Kidron and Tyropoeon. It was also near the Gihon Spring and close to the principal highways which ran from the Jordan rift to the coastal plains and from Shechem to Hebron.

During the conquest of Palestine, Joshua defeated a

Model of the Temple.

Jewish rulers' hostility in His previous visits had demonstrated their unwillingness to believe in Him. Indeed, on the last visit before this time they had sought to kill Him because He had healed a man on the Sabbath, so Jesus had deliberately avoided Jerusalem.

However, the Jewish leaders through their emissaries had kept in touch with Jesus' work in Galilee. Their hostility had continued to mount, and so some kind of crisis was anticipated at this feast. Therefore the Jewish rulers were searching diligently for Him throughout Jerusalem.

Model of the Antonia Fortress.

The multitudes themselves were not immune to the tense situation. Fearing their rulers, they did not dare to discuss Jesus openly, but they whispered among themselves about Him. Some championed His cause as a good man. They had either seen or heard of His good works, but others, having listened to their leaders, accused Him of leading the people astray.

About the middle of the week, Jesus suddenly appeared in the temple area teaching the people. In the listening crowd were some of the Jewish leaders, maybe some of their professional teachers. They wondered at Jesus' learning, and so they raised the question as to the source of His knowledge since He "hadn't been trained" (John 7:15). Here was a peasant carpenter who had attended none of their schools. Yet He posed as a rabbi. What is more, He was doing so great a job as to cause the professional rabbis to wonder. Since they did not teach Him, He must be self-educated. Nevertheless they accused Him of not being an accredited rabbi.

Jesus replied by disclaiming that He was self-taught. But He made a greater claim. He was taught of God. Furthermore, if any man would follow His teaching, He would discover that it had God for its source. A self-taught teacher presented his own ideas and aspired for recognition and glory, but Jesus sought only to glorify God. Then He pressed His argument by turning the tables on His accusers. They claimed to be authorities in the Law of Moses. Yet they did not keep that Law. As proof He cited their efforts to kill or murder Him on His previous visit to Jerusalem. In response the Jews denied any knowledge of such an attempt. "You have a demon! . . . Who wants to kill You?" (John 7:20), they asked. In essence they called Him insane.

However, Jesus' accusation had its effect upon the crowd. Even though their

coalition which included Adoni-zedek, king of Jerusalem (Josh. 10:1–10). There is no evidence, however, that Joshua ever occupied the city.

After Joshua's death the tribe of Judah captured Jerusalem (Judg. 1:8), but later the Jebusites reoccupied it (Judg. 1:21). The city remained Jebusite until David's conquest of it (2 Sam. 5:6–7). During the pre-Davidic period the Jebusites built a series of terraces with retaining walls on the slopes of the eastern side of the city. This construction allowed the Jebusites to build houses on a steep incline which otherwise would have been uninhabitable.

David began his reign in the late eleventh century B.C. in Hebron (2 Sam. 2:3–4). He led

Overview of entire city model.

an attack against the Jebusite-occupied city of Jerusalem and promised the leadership of his armed forces to the person who "smiteth the Jebusites" first (2 Sam. 5:8). David's uncontrollable half nephew, Joab, led the attack and became commander of the armed forces. David then took the "strong hold of Zion" (2 Sam. 5:7). The term *Zion* means "fortress" and described the citadel which David occupied.

David transferred his seat of government from Hebron to Jerusalem. He extended the fortified city to the north in the direction of the temple mount. He built a palace, renamed the city "the city of David" (2 Sam. 5:9) and built also in the area of the Millo. This last term

rulers sought to kill Him, yet they were allowing Him to teach openly and were doing nothing about it. Could it be that the rulers knew that Jesus was the Christ? On the other hand, so they reasoned, this could not be. For according to their popular, but unscriptural, theology, when Christ should appear no one would know from where He came—and they knew that Jesus was from Nazareth. Even if their theology had been correct, they apparently were ignorant of the place of His birth. Jesus replied that even though they did know some things about Him they were ignorant of the God who sent Him. This angered the multitude so that some in mob violence sought to seize Him, but since His hour had not yet come, they were unable to do so. Jesus would die according to a divine plan and purpose, not by means of mob violence. The immediate occasion of this unsuccessful attempt was a division within the crowd itself. Some raised the question as to whether even if Jesus were not the Christ, the Christ Himself would do greater things than Jesus was doing!

This reaction of some of the crowd alarmed the Pharisees who heard it. Therefore they sought the aid of the chief priests (Sadducees) to silence Jesus. Once again this unnatural and infamous coalition occurred. A detachment of temple police was sent to arrest Jesus and bring Him for trial before the Sanhedrin. Apparently He had won the crowd to a hesitant belief that He could be the Christ, so evidently there was a delay in carrying out the order to arrest Jesus. The temple police bided their time waiting for the right moment to do so.

Finally the last or eighth day of the feast arrived. One of the major features of the celebration was that each day for seven days the priests brought water in golden pitchers from the Pool of Siloam, through the city and into the temple. This pool may still be seen today just outside the east wall of the city. Originally its water flowed down the valley, but for military purposes Hezekiah had dug a tunnel which brought the water inside the city walls. In modern times this tunnel has been excavated, revealing on its walls an inscription which tells of the digging of the tunnel.

When the priestly procession arrived in the temple, the water was poured out in commemoration of the water which God had provided in the wilderness and to remind the people of the prophecies concerning the coming of God's Spirit upon His people. During this procession the priests chanted Isaiah 12:3, "Therefore with joy shall ye draw water out of the wells of salvation." However, these promises had not yet been fulfilled, so as a reminder of this on the last day of the feast, during a holy convocation, the priest repeated this ritual. Only this time their pitchers were empty. Salvation, the water of life, and the Spirit of God were still a hope for the future.

Jesus was standing and watching this ceremony. Suddenly the proceedings were interrupted by His cry: "If anyone is thirsty, he should come to Me and drink! The one who believes in Me, as the Scripture has said, will have streams of living water flow from deep within Him" (John 7:37–38). He proclaimed Himself as the fulfillment of the promises and the prophecy. Judaism ran into

Sunset over the temple mount in Jerusalem, taken from the Mount of Olives.

means "filling." It probably refers to the terraces built on the retaining walls of the eastern slope of the hill of Zion. David reinforced these walls and did additional building in the area.

David brought the ark of the covenant into the city, and the city of Jerusalem became the religious capital of the nation (2 Sam. 6:12). Near the end of his life, David consecrated the site on Mount Moriah as the location of a future temple to Yahweh (1 Chron. 21:28–22:1). David did not build the temple, but he gathered materials for construction which his son Solomon used (1 Chron. 22:2–5).

Foremost among Solomon's great contributions to Jerusalem was his extensive construction. He built the temple on Mount Moriah (1 Kings 6:1), a palace for himself,

and extended the walls of the city (1 Kings 3:1). He probably also built stable facilities (1 Kings 10:26) and provided for expanded water supplies to water his trees (Eccl. 2:6).

Jerusalem became the capital of the Kingdom of Judah after the revolt under the reign of Rehoboam, the son of Solomon (1 Kings 12:18). Under succeeding kings the city was expanded, repaired, and beautified.

In dealing with a desperate revolt under King Zedekiah, the Babylonians burned the temple, the palace, and most of the houses of the city (2 Kings 25:8–11). The destruction was complete, and no known remnant of this preexilic city remains.

In 537 B.C. Cyrus the Persian granted permission for the Jews to return and build again the temple of God in Jerusalem (2 Chron. 36:23). Under the influence of the

A model of Herod's palace in a model of Jerusalem.

prophets Haggai and Zechariah, the temple was completed around 515 B.C. (Ezra 6:14–18).

In the next century Nehemiah returned to rebuild the walls of Jerusalem. He quickly mobilized the people to complete the task in a record time of fifty-two days (Neh. 6:15). Nehemiah rebuilt these walls over an area smaller and closer to the peaks of the hills than the earlier walls had been.

In New Testament times Herod the Great and his Roman benefactors led a time of rapid growth in the size and magnificence of Jerusalem. Herod built several fortresses for guarding the city. One, the Tower of Antonia, dominated the temple area. Paul was taken to this refuge in order to escape a Jewish mob (Acts 21:34). Herod also constructed a lavish palace for himself and erected a new wall which enclosed a larger area.

Herod's most notable construction project was the reconstruction and expansion of the Jerusalem temple. He greatly increased its size and decorated it with elaborate appointments. He began the work in his lifetime (20 B.C.), but it was not completed until A.D. 64, only a few years before it was destroyed again in the first Jewish revolt (A.D. 66–70).

After Herod's death and the removal of his son, Archelaus,

a dead end of frustration, but in His death men should find the water of salvation. And He would send the Holy Spirit upon them. As in Galilee He had proclaimed Himself to be Bread for the hungry, so in Jerusalem He offered Himself as Water for the thirsty. It was a momentous occasion indeed!

Jesus' cry electrified the crowd. Immediately some of them declared Jesus to be "the prophet" promised by Moses; others plainly said that He was the Christ. But others, parroting the words of the Jewish rulers, once again raised the question as to Jesus' origin. He was a Galilean, and the Scriptures plainly taught that the Messiah would be out of the seed of David and from Bethlehem. They were still ignorant of the true facts concerning Jesus' birth. So the people were still divided concerning Him.

This division did not help the temple police in their mission to arrest Jesus, but their failure to do so was for quite another reason. Later when asked by the chief priests and Pharisees why they did not do so, they said, "No man ever spoke like this!" (John 7:46). This upset the Pharisees. Jesus had captivated the multitude, and now their own officers. Was it possible that some of the Sanhedrin were secret believers? Or any of the ultraorthodox Pharisees? One could expect no better of the ignorant, accursed multitudes, but was Jesus even making inroads among the intelligentsia? That the Pharisees were hopeful this was not the case is seen in their question: "Have any of the rulers believed in Him? Or any of the Pharisees?" (John 7:48). (The Greek text invites a negative answer.)

Whether one had done so, at least one was approaching that point. Nicodemus was both a Pharisee and a Jewish ruler, a member of the Sanhedrin. He may at this time have been a secret disciple of Jesus. At any rate he spoke directly on Jesus' behalf: "Our law doesn't judge a man before it hears from him and knows what he's doing, does it?" (John 7:51). Actually he said "the man" not "a man." Jesus had the right to be heard in His own defense. The others had no answer for this simple plea for justice. Their only answer was to ridicule Nicodemus: "You aren't from Galilee too, are you? . . . Search and see: no prophet arises from Galilee" (John 7:52). This was not true, of course, for Galilee had produced many prophets. It was a matter of their senseless rage and also an expression of Judean pride.

So the Feast of Tabernacles came to a close, and Jesus and the Jewish rulers were farther apart than ever before. Jesus continued to adhere to the Father's will; they stubbornly clung to their own empty system of religious thought. And except for Nicodemus and Joseph of Arimathea, it will continue this way until the end.

THE WOMAN TAKEN IN ADULTERY

New Testament scholarship for the most part is agreed that this event (John 7:53–8:11) is not a genuine part of John's Gospel. It does not appear in the oldest and best manuscripts but appears first in one of the later ones. Some put it at the close of John's Gospel, and some even include it in Luke. Nevertheless, since it is such a true picture of Jesus, it is generally regarded as a genuine event out of His life. And it is so treated here.

The day following the Feast of Tabernacles, Jesus was teaching in the temple area. While He was so engaged, the scribes and Pharisees brought to Him a woman whom they had caught in the act of adultery. Reminding Him that according to Moses' Law she should be stoned to death, they asked for His judgment. Under ordinary circumstances she would have been executed immediately, but they used her situation as bait by which to entrap Jesus. To them this was more important than punishing the woman.

It was one of those situations into which the Pharisees delighted to place an adversary, for according to them either way Jesus answered they had Him. If He counseled mercy, they could accuse Him of condoning her deed. If He agreed that she should be stoned, they could accuse Him of being unmerciful.

Jesus did not answer them immediately. Instead He stooped down and wrote on the ground. This is the only time that He is mentioned as writing. It is idle speculation as to what Jesus wrote on the ground, but while He did so, the accusers continued to demand His decision. So rising up, He simply said, "The one without sin among you should be the first to throw a stone at her" (John 8:7). He challenged such a person to be the executioner. Did Jesus mean only the sin of adultery? According to Him any one of them who had ever looked on a woman lustily was guilty of such in his heart. But Jesus did not specify the sin. He simply said, "The one without sin." It could be any sin.

Then leaving the accusers to ponder this matter, Jesus again stooped down and continued to write on the ground. One can imagine the furtive glances which passed among these men. Then one by one, the oldest first, they slipped away. Jesus and the woman were left alone. He arose and asked her, "Woman, where are they? Has no one condemned you?" (John 8:10). "Condemned" means to find guilty and sentence to death. No man did so. And neither did Jesus. He did not condone her sin, but with an admonition to sin no more, He sent her from Him. She called Him "Lord." Did she really trust Him as such? It can only be hoped that she did.

THE LIGHT OF THE WORLD

The language of John 8:12 naturally follows John 7:52. The remainder of John 8 could very well have happened on the last day of the Feast of Tabernacles, but it makes just as good sense to regard it as an event on the day after the Feast and following the matter of the woman taken in adultery. In either case it teaches a tremendous truth regarding the Person of Jesus.

Jesus was still in the temple area, the exact place being the Court of the Women in which were placed the treasury chests to receive the gifts of the worshipers. During the Feast of Tabernacles this court was brilliantly lighted by candelabra. This commemorated the fact that God, during the wilderness wanderings, was Israel's pillar of cloud by day and of fire by night, but now the candelabra were not lighted. This condition corresponds to the empty water pitchers which evoked Jesus' claim to bring the Water of life. So now He said,

from the throne, the Romans ruled Palestine through a series of procurators. Pontius Pilate ruled from A.D. 17 to 26. He constructed a major aqueduct from Bethlehem to Jerusalem. The construction of such a water supply removed Jerusalem from its dependence on the Gihon.

Jerusalem has a long and storied history. As archaeologists continue to explore, more of this history will be revealed and highlighted. For Bible students, therefore, the subject of Jerusalem will remain highly intriguing and ever expanding.

The late Thomas D. Lea was provost and professor of New Testament, Southwestern Baptist Theological Seminary, Fort Worth, Texas.

"I am the light of the world. Anyone who follows Me will never walk in the darkness, but will have the light of life" (John 8:12). Thus to His claims to be Bread and Water, He adds that of Light. These can only be understood as claims to deity, and the Pharisees so comprehended them.

Therefore, once again a debate ensued between them and Jesus. They accused Jesus of bearing false witness since the law required two witnesses to establish a truth. Jesus countered that both He and His Father bore witness to His Person. The Pharisees asked Him to identify His Father. In reply Jesus said that they did not really know Him or His Father. If they knew in their souls who He was, they would also know the Father in like manner. But they knew neither because of their sins; and unless they believed in Jesus, they would die in their sins. They had asked for proof as to Jesus' true identity, and as He had done twice previously in Galilee, so here He cited His death (and Resurrection) as proof. Furthermore, He said that they were the ones who would lift Him up on the cross. This Jesus had spoken to the Twelve, but here for the first time He says it to the Jewish leaders.

The Pool of Siloam

Cecil Ray Taylor

"Go, . . .wash in the pool of Siloam," said Jesus to the man born blind (John 9:6–7). This pool was linked to the spring of Gihon, the only important source of water near Jerusalem.[1] Under David, Israelites dug a basin near the spring to collect its waters which fed into a gently sloping[2] channel—the Aqueduct of Shiloh (Isa. 8:6–7)—that ran south along the city mound. These waters may have irrigated the Kidron Valley below through a series of lateral openings in the eastern wall of the channel. The remaining water drained into "the lower pool"[3] near the southern wall of the city.

Because the Shiloh ran outside the city walls, it was highly vulnerable to enemy attack. When the Assyrians threatened invasion (2 Kings 18:17) about 701 B.C., Hezekiah closed the older system and filled up the Gihon so the invaders could not use it.[4] Then he diverted its waters underground through the famous Tunnel of Hezekiah into a new pool inside new ramparts.[5]

The name *Siloam* (Hebrew *Shiloach* meaning "sent") apparently transferred from the older waterway to Hezekiah's new system and the western pool became known as "the pool of Siloam."[6] Cut from solid rock, it

Gihon Spring.

These words brought a twofold reaction among the Pharisees. Some of them began to believe in Him. To them Jesus said that if their faith were genuine they would in truth be His disciples. They would know the truth which would make them free, but others of the Pharisees were angered at Jesus' words. They asserted that they were Abraham's seed and had never been in bondage to any man. On the surface this was a ridiculous claim, for Israel's history had been one bondage after another. Even then they were a captive nation under the Romans. To give the Pharisees credit at this point, however, they did not recognize this bondage in their hearts.

However, Jesus brushed aside the political implication, declaring that they were slaves to their sin. It was freedom from this that Jesus promised, and then taking up the matter of Abraham, He said that they were not even a true seed of Abraham for they did not the works of Abraham. Because He spoke the truth, they were seeking to kill Him, something which Abraham had not done. No, they were doing the works of their father the devil. They could not answer this charge, so they resorted to slander. As an obvious slur upon Jesus' birth, they said, "We weren't born of sexual immorality. . . . We have one Father—God" (John 8:41). Jesus replied that if God were their Father they would love Him. Then pressing home His charge, He added, "You are of your father the Devil, and you want to carry out your father's desires. He was a murderer from the beginning and has not stood in the truth, because there is no truth in him" (John 8:44). Jesus called them liars, murderers, and tools of the devil. Note the growing intensity of the conflict between Him and the Pharisees.

Stung by these strong words, the Pharisees proved that they were the children of the Slanderer, the devil. They said that Jesus was a Samaritan and had a devil.

ran seventy-one feet from north to south and seventy-five feet from east to west. A set of steps along one edge of the pool was bisected by a central arcade which may have separated a section for men from a section for women.[7]

The system got its name probably because waters were "sent" along its course from the Gihon. John emphasized the name to reflect a theme common in this Gospel, namely, that Jesus was "sent" into this world from heaven.[8]

[1]Ronald Youngblood, "Siloam Inscription," *The Biblical World: A Dictionary of Biblical Archaeology*, ed. Charles F. Pfeiffer (Grand Rapids: Baker Book House, 1966), 529–30.
[2]According to Wiseman, *Illustrated Bible Dictionary*, 1452, this channel dropped only five centimeters in a linear run of three hundred meters.
[3]"King's pool" (Neh. 2:14) and "pool of Shelah" may be other names for this older pool; Barrois, 354.
[4]According to Wiseman, *Illustrated Bible Dictionary*, 1452, archaeologists have found traces of this blockage.
[5]See 2 Chronicles 32:3,30; Isaiah 22:9,11; Leon Morris, *Gospel According to John* (Grand Rapids: Wm. B. Eerdmans Publishing Co., 1971), 481 n. 21, called this the "upper pool," adding that it appears to have overflowed into the "lower pool" to which the former channel led. Modern buildings prevent a check on the latter.
[6]Barrois, 354.
[7]Youngblood, 531.
[8]Barrois, 352.

Cecil Ray Taylor is chairman, Division of Religion, Mobile College, Mobile, Alabama.

Herod's Temple

In plain language they called Him an insane Samaritan. To them this was to bemean Jesus indeed. The Lord denied the charge, stating that He sought to honor God while they dishonored Him. Jesus did not turn back but pressed His point even more strongly. Said He, "If anyone keeps My word, he will never see death" (John 8:51). In derision the Pharisees replied that now they knew Jesus was insane, for both Abraham and the prophets had kept God's Word, yet they were all dead. They demanded to know if He placed Himself above them.

Jesus answered with a tremendous claim: "Your father Abraham was overjoyed that he would see My day; he saw it and rejoiced" (John 8:56). He looked for Messiah's day and rejoiced in it. That day was before their very eyes, and they were angry. Not to be outdone, the Pharisees mocked Jesus: "You aren't fifty years old yet, and You've seen Abraham?" (John 8:57). But they were stunned by His reply: "I assure you: Before Abraham was, I am" (John 8:58), literally, "before Abraham was born, I always am." This was a claim to eternal being or to deity, and the Pharisees so interpreted it; for them this was blasphemy. So they took up stones intent on stoning Him to death. Mob violence without a trial! When they could not answer His arguments, they had but two choices—believe in Him or destroy Him, and they chose the latter course. This was not the first or the last time they would face this alternative, and their choice was always the same.

But Jesus' time had not yet come, so He left them in the temple area with murderous stones in their hands. However, these stones were but outward symbols of the murder that was in their hearts.

A blind beggar at the Damascus gate in Jerusalem.

ANOTHER SABBATH CONTROVERSY

While Jesus remained in Jerusalem His actions caused the old Sabbath controversy to break out again. It was probably the Sabbath after the Feast of Tabernacles, and Jesus met a man blind from birth. Jesus healed him by anointing his eyes with clay and telling him to rinse it off in the pool of Siloam. Having done so, the man returned with his sight. The matter was brought to the attention of the Pharisees, and upon their inquiry the man told them how his blindness had been healed. They had no concern about it except that it had occurred on the Sabbath.

They endeavored therefore to discount the whole thing. Some of them simply said that Jesus could not be from God since He broke the Sabbath, but others asked if a sinner could do such a miracle. Thus divided, they sought to deny that a miracle had taken place. It was simply a trick to deceive the people. To prove this the rulers sought out the man's parents. They confirmed the fact that their son had been born blind, but they avoided the question as to how the healing had occurred. They feared the Jewish rulers who had already agreed that anyone confessing Jesus as the Christ should be put out of the synagogue. A Jew might be put

The Pool of Siloam in Jerusalem.

out of the synagogue for thirty days, sixty days, or indefinitely. Apparently the third is meant here. It was to them a terrible thing akin to excommunication today. They were regarded as dead and, therefore, could have no dealings with other Jews. Furthermore, they were cut off from the congregation of the Lord. It is little wonder that the parents sidestepped this question.

Instead they told the Pharisees to ask their son because he was of age, and the son handled himself quite well. When asked if Jesus were a sinner, he replied, "Whether or not He's a sinner, I don't know. One thing I do know: I was blind, and now I can see!" (John 9:25). He did not know about their theology, but he did know about his experience. It is impossible to argue against results.

When the Pharisees continued to bombard the man with questions, he made sport of them. Why were they so persistent? Did they also want to become disciples of Jesus? In reply they avowed that they were disciples of Moses but disavowed any knowledge about Jesus, and the man taunted them all the more. They were supposed to be up on such matters, yet here was a Man who healed blind eyes, and they did not know about Him. Then he seized upon a bit of their own theology. They asked if he thought that Jesus was a sinner. Very well, said the man, "We know that God doesn't listen to sinners; but if anyone is God-fearing and does His will, He listens to him. Throughout history no one has ever heard of someone opening the eyes of a person born blind. If this man were not from God, He wouldn't be able to do anything" (John 9:31–33). With a slur that he was born in sins and yet proposed to teach them, the Pharisees drove this upstart from their presence. Apparently they did not cast him out of the synagogue, since this required a meeting of the Sanhedrin. But the incident ended on a beautiful note, for Jesus found the man, led him to believe on Him, and forgave his sins.

However, Jesus was not rid of the tenacious Pharisees. They continued to attack Him with their words, so Jesus called them false shepherds of Israel. They posed as the shepherds of the people, but their only purpose was to ravage them to their own gain. By contrast, in a series of mixed metaphors, Jesus described Himself as the true Shepherd and the Door to the sheepfold. As the good Shepherd He will lay down His life for His sheep to protect them from the wolves that seek to devour them. The wolves of sin were destroying the sheep. The false shepherds were concerned only for their own safety and power, but the good Shepherd will die to save the sheep—not only the sheep in Israel but also the sheep in the whole world.

The Pharisees were seeking to kill Jesus, but they could not take His life from Him. He will lay it down of Himself. He declared that He had authority within Himself to lay it down and to take it up again. This did not mean that Jesus would raise Himself from the dead but that both His death and Resurrection would be within His Father's will. Until God is ready, it is useless for the Pharisees to try to carry out their evil purpose. So Jesus departed from Jerusalem, leaving the Jewish rulers to squabble among themselves.

Silwan (Siloam) Village is situated on the rocky southeastern slope of the Kidron valley across from and above the Gihon spring.

Siloam inscription in limestone. Found in Jerusalem and dates from the 7th century B.C.

Following this latest controversy with the Pharisees, Jesus spent the greater part of three months in a brief but intensive ministry in Judea but outside of Jerusalem. At the close of this period, He returned to the city for the Feast of Dedication. This phase of the later Judean ministry is recorded only by Luke (10:1–13:21). One should not be surprised to encounter events similar to some which took place in Galilee. This is a distinct entity in Jesus' ministry among a different people. He did not propose to deprive them of the witness which had been given to Galilee.

1. The Mission of the Seventy

In Galilee Jesus sent the Twelve on a preaching mission. Here in Judea He chose seventy other disciples and sent them on a similar one. As in Galilee and Samaria so in Judea the harvest was great, but the laborers were so few.

Before sending these forth two by two, He gave them instructions similar to those given to the Twelve, only the instructions given here were limited to their immediate mission. Previously in instructing the

This outline of stone may be the foundation of a sheepfold.

Twelve, Jesus had looked beyond the present to the mission beyond His Resurrection and extending unto the end of the age, but this present mission was for the immediate need only.

The seventy did as they were told, and they returned rejoicing that even demons were subject to them in Jesus' name. It was a happy time for Jesus also, for in their triumphs He saw the eventual overthrow of Satan's power. This was not to be through the work of "the wise and prudent," such as the Jewish rulers, but through these simple "babes" who were willing to submit unto Him. Satan's power would be broken through Jesus' death and Resurrection, and this victory would be proclaimed by His followers and be realized unto salvation in the experience of those who believed the proclamation.

Jesus shared this joy with the Twelve, for privately He said to them, "Blessed are the eyes that see the things you see! For I tell you that many prophets and kings wanted to see the things you see, yet didn't see them; to hear the things you hear, yet didn't hear them" (Luke 10:23–24).

What a refreshing experience this was for Jesus! After the sophisticated resistance which He had encountered in Jerusalem, this was as a shower in the

desert.

2. The Parable of the Good Samaritan

Even though Jesus had left Jerusalem, the Pharisees continued to dog His steps, so on one occasion one of their number, a lawyer or one skilled in interpreting the Mosaic Law, tempted Jesus with a question. He addressed Him as "Teacher," asking what he must do to inherit eternal life. (Apparently Jesus had been teaching on this subject at the time.) Since the man was a specialist in the Law, Jesus threw his question back upon him by asking him what the Law said. Without hesitation the lawyer quoted what the Jews considered to be the heart of the Law: "You shall love the Lord your God with all your heart, with all your soul, with all your strength, and with all your mind; and your neighbor as yourself" (Luke 10:27).

Jesus commended him for his answer, saying that if he did these things he would live. The trouble was that the lawyer could not do them perfectly, and that was the point of Jesus' answer. Jesus did say that if one kept the Law perfectly, always, and without one slip he would inherit eternal life, but because of man's sinful nature, this is an impossibility. It is in this fact that Jesus' redemptive work became a necessity.

The lawyer did not wait long to reveal the flaw in his record. Evidently he saw Jesus' point, and so trying to hedge on the stringent requirement of the Law, he asked, "And who is my neighbor" (Luke 10:29). This was a typical Jewish hairsplitting trick. They saw no way to hedge on their attitude toward God, but they sought an outlet in the matter of their neighbor. They excluded from this group all Gentiles and especially all Samaritans. It was no matter to them that the word *neighbor* means "the one who is near." The Jews made exceptions on the basis of race. So the lawyer thought that he had found a loophole in the Law.

Jesus quickly plugged up the hole as He related the Parable of the Good Samaritan. This parable related a common experience for those who traveled the highway of blood from Jerusalem to Jericho. It was an area infested with highwaymen, who beat and stripped their victims of money and clothing, leaving them half dead. Obviously the victim in the story was a Jew, and without pressing every detail of the parable, one sees Jesus' condemnation of the entire Jewish religious system as He pictured the priest and Levite pass-

Road from Jerusalem to Jericho. The setting of Jesus' Parable of the Good Samaritan.

Village of Bethany. Home of Mary, Martha, and Lazarus, three of Jesus' closest friends. Jesus spent nights here the first part of Passion Week.

ing by the poor man without rendering aid. But the bombshell in the story was the character whom Jesus made the hero. A despised Samaritan! The last person who would have been expected to render aid to a helpless Jew! (One wonders whom Jesus would pick in a modern setting!)

At any rate He described the man's merciful ministry in detail, including his taking the victim to an inn and providing money to pay for his care until he was well. Having completed the story, Jesus let the lawyer himself apply its lesson. Obviously the neighborly man was the Samaritan who showed mercy on the poor Jew. One's neighbor, then, is anyone who needs his help, regardless of his race or of any other difference between men. So Jesus said, "Go, and do the same" (Luke 10:37). This is a lesson much in need today as it was then.

3. Jesus Visits Martha and Mary

As Jesus and the Twelve traveled about Judea, they came one day to a certain village called Bethany. It is located just over the crest of the Mount of Olives less than two miles east of Jerusalem. In this village lived two sisters, Martha and Mary, and their brother, Lazarus. Lazarus was probably not at home at this time, since no mention is made of him. In all likelihood this was Jesus' home when He was in the vicinity of Jerusalem. Tourists are shown the possible ruins of this home even today.

As was probably His custom, Jesus visited with the two sisters on this occasion. The scene is quite vivid. Mary sat alongside and somewhat in front of Jesus' feet as she drank in His every word. It was probably late in the afternoon, and Jesus had been walking all day. So Martha, ever the practical one, was busy in the kitchen preparing a meal for Him. It seems never to have occurred to Mary that while man does not live by bread alone he must have bread.

On the other hand Martha was distracted in her anxiety to prepare a sumptuous meal for the occasion. Suddenly she burst in upon the conversation between Jesus and Mary. The language of the text (Luke 10:40) indicates that she reproached Jesus for keeping Mary from helping her with the meal. This speaks for the friendly relations between Him and His friends. He was at home with them, and they enjoyed His company. So Martha's reproach was of a friendly sort.

It requires little imagination to see a friendly smile on Jesus' face as He, in turn, chided Martha. "Martha, Martha, you are worried and upset about many things, but one thing is necessary. Mary has made the right choice, and it will not be taken away from her" (Luke 10:41–42). In effect, Jesus said that only one dish was necessary for the meal rather than the many about which Martha was fretting. Mary had chosen the best dish, that of fellowship with Jesus, and it would not be taken from her. Clearly in this incident Jesus sided with Mary.

One's character should not be judged by one incident alone. From this one account Martha has been labeled as a "cook" only, while Mary is pictured as a spiritually gifted woman, but time was to prove the deep faith of Martha. It is possible to be a practical person and one of great faith as well.

4. A Busy Interval

The following weeks were busy ones for Jesus. In the interval between His visit to Bethany and His return to Jerusalem for the Feast of Dedication, He went about Judea teaching and healing. On one occasion after Jesus had ended a season of prayer, one of His disciples asked that He teach them to pray, as John the Baptist had taught his disciples. Jesus had taught them to pray, as in the Sermon on the Mount, but evidently they had not learned their lesson or else had forgotten it. Jesus replied by giving them the substance of the Model Prayer, followed by a parable designed to teach God's great desire to grant prayers that were prayed within His fatherly will.

However, not all of the events were as pleasant as this one. On one occasion Jesus healed a dumb demoniac, and as in Galilee His enemies accused Him of doing so by the power of Beelzebub. Some students would equate this with the incident in Galilee, but there is no reason to suppose that this accusation would not be made in Judea as in Galilee where it occurred twice. In this latter incident Jesus answered the charge in much the same manner as in Galilee except for one major exception. In Judea He said nothing of the unpardonable sin. Instead He used this as the occasion to point out the emptiness and failure of the Jewish religious system.

He pictured one who by the teaching of the Pharisees had been cleansed of an evil spirit. Later the spirit returned to find his life "swept and put in order" (Luke 11:25). It was swept clean morally and adorned with rite and ceremony, but it was left empty. The Pharisees gave the man nothing with which to fill his life, so the evil spirit brought into his life seven others more evil than it was. Thus the latter state was worse than the former. The man had tried Judaism only to find it empty. In his frustration he would be less likely to respond to any other form of religion.

Jesus was ever alert to seize upon an event of the moment to teach a great spiritual truth. On one occasion a man requested that He should make his brother divide the family inheritance with him. Evidently this request came from the younger of two brothers. It seems that the younger wanted an equal share, but Jesus refused to be an arbiter in this family fuss. He never sided forcibly with one sinner against another sinner. He preached to both the will of God, great moral and spiritual principles, leaving them to apply the truth to their own lives. In this situation He did not say to one or to the other what he should do. Instead, "He told them, Watch out, and be on guard against all greed, because one's life is not in the abundance of his possessions" (Luke 12:15). The trouble with both brothers was the sin of covetousness. So Jesus said, "Look out, and guard yourselves against it!" for even if one's abundance overflows, that is not life indeed.

To illustrate this truth Jesus gave the parable of the Rich Fool. So abundant was the yield of his fields that his barns could not contain it. He then determined to tear them down and build greater ones, and in selfish indulgence said, "You have many goods stored up for many years. Take it easy; eat, drink, and enjoy yourself" (Luke 12:19). Jesus did not accuse the man of dishonesty or of unfair labor practices. Neither did He condemn him for being wealthy. His sin was his desire for more that he might indulge his own selfishness. He had no sense of stewardship. Instead of recognizing God as the source of his blessings, he spoke of "my crops," "my barns," "my goods," "myself." He thought to feed his soul on things.

"But God said to him, You fool! This very night your life is demanded of you" (Luke 12:20). Literally, "This night they [things] are requiring your soul of you." How sad, yet how universally true. It is no wonder that Jesus concluded this interview with a warning to be ever watchful. God provides, but man receives all things as a steward of God, and he is held responsible for his stewardship.

Current events also provided Jesus with teaching situations. Just as He finished His previous discourse, some of His listeners came to Him with the news that Pilate's soldiers had slain some Galileans who were engaged in making sacrifices in the temple. Their own blood had been mingled with that of their sacrifices. No mention of this event is found in any other record outside of Luke (13:1–3), but it is true to Pilate's record nevertheless. In all likelihood these were revolutionaries who had been slain in the temple itself.

Doubtless His informers expected Jesus to express horror at such an act, a feeling which He most surely felt, but His comments were along an entirely different line. He turned it into a lesson on the necessity for repentance. Were these Galileans sinners above that of other Galileans? "No, I tell you; but unless you repent, you will all perish as well!" (Luke 13:3).

Then He brought the lesson nearer home. Apparently it was common knowledge that the tower of Siloam in Jerusalem had fallen killing eighteen people. So Jesus added this incident to His lesson. Were these poor people greater sinners than others in Jerusalem who were spared this tragedy? He again answered in the negative, calling upon all to repent.

Before returning to Jerusalem Jesus had one more run-in with the ruler of a synagogue over the Sabbath question. In the synagogue on the Sabbath He healed a woman who had had a curvature of the spine for eighteen years. She glorified God, but the ruler was angry with Jesus for violating the rules regarding the Sabbath. He cared more for his rules than for this poor woman, but even though he was angry with Jesus, he rebuked the multitude which had gathered about Him. Evidently he had heard how difficult it was to get the best of Jesus. Therefore, he ordered the people to come for healing on weekdays, not on the Sabbath. Evidently others, perhaps Pharisees, agreed with the ruler, and so Jesus showed him the same courtesy which had been accorded Him. He spoke to the others through him: "But the Lord answered him and said, Hypocrites! . . ." (Luke 13:15). He accused them of treating their animals better than they treated people. On the Sabbath they led their animals to water but denied to Him the right to heal this poor woman on that day. Once again He had bested His adversaries, and the multitude rejoiced at both the healing and His putting the hypocrites in their places.

This prompted Jesus to repeat the Parables of the Mustard Seed and the Leaven. He had made small beginnings in establishing the kingdom of God, as was shown by the response of the people, and it would grow until it filled the earth.

THE FEAST OF DEDICATION

The middle of December had arrived, and it was time for the Feast of Dedication. This was one of the lesser feasts among the Jews. It commemorated the dedication of the temple in 164 B.C. by Judas Maccabeus. Antiochus Epiphanes had defiled the temple by sacrificing a sow on Jehovah's altar. This along with other atrocities had precipitated the revolt which led to his defeat, so Judas Maccabeus, the hero of the revolution, had led the now free nation in cleansing and rededicating the temple. For the most part this feast was observed in the local synagogues with great rejoicing much like that associated with the Feast of Tabernacles, but since Jesus was in Judea at the time, He attended the feast in Jerusalem.

John notes that "it was winter" (10:22) and Jesus was walking along Solomon's porch in the temple area. This was a colonnaded area on the eastern side of the temple formed by a sort of balcony built out over the slopes which went down into the valley below. Since it was a covered area, it was usable in any kind of weather.

As Jesus walked along, He was accosted by the Jewish rulers. Apparently they were exasperated by Jesus. They had tried repeatedly to trap Him into an admission as to His true identity. So surrounding Him, they asked, "How long are you going to keep us in suspense? If You are the Messiah, tell us plainly" (John 10:24).

The point of their demand was "plainly." For the sake of argument they assumed that He was the Christ, so they demanded that He say so in plain words, "I am the Messiah." Jesus had refrained from using this word "Messiah" to them because of the political connotation which they put upon it. Had they been able to trap Him into using the word, they would have accused Him of plotting a rebellion against Rome, as indeed they did when He later admitted under oath to being the Messiah. So Jesus continued to avoid the word in His dealings with others.

However, He did answer their question about holding them in suspense. He reminded them that repeatedly He had claimed to be the Son of the Father and they had not believed Him. This title had no political meaning however, and so they were not satisfied. Jesus continued by citing His works which He did in the Father's name, but they did not believe them because they were not of His sheep. His sheep heard His voice and followed Him. He insisted that He gave them eternal life, they would never perish, and no one was able to snatch them out of His hand. Furthermore, His Father who gave them to Him is greater than all, and no man is able to snatch them out of His Father's hand. Then Jesus claimed oneness with the Father: "The Father and I are one" (John 10:30).

This last claim was more than the rulers could take. They knew that Jesus plainly claimed identity with God, and to them this was blasphemy—so they reached for their stones. Mob violence all over again! But Jesus stood His ground, asking them for which of His good works they proposed to stone Him. Not for good works, said they, "but for blasphemy, and because You—being a man—make Yourself God" (John 10:33).

There are those who insist that Jesus never called Himself God, but the Jews so understood Him, and so He did. Taking them at their word, Jesus challenged them that even if they would not believe Him at least they should recognize His works as benevolent ones, and so the works of God: "This way you will know and understand that the Father is in Me and I in the Father" (John 10:38).

But His words were wasted on them, for their only response was once again to try to arrest Him. However, once again He escaped their clutches, and Jesus left Jerusalem not to return until a few months later when He made His final challenge to the city and its rulers. The die was cast, but still His hour had not yet arrived.

"*I am the resurrection and the life. The one who believes in Me, even if he dies, will live. Everone who lives and believes in Me will never die—ever. Do you believe this?*"

John 11:25-26 (HCSB)

The Perean Ministry

7

An overview of a Jerusalem model found at the Holyland Hotel in Jerusalem.

The Ministry of the Great Physician

From Jerusalem Jesus traveled eastward, crossing the Jordan River into Perea. Here He entered again into the territory of Herod Antipas, but for the time being He was out of Judea and away from the center of power of the Jewish rulers. It was late in December of A.D. 29. About three and one-half months remained before the Crucifixion. The records of this period are rather sparse, but they picture Jesus continuing His ministry of teaching and healing, and this He carried out in a more favorable atmosphere than that of Judea. It must have been refreshing to Jesus to find that in Perea many people believed on Him because they had heard John the Baptist preach concerning Him. What a compliment it is to one's preaching about Jesus that men recognize Him thereby!

A WARNING AGAINST HEROD ANTIPAS

Shortly after Jesus arrived in Perea, a strange thing happened. Certain Pharisees warned Him to get out of Herod's domain because Herod sought to kill Him. In view of the general hostility of the Pharisees toward Jesus, this is a surprising turn of events. At least this was a new role for them to play. Certainly it suggests that not all Pharisees were so vehemently opposed to Jesus as they seemed to be as a class.

At any rate in His reply Jesus showed His contempt for Herod Antipas. He called him a "fox," indicating that He was aware of his cunning cowardice and of his evil designs toward Him, but He let it be known that Herod would not succeed in his purpose. Jesus' work must continue until He had reached the final time and purpose of His coming, and He wanted the Pharisees to realize this. Jesus did not court danger, but neither did He run from it. His life was held in the Father's will, and besides, "it is not possible for a prophet to perish outside of Jerusalem" (Luke 13:33). His destiny lay not in Perea but in Jerusalem.

The mention of Jerusalem evoked from Jesus the first of three laments which He uttered over the city. "O Jerusalem! Jerusalem! The city who kills the prophets and stones those who are sent to her! How often I wanted to gather your children together, as a hen gathers her chicks under her wings, but you were not willing! See! Your house is abandoned to you. And I tell you, you will not see Me until the time comes when you say, 'Blessed is He who comes in the name of the Lord'!" (Luke 13:34–35).

Jesus' heart was nigh unto breaking as He foresaw the end of the city so dear to the heart of every Jew. He saw the storm of her destruction coming. Repeatedly He had offered Himself as her Savior, only to be rejected. He would not enter the city again until His final visit at the beginning of Passion Week. It is worthy of note that although Luke up to this time has not recorded any visit of Jesus to Jerusalem during His public ministry, he anticipates the record of John's Gospel which was written years after Luke wrote his.

JESUS IN THE HOME OF A PHARISEE

The friendly attitude of some Pharisees toward Jesus is further evidenced by the fact that early in the Perean ministry He was the dinner guest in one's home who was a ruler among the Pharisees. The same thing had occurred one time in Galilee (Luke 7:36–50), although on the former occasion the host himself was critical of Jesus. Of further interest is the fact that both of these instances are told by Luke (14:1–24).

Clearly, however, in the Perean incident the Pharisee who was the host had apparently invited other "lawyers and Pharisees" also. As the story develops, evidently they were not friendly toward Jesus; for as they were eating, they were watching Him out of the corners of their eyes.

It was on a Sabbath day. Suddenly a man who had dropsy entered. Seeing him, Jesus asked these watchful lawyers and Pharisees if it were lawful to heal on the Sabbath. When they refused to answer, Jesus healed the man and let him go, and, as once before, He reminded them that they were kinder to their animals than they were to their fellow human beings.

Jesus had noted that when the guests had arrived they had sought out the chief reclining places at the table. They all wanted to be at the head table. Therefore, using this as the basis, Jesus taught them a lesson in humility, a subject about which they knew very little. If one seeks out the chief reclining place and a more honorable person comes, he may be shamed by being asked to give his place to the honorable person. It would be far better to take the least honorable place. It is possible, however, that the host may ask him to take a better place and thus he would be honored before his friends. "For everyone who exalts himself will be humbled, and the one who humbles himself will be exalted" (Luke 14:11).

Furthermore, Jesus used the occasion to teach a lesson in true hospital-

Reconstruction of a wealthy Jewish house.

ity. He had noted that the host had invited only his own kind to the dinner. Therefore He said that instead of inviting his friends, relatives, or rich neighbors, who in turn might invite him to a dinner, he should invite the poor, lame, and blind to whom he owed no social obligation and from whom he expected no invitation in return. For such an act he would receive no social favor, but he would receive a far greater spiritual blessing.

Jesus' words about a blessing deeply impressed one of the guests, so he exclaimed, "Blessed is the one who will eat bread in the kingdom of God!" (Luke 14:15). But knowing these Pharisees' attitude toward the kingdom, Jesus cooled his ardor with a parable which was very much to the point. The Pharisees regarded themselves as especially favored of God, so Jesus said that a certain man gave a dinner. He sent invitations to many, for it was customary to invite guests ahead of time. The story presumes that they had accepted the invitation. When the meal was ready, the host sent his servant to tell the guests to come, but they all began to make excuses as to why they could not come. One had bought a field and must go to inspect it. Another had purchased five yoke of oxen and must go to prove them. Imagine making such purchases without first knowing their value! A third said that he had married a wife and could not come. At least he had some excuse!

The point was that none of them really wanted to come, and the host was angered at their refusals. Therefore, he sent his

Watchtower overlooking grainfields near the valley of Lebonah. Jesus may have been in the vicinity of such a tower when He spoke of the necessity of counting the cost of being His disciple. He told His disciples that before a man built a tower, he would first sit down and count the cost to see if he had the resources to complete it (Luke 14:28-30).

Statue representing good shepherd. Greco-Roman Museum, Alexandria, Egypt.

servant into the street to gather poor unfortunates to eat with him. Still there was room. Then he sent his servant to invite chance passersby to come, but none of those who were first invited and excused themselves would taste of the supper.

Obviously the point of the story was that these Pharisees thought they were the privileged of God. They had in their own thoughts accepted God's invitation to be a part of His kingdom feast, but when the kingdom was ready, they refused to participate. So God will invite those who were despised and neglected by them. Because of their obstinate attitude the Pharisees would miss their opportunity.

ANOTHER GROUP OF PARABLES

Throughout His ministry Jesus placed great emphasis on parabolic teaching. At times, as on one occasion in Galilee, He used only parables, but there is scarcely any extended teaching of Jesus in which He did not use one or more vivid pictures in order to make truth live. The fact that so many of His teachings are remembered in connection with some parable shows how effective this method was in presenting truth in living color.

Jesus continued to employ parables in Perea as He had done in other areas wherein He ministered. Some of them are repetitions as He unveiled God's revelation to different audiences, but in a rather brief span of time He added new ones which have become some of His best remembered and most beloved parables. Whether by a set purpose or not, Jesus presented them in three groups of three.

The first group was designed to test the sincerity of the multitudes which followed Him. Jesus never made a play for the crowds. He was concerned about genuineness of purpose rather than the glamour of numbers, so He ever impressed upon men the price that they must pay in order to follow Him. This is seen clearly in an incident in Perea.

On one occasion "great multitudes" followed Him. Turning to them, He said that to be His disciple a man must choose Him above love for family or even life itself. He must be willing to be a crossbearer, or one on the way to his execution, if he would be a follower of Jesus. He urged these people to count the cost before making their commitment. Then He used the three parables.

Before a man begins to build a tower, he would be wise to sit down and figure the cost to determine whether he can complete it. Or a king would do well to do likewise before he starts a war. If he knows that he cannot win, he would be wise to negotiate with his enemy in order to reach the terms which are required for peace. "In the same way, therefore, every one of you who does not say goodbye to all his possessions cannot be My disciple" (Luke 14:33). Then to drive home His lesson, Jesus repeated the figure of salt. Salt is good or useful provided that it be salty. Otherwise, it is useless and fit only to be cast out, probably to make a roadbed or footpath. Such is the fate of those who are superficial in their commitment to Christ.

First-century coins. Representative of a coin the woman lost and diligently sought (Luke 15:8-10).

This is a necessary truth for every age. If it were followed, it would decrease the quantity of those who profess the faith, but it would certainly increase the quality of those who seek to practice it. It is no wonder that Jesus said, "Anyone who has ears to hear, should listen!" (Luke 14:35).

The second group of parables was given in response to the criticism of the Pharisees and scribes because Jesus was receiving publicans and sinners and even eating with them. These stories contrast their attitude with that of God regarding such people. While they rejected and despised them, God was ever seeking them to draw them unto Himself in repentance.

The first of these parables was that of the lost sheep. This is one of the most beautiful of all of Jesus' parables, one which has been illustrated in both art and music. A shepherd had one hundred sheep, but one was lost from the fold. So he left the ninety-nine to go in search for the one lost sheep, and when he had found it, in true shepherd fashion he placed it on his shoulder and with rejoicing brought it back to the fold.

Quite obviously the ninety-nine suggest the self-righteous Pharisees who regarded themselves as being safe in God's fold. The one lost sheep corresponds to the publicans and sinners whom the Pharisees regarded as being outside the fold of God. But Jesus concluded the parable by saying that there is more rejoicing in heaven over one repentant sinner than over the many who do not regard themselves as needing to repent.

The second parable was like unto the first. It pictured a woman who had ten pieces of silver but who had lost one of them. Jesus portrayed the diligent search of the woman until she had found the lost coin, and He repeated the lesson derived from the first parable.

The third parable, however, took on quite a different turn. Whereas the first two emphasized heaven's joy over finding one lost person as over against those who did not consider themselves to be lost, the third parable contrasted the Father's attitude toward the lost with that of the Pharisees. It is commonly called the Parable of the Prodigal Son, referring to the lost one. Actually Jesus placed His emphasis upon the merciless attitude of the elder brother.

The story is too familiar to need recounting, but certain elements will bear emphasis. The younger son, chafing under the father's discipline, went into a far country where he wasted his substance in riotous living. The degree of his degeneracy is seen in that he wound up feeding swine which were not his own. Imagine a Jew in such a predicament! Finally he realized what a mess he had made of his life, and in abject repentance he determined to return to his father's house. In unparalleled art Jesus pictured the yearning heart of the father. The son had determined to request, not that he be restored to sonship, but that he simply be allowed to be as a hired servant. Before he would finish his repentant request, however, as soon as he admitted his unworthiness to be a son, in compassion the father restored him to full sonship. Actually in the father's heart he had never ceased to be a son or the object of his father's love. It was only that his sin had separated him from his father's grace. His forgiveness and restoration waited only upon his repentance, and to celebrate the lost son's return the father made a great feast.

At this point the true lesson of the parable emerged. The elder brother, instead of rejoicing over his brother's return, sulked because even though he had served his father well he had never been so royally treated. He was not moved by his brother's need but was concerned only with what he considered to be his rights by virtue of his good works. However, the father said to him, "'Son,' he said to him, 'you are always with me, and everything I have is yours. But we had to celebrate and rejoice, because this brother of yours was dead and is alive again; he was lost and is found'" (Luke 15:31–32).

There are many truths to be derived from this parable, but as in all parables one should not press every item unduly. The one great truth which Jesus taught was the self-righteous son's attitude toward the sinful brother. In stern reality the Lord placed a mirror before the Pharisees to enable them to see themselves and their unmerciful conduct toward all sinners who are still the object of God's love.

The third group of parables deals with the subject of stewardship, and it may have been suggested by the wasteful attitude of the younger son in the preceding story. If so, the first of this third group may imply Jesus' censure of his lack of stewardship. But its meaning affords a much wider application, for it was spoken to Jesus' disciples.

The first parable is usually called that of the Unjust Steward, but it is nearer to Jesus' lesson to call it the parable of the shrewd steward. A steward owned nothing in his own right. He was a slave who had been entrust-

Jewish Inheritance Laws

Timothy L. Noel

What was the Jewish law in the first century that regulated the inheritance of a family estate? What distinction did the law make regarding the inheritance of the firstborn son as opposed to younger sons? Did the law make provision for the younger son to demand a share of his father's property? Clearly, the answer is no. The father could dispose of his property in either of two ways. The normal means of providing for inheritance for sons was through a will that would be executed at his death.

On the other hand, the father could provide for his sons by dividing the property before his death. But in such instances restrictions would be placed on the inheritance. If the property was passed on to the sons after the death of the father, a double share would go to the elder son. If the father had two sons, the elder would receive two-thirds of the inheritance, and the younger would receive one-third.

If the property was divided between the sons before the father's death, evidently different arrangements were made in the amount of the inheritance. Clearly the father could not give one-third of all he owned to the younger son and the rest to the older son. In that case nothing would be left for the father and mother's livelihood or for any other dependents such as unmarried daughters. Some deduction would have been made for the father and mother's maintenance until their death. And some provision would need to be made for the rest of the family.

According to Jewish law, all the advantages of property ownership, including all profits from the property, would remain with the

Signet ring.

Green farmland of central Israel with citrus groves between Beersheba and Jerusalem.

Huleh Valley.

father, even though the younger son held a portion of the title. The property might be signed over to the sons, but the father retained control.

Exactly what that meant as far as how much the younger son might have received from the father by asking for his portion before his father's death is not clear. Obviously it would have been less than the one-third he would have received had he waited until his father died, but how much less? Two-ninths of the estate has been suggested, but that figure is obviously conjecture.

Just as important, as far as the legality of what the younger son proposed, is the right of disposal of the estate. By law, the son could hold title to the property but could not dispose of it since the father would need to live on the property and make a living through it. The younger son, however, not only asked for ownership but also for right of disposal.

For the son to ask for his share of the inheritance was more than a request for independence. It was a confession that he could not live at home. Sons were expected to live at home and work for their father until they married. Then they were expected to work with the father until the father's death. The concept of a son's striking out on his own when he reached a certain age is a concept unique to our culture, not that of Jesus' day and time.

Timothy L. Noel is pastor, Lexington Avenue Baptist Church, Danville, Kentucky.

Sign and clay tablet from the 12th century B.C. describing an inheritance arrangement.

ed with his owner's property. The word for "steward" really means house manager or the overseer of an estate.

A steward who had wasted his owner's goods was called to an accounting, being told that he had lost his position of trust. What could he do? He was not strong enough to do menial toil, and he was too proud to beg. So he decided on a plan to ensure his own future. Going to his owner's debtors, he dishonestly reduced their indebtedness. His purpose was to feather his own nest, reasoning that when he was dismissed from his stewardship those who had benefited by his unjust acts would befriend him in turn. When his owner discovered what he had done, he did not condemn him. Instead he commended him for having acted shrewdly.

It is obvious that if every point of this parable be pressed then one is in difficulty, for it makes Jesus approve of dishonesty. But He was not dealing in details. He was simply drawing a word picture which could have been true to life, and then from that picture He brought forth one great truth. While the man still had control of his owner's goods, which were soon to be taken from him, he used them in such fashion as to ensure his own future.

Jesus' lesson is introduced with one phase: "For the sons of this age are more astute than the sons of light in dealing with their own people" (Luke 16:8). Then He added, "And I tell you, make friends for yourselves by means of the money of unrighteousness, so that when it fails, they may welcome you into eternal dwellings" (Luke 16:9). Man, at best, is but a temporary steward of God's possessions. The time will come when "it" will fail or man through death will no longer have these possessions to manage. In the meantime he should so use them as to ensure for him a welcome into heaven by those who preceded him by virtue of his proper stewardship. There is no thought here of one purchasing salvation, but he can so use material possessions as to enable others to receive eternal life. Here are evangelism and missions at their best. Man can best lay up treasures in heaven by investing them in people who are going there. Man cannot serve God and money, but he can serve God through money or through material wealth.

The Pharisees, being lovers of money, scoffed at the whole idea. So to them Jesus uttered the Parable of the Rich Man and Lazarus. The rich man, living in mirth and splendor every day, was their idea of the better life. His very wealth was to them an evidence of God's approval, but the poor, diseased beggar was to them an object of scorn, one whom they considered to be under God's judgment. However, by a sudden turn of events, Jesus pictured these two men in God's sight. For both of them died or entered into Hades, the abode of the dead; and there the positions were reversed. Lazarus was in Abraham's bosom, a Jewish symbol of heaven, but the rich man was in torment. Note that each entered into his condition immediately upon death.

Furthermore, whereas in this life Lazarus had begged for the crumbs from the rich man's table, now in Hades the rich man begged Abraham to send Lazarus to him to dip his finger in water, just a drop, and with it to cool his parched tongue. But Abraham reminded him that whereas in the world there existed between him and the beggar a social gulf of his own creation, in the afterlife there was also a gulf—one of God's creation. Eternity evened up the inequities of time, only everlastingly so.

Then Jesus made the primary point of His lesson. When the rich man

Thomas: A Brief Biography

Tony Tench

Without doubt, the apostle Thomas is best known as "doubting Thomas." Of course, there is some element of truth in that phrase. Yet, as William Barclay observed, "There is also something very much like a slander" in that description.[1]

Biblical and extra-biblical sources identify Thomas as a loyal and confident disciple of Jesus—an exemplary believer! Such sources describe Thomas as:

An Apostle of our Lord: Thomas is listed among the twelve apostles in each of the synoptic Gospels (Matt. 10:3; Mark 3:18; Luke 6:15) and among the number who gathered in the upper room to select Judas Iscariot's successor in Acts 1. He is also mentioned as a lead player in the dramatic stories of

Village of Bethany on the southeast slope of the Mount of Olives. Here Jesus raised Lazarus from death (John 11:1-46).

found no relief for himself, he requested Abraham to send Lazarus to warn his five brethren not to make the same mistake that he had made. But Abraham reminded him that they had Moses and the prophets. Let them hear them. The rich man said, "'No, father Abraham,' he said. 'But if someone from the dead goes to them, they will repent.' But he told him, 'If they don't listen to Moses and the prophets, they will not be persuaded if someone rises from the dead'" (Luke 16:30–31).

So with consummate skill Jesus drove home His lesson. The Pharisees in their smug complacency refused to heed their Scriptures. The end that awaits them is certain, and they will not even hear Him when He rises from the dead.

After a brief interlude, Jesus spoke to the disciples the Parable of the Unprofitable Servant. Lest they should think that through the right use of their stewardship they could purchase the favor of God, He declared that grace is not for sale. After working all day in the field, a slave is ordered to prepare the evening meal for his owner, but the owner does not thank the slave for doing that which is expected of him. Even so, when a man has done his duty, he should expect no special merit or credit. His only hope is in the grace of God, not in his own servile works.

THE RAISING OF LAZARUS

Suddenly the scene shifts back to Bethany. Lazarus was seriously ill, so Mary and Martha sent a messenger to Jesus in Perea asking Him to come to them. Even though Jesus loved these friends, He delayed going for two days. He knew that soon in Bethany He would glorify God through His greatest miracle and that He also would be glorified thereby, but it would also result finally in Jesus' Crucifixion by which both Father and Son would receive the greatest glory.

When finally Jesus prepared to return to Judea, His disciples warned against it. They remembered the Jews' efforts to stone Jesus, but He reminded them that He would not die before His appointed time. For the moment, "Our friend Lazarus has fallen asleep, but I'm on My way to wake him up" (John 11:11). Seizing upon this thought, the disciples suggested that if Lazarus was sleeping he must be getting better. Jesus plainly said that Lazarus was dead but that He was glad for His disciples' sake because it afforded an occasion to increase their faith in Him. Thomas then rose to heights of heroism when he suggested that if Jesus were going to what the disciples considered to be certain death they should go and die with Him.

When they arrived in Bethany, Lazarus had been buried for four days. Friendly Jews from Jerusalem had come to console the bereaved sisters during the seven days of mourning. As Jesus neared the village, He was met by Martha, but Mary remained in the house. Martha, ever the practi-

John's Gospel (11:16; 14:5; 20:24–28; 21:2).

A Teacher of the Church: Eusebius, the church historian of the third century, wrote that Papias, an early church writer, had recorded the teachings of the apostles. Eusebius quoted Papias:

> If anyone chanced to come who had actually been a follower of the elders, I would inquire as to the discourses of the elders, what Andrew or what Peter said, or what Philip or what Thomas or James or what John or Matthew or any other of the Lord's disciples [had said].[2]

A Missionary for the Lord: Two strands of tradition mark the church's knowledge of Thomas' ministry following the Resurrection of Jesus. The first strand begins with Eusebius' notation that when the disciples decided to which parts of the world they would proceed with the gospel, "Parthia was allotted to Thomas."[3] Parthia was a kingdom that stretched from the Indus to the Tigris rivers and from the Persian Gulf to the Caspian Sea.[4] The second strand takes Thomas beyond Parthia to south India. Sophronius, writing in the sixth century, said that Thomas preached

cal one despite her grief, was in charge of things; but Mary was helpless in her sorrow.

There was a note of both rebuke and faith in Martha's voice when she greeted Jesus: "Lord, if You had been here, my brother wouldn't have died. Yet even now I know that whatever You ask from God, God will give You" (John 11:21–22). Jesus assured her that her brother would rise again, but in her present grief, while it offered comfort in the overall, she still thought in terms of the final resurrection. Then in words which have ever been the pillar of faith upon which bereaved hearts have rested, Jesus said, "I am the resurrection and the life. The one who believes in Me, even if he dies, will live. Everyone who lives and believes in Me will never die—ever. Do you believe this?" (John 11:25–26).

the gospel "to the Parthians, Medes, Persians, Carmanians, Hyrcanians, Bactrians, and Magians and died at Calamina in India."[5] Though the term *India* was used vaguely in the ancient world, in south India there exists a church by the name "Christians of St. Thomas."

When the Portuguese explorer Vasco Da Gama arrived in India in A.D. 1500, he found this church and learned of its mysterious traditions. The church's own account of its origin remembered Thomas preaching the gospel to the natives and baptizing many believers. According to their tradition, Thomas traveled to China with great success, and on his return to India, he was opposed by the Brahmins. A riot was incited against him which resulted in his death at the point of a spear.[6] Other church fathers mentioned Thomas's contribution to the preaching of the gospel in India including Gregory of Nazianzen (A.D. 329–390), Ambrose of Milan (A.D. 333–397), Jerome (A.D. 342–420), and Isidore of Seville (A.D. 560–636).[7]

Personal Identity: The name "Thomas" is the Greek form of the Aramaic word which means "twin." John says that Thomas was known as Didymus (11:16; 20:24;

A Parthian gold ornament. Tradition has it that Thomas took the gospel to the Parthians.

21:2), which is the Greek word for "twin." Because there is an absence of evidence that shows these terms as proper names in the first century,[8] Thomas' actual proper name is unknown to us. In the ancient world first names were given accompanied by a second distinguishing name. Both Thomas and Didymus are distinguishing names ("twin"), thus we may assume that there is another name for Thomas.[9]

If Thomas was a twin and he had another name, why was he called "twin," and can his other name be found? Church historian Eusebius told that Thomas sent Thaddaeus to Edessa. He based this account on a Syriac document he found in the archives of Edessa which reads: "After the Ascension of Jesus, Judas—who is called Thomas—sent to him the apostle Thaddaeus." The name "Judas Thomas" also appears in the Syriac Doctrine of Addai.[10] Thus, some scholars have proposed that Thomas' first name was Judas. If so, why was Judas called "twin"? Such a reference would by implication suggest that his twin was more important than he. No evidence exists that would suggest Thomas was the brother of any of the other disciples. We do not know who Thomas' twin was; any attempt to name his twin

At this point the practical Martha rose to the superlative heights of faith, for she made the greatest confession ever made as to Jesus' Messiahship. Yes, even greater than Peter's. He made his from the exhilarating mountaintop of Jesus' wondrous deeds, but Martha made hers out of the depths of disappointment and despondency. Insofar as she could see at the moment, Jesus had failed her. She had sent for Him in her hour of greatest need, and He had not come. In spite of all of this, despite her lack of understanding, out of her pit of frustration, she still declared, "Yes, Lord, . . . I believe You are the Messiah, the Son of God, who was to come into the world" (John 11:27).

Presently Martha fetched Mary. When she came to Jesus in abject grief, she fell at His feet, saying, "Lord, if You had been here, my brother would not have died!" (John 11:32). But unlike Martha she uttered no note of hope. Jesus then asked to be shown the tomb, and amid all the sounds of grief, Jesus also "burst into tears." He shared the grief of His friends. Truly He was touched with the feelings of their human weakness, but even in such a tender scene unbelief raised its evil head. Some of the Jews questioned why One who had opened eyes of the blind could not have prevented the death of His friend.

By this time they had arrived before the tomb. Martha protested when Jesus ordered that the stone sealing the tomb be rolled away. By this time Lazarus' body had begun to decompose, for he had been dead for four days.

There is significance in this note of time, for according to one Jewish tradition, the soul hovered about the body for three days in hope of reentering it. On the fourth day the soul departed. There is no evidence that Martha believed this, but in all likelihood the unbelieving Jews did. At any rate there must be no question about what Jesus proposed to do. It would seem, therefore, that Jesus had deliberately timed His miraculous act so as to remove any possibility of gainsaying it. Lazarus was truly dead with no earthly hope of living again upon this earth.

Now Jesus thanked the Father for granting the miracle even before it was performed. Absolute faith of the Son in the Father's will and power! Then with a loud voice He cried, "Lazarus, come out!" (John 11:43). And he did so, still bound in the grave clothes in which he had been entombed. There was absolutely no reasonable room for doubters to deny the miracle, and at Jesus' word they unwound the grave clothes, and Lazarus lived again.

Was this a resurrection? Not in the true sense of the word, for Jesus Himself will be the firstfruits out of the realm of the dead. One is resurrected never to die again. Lazarus was raised but would die once more. In truth this was a resuscitation or the bringing back to life of one who truly had been dead. So Jesus is "life" as He is also the "resurrection."

What strange and diverse reactions there were to this miracle! Some

would be speculation.

Thomas' testimony from Scripture reveals a personality to be admired and imitated. Many authors mark Thomas a "pessimist." However, Thomas appears to this writer to be more a realist than a pessimist. Thomas saw the need to proclaim Christ's message in word and in deed even though the resultant danger loomed large. He was a realist. He took Jesus at His word and was prepared to "take up his cross daily."

A review of the biblical references also gives us a picture of Thomas's relationship with Jesus. Though he was not listed among the inner circle of apostles, Thomas was close to Jesus—wholly committed to Jesus as Lord of life. Jesus would later say, "No one has greater love than this, that someone would lay down his life for his friends" (John 15:13). Thomas was ready to go with Jesus to the death in this greatest expression of love (John 11:16). Thomas was comfortable enough with Jesus that he was able to ask questions when no one else would (John 14:5). Thomas desired a personal relationship with Jesus. He was absent from the other disciples when Jesus appeared following the Resurrection. Why was Thomas absent? He may have been grieving! He wanted to be close to Jesus; once Jesus was crucified, Thomas could not bear the pain of his loss. Thomas may have been so caught in the reality of death that he could not believe the words of resurrection. He needed to experience the reality of resurrection (as the other disciples had experienced it before him). As it was before the Crucifixion, Thomas was changed by his personal encounter with the resurrected Lord. His confession of faith ("my Lord and my God") was closer to the heart of Jesus than any other had been.

Thomas, "the twin," was an exemplary disciple because his ambition was to be an earnest follower of Jesus.

¹William Barclay, *The Master's Men* (New York: Abingdon Press, 1959), 47.
²Eusebius, *The Ecclesiastical History and the Martyrs of Palestine* (London: Society for Promoting Christian Knowledge, 1927), III.39.
³Ibid., 1.
⁴Barclay, 51.
⁵Barclay, 51; and F. L. Cross, ed., *Oxford Dictionary of the Christian Church* (London: Oxford University Press, 1958), 1272.
⁶Ibid., 52.
⁷Ronald Brownrigg, *The Twelve Apostles* (New York: MacMillan Publishing Co., 1974), 186–188.
⁸Edgar J. Goodspeed, *The Twelve: The Story of Christ's Apostles* (New York: Holt, Rinehart and Winston, 1957), 43.
⁹Barclay, 47.
¹⁰Brownrigg, 180.

Tony Tench is minister of education and missions, First Baptist Church, Shelby, North Carolina.

who saw it believed in Jesus, but others, unmoved by it, simply hastened to nearby Jerusalem to tattle to the Pharisees about what Jesus had done. Since the Pharisees believed in the resurrection of the dead, one would think that this would have been an occasion for rejoicing. But so blinded were they by their hatred for Jesus, the miracle was lost to them—instead it only called them to diabolic action.

THE APPROACHING PASSION

Apparently Jesus intended that the raising of Lazarus should be a direct challenge to the Jewish authorities, and particularly to the Sadducees who through the high priest controlled the Sanhedrin. On two previous occasions He had raised the dead, but these occurred in Galilee. It was always possible for the Sadducees to discount these reports as the idle tales of an ignorant people, but for Jesus to raise a man from the dead within two miles of Jerusalem and the temple was another matter indeed. How could the chief priests deny this fact when it became common knowledge at the very center of their domain? The people of Jerusalem flocked to nearby Bethany to see this man alive who was known to have died. So when Jesus performed this miracle, He sealed His doom insofar as the Sadducees were concerned. He must be done away with.

Whether the Pharisees alone would ever have put Jesus to death is open to question. On several occasions they had been enraged to the verge of mob violence, but even then they evidently lacked the resoluteness to carry out their evil purpose. They might have argued Jesus to death, but killing Him was another matter. On the other hand the Sadducees were realists. Up until this time they had joined with the Pharisees in opposing Jesus, but it was not until He dared to violate their position of denying the resurrection from the dead that they took charge of the situation with a firm resolve to put Jesus to death.

Therefore, when the Pharisees reported the raising of Lazarus to Caiaphas, the high priest, he immediately called the Sanhedrin into session. One senses their exasperated rage in their words: "What are we going to do since this man does many signs? If we let Him continue in this way, everybody will believe in Him! Then the Romans will come and remove both our place and our nation" (John 11:47–48). They were concerned about their place first, and then their nation. Evidently these words reflected the Sadducees' fears who enjoyed their position of power and wealth under the Romans. And if they did not do something to stop Jesus, they feared a revolution against Rome which to them would result only in defeat for the nation and their removal from power.

Then Caiaphas took charge. In their excited jabbering the Sanhedrin was finding no solution to their problem. So in coldhearted realism this wily politician reminded them that it was expedient that one man should die for, or as a substitute for, the people rather than to have the nation destroyed. He was perfectly willing to sacrifice Jesus to save his own skin, but he spoke more than he knew. Actually he prophesied the very nature of Jesus' forthcoming death. He used the word "for" (*huper*) which means a substitute. It was used of one throwing his own body over another to take the blow intended for him. Jesus Himself had used this word when He spoke of the Good Shepherd dying for the sheep.

So they had the solution. It was either Jesus or them, and they all voted for Jesus to be the Substitute. From that moment they took counsel

A traditional site for Lazarus' tomb.

Lepers in Jesus' Time

Bennie D. Craver

In Jesus' time a leper was a person whom only God could love. Why? We can trace the answer to the way the early Hebrews viewed lepers. The ancestors of Jesus' contemporaries despised lepers because of the physical symptoms associated with the disease. The priest declared lepers to be physically unclean (Lev. 13:3,27,45). Because of their infection, lepers were also ceremonially unclean and cut off from the community's life and worship (Lev. 13:46).[1] A leper's pain was not only a private matter; it was also a public matter.

Scholars disagree over what the biblical designation "leprosy" included. Part of the problem concerns the word used for leprosy in the Bible. The root meant "suffering from a skin eruption, struck with a skin disease."[2] Sometimes the definite article preceded the word for leprosy, and sometimes it did not. The biblical writers did not restrict the term *leprosy* to a specific disease. They applied it to any number of afflictions that resulted in religious and social exclusion.[3] In their minds,

Reinterment funerary inscription of King Uzziah, Israel's king who developed leprosy.

the term *leprosy* was a generic designation more than a specific description.[4]

Leprosy and the Individual

Initial symptoms included the development of tissue-crusts on the skin, a rash, or a whitish-red swollen spot. Any of these could be early warning signs of leprosy. According to the law of Moses, the sufferer was to appear before the priest for examination (Lev. 13:2).

The priest's diagnosis hinged on the extent to which the symptom had affected the skin. If the mark had penetrated the skin and if hair in the infected area had turned white, the priest would conclude that "it is an infection of leprosy" (Lev. 13:3). He would then pronounce the person unclean.

On the other hand, if the infection had not penetrated the skin and if the hair had not turned white, the priest quarantined the individual for seven days (Lev.

among themselves as they plotted His death.

Did Jesus hear about this conspiracy? Whether or not actual news of it came to Him, He knew the response that might be expected to His challenge. So until such time that He was ready for them to carry it out, He left the vicinity of Jerusalem. He planned to return to the city, but together with His disciples He took a roundabout journey which would consume the time until His hour had arrived.

JESUS IN SAMARIA AND GALILEE

The time for the Passover was only a few weeks away. Pilgrims from Galilee would soon be leaving for Jerusalem by the usual route through Perea and thence through Judea to the city. It was probably Jesus' purpose to join such a group. Therefore, He and the Twelve traveled northward out of Judea through Samaria into southern Galilee.

Shortly after arriving in Galilee they entered into a certain village. There Jesus was accosted by ten lepers pleading that He would have mercy on them and heal them. So again, in keeping with the law concerning lepers, Jesus told them to go and show themselves unto the priest. Even though at that moment they had not actually been healed, they had faith to believe that Jesus would comply with their request. They started for the priest, and instantly they were cleansed of the dreaded disease. So eager were they to get the priest to pronounce them healed, nine of them rushed away without even thanking Jesus, but one did turn back, glorifying God as in gratitude he fell upon his face at Jesus' feet. Evidently the nine were Jews, for Luke notes that the one was a Samaritan. In a wistful note Jesus commented on the fact that only this "stranger" or alien had returned to give glory to God. Then He added, "Get up and go on your way. Your faith has made you well" (Luke 17:19). The words "has made you well" may be rendered "has saved you." It would seem, therefore, that whereas the nine received only physical healing, the one Samaritan, in addition also received forgiveness of his sins, the leprosy of the soul.

Some ever-present Pharisees must have witnessed this miracle. Such a display of power prompted them to ask Jesus when the kingdom of God should come. He replied that it does not come through outward observation, for it is not some outward phenomenon, but an inward experience: "The kingdom of God is among you" (Luke 17:21). Then there followed a discourse in which Jesus warned against current errors regarding the coming of the Son of Man. Later, on the Mount of Olives, He repeated much of these same teachings to His disciples.

Why Jesus should suddenly give two parables on prayer is not clear. But He did. One was apparently directed to the Twelve, and the other was aimed at the Pharisees. The disciples were soon to be subjected to great trial. (This may have been the reason for the former parable.) So Jesus "told them a

Colorful Torah covers at the great Jerusalem Synagogue.

Unidentified man on a street in Tel Aviv.

13:4). If during that time degenerative changes occurred, the priest diagnosed the malady as leprosy (Lev. 13:8). If, however, there was no increase in the spot's size, the priest might diagnose another type of skin disease after another seven days' quarantine.[5]

Leprosy and the Community

Physical distress, however, was only one factor complicating the leper's life. Jewish attitude based on their interpretation of the Mosaic law placed greater concern on the leper's ceremonial uncleanness than on the infection of a skin disease.[6]

God expected His people to be holy (Ex. 19:6). The root of the word *holy* can also mean "to be pure, clean" in the sense of physical purity and cleanliness.[7] Anything unclean or unholy drastically affected the community's well-being. Further, God had instructed His people to "make a distinction between the holy and the profane, and between the unclean and the clean" (Lev. 10:10, NASB).

In the Old Testament, there were two kinds of uncleanness. Some references to physical uncleanness resulted in a temporary ceremonial separation (Lev. 15:31). For cleansing and restoration a defiled person needed only to trust God and follow His requirements (Lev. 15:13–15,28–30).

A leper's uncleanness resulted in permanent exclusion from the community (Lev. 13:46). The law required a leper's clothing to be burned (Lev. 13:52) and his house to be demolished (Lev. 14:45). The law also required lepers to behave like mourners. They moved about with torn clothing and unkempt hair. They covered their beards and mustaches and cried out, "Unclean! Unclean!" (Lev. 13:45). Most significantly, a leper's new dwelling place was "outside the camp" (Lev. 13:46). The leper was cut off from spiritual fellowship, without hope and without God.[8]

What insights do these events related to lepers

offer us about Jesus' attitude toward rituals and regulations, the world's outcasts, and the eventual course of His own ministry?

First, Jesus placed divine compassion above religious rituals. Ceremonial uncleanness was of no consequence to Jesus when compared with one who was physically unclean and in need of cleansing or healing (Mark 1:40). Repeatedly the Gospel writers depicted Jesus as unaffected by ritual and the accompanying regulations. To the Jewish leaders of His day, however, Jesus' attitude threatened to subvert the established order. They simply could not condone His actions.[9]

Second, Jesus was compassionate toward society's outcasts. In Him, grace, power, and compassion converge. Like the leper, contemporary outcasts can boldly come to Him (v. 40). Although sin did not contribute to the leper's physical condition, leprosy does seem to symbolize the sin that Jesus alone can cleanse.[10]

Third, Jesus wanted to make clear that His ministry was not primarily related to healing but to redemption from an enemy more devastating than leprosy—sin.[11] Sin separates people from God. Jesus' cleansing touch makes people whole again.

[1] R. K. Harrison, "Leprosy," The New International Dictionary of New Testament Theology, ed. Colin Brown (Grand Rapids: Zondervan Publishing House, 1986), 2:463.
[2] William L. Holladay, A Concise Hebrew and Aramaic Lexicon of the Old Testament (Grand Rapids: William B. Eerdmans Publishing Company, 1971), 310. The word, Holladay noted, "scarcely" refers to leprosy.
[3] R. G. Cochrane, Biblical Leprosy, 2d ed. ([Great Britain]: The Tyndale Press, 1963), 12.
[4] R. K. Harrison, Leviticus: An Introduction and Commentary in Tyndale Old Testament Commentaries (Downers Grove, Illinois: Inter-Varsity Press, 1980), 136.
[5] Harrison, "Leprosy," 2:465. Other types of skin disease included psoriasis, eczema, and acne.
[6] S. G. Browne, "Leprosy: The Christian Attitude," The Expository Times 73:8 (May 1962): 244.
[7] William Gesenius, Gesenius' Hebrew and Chaldee Lexicon to the Old Testament Scriptures, trans. Samuel P. Tregelles (Grand Rapids: Wm. B. Eerdmans Publishing Company, 1949; 1982 reprint), 725.
[8] Harrison, Leviticus, 145; see Ephesians 2:12.
[9] Brooks, 56. Jesus did, however, instruct the leper to show himself to the priest and make an appropriate offering for his cleansing and restoration (v. 44).
[10] Ibid., 55.
[11] Brooks, 56.

Bennie D. Craver is pastor, First Baptist Church, Wimberley, Texas.

Capernaum ruins.

parable on the need for them to pray always and not become discouraged" (Luke 18:1). The word *discouraged* means "to give in to evil, to turn into a coward or lose heart, or to behave badly." Any of these meanings makes sense here. They are warned not to do any of these things, and the following weeks reveal how timely was this exhortation. Instead of doing these things they were to pray.

The following parable emphasized that their prayers would surely be heard of God. A widow continually pleaded with a judge to give her justice against an adversary, and after so long a time, even though the judge neither feared God nor had respect for man, he granted her request merely to get rid of her. Then came the lesson. If such a man will grant a poor, helpless widow's request, how much more will the righteous God give heed to the repeated prayers of His own. However, when the Son of Man comes, will He find such a persistent faith on earth? This is a question for every child of God to ponder.

Then Jesus turned His attention to the Pharisees. Perhaps this latter parable was due to the fact that they had asked about the kingdom of God, and because of their self-righteousness they considered themselves to be a part of it. As for all other men, well, they regarded them as nonentities. Therefore, Jesus paid His respects to the Pharisees.

Two men went into the temple to pray. One was a proud Pharisee; the other was a despised publican. The Pharisee's prayer was a self-congratulatory soliloquy as to his own soul. He recited his many virtues. Though he addressed God in a formal sort of way, his prayer actually was to himself. It contained no fellowship with God. Not a note of repentance was heard. The only sins which he confessed were the sins of others. His only word of praise was thanksgiving that he was not like other men, and especially not like this publican. What a wonderful man this Pharisee considered himself to be. He

Scenes of Jordan River in north looking west just south of Galilee, in the region of Perea.

fasted twice a week, and tithed his entire income—even before taxes! God should be proud to have such a man even deign to pray before Him. One is amazed that in so few words Jesus could sketch so devastating a picture of the self-righteous man.

With equal skill He portrayed the publican. What a sense of unworthiness he had. Not worthy to approach the altar. Not worthy even to lift his eyes heavenward. In utter despair he beat upon his breast and cried out for mercy: "God be merciful to me a sinner" (Luke 18:13). It is actually, "the sinner," as though he were the only sinner in the world. The Pharisee thought of others as sinners; the publican regarded no one as a sinner but himself.

What was the result of these prayers? The publican went home justified or declared just in God's sight. The Pharisee? Well, had not Titus destroyed the temple, his prayer might still be beating an empty echo against its walls. It certainly was not heard of God: "For everyone that exalteth himself shall be abased; and he that humbleth himself shall be exalted" (Luke 18:14).

A QUESTION ABOUT DIVORCE

The time arrived when Jesus began His last journey toward Jerusalem, so in company with the Twelve, and probably other pilgrims, He left Galilee. They crossed the Jordan River and headed south through Perea. Great crowds followed Jesus as He both taught and healed on the way.

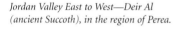

Jordan Valley East to West—Deir Al (ancient Succoth), in the region of Perea.

On one occasion a group of Pharisees came to Him with a knotty question concerning divorce. It was a much debated question among the Jews, and provided a most convenient trap into which they might ensnare Jesus. Their question was, "Is it lawful for a man to divorce his wife on any grounds?" (Matt. 19:3).

To understand this question it is necessary to recall the current teachings on the subject. Among the Jews there were two schools of thought. One teacher, Shammai, taught that divorce and remarriage were permissible only on the one ground of adultery, but another, Hillel, insisted that such was allowable "on any grounds." He based his position on the liberal interpretation of Deuteronomy 24:1—"When a man hath taken a wife, and married her, and it come to pass that she find no favour in his eyes, because he hath found some uncleanness in her: then let him write her a bill of divorcement." This "uncleanness" was indecent behavior short of immorality, but Hillel placed his emphasis upon "find no favour in his eyes." This he interpreted to mean anything which displeased the husband. It might be loss of beauty, boredom in her company, unruly conduct or even burning his meal.

Quite naturally this was the more popular of the two positions. Evidently the Pharisees expected Jesus to reject it, and thus they would discredit Him with the people. But once more He evaded their trap.

In His reply Jesus ignored both schools of thought. He went back to God's original purpose in marriage. In Genesis 1:27 it was recorded that God had made both male and female, and in marriage they became "one flesh." "Therefore what God has joined together, man must not separate"

Document recording the marriage of Ananiah ben Azariah and the handmaiden Tamut.

(Matt. 19:6). By the words "male and female" and "one flesh" Jesus pointed to the physical union in marriage. Of course, the spiritual and social aspects of marriage were implied or assumed, but the matter of "grounds" is the question related to adultery as over against lesser reasons.

The Pharisees, in turn, countered with another question. If no man was to sever the bonds made by God, why did Moses provide for a bill of divorcement? Jesus pointed out that Moses did not command divorce. He simply improved upon the current practice among the ancient Israelites. Prior to his provision a man simply sent his wife away. The lawgiver merely sought to protect the woman's rights, but, even so, Jesus said that he did this because of the hardness of men's hearts. He insisted that this was not God's original intent in the institution of marriage.

Then Jesus said, "Whoever divorces his wife, except for sexual immorality, and marries another, commits adultery" (Matt. 19:9). So in this statement as in the Sermon on the Mount, Jesus clearly allowed one cause for divorce and remarriage. In such a situation the innocent party could remarry, but the guilty one could not.

Some interpreters question the genuineness of the exception in these two passages, but the manuscript evidence is strong for their acceptance. It is objected that Luke 16:18 and Mark 10:11–12 do not include it, but in logic the argument from silence is the weakest of arguments. The question of "grounds" was not in the context of Luke's passage. Nor can it be contended that Mark's statement parallels that in Matthew. In the latter Jesus was answering the question of the Pharisees about "on any grounds," but Mark clearly says that the statement in his Gospel was made to the disciples "in the house" (10:10). Jesus had already dealt with the matter of grounds, and His remark in Mark 10:11–12 must be read in that light. It is even argued that this exception is not genuine because it makes Jesus side with Shammai against Hillel. Why not, if Shammai agreed with Jesus? But Jesus went behind Shammai to the original nature of marriage as given by God in the beginning.

Why did Jesus permit this one cause for divorce and remarriage? In its very nature marriage consists of spiritual love, a social contract and physical union, and in that order. To break a marriage in God's sight it must be in the reverse. One can be "one flesh" with only one person. Paul later warned against becoming one with a harlot (1 Cor. 6:15–16). As long as the oneness of flesh remains, the marriage cannot be broken; but when that basic provision (Gen. 1:27) has been destroyed, the innocent party is free to dissolve the other phases of the marriage relation if he so chooses. So when Jesus gave this one exception, He planted a safeguard to society, the home, the family, and the individual.

Apparently the disciples themselves were in sympathy with the popular view of Hillel, for they said to Jesus that in the light of His words, it is good or expedient not to marry. Jesus replied that for various reasons some are

"Haven't you read," He replied, "that He who created them in the beginning 'made them male and female,' and He also said: 'For this reason a man will leave his father and mother and be joined to his wife, and the two will become one flesh'? So they are no longer two, but one flesh. Therefore what God has joined together, man must not separate."

Matthew 19: 4-6 (HCSB)

not fitted for marriage, but the monogamous marriage is still the ideal for man and woman.

JESUS AND CHILDREN

In the wake of this discussion on marriage and divorce, certain parents brought little children to Jesus that He might put His hands on them and pray, but the disciples rebuked the parents. Maybe this was out of concern for Jesus that He not be unduly burdened. More likely they resented the interruption, since they wanted to hear more on the subject under consideration. At any rate they reflected the current trend to discount the importance of children.

However, Jesus was indignant at their action. By contrast He took the little ones into His arms and blessed them, saying, "Leave the children alone, and don't try to keep them from coming to Me, because the kingdom of heaven is made up of people like this" (Matt. 19:14). It was a brief but beautiful interlude, for Jesus was not only concerned about the home and marriage. He loved and blessed little children who are the crowning blessing of both.

THE RICH YOUNG RULER

While Jesus was still in Perea, a most touching incident occurred. Suddenly out of the crowd a young man ran and kneeled before Him. "Good Teacher, what must I do to inherit eternal life?" (Mark 10:17), asked the young man. His concept of "good" was inadequate. So leading him as a teacher does a pupil, Jesus reminded him that this quality in its absolute sense belongs only to God. By implication Jesus, however, accepted the tribute, for He Himself was/is God.

In reply to the question, Jesus told him to keep the Commandments; and when the young man asked, "Which?" (Matt. 19:18), Jesus quoted the last six, substituting for "covet" its larger sense of love for one's neighbor (Matt. 19:18–19). The young man said that from his childhood he had kept these, yet something was lacking. Then Jesus put His finger on the man's problem—his possessions, for he was wealthy. "If you want to be perfect, . . . go, sell your belongings and give to the poor, and you will have treasure in heaven. Then come, follow Me" (Matt. 19:21).

This should not be construed to mean that to become a Christian one must take the vow of poverty. Jesus was dealing with this man's particular besetting sin, love for his possessions. With another it may be quite a different sin. It is anything which replaces supreme allegiance to God.

When Jesus quoted the Commandments, He mentioned only those which have to do with one's relation to other men. He said nothing of those which relate one directly to God, namely, the first four. This omis-

Augustus denarius. Representative of the money that separates people from God.

sion was by design. The young man made a good score in his dealings with men, but what about his relation to God? Thus Jesus' prescription to him becomes understandable. Unknowingly he had broken the first four commandments by making his wealth his god. So Jesus told him to put this god of mammon out of his life, for no man can be a slave to God and to mammon.

On this score the young man failed the test. He went away sorrowful, but, nevertheless, he went away from Jesus. There was sorrow in the heart of the Savior also, not only for him but for all who trust in their wealth instead of God. For this reason it is difficult, though not impossible, for a rich man to enter into the kingdom of heaven. Jesus said, "It is easier for a camel to go through the eye of a needle than for a rich person to enter the kingdom of God" (Matt. 19:24). This picturesque statement troubled the disciples, for like their contemporaries they regarded wealth as an evidence of God's favor toward a man. If a rich man cannot be saved, "Then who can be saved?" they asked. Jesus replied that while it is impossible for man to enter heaven by virtue of his wealth, it is possible for God so to change his nature that he will give his supreme allegiance and love to God.

This thought of forsaking one's wealth for God suggested another problem to the Twelve. They had forsaken all to follow Jesus. So what would be their reward? Evidently some of them felt that such reward should be gauged by their length of service rendered to Jesus. Those who had followed Him from the first should receive more than those who came later. Jesus reminded them that they would surely be rewarded. However, the terms and degrees of that reward were in the wisdom and grace of the Father. Heaven's standards are different from those of earth. Therefore, "many who are first will be last, and the last first" (Matt. 19:30).

To illustrate this truth Jesus spoke the Parable of the Laborers in the vineyard. Early one morning a man employed laborers for his vineyard. They agreed to work for a denarius, or about seventeen cents, per day. At intervals throughout the day, the man hired other workers, telling them that he would pay them a just wage but specifying no figure. Finally, at the eleventh hour, probably one hour before sundown, he hired still others. To them nothing was said about wages.

The Mosaic Law required that poor laborers should be paid at the end of each day. So when the hour arrived, the owner paid the last group first, and to each he gave a denarius, the same amount that he gave to all of the others. The first group complained bitterly about this. Since they had worked all day in the heat, they felt that they should receive more. But the owner reminded them that they had made a bargain, and he had abided by it, so they had no basis of complaint. The money was his, and he could do with it as he chose. The other laborers had trusted him to deal fairly

Assortment of needles. Iron Age II artifacts. Jesus said it is easier for a camel to go through the eye of a needle than for a rich person to enter the kingdom of God (Matt. 19:24).

with them. The last group said nothing whatever about wages, but if he rewarded their faith in him, that was his business.

The lesson was quite clear. If one chooses to work for God on the basis of rewards, God will keep His bargain. The disciples need not worry at that point, but the fact is that a sovereign God rewards a man on the basis of grace rather than on that of works. That the Bible teaches rewards in heaven is true, but, even so, grace is God's impelling motive. For when the Christian does all that is required of him, he is still an unprofitable servant. He and all that he has belong to God in the first place.

THE REQUEST OF SELFISH AMBITION

The burden of the approaching passion rested ever more heavily upon Jesus. However, as though He were eager to meet it, He walked ahead of His disciples. Every step brought Him closer to Jerusalem and His final "rendezvous with destiny." The Twelve were both amazed and afraid as they noticed the strange look on Jesus' face. Finally He took them aside from the other pilgrims and once again reminded them of that which awaited him in Jerusalem, but strange to say they were still unable to comprehend His words. Despite Jesus' repeated instructions the disciples still thought in terms of a political kingdom.

This fact was quite evident in the request that James and John made to Jesus through their mother. Jesus' words about His coming suffering had been wasted on them, but they had seized upon His recent promise that the Twelve would sit upon twelve thrones to judge the tribes of Israel (Matt. 19:28). So they came to Jesus asking that He should command that these two brothers should sit one on His right hand and the other on His left in His kingdom. They wanted the two chief seats of power.

What was involved in this request? It has been suggested that Peter had been demoted since his rebuke of Jesus near Caesarea Philippi (Matt. 16:22), and so the mother of James and John wanted these principal seats for her sons. However, Peter's demotion is pure conjecture. A more reasonable explanation is possible—Was it not that they sought to gain an advantage because of a family relationship? Since their mothers were sisters, James, John, and Jesus were cousins. So, in effect, this request was a proposal that the seats of power in the coming kingdom should be kept within the family circle. The other ten disciples resented this request. Their resentment probably was not due to the fact that they had made this request at such an inopportune time. For none of them in their present state was fully capable of being sympathetic toward Jesus' passion. It more likely was resentment that James and John had beat them to the request and had sought an unfair advantage because of the family relationship.

What was Jesus' reply to the request? He told them that they were unaware of what they were really asking. Were they able to share the cup which He was to drink or to be baptized with the baptism which awaited Him? These, of course, had reference to His passion, but unaware of this, James and John glibly responded, "We are able" (Matt. 20:22). There was no martyr spirit in their reply. Jesus replied that indeed they would do so, even though at the time they were ignorant of the fact. However, it was not Jesus' prerogative to assign these chief seats. This had already been determined by the Father. And what was the basis of this determination? Not selfish ambition but selfless service.

To illustrate this truth Jesus related a parable. In doing so He contrasted the pagan standards of greatness with those of the kingdom of God. Among the pagan Gentiles their rulers lorded it over their subjects, and their high officials exercised authority over them. But in the kingdom of God one who aspires to greatness must become the most menial servant, and if one would be first in the kingdom, he must become a slave to his brethren. In essence, pagan greatness was determined by the number of people who served a person, but Christian greatness was to be determined by the number of people one served. Jesus Himself is the prime example of the latter, for the Son of man did not come to be served by menial slaves but to render such service to others and to give His life as a ransom for many. Truly the selfish ambition of the disciples appeared all the uglier when it was subjected to the pure light of self-renunciation on the part of Jesus.

THE HEALING OF BLIND BARTIMAEUS

Following this incident Jesus resumed His journey. With His company He traveled across the Jordan River into Judea. They had passed through the old town of Jericho and were nearing the new or Roman Jericho which had been built by Herod the Great. Alongside the road sat two blind beggars, one of them named Bartimaeus. From the crowd accompanying Jesus they heard the name of Jesus, so they began to cry out, "Lord, have mercy on us, Son of David!" (Matt. 20:30). They had heard how Jesus had healed the blind, and so they wished to make the most of their one opportunity. The crowd without mercy sought to silence them, but they simply cried out all the more.

Hearing their cries, Jesus stopped and called them to Him. His own interest in the blind men prompted others to lead them to Him. It was a pathetic moment as Jesus asked what they wished of Him. They had but one request, that they might receive their sight. Therefore, in compassion Jesus touched their eyes, and they saw. What a glorious experience it must have been for them, for the first thing that they saw was the glory of God in the face of Jesus Christ. It is no wonder that they praised God and followed Jesus in the way.

At this point in His journey Jesus was passing through Roman Jericho. This city was not only a tropical winter resort but also an important trading center for balsam and other items. Located as it was near the entrance to Judea from the east, it was a tax-collecting point not only for transient trade but for the local commercial enterprises.

Evidently Zaccheus was the head of tax collections something like a tax commissioner. Under him were other publicans serving in subordinate positions. Quite naturally Zaccheus was a rich man, made so by his oppressive methods of tax collecting, and for this reason he was a hated and despised man among his neighbors.

Zaccheus was also low of stature. He wanted to see this notable man, Jesus, but because of the crowds he was unable to do so. Luke in vivid language says that "he kept on seeking to see Jesus" (19:3, literal translation). He ran from one spot to another trying to find an opening in the crowd, but because of his stature he was unable to locate one through which he might peep. Finally, he ran ahead. He saw a sycamore tree whose low branches made it possible for him to climb into it and to get a vantage point.

When Jesus came to this tree, He looked up at Zaccheus, telling him to come down quickly because He proposed to visit the chief publican in his home. Overjoyed he did as Jesus had said, but as they entered into his house, the crowd became as a hive of buzzing bees. They were shocked that Jesus would enter into the home of so notorious a sinner. The people of Jericho must have been especially indignant, for there probably was not a man among them who had not suffered injustice at Zaccheus' hand.

The publican heard this grumbling. So as soon as he and Jesus were in

Overview of Herod's Winter Palace in NewTestament Jericho.

Larry Douglas Smith

Tax collectors appear frequently in the first three Gospels. Jesus greeted them, visited them in their homes, and joined them in meals. For these associations the Pharisees criticized Him. But both Jesus and His opponents pictured tax collectors as the worst of sinners. This article examines the nature of the Roman taxing system and the status of tax collectors within the Jewish communities of Jesus' day. However, local governments and the Jewish temple collected taxes. So the people paid taxes other than those described in this article.

Roman coins in a bowl.

Those reading the King James Version of the New Testament will note that the Greek word for tax collector (*telones* [te-LOW-nays]) appears as "publican." The word *publican* comes from *public*, here pertaining to the general interest or to government. The tax collectors were public servants.

Our knowledge of the Roman tax system is incomplete. Moreover, Roman tax collection seemed to have been changing during Jesus' life. Hence, our understanding of the publicans is not certain. Some use the term to refer to a small group of wealthy men who lived in Rome and who purchased the right to collect taxes. Others identify as publicans anyone within the tax collecting system. We will follow the practice of modern translations and use the term *tax collectors*.

Jewish political independence came to an end in 63 B.C. when the Roman general Pompey ended a brief period of Jewish independence. As was its common practice, Rome established a series of native leaders in power and attempted to rule and tax indirectly. The most powerful of these was Herod the Great, who was in power at the time of Jesus' birth. Upon Herod's death in 4 B.C., Judea was divided. The

Romans assigned Galilee to his son, usually called Herod Antipas, who governed as tetrarch from 4 B.C. to A.D. 39. He collected taxes for himself and for Rome. He was the immediate political figure in Galilee during Jesus' ministry.

The Roman need for tax revenue was great. Of course, corruption and misappropriation of revenue occurred. However, most of the money went to the many legitimate services provided by the state. Rome governed the entire Mediterranean basin, administering ordinary law and order, suppressing piracy, and defending the frontiers. Building and maintaining roads, temples, and public buildings took a large share of the state income. The Roman Empire was wealthy enough that even with these responsibilities the tax load should not have been too bad. However, the Roman tax system had two major structural flaws.

First, the tax burden was disproportionately placed on the poor who owned land. The members of the Roman Senate received a tax exemption on their large land holdings. The Romans did not trust merchants and what we would call businessmen, so they did not want the government to be dependent on them for taxes. Hence, their tax rate was low. Land was eternal and hence to be taxed—as long as

Imperial tax decrees etched on marble.

nobody important owned it.

The second structural flaw concerned the collection. The responsibility of collecting taxes was auctioned off to the highest bidder. Each bidder, whether an individual or corporation, had to pay the bid, regardless of whether that much was collected in the tax district. Those who did the bidding seldom took direct oversight in the collection process but passed that on to representatives living there. These in turn hired local agents who did the actual work of tax collecting. These local agents had their quotas and could keep overcharges. People could go to court against overcharges, and there were many such cases. However, this was a long and uncertain road for most. Most grumbled and paid. Some fled and abandoned their property. Others rebelled.

Taxes were collected in two principal ways. The first was according to the people and land. Hence, a census was necessary to know how much land and how many people were there to be taxed. This is the type of tax which was auctioned off from Rome. The

Views of Tax Archive (Rom. 13:3) at Caesarea Maritima.

other type of tax was commercial. All sorts of trade was taxed, and tolls were collected for safe passage. Since the tax collectors we meet in the first three Gospels were located in commercial cities, most scholars believe that these New Testament tax collectors were involved in collecting trade taxes from passing merchants. In addition, some evidence exists that by the time of Jesus the land and head taxes were collected by government agents and that only the trade tax was auctioned off to the highest bidder.[1]

Commercial taxes were usually collected along the trade routes, and this is where we find the tax collectors in the Gospels. Tax collectors examined merchandise and collected taxes due the government. Tax collectors could turn to the army to enforce the collection of taxes and could halt the transportation of goods if the collectors were not satisfied that the proper tax had been received. These men worked from crude facilities, sometimes only a table beside the highway.

[1]John E. Stambaugh and David L. Balch, *The New Testament in Its Social Environment* (Philadelphia: The Westminster Press, 1986), 19, 74–75.

Larry Douglas Smith is professor at Southeast Indiana State and adjunct, University of Louisville.

the house, he said, "Look, I'll give half of my possessions to the poor, Lord! And if I have extorted anything from anyone, I'll pay back four times as much!" (Luke 19:8). This was quite a confession of guilt, for the original language assumes that he was guilty of extortion. The Mosaic law required that such a person should return fourfold the amount so taken, and Zaccheus was prepared to do it. This was quite a change of character for him, but in addition he proposed to give half of his wealth to the poor. From a dishonest money-grubber he suddenly became a philanthropist. Such a change could only come from a changed nature.

In response to such evidence Jesus said, "Today salvation has come to this house . . . because he too is a son of Abraham" (Luke 19:9). He was a Jew by birth; he had become a true son of Abraham, the father of the faithful, by the new birth.

Apparently the multitude had stood just outside the house so as to hear the proceedings. Apparently, therefore, Jesus said to them, "For the Son of Man has come to seek and to save the lost" (Luke 19:10). This was Jesus' answer to their grumbling. Thus they could understand His reason for daring to show such a benevolent interest in a despised chief publican, and in so doing not only had He saved a lost man; He had served society as well. Now in place of an extortioner they had a child of God for their commissioner of taxes. This was ever Jesus' method. He proposed to save society by placing redeemed men and women in society, and nowhere is this more clearly seen than in His dealings with Zaccheus.

Furthermore, the work which Jesus did He expects His people to do. This is the sense of the Parable of the Pounds which He related on this occasion. Like the king in the story, Jesus was soon to leave His people. During His absence He will leave His work in the hands of His subjects. They are to use it for His purpose, and eventually there will come a day of reckoning. In keeping with how they attend to affairs, either they will be rewarded or else will be deprived of such. Faithfulness or the lack of it in their task will be evidence as to their true relation to Him. Blessed are they who are His true disciples! Woe upon those who are not!

With this Jesus departed from Jericho, traveling through the wilderness of Judea up the steep and winding road leading to Jerusalem.

A very old Sycamore tree in Jericho.

"O Jerusalem! Jerusalem that kills the prophets and stones those who are sent to her! How often I wanted to gather your children together, as a hen gathers her chicks under her wings, yet you were not willing!"

MATTHEW 23:37 (HCSB)

The Final Public Ministry

Traditional Palm Sunday entry road from Bethany via Mt. of Olives, Gethsemane, and into Jerusalem.

For three and one-half years the drama of divine redemption had been moving toward a grand climax. It was fitting that it should come in Jerusalem, and at what more appropriate time could it have occurred than in connection with the Feast of the Passover? This feast commemorated God's redemption of His people from Egyptian bondage, and that through the slaying of the paschal lamb.

Furthermore, the Passover was the most largely attended of all the feasts. Every male adult Jew living within twenty-five miles of Jerusalem was required to attend. Voluntarily they came from everywhere. No matter where a Jew lived in the world, it was his hope at least one time to celebrate the Passover in Jerusalem. Understandably, Jesus chose such a time for the dramatic finale to His redemptive ministry, for it was the season which involved not only the largest but also the most representative group of Jews which might be assembled in one place.

JESUS' ARRIVAL AT BETHANY

The year was A.D. 30. The season was springtime. The day was Friday before the Passover. Already Jerusalem was alive with pilgrims who had arrived early in order to perform certain purification rites before the Passover began. Among them was one major topic of conversation: Jesus, and whether He would come to this feast. Most people knew that the Jewish rulers had given orders that anyone knowing of His whereabouts should report it to them, for they purposed to head off any crisis by arresting Him on sight.

Jesus arrived in the vicinity on Friday, but instead of going into the city, He stopped at Bethany where He probably spent the night and Saturday with Martha, Mary, and Lazarus. Word soon spread that He was there. Therefore, many people flocked to Bethany not only to see Jesus but Lazarus also. This man whom Jesus had raised from the dead was quite a curiosity, in fact so much so that the chief priests had now determined to

Arab traveler along the Jericho road to Jerusalem with two donkeys.

put him to death along with Jesus. It was their only answer to a fact which they could not deny but would not accept.

THE ROYAL ENTRY

Finally Sunday morning arrived. The time for Jesus' final challenge to Jerusalem and the Jewish rulers was at hand. Jesus' entrance into Jerusalem on this occasion is commonly called His "Triumphal Entry," but as it turned out, it was everything but triumphant. The term "triumphal entry" suggests a king returning triumphantly to his capital city after a war. Such was done in great pomp and splendor with the king riding on a white horse followed by his trophies of victory. Jesus' Triumphal Entry was His arrival back into heaven following His Resurrection and Ascension (Eph. 4:8).

The Lord's entrance into Jerusalem may more appropriately be called His "Royal Entry," for He came as a King of peace. On previous occasions

Hosanna

Linda Oaks Garrett

The clearest use of the term *hosanna* in the Old Testament is found in Psalm 118:25, where it expresses a prayer for God's help. Similar calls for aid are found in Psalms 12:1; 20:9; 28:9; 60:5; and 108:6. The word is made up of two Hebrew terms, *hosha* [hoe shaw], meaning "save" or "help," and *na* [nah], which is a particle, showing the urgency of the need. *Na* could be translated "please." In the original setting of the word, which would have been familiar to the people who acclaimed Jesus' entry into Jerusalem, *hosanna* meant, "Help us, please, Lord."

Psalms 113–118 form a cycle of psalms that originally were chanted at the Feast of Sukkoth, or Tabernacles, and were known as the Hallel psalms.[1] During this festival these psalms would be sung in turn, and "the whole company used sometimes to answer at certain clauses, Halleluia."[2] Palm branches were shaken as the people circled the altar. The psalms were sung or chanted in simple, rhythmic phrases, much like those heard today in Jewish synagogue services or in Christian praise songs. At the Feast of Sukkoth the people called on God to provide the rain needed to support their

Lush green date palms.

The Illustrated Life of Jesus **205**

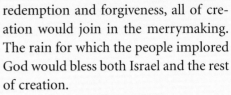

redemption and forgiveness, all of creation would join in the merrymaking. The rain for which the people implored God would bless both Israel and the rest of creation.

During the period of time between the Old and New Testaments, the Sukkoth festival became associated with Hanukkah, which was celebrated in the spring near what later became the Christian Easter holiday.

In 163 B.C. Judas Maccabeus led a Jewish revolt against the Seleucid king Antiochus IV. The Maccabean revolt was incited by Antiochus IV's sacrifice of pigs to pagan gods in the temple at Jerusalem. After the successful rebellion, the temple was cleansed, and the feast of Sukkoth was observed. This revolution allowed the Jewish people a brief time of political and religious freedom.

Hosanna was later chanted at Hanukkah as a slogan, in remembrance of a time when God provided political and religious aid to Israel. Loyal Israelites hoped for a deliverer like Judas Maccabeus who would restore religious purity and political independence.

By Jesus' time the term *hosanna* was connected closely with the idea of a messiah who would lib-

Along the traditional route of the royal entry.

Nicanor Gate.

crops. In this context their cry for help specifically referred to a plea for God to send rain.

The reason for shaking branches derived from an interpretation of Psalm 96:12, which says, "Then shall all the trees of the wood rejoice" (KJV). One ancient rabbi connected the activity of shaking tree limbs with celebration over the exoneration of Israel before God, the Righteous Judge.[3] It was thought that when God came to the people's aid, bringing

erate the people politically and restore the religious dominance Judaism knew in the Maccabean period. Significantly, in the context of Matthew 21, the cries of hosanna occurred just before Jesus cleansed the temple.

After hearing the people's cry for help, which quoted Psalm 118:25, Jesus cleansed the temple. He restored it to a condition in which it could serve as a place of honorable worship.[4] The people's cry implied a desire for Jesus to "be a modern Joshua

He had entered the city quietly and without any show of publicity, and while at those times He had taught and had demonstrated that He was the Son of God, even indirectly had admitted to being the Christ, He had refused to make such a claim "plainly." Now the situation was quite different, for an examination of His entry into Jerusalem on this occasion clearly demonstrates that with deliberate purpose He challenged the city and her religious leaders with the fact that He was their Messiah and King.

Hebrew prophecy taught that when Zion's King came He would not come as a mighty warrior riding upon a white charger. Instead He would come as King of peace, "gentle, and mounted on a donkey, even on a colt, the foal of a beast of burden" (Matt. 21:5; cf. Zech. 9:9). Jesus rode into Jerusalem in such a fashion.

In order to do so He had made definite but secret plans. Knowing the orders of the Jewish rulers about His arrest and being aware one year earlier that one of His own disciples would betray Him, He did not dare to take even the Twelve into His plans. He arranged with a man, probably in

and bring about a national deliverance."[5] They wanted Him to purge both the religious and political impurities from their greatest national symbol.

As is the case with so many other Old Testament concepts, Jesus revealed the true meaning of the people's cry. While most of the people who saw and heard Him did not understand the significance of His life, Jesus fulfilled the people's need for salvation in a way they could not understand until after His Resurrection. With the coming of the Holy Spirit, the church became aware that the salvation Jesus brought was salvation from sin and the freedom and power to live in right relationship to God on the basis of adoption into God's family.

Lighting of the candles at Hanukkah. Hanukkah, also called Feast of Lights or Feast of Dedication (John 10:22), is an eight-day festival that commemorates the cleansing and rededication of the Temple following the victories of Judas Maccabeus in 167/165 B.C.

[1]By Jesus' time it had become customary to sing these psalms "at the private paschal repasts in the homes," Sigmund Mowinckel, *The Psalms in Israel's Worship,* vol. 2, trans. D. R. Ap-Thomas (Nashville: Abingdon Press, 1967) 107.

[2]John Lightfoot, *Matthew—Mark,* vol. 2 in *A Commentary on the New Testament from the Talmud and Hebraica: Matthew—I Corinthians* (Grand Rapids: Baker Book House, 1979), 272.

[3]Ibid., 273. The Rabbi Asher is mentioned.

[4]By the time of Christ, Psalm 118 "was considered a direct prophecy of the coming of Christ" (Eric Werner, "'Hosanna' in the Gospels," *Journal of Biblical Literature* 64.2 [June 1946]: 114).

[5]F. D. Coggan, "Note on the Word [Hosanna]," *Expository Times* 52.2 (November 1940): 77.

Linda Oaks is a Ph.D. graduate of Southwestern Baptist Theological Seminary in New Testament and adjunct instructor in English at Jefferson State Community College, Birmingham, Alabama.

Bethany, to provide the necessary animals. In all likelihood, however, He did not tell the man what use He proposed to make of them. Instead, He arranged a secret sign by which he might recognize those whom Jesus would send for them. The sign was the words, "The Lord needs them" (Matt. 21:3).

So early on Sunday morning He and the Twelve were at Bethphage, a village near Bethany, where they probably had gone to join the multitude of pilgrims headed for Jerusalem. Jesus sent two of His disciples for the animals which were by prearrangement tied in a nearby village. As they were untying the ass and her colt, the owner asked what they were doing. They said, "The Lord needs them," and hearing these words, the man let them take the animals to Jesus.

A street in the old city of Jerusalem. Jesus may have ridden along a street like this as He made his royal entry.

The disciples placed their outer garments on the colt, and Jesus mounted it to ride into Jerusalem. John later reflected that at this point the Twelve did not understand the significance of this (12:16). He probably meant that the full meaning of it was not comprehended until after Jesus' Resurrection, but it is evident that the multitude did see in it a messianic act. They knew the prophecy of Zechariah, so they began to spread their garments in the path of the colt to provide a royal carpet. When the colt had walked over them, they ran and placed them before it again. Others cut branches from the palm trees, and with them did the same. And as they went along with Jesus, they were crying, "Hosanna to the Son of David: Blessed is He that comes in the name of the Lord; Hosanna in the highest" (Matt. 21:9). This showed that they were aware of the meaning of this Royal Entry, for these were messianic proclamations, and Jesus did not stop them.

The Pharisees also recognized the significance of the event. Things had gotten out of hand. Jesus had bested them again. Their plan to arrest Him had been thwarted. It seemed to them that the whole world had gone after Jesus. Therefore, they did the only thing that they could do. They called on Him to stop the whole thing. His only reply was that if He silenced them, the very stones would cry out the same thing, for His hour was approaching, and the machinations of mere men could not delay it.

At this point the procession reached the crest of the Mount of Olives. Before them the city was spread out in all its beauty, a beauty which was crowned by the beautiful Herodian Temple, and seeing it, Jesus burst into tears. Once again He lamented over the fate of the city and nation. He knew that soon they would reject Him. Rebellion was in the hearts of the people. The day would come when it would break out into a consuming conflagration. The Romans would besiege Jerusalem and utterly destroy her. This came to pass in A.D. 70, and all because she knew not the time of her visitation. When she rejected her Prince of Peace, she was doomed in the throes of war.

The procession which went down the mountain was met by one coming out of the city, and the two converged to usher Jesus into Jerusalem. Naturally this demonstration stirred the entire city. People ran from every direction to determine its cause. It is hardly conceivable that the dwellers in Jerusalem did not know Jesus, but the city was overrun with pilgrims from outside Palestine. Probably some of these asked, "Who is this?" (Matt. 21:10). Those about Jesus replied, "This is the prophet Jesus from Nazareth in Galilee!" (Matt. 21:11). It was quite a different answer from what they had been saying on their way into the city. They had clearly proclaimed Him to be the Messiah, but now they called Him "Jesus the prophet of Nazareth of Galilee." They said nothing about the Christ. Instead they called Him a "prophet." Furthermore, they said that He was from the despised village of Nazareth, and the Jewish rulers had said that no prophet came out of Galilee. It was probably out of fear for them that the crowd toned down their answers about Jesus. Everything that the multitude said about Jesus on this occasion was true, but they left unsaid so much more of the truth so as to water down their testimony that it lost its greatest meaning. They missed their greatest opportunity to proclaim Jesus as the Christ.

Jesus went into the temple area where He healed some blind and lame people, but the chief priests and scribes were unmoved by these wondrous works. Some children had been caught up in the spirit of the occasion. Even though their elders feared the rulers, the children were evidently immune to such. For right under the chief priests' noses they were crying, "Hosanna to the Son of David!" (Matt. 21:15). This only added to the rulers' anger. "Do You hear what these children are saying?" (v. 16) they asked Jesus. They wanted it stopped right then, but Jesus only reminded them of the messianic psalm which said, "From the mouths of children and nursing infants You have prepared praise" (8:2). What their elders failed to do these children did. And with this Jesus left Jerusalem and returned to Bethany.

A SECOND CLEANSING OF THE TEMPLE

Early on Monday morning Jesus returned to Jerusalem and to the temple. Entering the Court of the Gentiles, He once again found it filled with the bedlam of a marketplace. Those who sold sacrificial animals and doves and the money-changers were once again doing a land-office business. The Bazaars of Annas were still engaged in profiteering at the expense of the worshipers. Therefore, as at the beginning of His public ministry, so at its close Jesus drove them from the temple. Instead of making God's house a house of prayer, they had turned it into a den of robbers. Like attracts like, and it has even been suggested that thieves were using this sacred place as one where they met to plot their crimes.

Some interpreters insist that there was but one cleansing of the temple and that this is the same incident as the one reported by John at the outset of Jesus' ministry. However, there is no reason to question that this is the latter of two cleansings. In both cases the Messiah declared His authority over the temple.

Following this outburst a quieter atmosphere prevailed as Jesus continued to teach in the temple area. However, when word of His authoritative action reached the chief priests, they plotted all the more how they might destroy Him. Their initial plans had gone awry, since the people hung on Jesus' every word, but the rulers plotted and waited for the opportune moment to carry out their nefarious purpose.

Sometime during the day on Monday, an incident occurred which deeply disturbed Jesus. Some Greeks had come to Jerusalem for the Passover. They were probably God-fearers, Greeks who were studying Judaism but who had not yet accepted it as their religion. No doubt they had heard about Jesus, and learning that He was in Jerusalem, they wanted to see Him. So approaching Him they said to Philip, one of His disciples, "Sir, we want to see Jesus" (John 12:21). Philip told Andrew, and together they relayed the request to Jesus Himself.

Upon hearing that they wished to interview Him, Jesus was deeply moved in His spirit. He had previously said that His fold would contain "other

The Temple in Jesus' Day

George W. Knight

On the last Monday of His life, Jesus of Nazareth visited the temple of Jerusalem with His apostles and found there a scene of holiday activity in anticipation of the impending Passover celebration. Mark gave more detail in this account than either Matthew or Luke. Mark said Jesus halted all forms of selling and stopped the traffic through the temple precinct. He explained that the purpose and intent for the temple was to be a "house of prayer for all nations," and its purpose had been perverted to another function as a "den of robbers." The emphasis here is not on the honesty or dishonesty of the merchants but on the concept that the temple had become viewed as a safe haven for Israelites regardless of their behavior. Jesus challenged both

The model of the colonnaded court area of the temple.

their misuse of the temple and the reassignment of the Gentiles' prayer place for use as a marketplace. How did Israel come to this point, and how had this place of worship come to be considered a place to be managed for such an unworthy purpose?

The temple of Jerusalem where Jesus encountered the merchants stood in a long tradition of Jewish worship of their God. Their response to God's presence had its beginning in open-air worship sites such as the oaks of Mamre (Abraham, Gen.13:18) and Bethel (Jacob, Gen. 28:18–22). Later in Old Testament history portable worship shrines were used to demonstrate God's presence with the people of Israel, including the tabernacle and the tent of meeting. With the advent of the monarchy came the permanent structure that identified a centralized location to define God's presence and provide a place for people to worship Him.

When David built himself a house, he then proposed to build one for God. That was not to be, but he did provide the means for his son Solomon to carry out this dream and build the first temple for the Jewish people in Jerusalem. The design of the temple is described in some detail in 1 Kings 6–8 and 2 Chronicles 2–4. The location of the temple is described as Mount Moriah, on the threshing floor of Araunah the Jebusite where the Lord had appeared to David. This site is also identified with Abraham's offering of Isaac. The more common name of the place is Mount Zion or Ophel, the eastern hill facing the Mount of Olives across Kidron. The temple building was part of a larger complex of courts and supported buildings that continued to multiply in succeeding centuries.

The temple building itself appears to have been considered by the people to be God's dwelling place, and it was often called "the house of Yahweh." The design of the temple appears to carry out that view, reflected in the division of the structure into several rooms, with each progressing closer to the most holy presence of God. The dimensions of Solomon's building began with a porch as an entry that was open to the

A model of the Antonia fortress near the temple.

courtyard. It was ten cubits long, twenty cubits wide, and thirty cubits high.[1] In current measurements the entryway was fifteen feet long, thirty feet wide, and forty-five feet high.

The interior of the building was divided into two rooms, the first of which was larger and was the location of much of the worship activity. This

Robinson's arch in Jerusalem, an arch that supported a stairway from the temple platform down in Tyropoeon Valley.

main room was called *hekal*, a term that refers to a large or palatial dwelling and often to a king's residence. It came to be used to refer to a temple because the building was often considered the place where the deity lived on earth. In Solomon's temple then, this room was the holy place where God's presence was worshiped. It was sixty feet long, thirty feet wide, and forty-five feet high. It is described as having windows on both sides. The walls were covered with carved cedar wood depicting plants and flowers, and the floor was covered with gold. Entry into this room was through fifteen-feet-wide gold-covered cypress-paneled doors. The rituals of worship required several items of furniture. Located in this room were the incense altar, ten lampstands arranged five on the north side and five on the south side, and the table for the bread of the Presence, all covered with gold.

The final room was called the *debir* or the inner sanctuary, the holy of holies. It was in the shape of a cube thirty feet on each side and thirty feet high with the walls and floor overlaid with gold. The doors were gold-covered carved olive wood. Inside this room was only the ark of the covenant flanked by two fifteen-feet-tall gold-covered cherubim hovering wing tip to wing tip and wall to wall over the ark. Outside the two main rooms were storerooms arranged three-stories high with thirty rooms to a floor. The height of these rooms was about one-half of the temple and did not block off the windows of

the hekal. They served as storage and other support functions for the services.

The temple building was surrounded by courts where other worship activities took place. These are variously described and contained objects necessary for the rituals. Just in front of the entrance of the porch stood two bronze pillars almost thirty-five feet tall. The significance of these structures has been lost although their names, Boaz on the north and Jachin on the south, have been retained in the accounts. In the northeast part of the court was located a bronze altar for sacrifice thirty feet square and fifteen feet high.[2] Across the court on the southeast side was a "bronze sea," a basin fifteen feet in diameter and more than seven feet high, resting on four groups of three oxen that were facing outward to the north, south, east, and west. This served the purpose of washing and purifying. The other items were ten portable basins about six feet in diameter mounted on wheels. The basins had a capacity of about 250 gallons of water, which was used for purification of sacrifices.

Solomon's temple served to remind the people of Yahweh's presence among them. Although they did not generally think of God as limited to this particular place, this temple nonetheless provided them a place and opportunity for access to Him. It also served to centralize the worship of the people and to legitimate the monarchy. The history of Solomon's temple is checkered with devotion and abuse as his temple was plundered by foreign powers, such as Shishak of Egypt in 1 Kings 14:25-26, and their own kings, such as Joash who carried out repairs on the temple but later plundered its gold to buy off Hazael (2 Kings 12). This complex was destroyed by Babylonian King Nebuchadnezzar in

sheep" than Jews (John 10:16). Apparently in these Greeks He saw the promise of the multitude of Gentiles who would believe upon Him, and this realization brought down upon Him an increasing burden of His passion. His predestined hour truly was rapidly approaching. For only through His death on the cross could Greeks be brought to Him with full understanding of His saving work and power. So using the figure of a grain of wheat, Jesus described His own alternative. An unplanted grain could bear no fruit. It would abide by itself alone. Only as it fell into the earth and died to its own self could it bear a harvest. Even so, if Jesus saved His own life, He would defeat the purpose of His Incarnation. He would bear no fruit. To save a lost world He Himself must die.

In this disturbed state Jesus communed within His own spirit. The "hour" was before Him. He had anticipated it from the beginning, but now that He faced it, what should He say? "Father, save me from this hour" (John 12:27). What did He mean by this statement? Was it a prayer for deliverance from the cross? Or was it a soliloquy within His soul? It

587/586 B.C. The destruction of this temple caused a sense of grief and loss that shaped the nation for all time and provided an ideal for temple, nation, and city that may have never existed in history but only in the hope for the future of God's people.

The return from Exile allowed the people to rebuild the temple; and although the process was erratic and lengthy, it was completed in 515 B.C. This so-called temple of Zerubbabel was apparently much less impressive than the memory of Solomon's complex, and its history was marked as much by neglect and abuse as honor and pride of the people. It was not as ornate in decoration, nor did it have much of the furniture found in the earlier one. The holy place had only one seven-branched lampstand, and the door to the holy of holies had been replaced by a veil. More depressing for the people was the empty holy shrine that was missing the cherubim and, most important, the ark of the covenant. Noteworthy of abuse was the terrible desecration of the temple by Antiochus Epiphanes in 167 B.C. when a pig was sacrificed to Zeus on the altar. This "abomination of desolation" stood out in the religious history of the people, and its reparation is still celebrated in the Hanukkah festival. This second temple did not have the acclaim, nor is it commemorated in Jewish history as was the former temple of Solomon or the later temple of Herod; but interestingly, it was in use and served the religious purposes of the people longer than the other two

structures together, being used from 515 until 20 B.C.

Customarily, the third Jewish temple is included in the "second temple period"; but the complex constructed under the instigation of Herod the Great was an entirely different, larger, and grander structure than the previous one. As a part of his campaign to impress and obligate folk to him, Herod the Great undertook many enormous building projects, including the port of Caesarea Maritima and the fortress of Masada. However, nothing else approached the undertaking of building a new temple for the Jews in Jerusalem beginning in 20 B.C. In order for the structure to achieve Herod's purposes, it had to be large. To accomplish that primary goal, the entire mountain was extended.[3] The expansion of the area was achieved by building huge retaining walls to the east over the slopes of the Kidron and to the west into the Tyropoeon Valley. These walls were, in places, more than eighty feet high and sat on foundations some fifty feet deep. The area was then filled in and paved over, making an area of more than thirty-five acres upon which to build the new complex.

The plan of the new complex had the temple proper located to the western part of the area facing the east and enclosed in a series of terraces and walls. The interior dimensions of the building appear to have been left much as the previous structures with the *hekal* being sixty feet long and thirty feet wide while the *debir* remained thirty feet by thirty feet, although it appears that the height increased

depends upon how one punctuates it. If it ends in a period or a colon, then it becomes a prayer. But if it be ended with a question mark, it becomes a soliloquy. There is some manuscript evidence for either, but the context seems to favor the latter. Thus Jesus very likely did not pray to escape the cross. Instead He said, "What should I say—Father, save me from this hour? [Shall I say that?] But that is why I came to this hour. Father, glorify Your name!" (John 12:27–28). Not for one moment did Jesus seek to escape death! As will be seen later, even in Gethsemane His prayer related to something else.

His prayer to glorify God's name received an immediate answer. The people heard a noise, and some thought that it had thundered. Others said that an angel spoke to Jesus, but He, ever attuned to the Father's will, heard His voice: "I have glorified it, and I will glorify it again" (John 12:28). That Jesus did not pray to escape the cross is seen in the fact that He said that this voice came not for His sake but for the sake of the people. The crisis or judgment of this world is at hand. Within a few days it would receive the supreme test relative to Jesus, and Satan, who claimed world sovereignty, would see that claim refuted. For Christ being lifted up on the cross will draw all men unto Himself.

Once again the people were divided over Jesus. Some reminded Him that their Scriptures taught that Christ would abide forever. Now He was talking about being "lifted up," which they understood to mean His death. They asked Him to identify this "Son of man" who would be lifted up, but the light was gradually breaking through to some of them, for even some of the rulers (Nicodemus and Joseph of Arimathea?) believed on Him. However, out of fear of the Pharisees they continued to remain silent about their faith, for as yet they loved the glory of men more than they did the glory of God.

THE BARREN FIG TREE

During the early part of Passion Week, Jesus was in Jerusalem during the daytime; but His nights were spent outside the city, probably in the home of His friends in Bethany. On Monday morning about daybreak He and the Twelve were on their way back into the city. This was the hour of the first meal of the day among the Jews. It appears that they left Bethany before breakfast, and so they were hungry. Seeing a fig tree in full leaf, Jesus came to it expecting to find some figs with which to satisfy His hunger. According to Mosaic Law it was permissible for a passerby to pluck figs from another's tree in order to relieve his hunger, but Jesus found no figs.

A fig tree bears two crops each year. In Palestine the former comes in June, and the latter comes in September, but a unique thing about fig trees is that the fruit begins to form before the leaves appear. When the leaves are full, one expects to find figs. Now obviously, since this incident occurred in April, it was before the normal season for ripened figs, but

to ninety feet. The porch was described by Josephus as measuring 150 feet high and 150 feet wide, all covered with gold that reflected the sun so brightly that a person could not look directly upon it. The furniture of the holy place was the same as Zerubbabel's, and the holy of holies remained empty, still separated by a veil. Directly in front of the building was now an altar of burnt sacrifice measuring seventy-five feet square.

Several different plans of the arrangement of the courts in the temple have been suggested over the last century because the sources are unclear and at points contradictory.[4] Although the details are difficult to explicate, the overall understanding of the relationship of the courts to the temple proper is rather clear. Around the sanctuary and in front was the court of the priests. Beyond that was the court of Israel, which was limited to Jewish men. A semicircular set of stairs led down to another level that was occupied by the Court of Women, as close to the sanctuary and altar as Jewish women could go. From this terrace apparently there were stairs that led down to the next level. Entry to these stairs and thus the court was protected by a stone partition four and one-half feet high that had inscribed on it warnings in Greek and Latin prohibiting Gentiles from entering. Beyond this partition was the Court of Gentiles, which was

here was a tree ahead of the season as seen by its leaves. However, it had no fruit. So finding none, Jesus cursed the tree, saying, "May no fruit ever come from you again!" (Matt. 21:19). And the tree began to wither.

Herein lies a difficulty. Why did Jesus perform a destructive miracle? Furthermore, why did He curse a fruitless tree before the normal season for such fruit? However, the point in this incident is that the tree gave evidence of fruit yet produced none. It was promise without performance. It is generally agreed that this was an acted parable. The tree was symbolic of the Jewish nation. With all of its religious pretensions, it was bearing no fruit in God's purpose. Therefore, because of its promise without performance, it too was under the condemnation of God. Within a generation it would wither away as did the fig tree.

This thought gives meaning to the sequel to this event, for on Tuesday morning, as they were again going into the city, the disciples called Jesus' attention to the withered fig tree. He exhorted them to have faith in God. If so, they could say to "this mountain" for it to be taken up and cast into

a large part of the temple enclosure and was accessible to all people. In Mark 11 Jesus referred to this area as having become used as a marketplace and otherwise unsuitable for worship. By Jesus' time the rest of the temple platform included many other structures that added to the impressive complex. Inside the walls there were porticoes with colonnaded walkways, the best known of which is the Royal Porch or Portico of Solomon. It was located on the southern side and apparently served many purposes, including a business center, a place for exchange, and perhaps the meeting place for the Sanhedrin. Many gates were located in the walls and archaeological investigation has established a magnificent entry from the south up a monumental staircase that led into the two Huldah gates through underground passages that brought visitors into the temple court from below. One gate led through the western wall over a viaduct into the upper city, and another led through the southwestern part of the wall down a huge staircase that turned into the Tyropoean Valley. Another famous gate was the main gate in the eastern wall that led into the Kidron Valley and thus to Bethany. One other feature requiring mention was the Antonia fortress at the northwest corner of the temple that housed Roman soldiers and some Roman government offices. The entire complex was destroyed along with the city by the Roman general Titus in A.D. 70.

Herod's temple, the temple of Jesus' day, was a huge and magnificent structure, a wonder of the ancient world. It was an architectural marvel of overwhelming proportions that called attention not only to Jerusalem as the place where the Jewish people carried out their rituals of sacrifice but also to Herod the Great as the builder. In Mark 11 Jesus called for the temple to be a place of worship and a place for all nations because He came to seek and save those who were lost. While He began in Jerusalem and Judea, He pointed the disciples to the ends of the earth.

[1] The measurement for the cubit will be considered 18 inches although Carol Meyers has suggested 20.9 inches as the royal cubit and the one used in 1 Kings. However, for this article the conversion of the Old Testament dimensions will be into feet based on one and one-half feet per cubit. See Carol Meyers, "Temple, Jerusalem" in *The Anchor Bible Dictionary* (New York: Doubleday 1992), 6:356–7.
[2] This altar is not in the description of the temple in 1 Kings but is in the parallel passage in 2 Chronicles 4:1 and may be assumed in later statements in 1 Kings; for example, 8:64 and perhaps 9:25.
[3] The major primary source for this information is the first-century writer Flavius Josephus. He devoted a portion of *Antiquities* 8:3:6–9 and *Wars of the Jews* 1:7:6 to a detailed description of the temple and its construction. Josephus is accused of exaggeration in some of his descriptions, but his overall reports are of value in understanding the temple of Jesus' day.
[4] See for example, W. F. Steinspring, "Temple, Jerusalem," *Interpreter's Dictionary of the Bible*, ed. George A. Buttrick (Nashville: Abingdon Press, 1962), 4:534–60. See 4:556 for the suggestion by Vincent-Steve and page 558 for the attempt by Schick. Another possibility is given in Alfred Edersheim, *The Temple*, rev. and ill. with introduction by John J. Bimson (Grand Rapids: Kregel, 1997), 31.

George W. Knight is Cook-Derrick Professor of New Testament and Greek, Hardin-Simmons University, Abilene, Texas.

the sea, and it would be done (Matt. 21:21). Then there followed Jesus' assurance that believing prayer would surely be answered.

Did this mean that by faith the disciples could literally remove mountains? If so, it is strange that Jesus Himself never did this. More likely Jesus spoke in hyperbole. What was "this mountain"? Could it be Mount Moriah, the mountain on which stood the Temple, the symbol of Jewish religious power? If so, then the symbolic meaning of the barren fig tree is continued. The Temple and its power will fall. This obstacle to the progress of the kingdom of God will be utterly removed, and if Jesus' followers have faith in God, in both prayer and effort, they will see all other obstacles to the ongoing of the kingdom of God removed as they go from victory unto victory. It was a glorious promise then and throughout the ages.

A DAY OF CONTROVERSY

The time was Tuesday of Passion Week. The place was the court of the temple. It marked the close of Jesus' public ministry other than His words and deeds at the trial and Crucifixion, and significantly it occurred in the temple. In all likelihood, since this day of controversy ended in the Court of the Women in which were placed the treasury receptacles, it was in this court that the day of controversy occurred.

Since His royal entry Jesus had been the hero of the multitudes. Therefore, if the Jewish rulers were to accomplish their evil purpose concerning Him, it was necessary that they should discredit Him before the people. So one by one different groups of them confronted Jesus with situations which were designed to do so. In each case they posed a question for Him to answer.

1. The Question of Authority.

The first groups to challenge Jesus were the chief priests and scribes. They asked Him by what authority He dared to teach. According to their system they were in their rights to raise this question. For one to be an authorized rabbi, he must have been taught in one of their schools or by some accredited rabbi, and he should be authorized by the rabbi, a group of rabbis or by the Sanhedrin. The rulers knew that they had not so authorized Jesus. Therefore, they asked Him to name the person or group who had given to Him this authority.

Jesus countered with His own question, which, if they would answer, He,

A fig tree in Bethphage in early May 1994 soon after the local celebration of Easter. This suggests the normal stage of fruit development at the time of year Jesus' Crucifixion took place.

in turn, would answer theirs. Was the baptism of John the Baptist from heaven or from men? In effect, under whose authority did he do his work? The rulers saw immediately that Jesus had turned the tables on them. If they said "from heaven," then He would ask why they had not followed John. They were afraid to say "from men" because the people regarded John as a prophet. So they sought refuge in agnosticism, saying, "We don't know" (Matt. 21:27). Thus they admitted that they were incapable of judging a man's authority. If they did not know about John, how could they sit in judgment on Jesus? Therefore, Jesus refused to tell them the source of His authority.

But the effect of this encounter was to suggest that Jesus' authority was from heaven. At least this was the result with the multitudes, for they regarded John's authority as being from God. John had baptized Jesus and had heralded Him as the Christ. So if the Jewish rulers or the people were consistent, they must reckon John as the only possible man who could have authorized Jesus for His work. Therefore, in the minds of the people, His authority must ultimately be regarded as being from heaven itself. Rather than to discredit Jesus with them, the rulers only served to consolidate His hold on the multitude. However, He did not let the matter end there. Instead, in three parables He condemned the Jewish rulers and scribes before the people and in God's eternal purpose.

The first parable concerned the attitudes of two sons. Their father told them to go and work in his vineyard. One son refused, but later he regretted his decision and went and did as his father had said. The other readily agreed to go, but he did not do as he agreed. Then Jesus asked, "Which of the two did his father's will?" (Matt. 21:31). The rulers gave the only obvious answer, the first. Jesus then continued, "I assure you: Tax collectors and prostitutes are entering the kingdom of God before you! For John came to you in the way of righteousness, and you didn't believe him. Tax collectors and prostitutes did believe him, but you, when you saw it, didn't change your mind later to believe him" (Matt. 21:31–32). To place publicans and harlots before these self-righteous religious leaders was to them a bitter dose indeed, and they might well have wanted to break off the debate at this point. But Jesus was not through. Not only did they reject John—they were even then planning to kill Him, and so He compounded the first parable with another.

A certain man planted a vineyard. He prepared it with the greatest of care. He planted a hedge fence about it, made a winepress, and fortified it with a watchtower. Then he rented it to some husbandmen and went away to a distant land. (Jesus' listeners probably recalled Isa. 5.) When the time for grapes was drawing near, he sent various servants to collect his rent, but the husbandmen beat one, killed another, and stoned still another. The owner sent other servants with the same results. Finally, he sent his son, thinking that the husbandmen would honor him in his request. Instead they reasoned that if they killed him, the heir, they would be able to keep the vineyard for themselves. So they killed him.

Then Jesus drew the lesson. He asked the Jewish leaders what the owner of the vineyard would do to these wicked men. Again they gave the obvious answer. He would miserably destroy them and rent out his vineyard to those who would render to him the fruits of it. Jesus asked if they had never read in the Scriptures, "The stone that the builders rejected, this has become the cornerstone. This cornerstone came from the Lord, and is wonderful in our eyes" (Matt. 21:42; cf. Ps. 118:22–23). And then the roof fell in on these rulers, for Jesus said, "Therefore I tell you, the kingdom of God will be taken away from you and given to a nation producing its fruit" (Matt. 21:43).

Contemporary Jewish men praying at the Western Wall at Jerusalem. They wear phylacteries.

Thus He ended the covenant of service which God had made with Israel (Ex. 19). Repeatedly God had sent His servants to call her to honor this covenant, but she had refused, mistreating and killing those whom God had sent. Soon they will kill His Son. God rejected them only after they had completely rejected Him and refused to honor the conditions of the covenant. He, therefore, was under no obligation to fulfill its promise to Israel. Later Peter will show, in language which employs the terminology of both Exodus 19 and Matthew 21, that this new "nation" is the Christian people (cf. 1 Pet. 2:4–10).

The chief priests and Pharisees got the point, for "they knew He was speaking about them" (Matt. 21:45) and through them to the nation which they represented. If it wasn't for their fear of the multitude, they would have arrested Jesus on the spot.

However, Jesus not only stood His ground; He attacked again. This time He related the parable of the king's marriage feast for his son. The details were similar to the previous parable of the king's supper (Luke 14:15ff.), but the point of this new parable was that when one guest showed up at the marriage feast without the proper wedding garment he was cast into outer darkness. The lesson is that the Father is preparing a marriage feast for His Son as He takes unto Himself His bride, the Church, but these self-righteous people will be no part of it. They came clothed in their own righteousness and not in the righteousness of God in Christ Jesus.

2. A Question about Tribute.

The first skirmish was over. While the chief priests and scribes retreated in disorder, the Pharisees sent some of their prize students, together with some Herodians, to try their hand against Jesus. (Note how these various groups had merged in their common cause.) However, on at least one point the Pharisees and Herodians were in agreement—they were both opposed to paying taxes to the Romans. Therefore, they asked Jesus, "Tell us, therefore, what you think. Is it lawful to pay taxes to Caesar or not?" (Matt. 22:17).

This was one of those loaded questions designed to condemn one no matter how he answered it. Had Jesus said, "No," they would have accused Him of treason against Rome. Had He said, "Yes," they would have charged Him with treason against His own people. This position most certainly would have offended most of the Jews, but there was a deeper and subtler element involved. For had Jesus counseled paying Roman taxes, to the Jews it would have been a virtual denial of His messianic claims, because they said that the Messiah, being a King Himself, would not countenance the payment of taxes to another king.

However, Jesus evaded all of these pitfalls. He asked them to show Him the tribute money. Note that He asked them for it. Roman taxes could be paid only in Roman coins. The very fact that these Pharisees and Herodians had such a coin indicated that they were subservient to and dependent upon Rome. Furthermore, on one side of the coin was the

Tiberius denarius. The coin that Jesus saw when He asked whose likeness was on it and then said to give back to Caesar the things that are Caesar's and to God what is God's (Matt 22:17-22).

image of Tiberius Caesar; the other side bore his superscription. When Jesus asked His questioners to identify these, they said, "Caesar's." Then He said, "Give back to Caesar the things that are Caesar's, and to God the things that are God's" (Matt. 22:21). A man has obligations to both and should honor them each in its own sphere. Not only did Jesus answer His immediate questioners—He also spoke the words which have become the fountainhead of the principle of separation between Church and State.

The Pharisees and Herodians made no reply. They heard it, wondered about it, left Jesus, and went their way, but they left Jesus still in command of the field.

3. A Question about the Resurrection.

It was the Sadducees' or chief priests' turn again. They did not believe in the resurrection, and so they asked Jesus to solve a problem, probably one of their favorites in their continuing debate with the Pharisees.

Here was their problem. Moses had commanded that if a man died childless his brother should marry his widow and thereby raise up seed unto his brother. Now the Sadducees imagined a case in which there were seven brothers. The first died childless. Then the other six in turn married the widow, each of them also dying without having a child. Finally, the woman herself died. In the resurrection whose wife would she be?

Jesus answered their question by reminding them that they did not even understand their own Scriptures; neither did they know the power of God, for in the resurrection there is no such thing as the institution of marriage. All will be one big family of God.

Now did Jesus let them get away with their denial of the resurrection? He cited God's own words, "I *am* the God of Abraham and the God of Isaac and the God of Jacob" (Matt. 22:32). He did not say, "I was" but "I am." These three patriarchs still lived. So God is not the God of the dead, but of the living.

The Sadducees were silent, but the people were astonished at Jesus' teaching. Naturally the Sadducees were unhappy, but there were some happy people in the crowd. For the scribes (Pharisees) said, "Teacher, You have spoken well" (Luke 20:39). Even if they could not get the better of Jesus, at least He had put the Sadducees in their place, because they did not dare to ask Him any more questions.

4. A Question about Law.

Now the Pharisees must try their hand again. This time they sent one of their experts in the Mosaic Law. He asked Jesus, "Teacher, which commandment in the law is the greatest?" (Matt. 22:36). Or as Mark relates it, "Which commandment is the most important of all?" (12:28). Jesus answered with the words which were dear to every Jewish heart. He quoted the *Shema* (Deut. 6:4–5): "Hear, O Israel! The Lord our God is one Lord. And you shall love the Lord your God with all your heart, with all your soul, with all your mind, and with all your strength. . . . You shall love your neighbor as yourself" (Mark 12:29–31). On these, said Jesus, hang all the law and the prophets. The lawyer could only compliment Jesus for His answer. In turn Jesus said of the lawyer that he was not far from the kingdom of God. Not far—but not in. It is to be hoped that he did enter the kingdom of God, not through compliments but by faith in Jesus.

5. A Question about Christ.

It was now Jesus' turn to ask the Pharisees a question, and it concerned their opinion about the Christ: "What do you think about the Messiah?

A seat of judgment possibly from a Jewish synagogue. Jesus said, "The scribes and the Pharisees are seated in the chair of Moses" (Matt. 23:2).

Whose Son is He?" (Matt. 22:42). They replied that He is the son of David. Jesus quoted from the Messianic Psalm 110:1—"The Lord said to my Lord, 'Sit at My right hand until I put Your enemies under Your feet.'" Then He asked that if the Christ were his Son, how was it that David called Him his Lord? The Pharisees had no answer for this. Neither did they dare to ask Jesus any other questions. The Teacher had completely silenced His critics.

6. Jesus' Last Public Discourse.

Jesus then turned to the multitude and to His disciples. He recognized that the scribes and Pharisees sat in Moses' seat. They were the accredited teachers of the Jews. Insofar as they really sat in Moses' seat or taught in accord with Moses' Law, they were to be reverenced and followed. But the people were to beware of the multiplicity of rote rules which they devised, and especially of their own example in them, for they said but did not. They could always find ways to circumvent their own teachings. Furthermore, they laid heavy and grievous burdens on the people but did not even extend their fingers to help them to bear the burdens. They were good at prescribing, but they could not impart the power to enable their patients to live up to the prescription. Their only purpose was to impress others with their piety and to gain recognition for themselves. They unduly broadened their phylacteries and enlarged the hem of their garments in order to appear more pious than others. They loved the prominent place at the feasts and the chief seats in the synagogues. It was music in their ears to be greeted in public places and especially to be called rabbi, or "my great one" or "master."

Therefore, Jesus warned the people, and especially the disciples, against such vainglory. If someone called them "rabbi," that was one thing, but they were not to seek the title. One Jewish teacher said of this office that "men should love the work, but hate the rabbi-ship," but Jesus said that among His people there should be the equality of "brethren." Neither should they call any man their father or the source of their spiritual being. Only God is such. Nor should they set themselves up as supreme spiritual authorities, for this authority belonged only to Christ. If any one of them aspired to greatness, he should become a menial servant to others.

Then from warning the crowd and His disciples, Jesus turned upon the Pharisees, and in seven "woes" He excoriated them with the most merciless words which ever came from His lips (Matt. 23:13,15–36). They are all the more terrible since they came from Him who is the very essence of mercy itself. From the beginning the Pharisees had rejected and opposed Jesus, and they had stood as a barrier to others who would otherwise have believed in Him. His words were God's judgment upon them and their empty religious system. Like a whiplash He repeatedly hurled at them the term "hypocrites." They were mere play actors or pretenders portraying a role for men to see. Even now one shudders as he hears these words of the Lord.

The obverse side of a Jewish widow's mite.

"Woe to you, scribes and Pharisees, hypocrites!" (Matt. 23:13), because they slammed the door of the kingdom of heaven in the faces of men. They would not enter themselves—neither did they permit others to do so.

"Woe to you, scribes and Pharisees, hypocrites!" (Matt. 23:15). For they compassed land and sea to make one Gentile a proselyte to Judaism, but they lacked the spiritual power to redeem him from paganism. In their empty system they merely substituted for his pagan gods their own gods of ritual and ceremony. Therefore, he was twofold more a son of hell than they were. He was still a pagan but left without hope.

"Woe to you, blind guides" (Matt. 23:16–22), because in their system of graduated oaths they devised means of evading them as though one was less binding than another, when all the while God did not recognize their machinations. They made a mockery of what should have been a sacred and binding thing.

"Woe to you, scribes and Pharisees, hypocrites!" (Matt. 23:23). They were so meticulous in keeping the law of the tithe and all the while they ignored God's weightier laws concerning justice, mercy, and faith. They should not neglect the former, but they should keep the latter also. In their spiritual blindness they were so careful to filter out a little gnat from their cup, but they were oblivious to a camel which they gulped down—hair, hide, hoof, hump, and all!

"Woe to you, scribes and Pharisees, hypocrites!" (Matt. 23:25–26), for they so scrupulously cleansed the outside of their eating utensils, but within themselves they were filled with robbery and graft.

"Woe to you, scribes and Pharisees, hypocrites!" (Matt. 23:27–28). They were like whitewashed tombs. Outwardly they appeared so beautiful, but inwardly they were filled with decaying flesh and dead men's bones. For a Jew to touch a tomb made him ceremonially unclean and so unfit for worship for seven days. Therefore, as a warning to worshipers all tombs were whitewashed with powdered lime just before the Passover. This would be true as Jesus spoke, so that His words carried a vivid imagery. The Pharisees were like these tombs. Outwardly they appeared so righteous, but inwardly they were filled with putrid sin.

"Woe to you, scribes and Pharisees, hypocrites!" (Matt. 23:29–36), because they built sepulchres for the prophets and adorned the tombs of the righteous, both of which their fathers had slain. All the while they piously said that had they lived in those days they would not have done as their fathers did, but they were the true sons of their fathers. Said Jesus, "Fill up, then, the measure of your father's

Pottery grouping. Jesus accused the scribes and Pharisees of cleaning the outside of the cup and dish but leaving the inside full of greed and self-indulgence. He urged them to first clean the inside of the cup (Matt. 23:25-26).

sins" (v. 32). Thus He challenged them to go ahead with their plot to kill Him. This would be a fitting climax to this long line of murders, and then echoing the words of John the Baptist, Jesus said, "Snakes! Brood of vipers! How can you escape being condemned to hell?" (v. 33). Upon them Jesus placed all of the righteous blood which had been shed from the time of Abel throughout all of the Old Testament. A terrible indictment indeed, but a deserved one nevertheless!

Then Jesus uttered another lament over Jerusalem, as representative of the entire Jewish nation. She had killed all whom God had sent to call her back to His eternal purpose. Soon she would kill the Son of God Himself. Rebellion was in her heart. Jesus still saw the storm coming and frantically had tried to save this people, but they would neither hear nor heed: "See! Your house is left to you desolate" (Matt. 23:38). Israel had chosen to go it alone—without Christ. Very well! Her house was left to her—without salvation.

They would not see Jesus again, as He now appeared to them, until His Second Advent when He would come again in great glory and power. Then the true Israel or all who believe on Him shall welcome Him as "He who comes in the name of the Lord" (Matt. 23:39), but for that generation and for the outward Israel as such, Jesus fully and finally abandoned them.

7. A Closing Scene of Beauty.

The storm had passed. The critics of Jesus had slunk away. Evidently even the Twelve stood some distance apart from Jesus, for He was alone in the Court of the Women. It was a tender scene, for the Lord of the temple sat over against the treasury, watching the people cast in their gifts. Many of the wealthy cast in their gifts with no comment coming from Jesus. Then there came a poor widow to cast in two mites or lepta. She was a pauper whose gift was worth about two-fifths of a cent.

Seeing this, Jesus called the Twelve to Him. He told them that this poverty-stricken widow had given more than all of the others combined. They had given out of their overflow of wealth, but she out of her deep poverty had given all that she had, even her living itself. Truly Jesus does not count gifts; He weighs them in the scales of love! What a pity to see some rich person who claims to give the "widow's mite"!

With this touching scene Jesus left the temple, never to enter it again. Thus God abandoned the temple. It truly was left unto itself.

"I am the vine; you are the branches. The one who remains in Me and I in him produces much fruit, because you can do nothing without Me."

JOHN 15:5 (HCSB)

The Gathering Gloom

Mount of Olives and garden of Gethsemane across from the Old City of Jerusalem.

The Final Warnings

Except for Jesus' words at His trial and at Calvary, His public ministry was over. All that remained now was that He should enter into the ever-deepening shadows which led to the darkest day in the history of the world, the day when Christ died.

As would be expected Jesus spent these closing days among His friends, but even within this intimate circle the most diabolical of sins raised its evil head. The serpent was soon to bruise the heel of the seed of the woman, but in the end He would crush its head.

This period of gathering gloom extended from Tuesday afternoon until possibly after the midnight hour on Thursday, or until early Friday morning. And it was a time largely consumed by the teaching of Jesus to His inner circle of Twelve, or to the Eleven as the case might be. The Shepherd is soon to be taken from the sheep, and everything possible was done to prepare them for it.

JESUS' DISCOURSE ON THE MOUNT OF OLIVES

The Twelve had been stunned by Jesus' words of condemnation spoken against the house of Israel, and they understood this to include the temple itself. Therefore, as they were passing from the temple area, they pointed out its beautiful buildings, paying special attention to the large stones used in its construction. One may still see some of these Herodian stones which were later used in rebuilding the walls about Jerusalem. But Jesus told them that the time would come when not one of these stones would be left standing upon another. As impossible as this may have seemed to the disciples, it actually became true in the utter destruction of Jerusalem by the Romans in A.D. 70.

Jesus and His little band left the city through the eastern gate, crossed the Kidron Valley, and began their ascent of the Mount of Olives. At a point somewhere on this mount directly across the valley from the temple they sat down to rest. Here the disciples asked Jesus three questions: "Tell us, when will these things happen? And what is the sign of Your coming and of the end of the age?" (Matt. 24:3). As one follows the discourse of Jesus, it is well to keep these questions in mind, for even though at times He seems to be dealing with first one and then another, in large measure Jesus answered them seriatim.

"When will these things happen?" The destruction of Jerusalem. "What is the sign of Your coming?" The Second Coming of Christ. "And of the end of the age?" The end of the age. Jesus had touched upon all of these in His discourse to the Pharisees. So it is understandable that the disciples should inquire concerning them, and they were not left without an answer.

1. The Warning against False Signs.

The disciples had asked about signs. Therefore, before answering their specific questions, Jesus warned them against being misled by false signs, and this warning was most fitting then, as it is now.

Jesus warned against false christs. These are not the "antichrist," or those opposing Christ, but pseudo christs, those who claim to be the Christ. From time to time such have appeared through the ages. Josephus relates that Palestine was plagued with them just prior to and during the Jewish War against the Romans in A.D. 66–70. They not only contributed to the causes of the war but also added greatly to the Jews' suffering during it.

Furthermore, Jesus warned against cataclysmic disturbances between nations, in the social order and in nature. It is of interest to note that even today when these things occur there are those who herald them as signs of the approaching Second Coming of Christ. But Jesus said that "wars and rumors of wars . . . famines and earthquakes in various places" are but parts of the normal course of history. Christians are not to be troubled about these things, with respect to the end of the age, for "the end is not yet" (Matt. 24:6).

"All these events are the beginning of birth pains" (Matt. 24:8). The words *birth pains* were used by the Jews to refer to the sufferings of the Messiah which would precede His appearance. However, these, said Jesus, are not a sign of the end, but of the "beginning." This statement, then, introduced the thought of the sufferings which the followers of Christ would endure through the ages as they endeavored to carry out the Great Commission. He enlarged upon it in the following verses as He described many of the things which would happen to them in their endeavor (cf. Matt. 24:9–13; Mark 13:9–13; Luke 21:12–19). Those who endure to the end, or until death, "shall be saved." This word *saved* does not refer to soul redemption, for that is an established fact for the Christian. It speaks rather of the care of God for them in their trials and the successful culmination of their purpose in Christian witnessing.

The Mount of Olives

Thomas V. Brisco

Visitors to Jerusalem often ascend the Mount of Olives early in the morning to feast upon a truly spectacular scene. Stretching below them in panoramic fashion lies the city of Jerusalem bathed in the gold of dawn's first light. The view is utterly breathtaking, one that never fades in memory. For centuries pilgrims and conquerors alike have gained their initial glimpse of this timeless city from a similar vantage point. Yet a casual glance at the numerous churches and mosques that dot the nearby slopes testify that the Mount of Olives itself is a vital part of Jerusalem's story, deeply embedded in her religious memory.

The Mount of Olives is part of a two and a half mile- long ridge that looms above Jerusalem to the east. Deep valleys, including the Kidron, separate the ridge from the city itself. As a part of a larger mountainous spine which extends north to south through western Palestine, this ridge forms part of a great watershed. The western side of the ridge faces the Mediterranean Sea and consequently receives adequate winter rainfall to support groves of trees and olive orchards. Olive trees are particularly

View from the wooden scaffolding of a new water tower on the Hebrew University campus on Mount Scopus in Jerusalem looking toward the summit of the Mount of Olives (center, background).

Jewish cemetery on the Mount of Olives overlooking the Old City.

Mount of Olives.

suited to the alkaline soil formed from the decomposition of limestone which forms the ridge. However, the eastern side of the ridge is a part of the Judean wilderness—a dry, stark desert land devoid of water and vegetation. The contrast between the western and eastern sides of the ridge is dramatic.

Three distinct summits rise from the ridge, each distinguished from the others by saddles or depressions. Today the northern summit is called Mount Scopus (2,684 feet), crowned by the gleaming white buildings of the Hebrew University. Josephus used the term *Scopus* to describe a place or vantage point north of Jerusalem that served as a "lookout" over the city. The Roman General Titus gained his first view of Jerusalem from this portion of the ridge (Josephus, *Wars* II.xix.4,7).

A second summit, Jebel et-Tur (2,652 feet), rises south of the German hospice Augusta Victoria built in 1898. A slight saddle separates the peak from its norhern neighbor. Through this depression an ancient Roman road led from Jerusalem eastward down to Jericho. This sec-

The one sure sign that Jesus gave with respect to the end of the age, which involves the Second Coming of Christ, is that "this good news of the kingdom will be preached in all the world as a testimony to all nations. And then the end will come" (Matt. 24:14). But even here Jesus spoke not of time but of condition. He never set a time, but He did describe the condition, and with this Jesus proceeded to answer the disciples' three questions.

2. The Destruction of Jerusalem.

In answering the first question Jesus did not speak of time, even though He might have done so, for it happened just forty years after His Crucifixion. However, again He spoke of condition. He used the word *when* (*hotan*) which refers primarily to condition. In it the time element is conditioned by the condition.

"When you see 'the abomination that causes desolation,' spoken of by the prophet Daniel, standing in the holy place" (let the reader understand) (Matt. 24:15). Luke simply says that when they saw Jerusalem surrounded by armies, then they should know that Jerusalem's desolation was at hand. These, then, are the conditions which will herald the end of the city, and Jesus referred His disciples to the prophecy of Daniel in order that they might understand His meaning. To what did Jesus refer?

The prophet Daniel speaks of certain abominations when someone shall cause the sacrifices and oblations to cease in the temple (9:27; 11:31; 12:11). Some interpreters view this as the act of Antiochus Epiphanes, a Seleucid ruler (175–164 B.C.), who defiled the temple by erecting an altar to Zeus on the altar of Jehovah and thereon sacrificed swines' flesh. Furthermore, he converted the priests' rooms and the temple chambers into public brothels. No doubt Jesus' words called this to the minds of His hearers.

That this was not what Jesus had in mind is seen in the fact that He referred to some future event. Josephus relates that following the destruction of the temple Roman soldiers proclaimed Titus as emperor and offered sacrifices to their ensigns placed by the eastern gate. However, this was after the fall of the city. Jesus referred to something which immediately preceded this event.

When Jesus spoke of the "holy place," it does not necessarily refer to the Holy of Holies alone, even though it is included in His statement. It could include the entire holy city and its environs. If this be true, then the specific reference would be to the siege of the city by Titus, a siege

Roman soldier.

ond peak lies opposite the Temple Mount in Jerusalem and is more narrowly identified as the Mount of Olives. Though not appreciably higher than the highest points of Jerusalem, the deep cleft of the Kidron Valley sharply distinguished the mount from the city.

The modern road leading from Jerusalem to Jericho passes through a noticeable saddle separating the Mount of Olives from the third summit known today in Arabic as Jebel Batn el-Hawa (the mountain of the womb of the wind). The modern Arabic village of Silwan clings to the western slope of this summit. Beyond the Kidron, the ruins of the City of David—the original Canaanite/Jebusite settlement conquered by David ca. 990 B.C.—lie exposed by recent archaeological work. Traditionally known as the Mount of Offense (or Corruption), this most southern summit of the ridge may have been the locale of pagan altars built during Solomon's reign to meet the religious needs of his pagan wives and concubines (1 Kings 11:7).

Sources use different names to refer to the ridge or

Clay tile has "LXF," symbol of the 10th Legion of Titus.

which foretold the other events connected with its fall (Luke 21:20). Pagan armies with their pagan ensigns surrounding the city would truly be an abomination of desolation, which finally resulted in the end of the sacrifices and oblations. When the disciples should see this siege begin, they would know that the destruction of the city was near.

So when they shall see these armies approaching the city, they are to flee to the mountains. Eusebius says that the Christians actually fled to Pella at the foot of the mountains about seventeen miles south of the Sea of Galilee. Those who shall be on the housetop, probably looking for the approach of the Romans, should not go down into their houses to get anything to carry away with them. They should escape the city by what the rabbis called "the road of the roofs." Anyone working in the field, and who had laid aside his outer cloak or had left it at home, should not return for it. Haste would be of the essence. It would be difficult for pregnant women or those with suckling children, for this would slow them down. Furthermore, they were to pray that this would not occur in winter, lest fleeing their homes they should be exposed to the cold. Or that it should not be on a Sabbath day on which Jews are forbidden to travel more than a short distance. Some rabbis said that it was permissible to ignore these regulations in order to escape danger, but many would die rather than do so.

Jesus said that the tribulation suffered during and following this Roman siege would exceed anything ever seen on the earth up to that time or which would ever come in the future (Mark 13:19). This latter time element shows that here Jesus was not thinking of some "tribulation" in the last days of the age. He was speaking of the destruction of Jerusalem, and Josephus vividly describes these conditions, especially during the closing part of this siege and at the time of the fall of the city. Titus himself said that God was against the Jews on that day, and Jesus said that had not God shortened these days of suffering, "for the elect's sake" (Matt. 24:22), the Christians themselves would have been wiped out.

As mentioned above, false christs would appear preceding and during this terrible time, and they led many astray, adding to their suffering. However, Jesus told His followers beforehand in order that they might not be led astray (Matt. 24:25). At this point His warning extends beyond the immediate future to include all time until the end of the age. What follows may apply equally to the period through the destruction of Jerusalem, even up to and including the Second Coming of Christ (cf. Matt. 24:26–28).

3. The Second Coming of Christ.

Jesus introduced His answer to this second question by specific warnings against false predictions as to His return. The warning is particularly against any claims of a secret coming of Christ. Pretenders would/will appear either in some isolated place or in some secret place within a city. Such places would make it difficult or impossible to check on their claims. Even in modern times Pastor Russell claimed that the Lord came to him secretly, telling him to gather out the one hundred and forty-four thousand redeemed (cf. Rev. 7). Jesus warned against any such secret coming, for when the Son of man comes, He will be seen by all, as when lightning flashes it is seen from east to west (across the sky) by all simultaneously. Furthermore, He said that where the carcass is there will the vultures be gathered together. In other words, in this realistic picture He said that whenever conditions are right the Son of man will appear (Matt. 24:28).

Shofar, table of shew bread and the menorah being hauled from temple on Arch of Titus. Titus destroyed Jerusalem in A.D. 70 and the arch detailed above depicts his triumph in Rome from that victory.

Then Jesus began to speak in apocalyptic language, a sort of sign language commonly used by the Jews to portray divine events (cf. Rev.): "Immediately after the tribulation of those days" (Matt 24:29). What days? Not merely some days of tribulation near the end of the age. Jesus used the sweeping, panoramic language of prophecy to span the entire scope of time from His Ascension until His return. These are the days of tribulation which will be endured by His followers through the centuries (v. 8) as they witness to a lost world. Jesus did not say how long or how short this period would be. The matter of time was not in His thinking. He was thinking of condition.

Whenever that condition shall come, then, in apocalyptic language, He described certain phenomena in the heavens: "Then the sign of the Son of Man will appear in the sky" (Matt. 24:30). And what will that "sign" be? It will be "the Son of Man coming on the clouds of heaven with power and great glory" (24:30).

At this point Jesus dealt with both the destruction of Jerusalem and His Second Coming. It is as though He were summing up these two events before passing on to answer the third question. He said that when a fig tree puts forth its leaves one knows that summer draws near. Likewise, when one saw "these things" (Matt. 24:33, the conditions which preceded the destruction of Jerusalem), he would know that "He is near—at the door" (24:33). The text reads "He is near," but either "He" or "it" is an accurate translation. Although HCSB has "He" in the main text, it shows "it" as a valid alternative in a footnote to this verse. And since Jesus said that "this generation will certainly not pass away until all these things take place," it does not refer to Jesus' return. But the destruction of Jerusalem did occur within that generation, so the translation "it" is preferable.

Then Jesus spoke of His return when He said, "Concerning that day and hour no one knows—neither the angels of heaven—except the Father only" (Matt. 24:36). Mark adds that even the Son does not know (13:32). This latter statement involves the limitations of the Incarnation voluntarily assumed by the Son. But the certainty of both the destruction of Jerusalem and of the Lord's return is assured, for Jesus had predicted them, and even though heaven and earth would pass away, His "words will never pass away" (Matt. 24:35).

The date of the destruction of Jerusalem is a matter of history. The time of the Second Coming is hidden in the mind of God, but as the former came to pass, so will the latter do so. In the meantime, Jesus said, life will move along its natural course until without warning the Lord will return. When He does, there will be a sudden separation between those who are His and those who are not His. "Therefore be alert, since you don't know what day your Lord is coming" (Matt. 24:42).

4. The End of the Age.

Of course, the end of the age is simultaneous with the return of the Lord. As He spoke of the one, He spoke of the other. Therefore, to drive home this truth Jesus closed this Olivet discourse with a series of parables, followed by an actual description of the scene of the judgment which will occur at the end of the age.

Like a householder watching for a thief in the night, who comes unexpectedly, so should the Lord's people be alert to await His coming. No servant of His should be a "wicked slave" (Matt. 24:48) in abusing the responsibility entrusted to him. Such conduct could even mean that he was not truly the Lord's servant.

Furthermore, in the Parable of the Ten Virgins (Matt. 25:1–13) Jesus taught the importance of being properly related to Him. The five wise virgins were so related—they had oil in their lamps. But the five foolish ones were not— they had no oil in their lamps, and when the Bridegroom appeared, they had no further opportunity to make ready.

The Parable of the Talents (Matt. 25:14–30) teaches the importance of faithfulness in the responsibility placed by the Lord upon His servants, or slaves, in the interim between His Ascension and His return. At His return there will be a reckoning. Those who are faithful in their several capacities and responsibilities will be rewarded accordingly, but those who are unfaithful will lose not only their reward but also their further opportunity. Indeed, such unfaithfulness will even prove that they were not really servants of Christ at all. So instead of receiving everlasting reward, they will be cast from Him into everlasting punishment.

Then came the scene of the final Judgment (Matt. 25:31–46). When the condition is right for the coming of the Son of man, He will sit on the throne of His glory. Before Him will be assembled all nations or ethnic groups, and as a shepherd separates the sheep from the goats, so shall the Son of man separate all men, the "sheep" on His right hand and the "goats" on His left. Some see the following scene as the Judgment of the Nations, but nations as such are judged in the context of history. Therefore, this judgment may more likely be

Roman oil lamps of the kind that may have been used by the Ten Virgins.

portions of the ridge. Due to the abundant olive trees that graced the western slopes of the ridge, the predominate names reflect words meaning "olive" or "olive tree." One of the earliest references speaks of the ascent of the Mount of Olives (2 Sam. 15:30, NASB). Zechariah referred to the Mount of Olives, which is in front of Jerusalem on the east (Zech. 14:4, NASB). The New Testament used the terms Mount of Olives (Matt. 21:1, NASB) and the mountain called Olivet (or olive grove) (Luke 19:29, NASB). The term *Olivet* derives from the Latin term *olivetum*. In Jewish tradition the term *Mount of Ointment* suggests the oil produced from the olives. Because fire signals from the mountain were used to announce the new moon, Talmudic literature used the term *mountain of lights*. In Christian tradition the Mount of Olives has been called the Mount of Ascension (see Acts 1:12).

Sacred traditions associated with the Mount of Olives have a lengthy history. Second Samuel implies that the Mount of Olives was used for worship from at least the time of David. David fled Jerusalem eastward across the slopes of the Mount of Olives to the "summit, where God was worshiped" (2 Sam. 15:32, NASB). This suggests an open air cultic site (a high place) was located there; such worship centers often were located on mountains in ancient times. Later, Solomon built several pagan shrines for his wives on the southern summit of the ridge, the Mount of Offense

(1 Kings 11:7–8). A few scholars locate Nob, the village of the priest Ahimelech (1 Sam. 21:1–9), on Mount Scopus, an identification much disputed. However, whatever the sacred associations of the mountain in earlier periods, at least by the time of Josiah the shrines and altars were destroyed (2 Kings 23:13–14). A later Jewish tradition records that the ritual burning of a red heifer to obtain ashes used in cleansing ritual impurity (Num. 19) was performed on the steps of the Mount of Olives.

A noticeable feature of the Mount of Olives is the numerous graves located upon the western slopes extending down into the Kidron Valley.

Many traditions regarding the day of judgment are associated with the area. However, various speculations about the future entwined about the Mount of Olives cannot obscure the sanctity imparted to the mount by the past. True enough kings and prophets trod where conquerors encamped their troops along the olive tree-crested slopes. But still the teachings of Jesus which echo from the slopes and the memory of His agonizing decision reached in Gethsemane hallow the Mount of Olives forever.

Thomas V. Brisco is professor of biblical backgrounds and archaeology, Southwestern Baptist Theological Seminary, Fort Worth, Texas.

considered as one of several pictures of the judgment of individuals.

"Then the King will say . . ." Note that the Son of man is now called a King. What shall the King say? To the "sheep" He shall say, "Come, you who are blessed by My Father, inherit the kingdom prepared for you from the foundation of the world" (Matt. 25:34). The basis of this inheritance is the benevolent attitude which they have shown toward the King (Matt. 25:35–36), and this attitude is expressed toward Him in their treatment of those about them who are in need (vv. 37–40).

Conversely, to the "goats" He shall say, "Depart from me, you who are cursed, into the eternal fire prepared for the Devil and his angels" (Matt. 25:41), and the basis of this condemnation is the malevolent attitude shown toward the King, as expressed in this same attitude toward their needy fellowmen (vv. 42–46). In other words, in each case had these two groups been with Jesus in the flesh they would have acted toward Him as they acted toward their fellowmen.

What may be understood by this scene of judgment? The basis of judgment will not be one's works. It will be the kind of character one brings to the judgment, a character as revealed in his works. So the judgment will not determine character. It will only reveal it. The judgment will not decide whether one is saved or lost. It will reveal or declare one's saved or lost condition.

And the destination of each group will be fixed and final. The lost will enter into "eternal punishment: but the righteous into life eternal" (Matt. 25:46). Some people prefer to deny the fact of "everlasting punishment." If this denial be permitted, then one must deny the fact of "life eternal" also. For the same word (*aionion*, eternal) describes both punishment and life. The language is quite plain. Jesus spoke of both punishment and life as "eternal," and the thought of eternal punishment is all the more real when one remembers that it was expressed by Him who is infinite love and mercy.

So the Olivet discourse was ended. But before Jesus and the Twelve continued their journey toward Bethany, He told them that after two days the Passover would be observed, and the Son of man would be handed over to be crucified. Thus Jesus foretold the very day on which He would be crucified.

Probably at that moment the Sanhedrin was in session. It had been called by Caiaphas, the high priest, to plan how Jesus should be arrested subtlely and be killed. However, they agreed to wait until after the Passover, lest they

Goat herd on the hillside of ancient Samaria.

should find a revolt against their actions on the part of the people. Little did they know that the time and manner of Jesus' death was not theirs to choose. Both had already been predetermined by God.

A DINNER AMONG FRIENDS

It was Tuesday evening in Bethany. The place was the home of Simon the leper, one who probably had been healed by Jesus. The occasion was a dinner in honor of Jesus. Present also were Lazarus and the Twelve. As might be expected Martha joined in serving the meal.

During the meal Mary, in characteristic fashion, came with an alabaster cruse of very precious ointment or nard. It probably was her prized possession, a gift fit for a king. In a great expression of love she broke the cruse, and anointed Jesus' head and feet with the ointment. Then she wiped His feet with her hair. It was an act of utter devotion.

Seeing this act Judas criticized her, and the other disciples joined with him in the criticism. Failing to understand this deed of love, they regarded it merely as a "waste." Judas asked why it was not sold and the proceeds used to relieve the poor, but John notes that he had no concern for the poor. Instead, since he kept the money for the little band, he merely wanted to get his greedy hands on the money and steal it for himself.

Jesus rebuked His disciples by reminding them that they could minister to the poor at any time. Mary had anointed Him for His

Shepherd with sheep.

Alabaster

David D. Edwards

I remember wandering as a boy through the trails at Carlsbad Caverns in southern New Mexico. I was amazed by the wonderful formations of rock. Beyond all the picturesque designs I found in the miles of caverns, the simple stalagmites and stalactites best held my fascination. For years I kept in my bedroom a small figurine depicting these creations. Little did I realize the usefulness of the minerals contained in these rock cylinders and their connection to Scripture.

Alabaster aryballos (small Greek flask with flattened lip).

The alabaster stone of the ancient writers was a material mined from stalactites and stalagmites. In modern usage alabaster is a fine-grained gypsum consisting of calcium sulphate. It comes from evaporated seawater and is used in sheet rock for construction. Oriental alabaster, on the other hand, is calcium carbonate found in limestone caverns. When waters drip through the roof of a cave, the remaining calcium carbonate forms a stalactite. The same material rises from the floor of the cave when ground water dissolves, gradually creating a stalagmite. The stalactite hangs vertically, and the stalagmite grows upward until the two eventually meet.[1]

Over time, layers of crystals form as the cones grow. The colors of the stalactites and stalagmites change as other minerals become enmeshed with the rise and fall of the waters in the caverns. Pure alabaster is white or translucent. Impurities in the stone result in a variety of colors, including yellow, buff, brown, and gray. Red can also be found due to the presence of iron oxide in the stone. The colorful pattern gives each rock a unique appearance resembling onyx marble. Strictly speaking, alabaster is neither onyx nor marble, but often the ancient writers called onyx "alabaster" due to the visual similarities.[2]

Oriental alabaster is also called Egyptian alabaster because of the massive amounts produced in Thebes and at the quarries of Hat-nub near the town of Alabastron. (Most likely the material gave the town its name.)[3] Apparently, Egyptian alabaster was widely circulated in the ancient Mediterranean world. An archeological dig at the Canaanite city of Ai in 1934 discovered numerous alabaster vessels, including four bowls and a jar.[4] The type of alabaster and the shape of the jar link their origin to Egypt, probably from the first dynasty.

Through the centuries, primitive people considered alabaster a rarity. While they would use the more common clay vessels in their homes, they reserved alabaster for special purposes. For instance, the group at Ai most likely used the alabaster bowls as cultic utensils in Canaanite worship practices. The discovery of the pieces in their temple underscores this theory. Egyptians used alabaster in their sarcophagi (coffins made of stone) and in the walls of their temples and tombs.

Alabaster perfume jar from Jericho. Dates from 1800–1550 B.C.

burial, and wherever the gospel should be preached, this deed of love would be known as a memorial unto her. So this odor of a precious ointment did more than perfume the banquet hall. On the winds of time it has wafted down the centuries and throughout the world.

What a contrast is seen between Mary and Judas! Both had known the love of Jesus. Both had heard His words and had seen His wondrous works but with such diverse reactions. In all likelihood Mary and Judas were the first two who completely realized that Jesus was going to die, and with this realization each asked a question. Mary asked, "What can I do for Jesus to show that I love Him, understand, and sympathize with Him?" So she anointed Him for burial. Judas

The English Old Testament makes no reference to alabaster. However, the Greek translation of the Old Testament, the Septuagint, speaks of alabaster in 2 Kings 21:13. Our English Bible translates God's judgment on Judah, saying, "I will wipe Jerusalem as one wipes a dish." But according to the Greek version, God spoke through His prophets, saying, "I will wipe Jerusalem as one wipes an alabastros" (the Greek word for "alabaster"). When we remember that the Septuagint was written in Egypt, it makes sense. Writing to readers who were accustomed to alabaster, the translators simply called the vessel by a more specialized name. What is unusual is the designation of the plate as an "alabaster." Not just anything was called an alabaster. Normally an alabaster referred to a type of flask.

Craftsmen often used alabaster to make vases to contain types of perfume. Fashioning a long-neck bottle with a narrow lip or spout, they could pour the precious unguents. The artisan would seal the orifice to preserve the aroma and keep the contents pure. The ancients believed alabaster provided the best container to sustain the aroma of the ointment. The Roman historian Pliny wrote of nard as the most priceless among all perfumes, costing sometimes one hundred denarii per pound (*Natural History*, 12.26.43). The more expensive and desirable variety grew in India. To keep such a valuable commodity at its best, he suggested the use of an alabaster flask (*Natural History,* 13.3.19). Perhaps for this reason the vases

Double goblets made of alabaster dating from the 14th century B.C.

themselves eventually were called "alabasters."

The value of the alabasters themselves varied, depending on the beauty of the stone and the quality of the craftsmanship. Some alabasters were quite delicate and colorful, making them both extremely beautiful and costly. The size of the alabaster also contributed to the value. A larger cruse could hold a substantial amount of ointment, thus signifying the wealth of the owner.

The use of the alabaster in the Gospel account is consistent with the use by people through time. Because it was both precious and rare, it was ideal for those who brought offerings to the temple at Ai. So also it was fitting for the woman to use alabaster as a gift to Jesus. Alabaster was worthy not only for the kings of Egypt but for the King of kings.

[1] For a more technical treatment of the minerals found in alabaster, see Edward S. Dana, *A Textbook of Mineralogy* (New York: John Wiley and Sons, 1951), 514.
[2] For a discussion of the comparison between alabaster and onyx and how stalagmitic alabaster is formed, see "Alabaster" in *The Zondervan Pictorial Encyclopedia of the Bible*, vol. 1 (Grand Rapids: Zondervan, 1975), 95–96.
[3] See "Alabaster" in *Encyclopedia Biblica*, vol. 1 (New York: Macmillan Co., 1903), 108.
[4] See Ruth Amiran, "The Egyptian Alabaster Vessels from Ai," *Israel Exploration Journal Twenty*, nos. 3-4 (1970), 170–79.

David D. Edwards is pastor, Main Street Baptist Church, Georgetown, Texas.

asked, "In view of the fact that Jesus is going to die anyway, what can Jesus do for me? What can I get out of this debacle for myself?" So he betrayed Jesus for thirty pieces of silver, the price of a slave, for Judas went directly from this dinner to seek out the chief priests and drive a bargain with them for his dastardly deed.

At this point one wonders again why Jesus chose Judas as one of His disciples. Some have supposed that Judas was chosen for the express purpose of his betrayal, but this would relieve Judas of all guilt and make him a mere puppet on a string held in God's hands. Such a thought not only is contrary to the Gospel record; it is in direct opposition to God's nature and His dealings with men as personalities endowed with the privilege of choice. In trying to relieve Judas of guilt they make God guilty of an unrighteous act.

In truth one is driven back to a recognition that Jesus saw a peculiar worth in Judas, which, if surrendered to Him, would make Judas of definite value to the kingdom of God. But Judas never truly gave himself to Jesus. He remained self-centered to the end.

Some even see in Judas' betrayal an effort to force Jesus' hand. It seems that on other occasions he had tried to do so but to no avail. To his nationalistic mind Jesus had missed His chance to establish His kingdom on the occasion of His royal entry, so to Judas Jesus was an impractical dreamer. Perhaps if he created a situation which endangered Jesus' life, He would declare Himself. But again this

Hellenistic sarcophagus showing a man and woman reclining on a couch which forms a lid depicts reclining at table.

attributes to the betrayer a motive which is not borne out by the record.

More likely Judas felt that he had forsaken everything to follow Jesus, hoping that thereby he might receive a place of prominence in the new kingdom. His dreams however were soon to be trampled in the dirt, so he sought to cash in on the failure as best he could. For his perfidy he received a little less than twenty-five dollars. It was a sorry bargain indeed for him, but his treachery appeared to be a windfall to the chief priests. They had not hoped for betrayal from within Jesus' little circle of intimates. It was no longer necessary to wait until after the Passover. They now had only to wait until Judas could find an opportune moment to deliver Jesus into their hands.

THE TWO MEALS

THE PASSOVER MEAL

Nothing is known as to Jesus' actions on Wednesday of Passion Week. Perhaps He spent the day in seclusion as He rested and taught His disciples, but about noon on Thursday He made ready for His final visit to Jerusalem, a visit which would end in His death.

1. The Preparation for the Passover Meal.

On Thursday Peter and John were sent into the city to prepare for Jesus' last Passover meal with His disciples. They were told that there they would see a man carrying a pitcher of water. Following him they would be led to the house in which they were to make preparations for the meal.

Traditional Upper Room.

This fact is suggestive of previous preparation on the part of Jesus. Judas must not know this location in advance. A man carrying a pitcher of water would be most conspicuous, for it was customary only for women to do this. So this man evidently was to do this as a prearranged sign. Jesus called him "such a man." In the papyri this very phrase was used in the sense of "Mister X." It is so used in modern Greek.

Pottery bowl, the kind that may have been used in the Passover Feast to dip bread in the stew.

There they made ready for the meal. They went to the Temple and secured a lamb which was slain by a priest. The lamb, in turn, was roasted, and together with certain other specified food this comprised the Passover meal.

2. The Arrival for the Passover Meal.

About 6:00 P.M. Jesus and the other disciples came to the home and entered the Upper Room. A contention ensued among the Twelve as each sought to get the chief place next to Jesus about the table. But Jesus rebuked them with a lesson concerning greatness in the Kingdom, and then He proceeded to demonstrate His lesson.

On such a festive occasion it was customary for the host to provide a slave to rinse the dust from the feet of the arriving guests, but since Jesus had no such slave, He assumed that role Himself. He laid aside His outer garments, girded Himself with a towel, filled a basin with water, and began to rinse the disciples' feet. But when He came to Peter, He was met with a protest. That disciple refused to let Jesus render so menial a service for him.

One can almost see a twinkle of humor in Jesus' eyes in the play upon words which followed. Peter said, "Thou shalt never rinse my feet" (John 13:8). Jesus replied, "If I rinse thee not, thou hast no part with me" (v. 8). Then Peter, in characteristic fashion, said, "Lord, not my feet only, but also my hands and my head" (v. 9). Give me a bath all over! And then Jesus replied, "He that took a bath needeth not save to rinse his feet" (v. 10). In other words, if Peter took a bath before coming to supper, he needed only to have his feet rinsed free of dust (author's translation).

Then Jesus added that not all among them were clean. Thus He spoke of Judas and his purpose of betrayal. Jesus ended this episode by applying the lesson. As He had rendered a menial service to them, if they wished to be great in the kingdom, they must do so to one another. In this act Jesus did not give to His followers an ordinance. He merely taught them a lesson in humility.

3. The Betrayer Indicated.

Jesus and the Twelve were now reclining about the table as they ate the Passover meal. In all likelihood the Lord, as the host, had already recounted the events which were commemorated in the meal. While they were eating, Jesus tossed a bombshell among them as He said, "I assure you: One of you will betray Me" (John 13:21). This must have been greeted by a moment of stunned silence as the disciples looked about at each other, and then one by one they began to ask, "Surely not I, Lord?" (Matt. 26:22). The form of the question invited a negative answer. "Surely not I, Lord?" Such a thought was incredible to the Eleven. Jesus replied by saying that it was one who was dipping his hand into the dish with Him. This did not specifically point out Judas, since all of them were doing this. It merely indicated the intimacy which was to be betrayed. That Judas was not a puppet in the hands of fate is seen in Jesus' following words: "The Son of Man will go just as it is written about Him, but woe to that man by whom the Son of Man is betrayed! It would have been better for that man if he had not been born" (Matt. 26:24).

Up to this point Judas had remained silent, but lest his silence indict him he finally asked, "Surely not I, Rabbi?" (26:25). His question also invited a negative answer. He had to try to bluff it out, but there is one decided difference in his question. Whereas the others addressed Jesus as "Lord," Judas merely called Him "Rabbi." To him Jesus was a rabbi and nothing more. This fact is reflected in Jesus' reply, "You have said it yourself." This means "yes."

Just prior to Judas' question there was a

A first-century water or wine dipper juglet.

movement about the table, for Peter came to John who was reclining on Jesus' right side, the place of honor. He asked him to ascertain from Jesus the name of the traitor. The Lord said to John, not to Peter, "He's the one I give the piece of bread to after I have dipped it" (John 13:26). All were dipping their bread in a common bowl of gravy. Customarily on such occasions the host honored a guest by dipping a morsel in the gravy and giving it to him. So Jesus did this for Judas. Was this a last effort to reclaim Judas from his evil purpose? At any rate the act would carry no particular significance to Peter and the others. Otherwise Judas might well have been mobbed on the spot. But Judas knew. At this point he asked his question, "Rabbi, is it I?" So when he knew that Jesus was aware of his purpose, "Satan entered him" (John 13:27). Satan was already there, but this was John's way of saying that there was no longer any hindrance to the traitor's embarking on his purpose. So he prepared to leave the room.

Seeing this Jesus said, "What you're doing, do quickly." It was customary at the Passover to buy food to give to the poor. The disciples thought that Jesus was sending Judas on such an errand of mercy. John notes that as soon as Judas received the sop, he left immediately, and then he commented that "it was night" (13:30). Since it was the time of the full moon, this can hardly refer to natural darkness. It was John's mystical way of noting the darkness in the soul of Judas.

With the departure of Judas Jesus turned His interest to the Eleven. He spoke of the imminency of His rapidly approaching Crucifixion and of their need to love one another. Then He said that that very night all of them would be caused to stumble because of what would happen to Him. The Shepherd would be smitten, and the flock would be scattered. However, Jesus promised that after His Resurrection He would meet them in Galilee.

The idea of stumbling brought a protest from Peter. Even though all others might forsake Him in His hour of danger, he said that he would never do so. He was ready to go to prison and death for his Lord. But Jesus knew him better than he knew himself, so He said that before the cock should crow before daylight

Pottery bowl of the type used in serving a meal.

Peter would deny Him three times. Still Peter continued to avow his loyalty, and the other disciples joined with him in it.

Jesus was aware of the danger for Him which stalked the streets of Jerusalem that night. Soon under Judas' guidance the temple police would be searching for Him. In this light one may understand Jesus' words in Luke 22:35–38. Jesus was going to die, but it would be according to God's plan and not by mob violence. So He reminded the Eleven that on a previous occasion when He had sent them forth to preach, they went without purse, wallet, or extra shoes and they had lacked nothing. "Then He said to them, 'But now, whoever has a money-bag should take it, and also a backpack. And whoever doesn't have a sword should sell his robe and buy one" (Luke 22:36). In the original Greek it is clear that Jesus said that if any of them had either a purse or a wallet, he should buy a sword, but if he had neither, then let him sell his robe and buy one.

In the light of the extreme pacifism so often attributed to Jesus, these words appear strange indeed. Some interpreters endeavor to tone them down by comparing them to Jesus' words to Peter in the Garden of Gethsemane (Matt. 26:52). But these are plain words and must be interpreted in their context. Light is thrown upon them by the statement which follows: "For I tell you, what is written must be fulfilled in Me: 'And He was counted among the outlaws. Yes, what is written about Me is coming to its fulfillment" (Luke 22:37; cf. Isa. 53:12). Jesus has a goal ("end") which must be fulfilled by His death on the cross (between two thieves). Nothing must prevent it. The Gethsemane experience still awaits Him, and He must not be arrested until it is finished.

So Jesus told the disciples to get a sword. They were to protect Him until He was ready to be taken. The sword was for defensive purposes only. He would not establish His kingdom through the sword, but for the present situation a sword might be necessary in order that the kingdom should be established according to God's will.

In response to Jesus' admonition, the disciples said, "'Lord, . . . look, here are two swords.' 'Enough of that!' He told them" (Luke 22:38). Probably they found two swords belonging to the owner of the house in which they were gathered, so the disciples took the swords in accordance with Jesus' instruction.

THE INSTITUTION OF THE MEMORIAL SUPPER

Judas had left the room to go on his evil errand. This left only Jesus and the eleven believers. Judas, along with the others, most likely had been baptized; but he was not a believer, so this memorial supper was observed only by Jesus and these baptized believers.

As they were eating the Passover meal, Jesus took bread, blessed it, and broke it, and gave it to His disciples, saying, "Take, eat; this is My body" (Matt. 26:26). Then He took the cup, saying, "Drink from it. . . for this is My blood of the covenant, which is shed for many for the forgiveness of sins" (Matt.

26:27–28). Thus in the simplest of action and language He instituted the ordinance of the Lord's Supper.

It would be to violate the nature of the Lord's teachings to say that these elements actually became the body and blood of Jesus. In poetic, symbolic language He said that these elements represent His body and blood. They were not to be regarded as some fetish but as a memorial calling to the worshiper's remembrance that which Jesus did for man's redemption. They were to proclaim His death until His return. Thus this Supper in faith points back to His death and points forward to His Second Coming.

A practical question presents itself. What was the ingredient contained in the "cup"? At the Passover meal wine diluted with water was drunk. Was this that which the cup contained? The New Testament never refers to it as "wine" but as the "fruit of the vine" (Matt. 26:29). Certainly the bread used was unleavened bread. These dual elements represented the sinless body and blood of Jesus. May it not, therefore, be concluded that the content of the cup was the "fruit of the vine" uncontaminated by the fermentation brought about by bacteria? It is of interest to note that while Mark and Matthew speak of "a cup," Luke and Paul (1 Cor. 11:25) speak of "the cup" as though it were a cup set apart from other cups used in the meal. It may well be that this was "the cup" filled with unfermented fruit of the vine and which was provided for the memorial supper.

Jesus concluded this beautiful moment by saying, "I will not drink of this fruit of the vine until that day when I drink it new in My Father's kingdom with you" (Matt. 26: 29). But His followers are to "eat this bread, and drink the cup . . . till he come" (1 Cor. 11:26).

THE FAREWELL DISCOURSE

The memorial supper had been instituted, and the hour was rapidly approaching when it would find meaning in the grim reality of Jesus' death. He was now ready to give to the disciples His final teaching before the Shepherd was to be taken from the sheep, and this final discourse may be divided into two parts.

1. In the Upper Room.

The words and deeds of Jesus this night had plunged the disciples into gloom. The passion which all the while had been so real to the Savior was finally taking hold upon them. So Jesus sought to comfort and encourage them, not only for the hours immediately ahead of them, but for the unfolding years ahead. Indeed, He enveloped the centuries as He spoke to His followers until the end of time.

"Your heart must not be troubled. Believe in God; believe also in Me. In My Father's house are many dwelling places; if not, I would have told you. I am going away to prepare a place for you. If I go away and prepare a place for you, I will come back and receive you to Myself, so that where I am you may be also" (John 14:1–3).

One might as well try to adorn an American Beauty rose as to comment on these words, for they were a pillow for broken hearts then, as they have been through the centuries and will be until the end of time.

But quizzical minds did inquire after them then, even as they do so now, and the answers received are eternal gems of truth. Jesus said, "You know the way where I am going." Thomas said that since they did not know where Jesus was going, how could they know the way? Jesus replied, "I am the way, the truth, and the life. No man comes to the Father except through Me." He then said that He fully revealed the Father. If they knew Him, they knew the Father also. These words evoked a prayer from Philip: "Lord, show us the Father, and that's enough for us." In turn this evoked surprise from Jesus that after all this time the disciples did not yet know the intimate oneness of Father and Son: "The one who has seen Me has seen the Father. How can you say, 'Show us the Father'?"(vv. 4–9). This led Jesus to emphasize again this oneness. Both His words and His works were of the Father, and if they did not believe His words, at least they should see God's presence in His works.

Furthermore, if they committed themselves to Him, they would do even greater works than He had done, not greater in kind but in scope, and this was because He was going to the Father. In His absence He promised that what-soever they should ask in His name He would do, that the Father might be glorified in the Son.

The thought of His bodily absence introduced Jesus' promise of the abiding presence of the Holy Spirit. He said, "And I also will ask the Father, and He will give you another Counselor to be with you forever. He is the Spirit of truth, whom the world is unable to receive because it doesn't see Him or know Him. But you do know Him, because He remains with you and will be in you. I will not leave you as orphans; I am coming to you" (John 14:16–18).

Even though Jesus was going away, they were not to be left as orphans after all. He would come to them in the presence of the Holy Spirit, who would be their Comforter or Encourager. He would be "another Counselor" or "anoth-er" of the same kind as Jesus. B. H. Carroll called the Holy Spirit "The Other Jesus." Marcus Dods called Him "Jesus' alter Ego" or "Jesus' other Self." And note that the disciples were not to pray for the coming of the Holy Spirit. Jesus said, "And I also will ask the Father, and He will give you another Counselor."

Jesus then spoke of Christian love. This is the love which God has for man, to which man responds in love for God through Christ, and they would show their love for Him by keeping His commandments. If they do, then they will know the abiding love of God in Christ who will indwell them. Jesus spoke these words during His bodily presence, but "the other Jesus," even the Comforter, will teach them all things and will bring to their remembrance all that Jesus had said to them throughout His sojourn with them.

Finally, Jesus left with them the legacy of His peace. It is not the temporary, shallow peace of the world, but the abiding peace of His spiritual presence.

Therefore, they were to be neither troubled nor afraid. If they truly love Him, they would not grieve because He was leaving them. Instead, they would rejoice because He was returning to the bosom of the Father. He told them now of His impending departure in order that when it occurred they would believe.

Hereafter He would not talk much with them, because He would soon be taken from them by the power of evil. He was ready for it in order that the world might know fully God's redeeming purpose.

"Get up; let's leave this place" (John 14:31), and with these words Jesus led His little band of sheep from the safety of the Upper Room to go to the tryst which awaited Him in Gethsemane.

2. On the Way to Gethsemane.

Jesus often used the peripatetic method of teaching. That is, He taught as He walked along. So on the way to Gethsemane, as they walked along Jerusalem's dark streets, He continued to teach.

He had already spoken of His departure and of the coming of the Holy

Olive garden on Mount of Olives.

Spirit, and in His power they were to witness concerning the gospel in the unfolding future. This they would do as in the Spirit they abode in Him.

Jesus likened Himself to "the true vine, and My Father is the vineyard keeper" (John 15:1). The followers of Jesus are the branches on the Vine, and the Father expects them to bear fruit. This they will do as they abide in Jesus, for apart from Him they will be fruitless. Failure to do so will result in lost usefulness. The result will be that they will be pruned from the Vine and their useless works will be burned. This does not refer to a lost redemption but to a lost opportunity. In fact, they had been chosen for the express purpose of bearing much fruit to the glory of God, and in their efforts at fruitbearing they have the assurance that God will give them the object of their prayers, as long as they come to God by the merits and in the authority of Jesus' name.

As they seek to witness, they must expect to endure the enmity of the world. It hated Jesus; it will hate them. It persecuted Jesus; it will persecute them. Nevertheless, they will not be alone in their work, for the Comforter will be

with them. He will testify of Jesus, and in His power and presence they shall bear witness also.

Then Jesus reiterated the necessity of His departure. It was in order that the Holy Spirit might come. Of course He had been present all the while, but in a special way He will now work in and through the followers of Jesus.

He will reprove or convict the world of sin, righteousness, and judgment (John 16:8). "Of sin," because the world believes not on Jesus—and this unbelief is the greatest of sins. "Of righteousness," because Jesus goes to the Father, and the world shall see Him no more—but with Jesus' righteousness as the standard, the world will be made to realize its lack of righteousness before God. "Of judgment," because Satan is judged permanently—and those who cling to him are judged accordingly.

There were many things which Jesus would have spoken to the Eleven, but they were unprepared to receive them. However, the Holy Spirit would continue to teach them. He would guide them into all truth. He will not speak of Himself but of Jesus. He will not glorify Himself but Jesus. He will receive the things of Jesus and will show them to the disciples.

Then with a final promise of answered prayer, Jesus said, "Look: An hour is coming, and has come, when you will be scattered each to his own home, and you will leave Me alone. Yet I am not alone, because the Father is with Me. I have told you these things so that in Me you may have peace. In the world you have suffering. But take courage! I have conquered the world" (John 16:32–33).

Young grapes growing near Tel Lakhish. As Jesus and His disciples walked from the Upper Room to the Garden of Gethsemane, He said, "I am the vine; you are the branches. The one who remains in Me and I in him produces much fruit, because you can do nothing without Me" (John 15:5).

Jesus had been walking as He taught, so possibly by this time they were somewhere in the vicinity of the Temple area. If so, this adds meaning to that which ensued, for Jesus began to pray. This has been called His high priestly prayer. He will soon become the Sacrifice, but now the prayer of the High Priest rises as sweet incense to gladden the heart of God.

First, Jesus prayed for Himself. "Father, the hour is come. Glorify Your Son so that the Son may glorify You" (John 17:1). He came to give eternal life to all who should believe on Him. "This is eternal life: that they may know You, the only true God, the One You have sent—Jesus Christ" (John 17:3). He had fully done the Father's will, a will which anticipates the cross. Now the Son prays that the Father will glorify Him "with that glory I had with You before the world existed" (v. 5).

Second, Jesus prayed for the Eleven, and for all those who at that time had believed on Him.

"I pray for them" (John 17:9). He will soon leave them alone in the world, so He prayed that the Father would keep them. Because they are not of the world, the world will hate them. He did not pray that the Father would take them out of the world but that He would guard them from the evil one. He asked that they should be sanctified or dedicated (set apart for God's service) through God's Word which is truth. Jesus was sending them into the world to declare God's truth, even as God had sent Him into the world to reveal it. And for their sakes He dedicated Himself to the cross.

Third, Jesus prayed for all who in the future should believe in Him. He prayed that they should know unity in spirit, even as He and the Father were one. Furthermore, He prayed that all who believe in Him should be with Him in glory. He wants them to behold His glory which the Father has given to Him, "because you loved Me before the world's foundation" (John 17:24).

Then Jesus closed this prayer with words of wondrous beauty: "Righteous Father! The world has not known You. However, I have known You, and these have known that You sent Me. I made Your name known to them and will make it known, so that the love with which You have loved Me may be in them, and that I may be in them" (John 17:25–26).

What a beautiful way to close His public ministry! Having done so, Jesus went through the eastern gate of Jerusalem to meet His rendezvous with destiny—a destiny which would give His greatest revelation of the love of God.

THE AGONY IN GETHSEMANE

It was now possibly past midnight when Jesus and the Eleven arrived at Gethsemane. This was a garden just across the Kidron brook from Jerusalem. Tourists today may visit such a garden in which stands the Church of All

Nations. Gnarled olive trees may still be seen there, and one may view the Rock of Agony, reported to be the very rock on which Jesus prayed. Whether this is the actual spot or not, it must have been one nearby.

The word *Gethsemane* means "olive press," so evidently this was an olive orchard. It could have belonged to some friend of Jesus. He had often retired within its shaded retreats to spend time in prayer.

When Jesus arrived at Gethsemane, He left eight of the disciples near the entrance, probably as an outer guard against His being interrupted before He was ready to be arrested. Did this group have one of the two swords?

Then going farther into the garden, He left Peter, James, and John. Their near presence not only would strengthen Jesus but would also afford Him further protection. It is a fact that Peter carried one of the two swords. Luke says that Jesus told them to "pray that you may not enter into temptation" or trial (22:40). Both Matthew and Mark note that he told them to remain in that spot and "watch" or be on the alert.

Then with great sorrow of soul Jesus went still further into the shadows. There with only God to see He knelt, fell on His face, and prayed. With a physician's touch Luke says that His "sweat became like drops of blood falling to the ground." He broke out into a bloody sweat which became clotted blood.

Three times Jesus prayed, and there is a progression in His prayers. The first prayer was, "My Father! If it is possible, let this cup pass from Me. Yet not as I will, but as You will" (Matt. 26:39). He prayed for the cup to pass away if it be possible.

The second and third prayers were, "My Father, if this cannot pass unless I drink it, Your will be done" (Matt. 26:42). The original language reveals that, realizing that the cup cannot pass away, "unless I drink it," He was resigned to drinking it although He had not yet done so.

Was this struggle in prayer between Jesus and Satan? Or between Jesus and the Father? Or was it a struggle within Himself, within His own soul? Some hold that in Gethsemane Satan again tempted Jesus to avoid the cross. True, he did not want Jesus to die on the cross, but the struggle at this point does not seem to have been between Jesus and Satan. Nor can one say that it was a struggle between Jesus and the Father. There is no evidence of conflict between their wills. Indeed, in each prayer Jesus prayed that God's will should be done. Therefore, it would seem that the struggle was one within the soul of Jesus Himself.

This struggle is depicted in that which the "cup" involved. Does it mean that Jesus feared physical death? The entire record of the Gospels is to the contrary. It is more likely that it entailed that which His death involved. It meant that He must become sin for a lost world. His sensitive and sinless soul drew back from the prospect of becoming the very essence of sin itself. If there were any other way! Since there was not, He willingly surrendered Himself to the Father's will. He took the "cup" to drink its last bitter dreg.

After each of the first two prayers, Jesus had come to the three disciples to find them asleep. Physical exhaustion had taken its toll. The first time He found them asleep He awakened them and cautioned them to be on the alert, but the second time He did not bother them. The spirit was willing, but the flesh was weak.

However, the third time, with the victory fully won, He said to them, "Are you still sleeping and resting?" (Matt. 26:45). He no longer needed their protection, for "the time is near. The Son of Man is being betrayed into the hands of sinners. Get up, let's go! See—My betrayer is near" (vv. 45–46).

The hour truly had come. And the Son of Man was ready.

When the centurion and those with him, who were guarding Jesus, saw the earthquake and the things that had happened, they were terrified and said, "This man really was God's Son."

MATTHEW 27: 54 (HCSB)

The Crucifixion of Jesus

Gordon's Calvary, a place many believe Jesus was crucified.

The actual Crucifixion of Jesus consumed a period of about six hours. It began about nine o'clock on Friday morning, and Jesus died shortly after three o'clock in the afternoon of that day. But the larger picture involves the time from His arrest until His death and burial, and the arrest took place sometime after midnight and long before dawn on Friday.

The Trial of Jesus

Even as Jesus said, "Get up; let's go," Judas appeared, accompanied by the temple police and a cohort of Roman soldiers. Since leaving the Upper Room, Judas had been quite busy. In all probability he went first to the home of Caiaphas where he received a detachment of temple police. It took time for the high priest to secure the cohort of Roman soldiers from the Tower of Antonia. Perhaps these were sent along in case of a riot among the friends of Jesus.

Judas likely led this armed band to the home where he had left Jesus, but when they arrived, He and the Eleven had departed. Remembering Jesus' custom of praying in Gethsemane, Judas must have surmised that He had gone there again, so he led his group to the garden. They got by the outer guard of disciples who, like the inner guard, may have been asleep.

When they came to Jesus, He asked whom they were seeking. They said, "Jesus the Nazarene" (John 18:5). He replied, "I am He." Upon hearing this the guard, in fearful awe, moved back so quickly that they fell to the ground. Regaining their composure, they again, in answer to a second question from Jesus, said that they sought Him.

Judas had agreed to point out Jesus to them by kissing Him, and even though Jesus had identified Himself to them, Judas stepped up to Him and said, "Greetings, Rabbi!" (Matt. 26:49; to him Jesus was still only a rabbi) and with that he kissed Him. Actually, he "kissed him much." Since Judas called Jesus "Rabbi," he probably kissed Him on the hand, the customary greeting of a pupil to his rabbi. With that the officers seized Jesus.

By this time the disciples were wide awake. They asked Jesus if they should smite with the sword. Since they had been asleep, they were unaware that Jesus was now ready to be taken. Without waiting for an answer from Jesus, Peter, who may still have been somewhat dazed from sleep, pulled out his sword and swung away. He was trying to cut off somebody's head, for when he swung, Malchus, the high priest's slave, dodged expertly toward the direction from which the blow came, so that instead of being beheaded, he lost only his right ear. Jesus quickly healed the ear, and then He rebuked Peter. He took him in hand as He said, "Put your sword in place because all who take up a sword will perish by a sword" (Matt. 26:52).

Why did Peter react as he did? And why did Jesus rebuke him? When Peter saw Jesus being taken, and not knowing that He was now ready for it to take place, he did exactly what he understood that Jesus had told him to do. He was protecting Him from His enemies. But Jesus had now accomplished His purpose in coming to Gethsemane. He no longer needed this protection, so He told Peter to put up his sword lest he get himself killed.

Note Jesus' further word: "Or do you think that I cannot call on My Father, and He will provide Me at once with more than twelve legions of angels?

Greek sword of the kind Peter may have wielded in Jesus defense when the Temple Police came to arrest Him.

How, then, would the Scriptures be fulfilled that say it must happen this way?" (Matt. 26:53–54). More than twelve legions of angels! Over seventy-two thousand! One legion for each disciple, including Judas. He no longer needed guarding. Had He spoken just one word to the Father, the very forces of heaven would have rescued Him, and against such an assemblage what could a few temple police and Roman soldiers have done? No, Jesus was ready—His hour had come. The Scriptures must be fulfilled in Him. No man took His life from Him—He laid it down of Himself.

So with a word of rebuke for His captors, He permitted them to bind Him and lead Him away, and despite the disciples' avowals of loyalty, they all forsook Jesus and fled. They could with a sword dare the power of the armed band, but they lacked the moral courage to stand helpless in the face of evil.

Mark notes that a young man fled naked, as some officer grabbed after him (14:51–52), but he only got hold of a loose linen cloth which the lad had thrown about his body. Was this John Mark himself? If so, he had probably been awakened from sleep when the band came to his mother's home. With

Jewish Law and the Trials of Jesus

G. Al Wright, Jr.

Walk with me through the words of this article into a trial of disorder. The Gospels inform us that after Jesus' arrest He was taken to the chief priest and his cohorts, known as the Sanhedrin, in order to be tried.

The Sanhedrin was the primary governing body for the people of Israel. Composed of seventy of the elders drawn from a variety of circles, its primary role was to maintain the peace. Working in subservience to Rome's rulers, the goal of this group was to appease the politically appointed Gentile leaders in their city so their way of life could be maintained without interruption. Because the chief priest was a Roman appointee and based on the reality that the primary role of the Sanhedrin during those days was to appease Rome, we can safely conclude that there were people in this group on that night when Jesus stood before them who were operating with mixed motives. The gathered group was a mixture of insincerity, self-protective cunning, honest religious devotion, conscientious soul-searching, and fanaticism.

The purpose of this article is to examine the character and conduct of Jesus' trial before the Sanhedrin with particular attention to the function of Jewish law

Tombs of Jewish Sanhedrin. A typical tomb of the wealthy in Jesus time.

and custom. The issues include the nature of this trial as a formal proceeding or an informal hearing, the role of the chief priest, the function of the witnesses, the word of Jesus about the temple, the swearing of an oath, the ripping of the robes, and the ultimate charge of blasphemy that led to Jesus' being carried away to Pilate.

The first and most critical issue is whether this gathering of the Sanhedrin was a formal hearing. The dilemma is simply that rules were adopted for a formal gathering of the Sanhedrin around A.D. 200 that could reflect the practice of prior periods. If the rules for the operation of a Sanhedrin codified around A.D. 200 were in effect during Jesus' day, then we can safely conclude that this hearing before the Sanhedrin was not a formal proceeding. If we conclude that the rules of A.D. 200 do not apply here, then we are left with the ambiguity of being unable to judge either way. Since, however, so much of what is reported in later Jewish writings does reflect the ongoing practice of

Excavations of Herod's Palace on the west side of old Jerusalem adjacent to the Tower of David They reveal the Herodian foundations intersected by later levels of occupation. Jesus most likely was sent here by Pilate to Herod-Antipas of Galilee.

Stairway from city of David up to the western hill to the church of St. Peter's Engalacatu. Some Bible students suggest Jesus walked up this stairway to His trial before Caiaphas.

prior periods, we may safely conclude that at least some of the rules of the Sanhedrin that became law in A.D. 200 were at least in operation during Jesus' days. Operating on that assumption, the gathering of this group violated several basic rules: (1) meetings of the Sanhedrin could not be held at night—this meeting was clearly conducted under the cover of darkness; (2) the Sanhedrin did not gather during festivals—this trial was most certainly during one of the most sacred seasons of the year for the Jewish faithful; (3) the Sanhedrin was required to meet during successive days—this meeting was short and to the point; (4) witnesses who came before the Sanhedrin were examined privately—the witnesses in this situation were sought without screening and spoke their witness publicly. The most simple, most widely accepted conclusion to be drawn from the above violations of the rules for the gathering of the Sanhedrin is that this trial was an informal hearing to execute a foregone conclusion. Caiaphas made one decision: to arrest and execute Jesus. Jewish law and custom during this time help clarify this rapidly reached conclusion.

The office of chief priest during this period was not as much a religious office as it was a political appointment. Rome would leave alone any region that kept the peace. The role of the chief priest was precisely defined in terms of this peace-keeping mission. Any threat to the peace that carried any potential toward the incitement of riot was to be suppressed swiftly and surely. When the chief priest and the parties in partnership with him heard the words and saw the ways of Jesus, they perceived Jesus and all that He was about as a threat to the peace. Trouble caused by Jesus through the incitement of a riot would mean really big trouble for Caiaphas and his people. Thus to protect himself and his turf, he knew that Jesus had to be eliminated. The first step in the process from the perspective of Jewish law was to get an acceptable accusation to bring Him before the Roman government.

The Sanhedrin gathered and began listening to witnesses. All the gospel accounts concur in the disagreement of the witnesses until two were found who brought the same testimony. The testimony of the two was not as important as was their agreement. The Jewish faithful relied on texts like Deuteronomy 19:15: "One witness is not enough to convict a man accused of any crime or offense he may have committed. A matter must be established by the testimony of two or three witnesses" (see Deut. 17:6, NIV; Num. 35:30).

The witness that was given had to do with the most sacred building in any city inhabited by the Jews. A threat to the temple would tear apart the Jewish way of life. Since the temple was seen as the center of the universe and the most sacred place in all the earth, its destruction would represent potential devastation for God's people. These words from the witnesses were taken seriously.

When Jesus refused to respond to the accusations, the chief priest invoked an oath. The invoking of an oath was common in courtroom procedure but was also practiced in the practical affairs of daily life. That the oath was issued in the name of the living God is also important. This Old Testament term put the one under oath in the presence and beneath the power of that One who would judge him impartially and severely if he committed perjury.

The chief priest demanded a response in the delivery of the oath. He addressed the one, however, who had commanded his followers not to swear an oath. Jesus refused to walk beneath the yoke of the oath which was, in effect, a rejection of the authority of the chief priest and the accepted rules within which he operated. Jesus instead invoked the higher authority of Scripture and spoke with the authority that had all along amazed the crowds and angered the Pharisees. Refusing to submit to the chief priest's clear command, Jesus communicated the Word of God with Himself alone as the interpreter of its meaning. When the chief priest heard spoken in his presence what he probably had heard about previously, he ripped his robes.

The chief priest ripped his robes because what he heard was not just an outrage toward him but an offense to God. Jesus neither denied the testimony of the witnesses nor responded to the invoking of the oath. He stood His ground, refusing to bow to what the law demanded or custom dictated. Tearing one's garments was a powerful sign of mourning, and showing the signs of mourning had persuasive power. For the high priest to tear his clothing was the most extreme sign of mourning, since the Bible forbids him to tear his garments, or even to dishevel his hair (Lev. 21:10). Caiaphas' transgression of the law showed horror. Few Jews would have denied him what he wanted, and certainly, not his own counsellors.

The charge of blasphemy covered transgressions ranging from naming the name of God inappropriately to placing oneself in the position of God. As the chief priest saw it, Jesus' blasphemy had run the gamut. He had spoken against the temple. He had refused to acquiesce to Jewish law and custom. He had proclaimed the truth of Scripture with Himself alone as the interpretive authority.

There is little evidence to support that the hearing before the Sanhedrin was a formal court proceeding. It most likely was an informal gathering of at least some of those who for some time had been seeking a charge against Jesus that would support killing Him. Jewish law and custom were at the center of the confrontation as witnesses were sought and found, an oath was invoked, and a charge communicated that had solid foundation as blasphemy as the religious leaders understood blasphemy. The chief priest operated with the principle that it is better for one man to die than for many people to suffer.

G. Al Wright, Jr., is pastor of First Baptist Church, Waynesboro, Georgia.

---

a boy's curiosity perhaps he hurriedly put this linen cloth about his body and followed them to Gethsemane. At least, it is an interesting theory.

As the armed band led Jesus away, He said to them, "This is your hour—and the dominion of darkness" (Luke 22:53). Jesus had taken the "cup," and for all practical purposes had become sin. Until this time God had kept evil on a leash. He permitted it to go so far in its wicked purpose, but no farther. Now it seems that He unleashed evil to let it do its worst. It is as though God were saying, "Do your worst. You want to destroy God. Now you have your chance. But when you have expended all of your tyrannical power, I will still triumph over you!" It is thus that one can understand the utter abandon of evil in the hours which followed. In this light both the cross and the empty tomb take on their ultimate significance.

THE TRIAL ITSELF

The trial of Jesus comprised two phases, the Jewish and the Roman, and each of these was composed of three stages.

1. The Jewish Trial.

(1) The Preliminary Examination.

Jesus was taken first before Annas, the father-in-law of Caiaphas. It was before dawn on Friday. Even though Annas had been deposed as high priest by the Romans, he continued to wield great power with both the Jews and the Romans. So any charge brought against Jesus having his support would bear weight with both groups.

Furthermore, the sudden turn of events brought on by Judas' treachery had probably caught the Sanhedrin unprepared. Therefore, it was deemed wise by them to let Annas hold a preliminary examination in order to try to learn some definite charge to bring against Jesus.

When Christ appeared before him, Annas asked Him about His disciples and His teachings. Jesus reminded him that He had always spoken openly in the synagogues and the temple itself, so let those who had heard Him answer Annas' question. One of the temple police struck Jesus with a rod for thus answering the high priest. "If I have spoken wrongly," Jesus answered him, "give evidence about the wrong; but if rightly, why do you hit Me?" (John 18:23).

It was evident that Annas had failed to evoke a charge from Jesus. Therefore, he sent Him on to Caiaphas.

(2) The Predawn Trial before the Sanhedrin.

This stage of the trial was held in the home of Caiaphas. When word reached him that Jesus had been arrested, he hastily summoned the Sanhedrin, excepting Joseph of Arimathea and Nicodemus, to his home. It would appear that they had prepared two men to bear witness against Jesus, but events were moving so rapidly that they had not yet arrived. Therefore, the Sanhedrin sought to get other witnesses to bring some testimony against Jesus which would justify the death sentence. Apparently they had difficulty finding such, and even those who came forward gave conflicting testimony.

By this time the coached witnesses arrived, but even their testimony did not agree. One reported Jesus as having said, "I can demolish God's sanctuary and rebuild it in three days" (Matt. 26:61). The other's account was that He had said, "I will demolish this sanctuary made by hands, and in three days I will build another not made by hands" (Mark 14:58). Evidently the chief priests had remembered but misunderstood Jesus' words at the first cleansing of the temple. However, the witnesses did not do so well in following their coaching.

So failing here, the high priest took charge. As though to imply that these witnesses had produced damaging evidence, he asked if Jesus could answer the charge. But He remained silent. Then in desperation Caiaphas put Him on oath: "By the living God I place You under oath: tell us if You are the Messiah, the Son of God!" (Matt. 26:63). Had Jesus remained silent at this point His silence would have been equal to a denial of His Messiahship, the Son of God. So under oath He admitted that He was, saying, "You have said it yourself" or "Yes."

This would have been enough evidence for Caiaphas. But he received more than he expected, for Jesus continued, "But I tell you, in the future you will see 'the Son of Man seated at the right hand' of the Power, and 'coming on the clouds of heaven'" (Matt. 26:64). The day will come when He will be the Judge and Caiaphas will be the judged.

Caiaphas had heard enough. So charging Jesus with blasphemy, he asked as to what further evidence they needed. Then he began to tear his garments. When they heard blasphemy, the Jews were supposed to tear their garments and never wear them again. In all likelihood the remainder of the Sanhedrin followed their high priest's example, and when Caiaphas asked for their verdict, they all cried, "He deserves death" (Matt. 26:66).

Then pandemonium broke loose. They began to spit in Jesus' face and to beat Him on the neck. The temple police joined in the debacle. After blindfolding Jesus, they beat Him with rods and mocked Him, saying, "Prophesy to us, You Messiah! Who hit You?" (Matt. 26:68). It was a sickening spectacle. A court of justice had become a kangaroo court of injustice. What should have been a dignified occasion had become mob violence. It was the hour of the tyranny of darkness, as these men vented their hatred upon the Holy One of God.

While all this was transpiring within Caiaphas' house, a tragic event was taking place in the court outside. Peter, after a momentary panic, had followed afar off to see the outcome of Jesus' arrest. Three times he was asked by those around him if he were not one of Jesus' disciples. He first pretended not to understand the question. Later he took an oath that he did not know Jesus. Finally someone noted that he was a Galilean, because his peculiar dialect proved it. Apparently Peter then decided if language had anything to do with it he would show them some language. His fisherman's vocabulary came to the surface as he began to curse and swear, saying, "I do not know the man" (Matt. 26:74). Then from somewhere, probably outside the city, he heard a rooster crow. With this he recalled Jesus' words about his three denials.

Evidently Jesus heard it also, for He turned and looked at Peter, who was also looking at Him. That look broke Peter's heart, and weeping bitterly, he slipped away into the darkness.

(3) The Post-Dawn Trial before the Sanhedrin.

This stage of Jesus' trial was a mere formality, for the Sanhedrin had already decreed that He was liable to death. But Jewish law forbade that trials should be held at night, so to ratify the action already taken under cover of darkness, and to preserve the semblance of legality, after dawn the Sanhedrin assembled in its regular chambers and formally pronounced Jesus to be liable to death. It was after dawn, indeed, but it was the dawn of the blackest day in the history of the world!

A post mortem to the Jewish trial of Jesus was the remorse and suicide of Judas. When he saw that Jesus was condemned to death, "he repented himself" (Matt. 27:3, KJV). The word rendered "repented" is not the word for true repentance, meaning a change of mind, heart, and attitude. It is one which means "regret" but which involves no change within the person. Paul says that it may lead to true repentance (2 Cor. 7:8–10) but not necessarily so. Judas's regret did not do so. He regretted that he got caught in his deed. He suffered remorse, but he did not truly repent. Like some rapist who suffers remorse after he has satisfied his lust, but will commit his foul deed again, so Judas suffered remorse. However, it involved no change of heart, mind, or attitude.

In his fit of remorse he sought to ease his conscience by returning the thirty pieces of silver, but the chief priests would have none of it. They had used Judas in their nefarious deed and now were through with him. So he flung the blood money at their feet and went out and hanged himself. He is one of five suicides mentioned in the Bible, the only one in the New Testament. Where

The Church of St. Peter in Gallicantu on the north slope of the Hinnom Valley, the place, according to tradition, where Peter denied Jesus.

he did this is not known. Tradition places it in the Valley of Hinnom. Such a place is still pointed out to tourists. This would have been a fitting place for so foul an end, for it was Jesus' symbol of hell, the eternal destiny of Judas as he went "to his own place" (Acts 1:25).

The chief priests never appeared more hypocritical than at this point. They had probably taken this blood money from the sacred treasury or Corban. They had no compunction of conscience in using God's sacred money to carry out their evil purpose to destroy an innocent man, even the Son of God. Yet when it was thrown back at their feet, they said, "It's not lawful to put it into the temple treasury, since it is blood money" (Matt. 27:6), a price which they themselves had paid. So after taking counsel, they used it to purchase a potter's field in which to bury, not Jews, but foreigners! (v. 7; cf. Acts 1:18–19). They did not even name it "Judas' Memorial Cemetery!" Judas selfishly reached for the stars, but he got nothing. Yea, less than nothing; for he lost even that which he had, including his immortal soul.

Governor Pontius Pilate

Joel F. Drinkard, Jr.

Pontius Pilate was the fifth governor of Judea after Herod's son Archelaus was deposed in A.D. 6 and the Romans took over direct rule of Judea. The traditional dating for Pilate's rule is A.D. 26 to 36,[1] and he must have been relatively effective since he remained as governor for at least ten years.

Nothing is known of the background or personal life of Pontius Pilate before he appears on the pages of the New Testament. Apart from a brief mention in the Annals of Tacitus, a Roman historian who wrote about A.D. 115, all the references to Pilate come from the New Testament, the Jewish writers Philo and Josephus, and later Christian traditions.

It is possible to surmise a couple of items about Pilate's background just from the office he held—that of governor of the province of Judea. Beginning with the reign of Augustus, 27 B.C. to A.D. 14, the emperor appointed some of the provincial governors directly, rather than the Roman senate appointing

The original and only Latin dedicatory inscription yet found which mentions Pontius Pilate, the fifth Roman procurator of Judea, governing from A.D. 26 to 36.

them. Judea was one of the provinces where the governor was appointed directly by the emperor.

Furthermore, these provincial governors were appointed from the equestrian order, a wealthy class, but not from the aristocratic families that made up the Roman senate. Members of the equestrian order were required to have at least four hundred thousand sesterces of property. A sesterce was one-fourth of a denarius, and a denarius often was used as the typical daily wage for a peasant or common laborer. So the member of the equestrian order had to hold property valued at one hundred thousand days' pay for a worker. To put the matter in oversimplified terms, and to use our categories, such a person would have to be a millionaire or a multimillionaire. Pilate belonged to a wealthy family and probably had great personal wealth himself.

The New Testament notes that Pilate had a wife (Matt. 27:19). Her name is not given in Scripture, but later Christian tradition gave her name as Procula. She appears in the narrative as having had a dream the night before Pilate tried Jesus. Her dream troubled her, and she urged Pilate to have nothing to do with that "righteous man."

The New Testament informs us of only three events involving Pilate from the time he served as governor of Judea. In Luke 3:1–2, a date formula for the beginning of the ministry of John the Baptist and for Jesus' baptism by John specifies that these events took place in the fifteenth year of the reign of Tiberius, about A.D. 29.[2] Pilate was governor of Judea.

The second reference to Pilate comes in the midst of Jesus' ministry. While Jesus was teaching the crowds, some of those present told Him "about the Galileans whose blood Pilate had mixed with their sacrifices" (Luke 13:1).[3] This episode is not reported in any of the Jewish sources, although some have related it to one of the episodes. It seems obvious that Pilate slaughtered a group of Galilean Jews for some unstated reason while they were offering their sacrifices. Jesus used the episode to teach that those Galileans who were slain were no more sinful than any other people—that suffering and death are not always the result of some terrible sin a person has committed.

The final set of references to Pilate, and by far the most numerous, are those during the trail and crucifixion of Jesus. These are found in Matthew 27; Mark 15; Luke 23; John 18–19; and later reports of the trial found in Acts 3:13; 4:27; 13:28; and 1 Timothy 6:13.

More information on Pilate is provided in the writings of Philo and Josephus. Josephus related an incident apparently from a time just after Pilate took up his responsibility in Judea (Ant. 18:3.1). The Roman administrative center of Judea was at Caesarea Maritima, as was the official governor's residence. On certain festival occasions the governor brought a contingent of his troops and took up temporary residence in Jerusalem, at Herod's former palace. This action demonstrated a Roman presence at the festival and also probably prevented any popular uprising during crowded festival seasons. The Roman governors prior to Pilate showed concern and sensitivity to Jewish customs regarding images. One chief belief of the Jews was that all images, whether human or divine, were forbidden by their law.

Whether Pilate was unaware of the Jewish law because he was new to his post or was demonstrating Roman might and Jewish subordination, he marched his troops into Jerusalem and to the governor's residence with Roman standards at the head of the troops. This Pilate did at night without the Jews' knowledge. When the Jews learned what he had done, they protested to Pilate, who by now had returned to Caesarea. For five days they asked him to remove the offensive standards, but he refused. On the sixth day Pilate ordered his soldiers to surround the Jewish protesters with their weapons concealed but ready to use. When the Jews again raised their protest, Pilate sig-

Roman arches at Caesarea Maritima where Pilate's primary residence was located.

2. The Roman Trial.

(1) The First Time before Pilate.

Under Roman rule the Sanhedrin was permitted to try cases which involved civil and religious matters, but the Romans reserved to themselves the right to try criminal cases involving capital punishment. So even in this light the Jewish trial was a farce. The most that it could accomplish was to determine some capital charge against Jesus to present to the Roman governor Pilate.

Since it was early on Friday morning when the chief priests brought Jesus to Pilate, the place was probably the Herodian palace. Lest they be defiled for the Passover the chief priests refused to enter the dwelling of a Gentile. Therefore, when they arrived, Pilate came outside to meet with them.

The interplay of scorn between Pilate and the Jewish rulers is quite evident in the proceedings. In response to the governor's question as to the charge against Jesus, they said that had He not been an evildoer they would not have brought Him to Pilate. However, of necessity they stated a charge: "We found this man subverting our nation, opposing payment of taxes to Caesar, and saying that He Himself is the Messiah, a King" (Luke 23:2). They themselves had accused Jesus of blasphemy, but they knew that Pilate would consider only a charge involving political implications. However, even the charge which they named was a false one.

Pilate sensed that the whole thing involved only religious matters, so he told them to judge Jesus according to their own laws. Even though the Roman had not yet examined Jesus, the Jews reminded him that they had no authority to handle capital cases. To them Jesus was condemned without a legal trial.

So Pilate had Jesus on his hands. Therefore, he took Him inside the palace to examine Him. Here, then, is one of the most dramatic moments in history—Jesus, the Son of God, before a pagan Roman governor. Pilate thought that Jesus was on trial before him, when all the while he was on trial before Jesus. Take interest in the regal bearing of Jesus throughout this entire series of trials. It is evident that He, not His judges, was directing the proceedings. He would die, but it must be as a King.

The governor never asked Jesus about the charge of forbidding the payment of Roman taxes. This is significant, since this was a particularly tender spot for the Roman Empire. It shows that Pilate realized the falseness of the charge and that the matter was religious in nature. However, the chief priests had charged that Jesus made Himself a king, so the governor asked if He were the King of the Jews. Jesus replied that according to Pilate's own words He was; but He emphasized the fact that His kingdom was one of truth and not of politics. However, the fact remained that both the Sanhedrin and Pilate had called Jesus a King.

With a contemptuous question as to "what is truth?" Pilate led Jesus outside again. He told the Jews that he found Him guilty of no crime. The chief priests and elders, Sadducees and Pharisees, repeated their charge, which met only the silence of Jesus. Evidently expecting a denial from Him, Pilate asked if He had anything to say about the charge. "But He didn't answer him on even one charge" (Matt. 27:14). Once He had led them to charge Him with kingship, Jesus had

naled the soldiers and threatened the protesters with immediate death unless they desisted. The Jews practiced a nonviolent form of civil disobedience: they laid down on the ground and bared their necks, preferring death to the insult of seeing their religious laws broken. When Pilate saw their strong resolve, he reconsidered. Perhaps he did not want the report of such a massacre to get back to Rome, especially over a matter he had caused, whether deliberately or inadvertently. Pilate ordered the standards removed from Jerusalem and brought back to Caesarea.

In yet another incident Josephus recorded that Pilate decided to build an aqueduct to bring additional water to Jerusalem from a distance of about twenty-five miles (Ant. 18.3.2). To help finance the project Pilate used some of the temple treasury, money that had been contributed as offerings and upkeep for the sacred precincts. A rebellion broke out over this action. Josephus stated that many tens of thousands of people protested. Again Pilate sent his armed troops to surround the people. When he ordered the people to disperse, they protested more loudly and increased their verbal assaults on him. Pilate signaled his troops to attack the crowd and disperse them. The troops did so, but using much more force than Pilate had ordered. As a result, many of the protesters were killed along with many innocent bystanders. However, the protest was broken. Some commentators feel this incident is the same as the slaughter of the Galileans mentioned in Luke 13:1.

Philo recorded that Pilate brought into Herod's palace in Jerusalem some gold-plated shields (Embassy to Gaius, 38.299–305). These he dedicated to Tiberius, not so much to honor Tiberius as to provoke the Jews. Now the shields had no image on them, only an inscription mentioning the name of the person to whom they were dedicated and the name of the person who dedicated them. Nevertheless, the Jewish community protested this action to Pilate. Among the protesters were Herod's four sons and other descendants and many Jewish leaders. When Pilate refused to take the shields down, perhaps because to do so would seem an insult to the emperor, the Jews threatened to send a report directly to Tiberius. Pilate was in a bind: he did not want to insult the emperor or to appear weak to the Jews, and he did not want a major incident either. Pilate's administrators sent word directly to Tiberius, begging his understanding. Tiberius immediately sent word to Pilate, severely rebuking him and ordering the shields be

nothing more to say. This silence caused the governor to marvel greatly.

Apparently the Jews sensed that Pilate was about to release Jesus. Therefore, they began to say more urgently, "He stirs up the people, teaching throughout all Judea, from Galilee . . . to here" (Luke 23:5). When Pilate heard the word *Galilee,* he saw a way out of his predicament, for Galilee was under the jurisdiction of Herod Antipas, and he was in Jerusalem at that moment. Even though the two men were not on good terms, Pilate sent Jesus to Herod for judgment. He cared little for showing the puppet tetrarch any courtesy. He merely wanted to get Jesus off his hands.

(2) The Appearance before Herod Antipas.

Herod Antipas was quite pleased when Jesus was brought before him. He had long wished to see Jesus, hoping that He would perform a miracle in his presence; but even though he questioned Him at length, amid the repeated charges of the Jewish rulers, Jesus did not so much as speak one word to him. Knowing Herod's true nature, He ignored him altogether.

Herod soon became bored with the entire proceedings. Therefore, he and his soldiers began to treat Jesus with contempt. They regarded Him as nothing, a zero. So they mocked Him, their supreme mockery being to array Him in robes of regal splendor. A king indeed! Therefore, they dressed Him as one, and then they sent Him back to Pilate. The Roman governor still had Jesus on his hands.

(3) The Second Time before Pilate.

When Jesus again stood before Pilate, the governor called a counsel with the Jewish rulers. He told them that neither he nor Herod had found Jesus guilty of their charges, but to placate them he proposed to whip Him and then to release Him. Whip an innocent man? But such was the conniving of an evil mind and a weak character. Of course the Jews would have none of this.

In desperation Pilate sought some other way to escape his uneasy predicament. Suddenly he remembered a custom of the Romans. On festive occasions, in order to placate the Jews, they would release some prisoner of their choosing. At that moment Pilate was holding a notable prisoner named Barabbas. He was guilty of insurrection, robbery, and murder, and, together with others, probably was scheduled to be crucified that very day. He may have been one of the false messiahs whose mission had failed, and like so many others of his kind, he had become the leader of a robber band which pillaged and murdered. Pilate thought that the Jewish people surely would not want him turned loose on them again.

Therefore, he proposed to release either Jesus or Barabbas. The Jews could have their choice. It may well be that the people were about to select Jesus for release, but at that point the proceedings were interrupted. For at that moment Pilate received a message from his wife. She urged him to have nothing to do with this righteous man. In a dream she had suffered many things because of Him, and since the Romans placed much importance on dreams, this disturbed Pilate all the more.

The Jewish rulers had used this interruption to advantage. Moving among

removed to Caesarea.

This incident probably occurred after October of A.D. 31 when Sejanus, Tiberius' anti-Semitic prefect, had been executed. Tiberius would permit no semblance of anti-Semitism, whether intended to not.

Josephus recorded a final incident concerning Pilate that occurred at the end of Pilate's term as governor (Ant. XVIII.4.1). Indeed, the incident apparently was what ended his years of service as governor. A prophet, or imposter, aroused the Samaritans by telling them he would show them sacred vessels buried on Mount Gerizim (their sacred mountain). Many Samaritans gathered in the vicinity of Mount Gerizim, some armed. Pilate had his troops block the road to the site and then had the troops attack the Samaritans. Some of the people were killed and many more taken captive. Later Pilate had leaders of this group killed. The unrest was ended. However, the local Samaritan council appealed the matter to Vitellius, the Roman legate to Syria. Vitelius ordered Pilate to Rome to answer the charges before Tiberius and replaced him with Marcellus.

In 1961, in the excavation of the theater in Caesarea Martima, a stone inscription mentioning Pilate was found in secondary use. The inscription is not complete, but reads in Latiin: TIBERIVM "A Tiberium. TIVSPI-LATVS Pontius Pilate. ECTVSIVDAE Praefect of Judea."

The inscription apparently refers to a building dedi-cated to Tiberius (the Tiberium). Enough of Pilate's name remains to make the identiy certain. Also, Pilate's title in the inscription is prefect, rather than procurator as often assumed.

Governor Pontius Pilate was a ruthless, aggressive politician. Although he apparently thought little about it at the time, he made one of the most infamous decisions in history when he permitted Jesus to be crucified unjustly. How ironic that his life had so little impact on history that the historians took little note of the once-powerful Roman governor. Yet the one he condemned to death continues to be the object of more literature than any other person who ever lived and is worshiped as Lord by millions.

[1]A new chronology dates his rule as beginning in A.D. 14. See Daniel Schwarts, "The Appointment of Pontius Piltae and the Chronology of Antiquities of the Jews, Books 18–20," *Zion* 48 (1982), 333.
[2]A suggested textual variation has 2 rather than 15, based on the peculiar Greek spelling *pentekaidekato* in Luke 3:1 rather than the normal *dekapente*.
[3]From the *Holy Bible, New International Version*, copyright 1973, 1978, 1984 by International Bible Society. Subsequent quotations are marked NIV.

Joel Drinkard, Jr., is Professor of Old Testament Interpretation, The Southern Baptist Theological Seminary, Louisville, Kentucky.

North wall of the city of Caesarea Maritima in foreground with aqueduct to the city in the background. After Archelaus was removed in A.D. 6. Caesarea Maritima became the capital of the province of Judea and served as the official home of the procurators among whom was Pontius Pilate.

the people, they urged them to choose Barabbas. Thus when Pilate asked them to make their choice, they chose Barabbas for release. In consternation Pilate, perhaps hoping that their choice might even extend to Jesus, asked, "What should I do then with Jesus, who is called Messiah?" (Matt. 27:22). Unanimously they cried, "Crucify Him!."

What was the choice that they made? It involved more than a man, for they proposed to release one who had claimed to be their kind of messiah and to crucify the Messiah of God. It is interesting to note that Origen claims to have seen a Gospel of Matthew which called Barabbas "Jesus Barabbas," and some manuscripts in existence today so read. There is tremendous suggestion in this thought.

The word *Jesus* means "Jehovah is salvation." *Barabbas* means "son of father." So here was "Barabbas, the son of his father" and "Jesus, the Son of His Father." The former offered himself as a political messiah; the latter offered

Dungeon where according to 4th century tradition, Jesus would have been scourged by Pilate.

Himself as a spiritual Messiah. The one proposed to give political redemption; the Other proposed to give redemption from sin. The one brought revolution; the Other brought regeneration. Jesus Barabbas offered to save the Jews by the shedding of their blood. Jesus Christ would save them by the shedding of His own blood. But the Jews chose Jesus Barabbas and rejected Jesus Christ. Truly, they chose, and rejected, more than they knew.

Still Pilate made one last effort to release Jesus—he beat Him unmercifully. This was done by tying Him to a post, having first bared His back. The whip was made of leather thongs. In the end of each thong was placed a piece of bone or metal. With each lick these pieces tore out bits of flesh, leaving the back of the victim a bloody, lacerated mass. In such a condition Jesus would appear to be everything else but regal. So, partly in derision of the Jews and perhaps also hoping to appeal to their sympathy for so pitiful a spectacle, Pilate brought Jesus before them, saying, "Here is the man!"

But Jesus was to know no sympathy that day. Instead, the mob cried, "Crucify Him." Still protesting the innocence of Jesus, Pilate tried to escape a decision by a weak yet taunting suggestion that the Jews should crucify Jesus. "See to it yourselves," he said. But they could not put anyone to death, let alone crucify them. And they would not let Pilate escape. By their law Jesus should die because He had made Himself the Son of God. Hearing this the superstitious Roman feared all the more. Again taking Jesus inside the palace, he questioned Him once more, but no answer came from Him. Pilate reminded Jesus that he had the power either to release or to crucify Him. Then Jesus spoke the second time to the governor. He reminded him that the only power which he had over Him was not from Rome but from heaven. Pilate's abuse of that power was a sin, to be sure. However, since he was a pagan who was ignorant of the revelation of God, those who knew that revelation and yet had handed Jesus over to Pilate for crucifixion must bear the greater sin.

When the governor sought once again to release Jesus, the Jews reminded him that if he did so he was no friend of Caesar. Here was a veiled threat to bring this whole matter to Caesar's attention, along with Pilate's other misdeeds. That did it! Because as a procurator he was directly accountable not to the Roman senate but to Caesar.

So Pilate gave up the struggle. He caused his judgment seat to be brought forth for the purpose of sitting thereon as he pronounced upon Jesus the sentence of death by crucifixion. Before he did so, however, in scornful defiance of the Jews, he pointed to Jesus saying, "Here is your King!" The chief priests completely denounced the kingship of Jesus, even of God Himself, as they said, "We have no king but Caesar" (John 19:15).

When, therefore, he saw that the case was hopeless, Pilate performed a customary ritual to declare his innocence in the whole debacle. Calling for a basin of water, he washed his hands before the multitude, saying, "I am innocent of this man's blood. See to it yourselves" (Matt. 27:24).

But Pilate could not escape his guilt so easily. In his cowardly surrender to mob violence, he made a travesty out of Roman justice. He continued on his evil way, until in A.D. 36, just six years after he had sought so tenaciously but weakly to escape the judgment of Caesar, he was recalled to Rome and banished to Gaul. Just outside Lucerene, Switzerland, stands Mount Pilatus. Tradition says that when storms rage on that mountain Pilate's ghost in the rain seeks to wash the guilt from his hands, saying, "It won't come off! It won't come off!" Nor will it ever do so.

What about the Jews who stood before him on that terrible day in Jerusalem? All the people answered, "His blood be on us and on our children!" (Matt. 27:25).

This is all the more terrible when one remembers the teaching of the Mosaic Law in this regard. Pilate knew nothing of it; but the Jewish people knew. In Deuteronomy 21 the law took account of the problem of innocence in cases of unsolved murder. If someone was found slain in the field by an unknown slayer, the distance should be measured from the body to the surrounding cities. The one nearest to the body was regarded responsible. So to be cleansed of guilt the elders of the city were to follow a prescribed rite. A heifer was to be slain in an uncultivated valley. This was to be done in the presence of the priests, the sons of Levi. Then the elders were to wash their hands over the slain heifer, all the while saying, "Our hands have not shed this blood, neither have our eyes seen it. Be merciful, O Lord, unto thy people Israel,

The eastern wall of Jerusalem taken from the Mt. of Olives. The closed Eastern Gate is visible in the wall.

whom thou hast redeemed, and lay not innocent blood unto thy people Israel's charge. And the blood shall be forgiven them" (vv. 7–8).

In the case of the innocent blood of Jesus, neither the people nor the priests did this. They all said, "His blood be on us, and on our children." A terrible legacy indeed!

Pilate released Barabbas, but he caused Jesus to be scourged and crucified. The soldiers made quite a sport of the whole affair. So Jesus was a king, was He? A king should have regal robes! Therefore, they put about Jesus a scarlet cloak belonging to one of the soldiers. He should have a crown! So they plaited one out of thorns and thrust it on His head, the thorns gouging into His brow. He should have a scepter! A reed of grass growing nearby was plucked and placed in His hand. Then in procession the soldiers passed by, kneeling before Him, hailing Him as King of the Jews, spitting on Him, and beating Him on the head.

When they had tired of the cruel sport, they led Jesus away to be crucified. The ordeal to which He had been subjected took its toll, for on the way He fell under the weight of His cross which He was required to carry. A passerby, Simon of Cyrene, probably a Jew from North Africa who had come to Jerusalem for the Passover, was made to carry the cross for Jesus. Two malefactors, perhaps companions in crime with Barabbas as their leader, were also taken to be crucified. So they came to Golgotha, a hill shaped like a skull. (The

Latin name is Calvary.)

No one knows for certain the location of this place. Tradition places it at the site of the Church of the Holy Sepulchre. In modern times Gordon's Calvary has been mentioned as a possibility. This is a small knoll outside the city wall, which to this day has the appearance of a skull. It is now the site of an Arab cemetery. A guide told the writer that this was once the place where the Jews executed by stoning. The Romans continued to use it, only they employed the method of crucifixion. One thing is known. Calvary was outside the city wall (Heb. 13:12). Archaeologists are not agreed as to whether the Church of the Holy Sepulchre stands outside the wall of that day, but most certainly Gordon's Calvary does.

THE DEATH OF JESUS

1. Some Significant Matters.

A benevolent society of women in Jerusalem always provided a drink of drugged wine for crucifixion victims in order to dull the pain, but when it was offered to Jesus, He tasted it and then refused it. He would endure the cross in full possession of His mental powers. Upon this refusal the soldiers proceeded with the crucifixion, an ordeal so terrible that Roman law forbade that it should be used in executing a Roman citizen.

One end of the upright part of the cross was placed in a hole in the ground. The crosspiece was placed flat on the ground. After stripping the victim of his clothes, he was made to lie flat on the ground with his arms outstretched along the crosspiece. In order to render him helpless, his arms and legs were jerked out of joint. Then, after his hands had been nailed to the crosspiece, his body was drawn up into a position, perhaps two feet above the ground, where the crosspiece was fastened to the upright part. Finally, his feet were crossed, and a spike driven through them into the wood. Then a board, on which was written the victim's crime, was nailed above his head. In the case of Jesus it read, "JESUS THE NAZARENE THE KING OF THE JEWS." Thus Jesus, stark naked, was nailed to a cross between two thieves. Truly, He was numbered with the transgressors.

The crucifixion detail was composed of four soldiers under the command of a centurion. Customarily the four soldiers divided among themselves the clothes of their victims. Usually such clothing consisted of five garments: head gear, sandals, girdle, an outer garment, and an inner garment. Each of the soldiers took one of the first four items, but Jesus' inner garment was seamless or in one piece. Therefore, rather than tear it, the soldiers gambled for it. Little did they know that they were fulfilling Psalm 22:18.

In the meantime the chief priests returned to Herod's palace to protest the wording written on the superscription above Jesus' head. They insisted that it should not read, "THE KING OF THE JEWS," but that He said, "I AM KING OF THE JEWS." However, Pilate stood his ground. Therefore, the official

Roman crime for which Jesus died was that He was King of the Jews.

John notes that this "title" was written in Hebrew (Aramaic), Latin, and Greek. Obviously Pilate's purpose in using this trilingual title was that the crime of Jesus might be known to all. Aramaic was the language spoken in Palestine at that time. Latin was the official language of the Empire, and Greek was a somewhat universal language which would be understood by all who did not read the other two.

However, knowing John's mystical nature, one can but wonder if he did not mention these languages with another purpose in mind. Was it not to point out the universal guilt for Jesus' death? Hebrew, Latin, and Greek suggest the three great streams of life in the Roman world. At least these languages suggest that the three great streams converged to nail Jesus to the cross. Hebrew was the language of religion; Latin was the language of government; Greek was the language of pagan culture. Religion rejected Jesus; government crucified Him; pagan culture ignored Him. Surely there was/is guilt enough for all.

What of the ordeal of the crucifixion itself? During this time Jesus spoke seven times, and in these "seven words from the cross" one may understand partly that which transpired as "God was in Christ, reconciling the world unto himself."

2. The Seven Words from the Cross.

(1) "Father, forgive them, because they do not know what they are doing" (Luke 23:34).

This was a prayer prayed by Jesus, probably while He was being fastened to the cross. Over and over He prayed it. It was a prayer that God would forgive all whose sin helped nail Him to the cross.

An artist's conception of Roman crucifixion based on an archaelogist's find of a nail driven through the side of an ankle bone.

In a distinct way, however, it was a prayer for those who had an actual part in the crucifixion itself, and especially the Jews. The basis upon which He asked this forgiveness was that they did not "know" what they were doing. Paul says that had the rulers of this world known, they would not have crucified the Lord of glory.

When Jesus prayed, He used a word for "know" which means to perceive through experiential knowledge until it becomes a conviction of the soul or soul knowledge. In their sin-mastered state they did not know in their souls what they were doing. They had asked for a sign from heaven as to Jesus' deity. That sign would be His bodily Resurrection. Thereafter they would have a basis upon which to acquire soul knowledge. If then they repented, they should be forgiven. Otherwise, there would be no forgiveness.

Another dual thought is suggested in the word *forgive*. It is the same word used in Matthew 27:49 for "let be" or "wait." Furthermore, it is akin to the word *suffer* or *permit* found in Matthew 19:14. Therefore, it is not out of line to understand this word *forgive* in these senses. With respect to the crucifiers it could mean, "Wait until after the resurrection." But another thought may well be involved. Jesus had said that He could call for more than twelve legions of angels to rescue Him. Was this not then a cry to heaven that the angelic hosts should "wait" or "let be" that the crucifixion might be permitted to continue according to the will and purpose of God?

At any rate it did continue. The people passing by on the nearby road railed upon Jesus, calling upon Him to come down from the cross. Even the chief priests, scribes, and elders, having returned from their fruitless mission to Pilate, joined in. They said literally, "He is the King of Israel! Let Him come down now from the cross, and we will believe in Him" (Matt. 27:42). They even dared God to save Him. "He has put His trust in God; let God rescue Him now—if He wants Him! For He said, 'I am God's Son'" (v. 43). The two thieves dying on either side of Jesus joined in with His tormentors.

This raises the question as to who or what nailed Jesus to the cross? Certainly it was in the will and purpose of God, but this is not to say that He actually did it. One might say that Satan did it. He had tried repeatedly to kill Jesus, but in no sense did he want Him to die on a cross. From the outset he tried to steer Jesus away from it. Even now through the crowd about Calvary he was challenging Him to leave the cross, for he knew that it was in such a death that God would utterly defeat him. In this light one can only say that evil running rampant nailed Jesus to the cross. It had even gotten out of Satan's control. God had unbridled evil to let it do its worst, and even then He would triumph over it and destroy its power.

Could Jesus have come down from the cross? He could have, but He would not, for He was on the cross to die for the sins of the world. If He saved Himself physically, He could not save man spiritually. So, in fact, He was held to the cross, not by spikes, but by divine love expressing itself in God's saving will and purpose.

(2) "Today you will be with Me in paradise" (Luke 23:43).

The howling mob continued, but to Jesus through its din came the voices of the two thieves. At first they both reproached Him, parroting the words of the Jewish rulers. Suddenly there was a change, for in one sense of the word both men began to pray to Jesus. They were asking that He do something for them.

One thief "railed on" Him or cursed. Imagine beginning a prayer with a curse! This man did. He demanded that since Jesus claimed to be the Christ, He should save both Himself and them. There was no note of repentance and confession. He said nothing about sin, only about his present peril. There was no change in his heart. He only wanted off that cross. Jesus heard him with His ears but not with His heart. There was no basis whatever for a divine response, so this thief entered hell with a so-called prayer on his lips.

A first-century storage jar of the type in which vinegar or wine might have been taken to the crucifixion site.

The other thief prayed quite differently. He rebuked his companion in crime, admitted their sin, but confessed the sinlessness of Jesus. Then he prayed, "Jesus, remember me when You come into Your kingdom!" (Luke 23:42). The light had broken through to his soul. He knew that Jesus was the Christ of God. In that knowledge he forgot all about his present predicament. His one thought was for his soul. On the cross both he and Jesus would surely die, yet his only desire was to be remembered by Jesus in His kingdom.

However, he received more than he asked for. Jesus said, "Today you will be with Me in paradise." He prayed for remembrance; he received fellowship. He thought of a far distant kingdom; Jesus said, "Today." Before the sun set on that day, Jesus and the redeemed sinner walked arm in arm through the gates of glory.

(3) "Woman, here is your son! . . . Here is your mother" (John 19:26–27).

There was a little island of love in that ocean of hate, for three women and a man had drawn near to the cross. One woman was Jesus' mother, and the man was John the beloved disciple. When Jesus saw them, He spoke to them words of comfort and courage.

Mary had learned to lean on Jesus, her eldest son. Now He was dying. The sword truly was piercing through her soul. The future must have been bleak indeed. To whom could she turn, for her other children did not believe in Jesus as the Christ!

John also was bent down with grief, for the One whom he loved with a passion was now hanging on a cruel cross. What could life possibly hold for him?

Then they both heard Jesus' blessed words. To Mary they meant that she could now turn to the one person on earth who, beside herself, loved and understood Jesus the best. To John it meant the comfort and encouragement of a committed responsibility. Jesus had faith in him so that to him He entrusted His dearest and best. As Jesus was his substitute on the cross, so John would be Jesus' substitute in caring for His mother.

From that hour he took Mary to live in his own home. One tradition says that she lived with John in Jerusalem for a few years and then died there. Another holds that she died at an advanced age in Ephesus, where she had continued to live with the beloved disciple. In either case they most surely were a comfort and strength to each other, and they had fellowship together in their living Lord.

(4) "My God, My God, why have You forsaken Me?" (Matt. 27:46).

These are the opening words of the twenty-second psalm, a psalm which describes the Crucifixion in vivid detail. It must have been much in Jesus' mind and heart throughout His life, but this was not a mere recital of a verse of Scripture. It came up from the very depths of Jesus' soul. Matthew gives this verse from the original Hebrew, but Mark gives it in Aramaic, the native tongue of Jesus. Either is correct, but more likely Mark gives it exactly as Jesus uttered it. In His deep grief and suffering, the Lord, who doubtless spoke Greek, went back to the language of His childhood to give utterance to this cry.

With this saying one enters into the very Holy of Holies of Calvary. A strange darkness had hovered over the land since the noon hour, as though the sun itself covered its face before such a scene. It was now about three o'clock in the afternoon. It was indeed the hour of darkness both natural and spiritual.

It is impossible for mere man to plumb the depths of the meaning of this word of Jesus, but note that He no longer called God "Father." In some indefinable way the Father had forsaken the Son, so that now He can only say, "My God." Even this was a cry of faith, although there is the difference in relationship.

Was it not that Jesus now had drunk the last dregs of the bitter "cup"? He had become sin. A holy God cannot look with favor upon sin. In that moment the Son of God wrestled with sin in its deepest depths. The Son of man, now become sin, endured the sufferings of hell as all of the vial of God's abiding wrath was poured out upon sin. It was for only a moment, but it was the infinite God suffering infinitely for the infinite guilt of finite man. In a very real sense Jesus had been left by God in the lurch, which is itself a good translation of this cry.

(5) "I'm thirsty!" (John 19:28).

At the outset of the Crucifixion, Jesus had refused drugged wine, but now He asked for something to drink. While the struggle with sin raged, He gave no thought to His own physical needs. Now that the battle was over, and the victory won, He called for some liquid.

This was a natural thing for Him to say, for thirst was one of the greatest sufferings which accompanied death on the cross. Through bleeding Jesus lost body fluid. The suffering and nerve-racking experience caused Him to perspire profusely. Every ray of the hot sun became a leach sucking water from every pore of His naked body, so that His lips were parched and cracked. His mouth was dry, and His tongue thickened. Fever ravished His body, and His inflamed vocal cords became raspy.

There were two reasons Jesus uttered this one word (*dipso*). John says that Jesus knew all things were now finished, that is, the purpose of His being on the cross had been achieved, but he added also "that the Scripture might be fulfilled" (cf. Pss. 22:14–15; 69:21). Except for the acts of dying and being raised again, every prophetic Scripture concerning His redemptive work other than those connected with Jesus' thirst had been fulfilled. So when He said, "I'm thirsty," the picture up to that point was complete. Jesus did not utter this as a merely mechanical recital of Scripture, but coming, as it did, out of His physical agony, it did fulfill Scripture.

However, there was another reason for this word. Jesus was about to utter the word of victory or completion. He wished it to be not the rasping utterance of one who was completely spent. It must be clearly enunciated in order that it might be heard and understood.

There was also a touch of pity in this gruesome scene. A soldier took a sponge and dipped it in the vinegar provided for the Crucifixion detail. Then placing it on a reed, he pressed it to the lips of the Savior.

(6) "It is finished!" (John 19:30).

This was Jesus' word of completion. It means that "it is finished and stands finished." It was a word of full and final completion. Nevermore will Jesus die on a cross. Nevermore will He suffer for the sin of the world. He had made the once-for-all sacrifice. All that was necessary for the Son to do for man's redemption had been accomplished.

The Greek papyri add greatly to the meaning of the word (*tetelestai*). It belongs to a family of words which was used in the legal and commercial life of Jesus' day. One word of this family was used to express the idea of completing a legal deed by dating and signing it. In a very real sense, before the foundation of the world, God had drawn up a deed of redemption for all men who would receive it, but the deed had never been dated or signed. So just before Jesus died He inserted the date of His death, and He signed it in His indelible blood.

The word uttered by Jesus was used in the sense of making full and final payment of a note. Again, in eternity the Son had made out a promissory note of redemption. In this light one may understand the manner of salvation for those who died before Calvary. They were saved on credit, the credit of the Son of God, looking toward that day when He would pay the note. Therefore, all the Old

First-Century Tombs in Judah

Joel F. Drinkard, Jr.

The most common type of tomb in Judea in the first century A.D. was the family tomb that could be used by members of an extended family over several generations. Typically, this tomb was a rock-cut, artificial burial cave. Although natural caves were used for burial, and small natural caves may have been enlarged to form some burial caves, the artificial cave cut into rock was more common.

Many of the hillsides near the towns and cities were dotted with these burial caves. The relatively soft limestone common to the region was easily worked with simple cutting tools. Not all burial caves were cut into hillsides. Some were formed by cutting steps down into the bedrock, then cutting a small entrance court, and finally cutting a burial chamber into the vertical wall created by the steps and entrance court. While no general description can cover all the variations of the burial cave, certain features were common in most of these burial caves.

The burial cave in general was for the wealthier members of society. The poorer people were simply buried in an unmarked pit outside the city. The wealthiest had the largest burial caves, often decorated with a monumental facade cut into the hillside. The burial

Tomb of Ben Hazir, a tomb with a monumental facade, a typical first-century tomb of a wealthy family.

be removed from the burial niche, freeing it for another burial, and would be placed in a bone repository within the tomb or in an ossuary. This secondary burial after a year marked the end of the official mourning rites for the individual and was to be performed by the immediate family.

The practice of gathering the bones of family members over several generations into a single bone repository may well explicate the common phrase from the Old Testament of "being gathered to one's fathers (or ancestors)." Literally, the deceased person's bones were gathered and placed with the ancestors' bones. Because burial caves were usually intended for extended family use, they would have numerous *loculi*; one is reported to have had 70 *loculi*.

The use of ossuaries for reburial of bones seems to have been introduced in Judea about the time of Herod the Great (37–4 B.C.) and remained common until the destruction of the temple by Titus in A.D. 70. The ossuary was a small limestone box, often beautifully decorated, with a stone cover; it was designed to hold the bones of the deceased. The use of ossuaries was related to the rise

complexes at Beth Shearim have elaborate entrance facades. Although a couple of centuries later than our target time period, these tombs show designs developed from first-century tombs. Large freestanding monuments were formed by cutting away the natural rock from the burial site, leaving an elaborate stone building. Examples include the so-called Absalom's Tomb and Zechariah's Tomb in the Kedron Valley just southeast of the Temple Mount in Jerusalem.

The typical burial cave had a small rock-cut entrance one to two feet wide and three to five feet high. The entrance would lead into a main chamber. The inner chamber would have one section with a sunken floor, usually at the entrance, providing sufficient height for the family members to stand. The ceiling would be five to six feet above this sunken floor. Along the walls of the chamber would be a number of burial niches called *loculi* [LOW-cu-lie] (the singular is *loculus*) or *kokhim* [koke-EEM] (the singular is *kokh*). These individual burial niches would be cut horizontally back into the rock of the wall about five to six feet deep, one and one-half feet wide, and two feet high. The body of the deceased would be placed in one of these niches. The niche would be sealed with a stone slab or with smaller unworked stones. The body would remain in the burial niche for a year; the bones would then

Interior of the garden tomb where some believe Jesus was buried.

Testament righteous, like Abraham, had looked forward in joy to Messiah's day.

Now on the cross the promissory note had been paid. So Jesus wrote across it *TETELESTAI!* Nevermore can payment again be demanded! All who lived before that hour, and since that hour, may in faith receive the redemption which God in Christ provided as He died on the cross.

Even more to the point is a papyrus usage of this verb where a father sent his son on a mission, saying, "Until you accomplish this for me." It is inferred that upon the successful completion of the mission the son reported, "It is finished."

In the above examples, therefore, Jesus' sixth word from the cross takes on added meaning. To the Father He said, "Mission accomplished!" To the host of Old Testament saints who were in heaven "on credit," He said, "The note has been paid and receipted. The deed to redemption has been dated and signed." As this word *TETELESTAI* gave assurance to those who in faith looked forward to Calvary, even so it continues to give assurance to all after the event who look back to it believing in the Savior.

(7) "Father, into Your hands I entrust My Spirit" (Luke 23:46).

Having uttered this word Jesus died. Mark and Luke say that He "expired" or "breathed His last." John says that He "yielded up His spirit," but Matthew says that He "gave up His spirit." In other words, when His mission was accomplished, He permitted His spirit to return to the Father. King all the way!

What did Jesus mean when He said, "Father, into Your hands I entrust My spirit"? You will notice that once again He addressed God as Father. There never was a time when He and the Father were not one, but now that the struggle is over the representative Prodigal of prodigals has been clasped to the Father's bosom. The Son committed or placed His spirit alongside the Father.

The papyri add meaning to this statement also, for this word *commit* was used in the sense of filing a report or of inserting something in the register. The Son, therefore, filed the report of His completed mission. The receipted note and completed deed He inserted in the register of heaven.

Another such use of this word was to commit a thing to another to be safeguarded and used for its intended purpose. A derivative of this word is used of a "deposit," as in a bank. The Son deposited His redemptive work in the bank of God's grace, to be kept safe and used for the redemption of all who shall believe in Him as Savior.

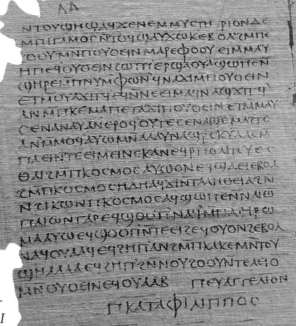

Greek papyrii on which popular material was recorded.

What these various words meant to those who first heard them from the cross enhances their meaning through the ages. They are the substance of the Gospel itself, and they are committed by the Father to all who receive the Son in faith, that through the Holy Spirit they may be the power of God unto salvation to everyone who believes in Him who became everything that men are, apart from sin, that they may become everything that He is.

THE PHENOMENA ACCOMPANYING JESUS' DEATH

When Jesus died, strange things happened in and near Jerusalem. Nature itself responded to the death of its Creator. The earth quaked, and the rocks were rent. The temple itself must have reeled, for the veil of the temple, which separated the Holy of Holies from the Court of the Priests, was torn in two from top to bottom. This signified that through the redemptive work of Christ every man might come to God with boldness.

Josephus tells of a quaking of the temple before its destruction, and the

---

of a belief in resurrection among the Pharisees. An ossuary kept the bones of individuals separated and would maintain the ritual purity of a righteous individual in view of a coming resurrection of the righteous. Some ossuaries held the bones of several individuals, probably close family members.

Some first-century tombs have a burial bench cut into the length of the wall, usually with an arch-shaped ceiling. This type structure is called an arcosolium. The arcosolium-type tomb became more

Limestone sarcophagus or ossuary at Tiberias in Israel.

popular after the first century.

Especially from Jericho, we have evidence that primary burial in wooden coffins was practiced from the first century B.C. to the beginning of the first century A.D. Most of these burials were not followed by the gathering of the bones or the use of ossuaries after the flesh had decayed. However, there is no evidence for the use of wooden coffins in the Jerusalem area.

The entrances to the burial caves were usually sealed with large stone slabs or with rolling stones. These blocking stones would prevent grave robbers from gaining easy entry into the tomb and would also prevent wild animals scavenging on the burial.

Obviously, such burial chambers had to be prepared well in advance of their intended usage. Their preparation would require months, or even years in the case of elaborate structures. Since the Jewish practice usually dictated the burial of the person within a day of their death, prior preparation of a tomb was mandatory.

Normal burial practice involved washing the body of the deceased; anointing the body with oils, spices, or perfumes; and wrapping the body in linen cloths or strips. Grave goods were often placed in the tomb, including oil lamps to light the tomb, small bottles and juglets to hold the spices and perfumes, and

Jewish Talmud even says that such a phenomenon happened forty years before its destruction. This would mean A.D. 30, the very year that Jesus died!

Furthermore, tombs about Jerusalem were opened as the earth heaved, and many of the saints who had died came forth to appear to many in Jerusalem. Apparently they were raised after Jesus' Resurrection, since He was the "first-fruits" from the dead (1 Cor. 15:23).

Quite naturally the earthquake frightened the people. Probably someone came running with the news about the temple veil. The centurion who commanded the Crucifixion detail, together with the soldiers, said, "This man was God's Son" (Matt. 27:54). It is to be hoped that they came to know Him as the Son of God.

The multitude which had raged about the cross returned to the city, smiting their breasts in great grief. Well they might, for they had participated in the crime of the ages. But far out on the edge of the crowd stood a little band of women, faithful to the end, and their faith would soon be rewarded with assurance.

THE BURIAL OF JESUS

The Jewish rulers were meticulous to the end. Since it was the "Preparation" (John 19:31) or Friday, they requested that the three bodies should not remain on their crosses over the Sabbath. When they wished to hasten death, the soldiers did so by breaking the legs of their crucified victims. If left to die naturally on a cross, they might even linger for days. Therefore, the soldiers broke the legs of the two thieves, but when they came to Jesus, they found that He was already dead. So they did not break His legs, but one of the soldiers ran a spear into His side. These also were fulfillments of Scripture—that none of His bones should be broken and that they should look on Him whom they had pierced (John 19:36–37).

However, an even more significant thing happened. When Jesus' side was pierced, there came out blood and water. In dealing with the physical cause of Jesus' death, a medical doctor says that the spear pierced His left side near the heart. He concluded that since blood and water came out together, this shows that the inner walls of Jesus' heart had ruptured. Thus He actually died, not from the throes of the Crucifixion itself but from a broken heart.

Nevertheless, when it was found that Jesus was dead, Joseph of Arimathea requested of Pilate that he be permitted to bury His body. Had not he, or some other person, claimed the body, it would have been thrown into the Valley of Hinnom. But having received permission, Joseph and Nicodemus prepared Jesus' body for burial and placed it in Joseph's new tomb in which no body had been buried.

even cooking pots, either to hold food or perhaps some of the spices and ointments.

The tomb where Jesus was buried is described as a hewn rock tomb (Mark 15:46; Matt. 27:60) which had never been used previously (Matt. 27:60; John 19:41). The entrance was sealed with a rolling stone (Mark 15:46; Matt. 27:60). The body of Jesus was wrapped in linen cloths filled with spices and ointments (John 19:39–40). Mark implies that the women were coming to the tomb on Sunday morning to complete the burial so hastily conducted before the beginning of Sabbath (Mark 15:47–16:2).

Joel F. Drinkard, Jr., is Professor of Old Testament Interpretation, The Southern Baptist Theological Seminary, Louisville, Kentucky.

Drawing of a typical rock-cut tomb in Israel (first century A.D.).

Where was this tomb located? Tradition says that it was on the site of the Church of the Holy Sepulchre. The same problems exist here as are found in the attempt to locate Calvary. Perhaps the location will never be known. Maybe God does not intend that it should.

One thing is certain. It was located in a garden near Calvary. Adjacent to Gordon's Calvary one may visit Gordon's Tomb. It is today located in a beautiful garden. The writer has visited both the Church of the Holy Sepulchre and Gordon's Tomb. (For what it may be worth, it is of interest to examine these purported burial places of the Savior.)

Joseph of Arimathea was a married man, and he may have had children. If such a person were preparing a tomb would he not prepare for others than himself? The tomb in the Church of Holy Sepulchre provides for only one body, but Gordon's Tomb has places for two bodies on one side and two on the other. Furthermore, one side is unfinished, as though the "new tomb" (John 19:41) had been put to use hurriedly and unexpectedly. Just outside this tomb has been excavated a small chapel of the Byzantine period. Evidently at that time the place was considered as a Christian shrine. To be sure, this is not conclusive evidence that this was considered to be the tomb in which Jesus' body was placed, but it is interesting nevertheless.

After the tomb was closed by rolling a stone across the entrance (Gordon's Tomb has a groove for such a stone), some of the faithful women lingered before it. Theirs was a love that would not let go.

However, there were other feelings concerning this tomb, for the chief priests and Pharisees went to Pilate with a request. They claimed to have

Courtyard of the Church of the Holy Sepulchre.

remembered suddenly that Jesus had said that after three days He would rise from the dead. Had it ever been out of their minds? However, they asked that the tomb be sealed with the Roman seal and that a Roman guard be placed before it. They feared that the disciples might steal the body. Then, according to them, the last "error" would be worse than the first.

Pilate granted their request: "You have a guard of soldiers . . . Go and make it as secure as you know how" (Matt. 27:65). Literally, "Make it sure for yourselves, as you know how." Therefore, they made the sepulchre sure, sealing the stone, with the guard watching them do it, and the guard was left to protect this seal of Roman authority and power. Poor soldiers! Was ever a detail assigned to so hopeless a mission!

The Jewish rulers were careful to protect their place and power, but in so doing they furnished one of the greatest proofs of Jesus' Resurrection from the dead.

"These are My words that I spoke to you while I was still with you, that everything written about Me in the Law of Moses, the Prophets, and the Psalms must be fulfilled." Then He opened their minds to understand the Scriptures.

LUKE 24: 44-45 (HCSB)

The Resurrection and Ascension of Jesus Christ

The tomb and monument that Herod built for his family.

The day on which Jesus Christ died is the blackest day in the history of the world, but the brightest day is that on which He arose from the dead. As someone has said, these days are but one day apart. According to the ancient Jewish method of reckoning time, any part of a day was considered as an entire day. Jesus was buried late on Friday—first day. He remained in the tomb throughout Saturday—second day. He arose from the dead early on Sunday—third day. When Jesus spoke of being in the heart of the earth "three days and three nights" He was speaking within the context of the thought of His day. The grand truth is that even though He was "killed," He was "raised again the third day."

THE DAY THAT CHRIST AROSE

Late on the Sabbath day Mary Magdalene and another Mary visited the tomb of Jesus. It was more than a Sabbath day's journey from Bethany to the tomb. The Sabbath ended at 6:00 P.M. Therefore, after this hour these two

A tomb with a rolling stone at Bethphage.

women and Salome went to buy spices to use in a further anointment of Jesus' body after the hasty burial on Friday. Then before dawn on Sunday these two Marys left Bethany to go to the tomb bent on their errand of love.

In the meantime, even before daylight, there was a great earthquake, as two angels from heaven came down and rolled away the stone. Their brilliant appearance, along with the earth tremor, frightened the soldiers almost to death. Therefore, they fled from the scene in terror.

As the women made their way to the tomb, they wondered who would roll away the stone for them. In their fondest dreams they did not anticipate the scene which awaited them, for when they arrived, they found the tomb opened. Even while they wondered about this, they saw the angels and became

Mary Magdalene

Julie Nall Knowles

Mary Magdalene may have met the Master as He walked through Magdala on the way to Capernaum. Freed from "seven demons" (Luke 8:2), Mary served Jesus from the days of His earliest Galilean ministry. Though "Mary from Magdala" distinguishes her from other Marys in the Gospel accounts, the fishing and ship-building village encouraged some of the speculation concerning Mary's character. Located at the juncture of roads from Nazareth and Tiberias, where the northwest coast of the Sea of Galilee curves inland, Magdala acquired substantial corruption as its trade flourished. Considering Magdala's reputation, medieval writers assumed Mary's afflictions had included prostitution; her identity merged with the unnamed sinful woman of Luke 7:37–50.

Yet in the Gospels Mary Magdalene is nothing but respectable; her remarkable healing (mentioned also in Mark 16:9) and complete conversion surely amazed all who knew her. Evidently she owned enough personal wealth to help support Jesus and

Vaulted Roman building at Tiberias.

His disciples' Galilean ministry (Luke 8:1–3) as well as to follow Jesus to Jerusalem. Besides, it is not very likely that Joanna the wife of Chuza would be traveling about Galilee with a notorious courtesan.

Joanna could not have moved about Galilee with much anonymity because she was recognized as the wife of the steward of Herod Antipas, the Roman tetrarch. Somewhere by the Sea of Galilee, Joanna had been touched by the healing power of Jesus. Chuza's income from supervising Antipas's proper-

Floor mosaic from the church at Tabgha in Galilee, Israel, showing birds amidst water flowers.

frightened. But one of them allayed their fears as he spoke to them: "Don't be afraid, because I know you are looking for Jesus who was crucified. He is not here! For He has been resurrected, just as He said. Come and see the place where He lay" (Matt. 28:5–6). He was lying in the tomb, but now the tomb was empty. The angel reminded them that Jesus had repeatedly told them that this would be so, and then they remembered His words. They went into the tomb and found that Jesus' body was not there.

This naturally raises the question as to why the angels rolled away the stone. Was it to let Jesus out? No mention is made as to the exact moment that He came forth, but the entire tone of the Gospel record is to the effect that Jesus came forth, unassisted, except by the power of God. It would seem, therefore, that the tomb was empty even before the stone was removed. Therefore, the purpose of rolling away the stone was not to let Jesus out but to let the women in. They received proof that the body was not there.

Having shown the women the empty tomb, the angel told them to go quickly and tell the other disciples, and that He would meet them in Galilee. With this the angels departed. Their mission concerning the risen Lord was finished. Thereafter it was up to the disciples to tell the glorious news to all the world.

Accepting this commission the women ran to tell the apostles. Apparently, they found only Peter and John. At first their report seemed to the two apostles as nothing more than the talk of hysterical women, and they did not believe it. Nevertheless, they would investigate the matter, so they ran to the

tomb. John, being the younger, outran Peter and came to the tomb first. However, he hesitated at the entrance, only peeping in and glancing about. But Peter, when he arrived all out of breath, rushed in and looked around. The tomb was empty, all right, but he saw nothing more in the spectacle. Insofar as he was concerned, it could have been a grave robbery or something else. Then John, perhaps emboldened by Peter's example, went into the tomb, and with a discerning eye he saw more. He saw the linen clothes in which Jesus' body had been wound. Evidently they were lying in the form of a body but with the body removed. Then he noticed the napkin which had been on Jesus' head. It was not lying with the linen cloth but was carefully rolled up in a separate place in an orderly fashion. To John this meant that the empty tomb was not due to grave robbers. It indicated to him that Jesus truly had been raised from the dead. Peter went away still wondering, but John went away believing in the bodily Resurrection of Jesus.

THE REPORT OF THE GUARDS

While these events were transpiring, another more sinister one was taking place. Some of the guard detail which had been posted at the tomb, having overcome their panic, had gone to report the supernatural event to the chief priests, but instead of visiting the tomb to check on their story, they called a meeting of the Sanhedrin. The discussion which developed must have been an odd one. Quite naturally the Sadducees would want to deny that a resurrection had taken place. It would seem, however, that the Pharisees would have welcomed the guard's report. Here was proof positive that they were right and the Sadducees were wrong. However, they were partners in crime, and their blind hatred of Jesus united them on the very thing which divided them. Both groups had their "sign from heaven," but they refused to believe it.

Therefore, they came up with what to them was a brilliant idea. They had

A Roman period mosaic of a boat on the sea of Galilee from Magdala.

ty must have been substantial enough for his wife to join "many others, which ministered unto him of their substance" (Luke 8:3, KJV). Joanna witnessed the empty tomb (Luke 24:10). Like Mary Magdalene, she also became one of Jesus' most devoted female disciples.

This article was originally published as "Women in Jesus' Ministry." Julie Nall Knowles is retired professor, English, Troy State University, Phenix City, Alabama.

A tomb at Bethphage with benches along the wall where bodies were placed.

warned Pilate of the possibility of a grave robbery, so now they bribed the soldiers to say that while they slept, the disciples had stolen the body of Jesus. If the soldiers were asleep, how did they know?

Where did the Sanhedrin get the "large money" for the bribe? Most likely it came from the sacred treasury. Probably they had taken the money from it to pay Judas for his act of treachery. Now they did the same to buy a denial of the Resurrection, and if Pilate heard of the failure of his soldiers, they could always use the Corban to seal his lips. They knew from experience that he was not above receiving a bribe, and they were not above giving it.

The soldiers did their job well, for years later, when Matthew wrote his Gospel, the concocted story was still being spread abroad. Nor did it stop with that generation, for more than a century later Justin Martyr mentions that this report was still being spread among the Jews by "chosen men" who had been sent throughout the Roman empire to propagate it.

This event suggests that through the centuries various theories have been proposed as denials of Jesus' Resurrection. Some have suggested that Joseph of Arimathea removed the body to another place, but why would he change his attitude so suddenly? Even had he done so, what about the guard? Another theory says that the women got lost and went to the wrong tomb. Did Peter and John also lose their way? One proposal is that the disciples made up the story to prove the deity of Jesus. However, in the first place, none of them expected Jesus to rise from the dead. In the second place, it would have been psychologically impossible for them to have endured untold suffering in preaching the Gospel, had they known that it was based on a fraud. One strange story is to the effect that Jesus did not really die. He merely fainted, later revived, and came from the tomb. But the soldiers, who were experts in killing, said that He was dead. Had this theory been true, how could Jesus have gotten out of the grave clothes, or even the tomb itself? Furthermore, it is inconceivable that such a risen Savior, broken and emaciated, could have commanded the faith of His followers. Then there is the theory that the entire story is based upon hysteria brought on by grief. Indeed, Peter and John did think, at first, that the women were hysterical, but a visit to the tomb confirmed their story. Were all to whom Jesus appeared victims of such an emotional disturbance? Even more than five hundred at once? On the face of it these theories are preposterous.

Perhaps the most widely held position today, which would discount the Resurrection account, is that the Resurrection does not mean that Jesus' body arose from the grave. It means that His spirit lives on. However, the word *resurrection* means that something or someone who was once dead is alive again. No one claims that Jesus' spirit died. Such a theory robs Jesus of His uniqueness, for all men's spirits live on, and if this be the meaning of Jesus' Resurrection, then why believe in Him? Why not believe in Buddha, Gandhi, or some other great teacher? Jesus has influenced history and the human race as no other person has done. If one denies His unique deity, as proved by His

Resurrection, then there is no reasonable explanation for this.

However, when men have exhausted their theories, they still must explain the empty tomb. All of the Gospels, which are credible historical documents, say that Jesus' body was placed in the tomb on Friday. It was found empty on Sunday, and all of the wisdom of men has never improved on the explanation of that which was given by the angel: "He is not here! For He has been resurrected, just as He said. Come and see the place where He lay."

THE APPEARANCES OF JESUS

For forty days after His Resurrection, Jesus remained bodily on the earth. During that time He made ten appearances to various of His followers, ranging all the way from one person to more than five hundred at one time. The first five occurred on Resurrection Sunday. The others were scattered over the remaining period of His sojourn on earth.

1. The Appearance to Mary Magdalene.

When Peter and John ran to the tomb, they were followed by Mary Magdalene. After these men had left, she stood outside the tomb weeping. Hers were not tears of joy but of sorrow, for, not yet believing that Jesus was risen, she thought that someone had removed His body to a place unknown to her. Finally, she turned to leave the tomb. Before her stood Jesus, but, perhaps because of tear-blinded eyes, she did not recognize Him. He asked her why she was crying. Thinking that He must be the gardener, she said, "Sir, if you've removed Him, tell me where you've put Him, and I will take Him away" (John 20:15). Then Jesus spoke her name. Mary! Recognizing His voice, she said, "Rabboni" or "My Teacher." Evidently she fell at His feet, and clung to Him, for He said, "Don't cling to me." He said this because He had not yet ascended to His Father. This suggests that no longer should she know Him merely by sight, sound, and touch. Their fellowship was to be a spiritual one. His final state of glory had not yet begun. It would do so after His Ascension. Thereafter she would know a more intimate relationship through the Holy Spirit.

Instead of clinging to His person, she was to go and tell His "brothers" that He would soon ascend to His Father and their Father, to His God and their God. This is suggestive of that more intimate fellowship in the Heavenly Father through the Spirit.

So Mary ran to tell them that she had seen the risen Lord. It was His first appearance, and it had been made to a lingering love.

Of interest at this point is that after the Resurrection of Jesus, no enemy of His ever visited the tomb. They were afraid that they might find it to be empty. After Mary Magdalene left the tomb, having seen Jesus, no friend of His is recorded as having returned to it, for they knew that it was empty.

2. The Appearance of Jesus to Other Women.

At some time early on Sunday morning, Jesus appeared to a group of women. Matthew records this as coming immediately after the women had discovered the tomb to be empty, but in harmonizing the four Gospel accounts, this probably came after the appearance to Mary Magdalene. At any rate Jesus met them and greeted them with "All hail." This could be rendered "Rejoice" or as merely "Good morning." Either makes sense. They should rejoice because He was risen. Or Jesus greeted them by saying, "Good morning," on this new day when the Son of righteousness had risen with healing in His wings. With this greeting, Jesus told them to bear the news to His disciples that He would keep His promise to meet them in Galilee.

3. The Appearance on the Road to Emmaus.

Sometime on Sunday afternoon two disciples, Cleopas and perhaps his wife, were walking along the road to Emmaus, a village located about seven miles from Jerusalem. They had been in the city during the last few terrible days, but they had left before the news of the Resurrection had been confirmed. Theirs was a gloomy walk, as they tossed words back and forth about the recent tragedy.

Jesus also was traveling that road, but when He drew near to them, for some reason they failed to recognize Him. As He walked along with them, He inquired as to their conversation. They expressed surprise that He seemed to be unaware of the events of recent days. When He asked what they meant, they recounted the death of Jesus, and one sees the depth of despair in their hearts as they said that they had hoped He should redeem Israel. But now He had been dead three days. True, word had come about the angels and the empty tomb. Some of the disciples had even investigated the report and had found the tomb to be empty, but to their knowledge no one had seen Jesus alive.

They had informed Jesus of recent events. Now He proceeded to teach them about the significance of these events. He gave to them an exposition of the messianic Scriptures which taught that these very things would happen to the Christ. How fortunate they were to hear these things from Christ Himself!

Presently they were in the village, at the door of their home. Jesus acted as though He would go by it, but upon their invitation He entered the home with them. As they sat down to eat, Jesus took a loaf of bread, blessed it, and gave some to them. Suddenly they recognized Him in the breaking of the bread, but just as suddenly He vanished from their sight. Then they noted how their hearts had burned within them as He had opened to them the meaning of the Scriptures.

4. The Appearance to Peter.

These two disciples of Emmaus hastened back to Jerusalem to tell the other believers the glad news, but upon arrival they found that they already knew about the risen Lord. It was now Sunday evening, and the group had assembled behind closed doors to share experiences. Therefore, when these two from Emmaus arrived, they were greeted with the news that Jesus had appeared to Simon Peter.

Peter had known that the tomb was empty, but apparently he did not believe that Jesus had risen until He appeared to him. The despair which had gripped this little group was now turned into exceeding joy, and they must have hung on every word of the disciples of Emmaus as they related in detail their experience with Jesus that day.

5. The Appearance to the Assembled Disciples.

Their greatest experience of the day was yet to come. As the group eagerly drank in every word of this report, suddenly Jesus Himself stood in their midst. Evidently the door was locked because of the disciples' fear of the Jews, but unlike the arrival of the disciples from Emmaus, who must have gained entrance by knocking on the door and giving proof as to their identity, Jesus was suddenly in their presence without having entered through an open door.

Thinking that they were seeing a spirit, naturally the group was terrified. But Jesus allayed their fears by giving to them the customary Jewish greeting: "Peace to you" (John 20:19). To prove to them that He was more than a spirit He showed them His hands, feet, and side. He challenged them to handle Him that they might know He possessed an actual body with flesh and bones. Here, then, was actual proof of the bodily Resurrection of Jesus.

It was too good to be true! But it was true, and as further evidence of it, Jesus ate some broiled fish which they gave to Him upon His request.

In this picture certain things may be learned as to the nature of Jesus' resurrection body. It was not subject to time, space, or density. He could appear and disappear suddenly. He entered the room without opening the door. Yet He could be seen with the natural eye. He could speak and be heard. He was conscious of His surroundings. He had a body of flesh and bones and was subject to the touch of others. He could eat food. And, most interesting of all, His body still bore the wounds inflicted at His Crucifixion.

Whether these things should be pressed as to the resurrection bodies of all believers, they are suggestive nevertheless. Paul said that these bodies will be of such nature as to be suited to the conditions which will exist in the post-resurrection manner of life (1 Cor. 15:38–41).

The disciples were overjoyed. They must have listened intently as Jesus repeated His legacy of peace: "Peace to you" (John 20:21). It was at this time that He gave to them the first of three commissions. As the Father had sent Him into the world, even so was He sending them into the world. His language reveals that He is still sent, but they are to go for Him. Then He breathed upon them saying, "Receive the Holy Spirit. If you forgive the sins of any, they are forgiven them; if you retain the sins of any, they are retained" (John 20:22–23). He gave them a foretaste of Pentecost as He repeated the charge concerning their use of "the keys of the kingdom" which He had given twice before. Then He left them.

One of the apostles, Thomas, was absent from this gladsome event. It is not told where he was. He simply was not there, and what a blessing he missed! When later he heard of Jesus' appearance, he said, "If I don't see the mark of the nails in His hands, put my finger into the mark of the nails, and put my hand into His side, I will never believe!" (John 20:25). For such a stupendous thing he demanded proof, but he was no more a doubter than the others, for he only demanded the proof which they had already received.

6. *The Appearance to the Eleven, including Thomas.*

The next Sunday night the disciples were together again, and this time Thomas was with them. Once again the door was shut. As He had done on the previous Sunday, Jesus suddenly appeared among them. Following the Jewish greeting of peace, immediately He spoke to Thomas: "Put your finger here and observe My hands. Reach out your hand and put it into My side. Don't be an unbeliever but a believer" (John 20:27). It was as though Jesus had heard Thomas' condition of faith, for He challenged him with almost the exact words which Thomas had used.

This was too much for Thomas. Confronted with the evidence of the bodily Resurrection, he forgot his demand. Instead of making the physical examination, he confessed, "My Lord and my God" (John 20:28). He believed through sight, not touch, but he had missed the higher blessedness which would have been his had he believed without seeing.

Nevertheless, one cannot discount the faith of Thomas. Unfortunately, he

has become a byword in modern language which refers to him as "Doubting Thomas," but even time cannot erase the fact that this heroic man, who once was ready to die with Jesus, made the greatest confession of the deity of Jesus that is recorded in the Gospels. No other faith reached the height of his faith as he confessed, "My Lord and my God."

7. The Appearance by the Sea of Galilee.

Jesus had said that He would meet His disciples in Galilee, so after the appearance on the second Sunday night, they evidently returned to Galilee to await the appointed time. As they waited, one evening Peter announced that he was going fishing. This was a natural thing for him to do, since fishing had once been his trade. There were six other disciples, including John, with him, and all seven spent the night in an effort to catch some fish. They caught none.

At daybreak Jesus stood on the beach. However, because the disciples were some distance from shore, with possibly a morning fog hovering about, they did not recognize Jesus. He called to ask if they had any meat, and when they answered in the negative, He told them to cast their net on the right side of the ship. When they did, they caught so many fish that they were unable to draw them in.

Remembering a similar occasion John told Peter that the one on the shore was the Lord. Peter was stripped for work, but hastily donning a coat, he jumped into the water and swam ashore. The others brought in the boat, dragging the filled net behind them.

According to the Sinai manuscript, Emmaus (Imwas) is thought to be the site of the house of Cleopas. Ruins of a Byzantine church stand on the site of the house. Here Jesus broke bread with two of the disciples following His resurrection. Profound sorrow was turned to joy when, in blessing the loaves, they recognized Jesus.

When they got to shore, they found that Jesus had already built a fire, had cooked a fish, and had bread with which to eat the fish. So in the early morning the seven disciples ate breakfast together. It is not stated that Jesus ate with them, but the assumption is that He did.

After they had eaten, Jesus spoke to Simon Peter: "Simon, son of John, do you love Me more than these?" (John 21:15). "These" could refer either to the boat, net and fish, or to the other six disciples. In all likelihood it is the latter. Peter had boasted that his devotion to Jesus exceeded that of all others, but his subsequent denials proved how utterly wrong he had been. Now Jesus gently reminds him of that fact. He asked him if he now feels that his love is greater than that of the others.

Peter ignored the "more than these" as he replied, "Yes, Lord . . . You know that I love You." Jesus said, "Feed My lambs." A second time Jesus asked, "Simon, son of John, do you love Me?" Not "more than these," but do you love Me? Again Peter gave the same reply. Jesus said, "Shepherd my sheep." A third time Jesus asked, "Simon, son of John, do you love Me?" Peter was grieved because Jesus asked him the third time if he loved Him, but he replied, "Lord, You know everything! You know that I love You."

Why did Jesus' third question grieve Peter? It could have been because His questions matched in number the denials of Peter, but the original language reveals a deeper reason for his grief. In this interplay of questions and answers, two different words are used for "love." The one expresses a superior love. It is akin to the word which John used when he said, "God is love" (1 John 4:8). The other word for "love" expresses the love as of a friend. In the first two questions Jesus used the verb for this superior love, but Peter answered with the verb meaning love as of a friend. In His third question Jesus changed to the verb which Peter had been using. When he failed to rise to the level of love for which Jesus asked, then Jesus came down to Peter's level. He did not ask if he loved Him with this God-kind-of-love but did he even love Him as a friend. Peter, then, was grieved, not because of the three questions but because of his failure. It certainly taught him a lesson in humility.

Having taught this lesson, Jesus then told Peter that the time would come when, in his old age, he would be taken by another where he did not want to go. John, writing long after Peter's death, interpreted this to mean the manner of death which Peter would die. Tradition says that he was crucified head downward at his own request. His Lord had been crucified upright, and since he had denied Him, Peter said that he did not deserve to die in the same manner as did Jesus. However, this is only a tradition.

Peter had been humbled, but it did not lessen his curiosity. Therefore, looking at John, he asked Jesus what would happen to him. In effect, Jesus told him that this should not be his concern. If He willed that John should live even until His return, "What is that to you? . . . follow Me" (John 21:22).

8. *The Appearance to More Than Five Hundred.*

This probably was the appearance mentioned by Paul (1 Cor. 15:6). At the time he wrote, many of these people still were alive. In a sense Paul was saying that if anyone wanted proof as to the bodily Resurrection of Jesus, eyewitnesses were still available to avow the truth.

This was the appearance to which Jesus referred even before His death, and of which the angel reminded the women following the Resurrection. It occurred on a specified mountain in Galilee. Possibly as the Eleven, and others who had seen Jesus alive in Jerusalem, journeyed to the appointed place, they had been joined by other disciples from Galilee, so that when Jesus appeared to them "they worshiped, but some doubted" (Matt. 28:17). This latter group would be those who saw Jesus for the first time after His Resurrection. It was simply too good to be true!

Then Jesus spoke to them: "All authority has been given to Me in heaven and on earth. Go, therefore, and make disciples of all nations, baptizing them in the name of the Father and of the Son and of the Holy Spirit, teaching them to observe everything I have commanded you. And remember, I am with you always, to the end of the age" (Matt. 28:18–20).

The word *authority* means "out of being." So out of His being as the crucified, resurrected, and living Lord, Jesus gave this Great Commission. It was given not to the apostles only but to all who believe on Him. The commission was not to "go." This word is a participle meaning "as you are going." He assumed that they would go to declare the blessed news. The only imperative form in these verses is "make disciples." This is Jesus' command, and by a further series of participles, He told them what to do. As they discipled all nations, they were to follow this by baptizing and teaching them. "To observe" means to preserve and pass on to others His commandments, and in the doing of it they were assured of His presence until the consummation of the age.

9. The Appearance to James.

This little gem is preserved only by Paul (1 Cor. 15:7), but it speaks volumes. James was a half brother of Jesus. Along with his other brothers and sisters, he did not believe that Jesus was the Christ. There is evidence in the Gospels that Jesus' mission was an embarrassment to the half brothers and sisters and that this may even have caused a strained relationship to exist between Mary and these children. These things all enter into the reason for Jesus' special appearance to James.

That James thereafter did believe in Jesus is quite evident. Afterward he became a leader of the Church in Jerusalem. Furthermore, he wrote one of the books of the New Testament, and his testimony about this appearance must have led his other brothers and sisters to share his faith in Jesus, for another brother, Jude, also wrote one of the New Testament epistles. But neither James nor Jude in their epistles mention their family relationship to Jesus. They call themselves a "servant" or "bond slave" of Jesus Christ. Through faith in Him they had found that higher relationship of which He had spoken.

10. The Last Appearance in Jerusalem.

At the end of forty days following the Passover, Jesus appeared to His disciples who had returned to Jerusalem. This probably occurred in the Upper Room where Jesus had instituted the Lord's Supper. In this appearance He evidently spent quite some time with them, for He opened their minds concerning the Old Testament Scriptures as they related to the redemptive work of Christ, including both His death and His Resurrection. Now this gospel of redemption is to be preached unto all nations, beginning from Jerusalem. The Eleven had seen these things, and, therefore, were to share their knowledge and experience with others.

Then Jesus promised to send the Holy Spirit upon them, even as the Father had promised. In turn, they were to wait in Jerusalem "until you are empowered from on high" (Luke 24:49). Actually, Jesus said, "Until you get yourselves clothed with power from on high." The Father will send the Holy Spirit unto them at Pentecost, but they must surrender to His power in order that He may do His work through them. The intervening ten days until the Day of Pentecost must have been days of earnest self-examination on the part of this little group and other fellow believers, because when the Holy Spirit did come in mighty power, they were instruments of God surrendered to His will.

Once again Jesus and the Eleven left the Upper Room to walk through the streets of Jerusalem. Apparently they went unnoticed by the people of the city, who long since had put the unpleasantness of forty days ago behind them. The little group went past the temple area, leaving the city by the eastern gate, but this time they went on by the Garden of Gethsemane. They continued on up the Mount of Olives, probably following the route which Jesus had taken into the city on His royal entry.

In spite of all that had happened, the disciples were still looking for an earthly kingdom, because, as they walked along, they asked Jesus if He would at this time restore the kingdom to Israel. He told them that they should not be concerned to know about this. This was a matter which the Heavenly Father had appointed in His own authority. In the meantime, they had another responsibility, that of being used to bring the kingdom into the hearts of men. He repeated the promise about the Holy Spirit's coming upon them in power: "And ye shall be witnesses unto me both in Jerusalem, and in all Judea, and in Samaria, and unto the uttermost part of the earth" (Acts 1:8).

By this time they had arrived at a place just across from Bethany. There

Sunrise on the Sea of Galilee at Tiberias. Here Jesus appeared to some of the disciples who had been fishing all night. The Risen Lord was preparing breakfast for them.

Jesus lifted His hands and pronounced a final benediction upon His disciples. Even as He was blessing them, He began to ascend into heaven. With eager and longing eyes they followed Him until a cloud obscured their vision, and they could see Him no longer. But their eyes continued to focus on the spot where they had last seen Him.

As they stood with fixed gaze into the heavens, two angels (were they the ones at the empty tomb?) appeared, standing beside them. They said, "Ye men of Galilee, why stand ye gazing up into heaven? This same Jesus which is taken up from you into heaven, shall so come in like manner as ye have seen him go into heaven" (Acts 1:11). Implied in these words is the truth that their responsibility was not merely to stand gazing into the heavens where the Lord had gone and whence He will return. They were to be busy about the task of spreading the glad tidings of salvation to all men, and through the age they and their successors in the faith are to continue to do so until they see the Lord in the air, coming in the clouds with the angelic hosts, in great power and glory, at the consummation of the age. "Even so, come, Lord Jesus" (Rev. 22:20).

THE TRIUMPHAL ENTRY

Even as the disciples gazed into the heavens, other eyes were looking over the ramparts of glory to welcome the Conqueror home. Heaven's streets rang with shouts of joy as the hosts of heaven viewed His triumphal entry.

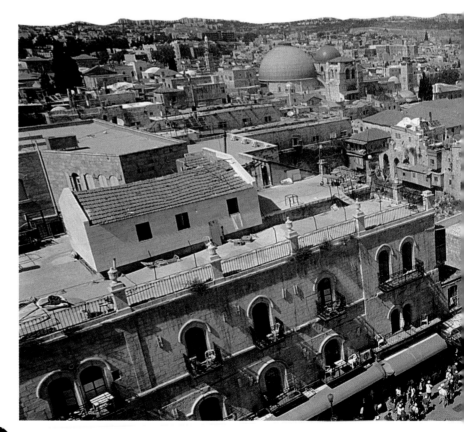

Panoramas of Jerusalem, the city where Jesus last appeared to His disciples.

Paul describes it when he says, "When he ascended up on high, he led captivity captive, and gave gifts unto men" (Eph. 4:8). In ancient times a returning conqueror rode through the streets of his capital city amid the shouts of acclaim from the populace. As evidence of the completeness of his victory, behind his chariot in chains walked notable prisoners, maybe even a defeated king, and the Conqueror tossed gifts to his rejoicing people.

Through the streets of heaven rode the triumphant Jesus. In chains behind His chariot trudged sin and death. The procession proceeded up to the throne of God, before whom the Son placed the evidence of His redemptive work as an abiding intercession for the souls of men. Then He sat down on the right hand of God, where He sits through the ages, expecting, until His enemies shall become the footstool of His feet.

What about the gifts given by the conquering Christ?—"and gave gifts to men." He gave them not to the heavenly hosts, but "to men." Men who were yet on earth waiting to hear the gospel of redemption, of justification, sanctification, and glorification—complete salvation, both here and hereafter. What were these gifts?—"And he gave some, apostles; and some, prophets; and some, evangelists; and some, pastors and teachers; For the perfecting of the saints, for the work of the ministry, for the edifying [building up] of the body of Christ; Till we all come in [into] the unity of the faith, and of the knowledge of the Son of God, unto a perfect [mature] man, unto the measure of the

Triumph scene of Marcus Aurelius. Paul had this kind of event in mind when he wrote of Jesus, "When he ascended up on high, he led captivity captive, and gave gifts to men (Eph. 4:8).

stature of the fulness of Christ: That we henceforth be no more children, tossed to and fro, and carried about with every wind of doctrine, by the sleight of men, and cunning craftiness, whereby they lie in wait to deceive; But speaking the truth in love, may grow up into him in all things, which is the head, even Christ" (Eph. 4:11–15).

Therefore, "Let this mind be in you, which was also in Christ Jesus: Who, being in the form of God, thought it not robbery to be equal with God: But made himself of no reputation, and took upon him the form of a servant, and was made in the likeness of men: And being found in fashion as a man, he humbled himself, and became obedient unto death, even the death of the cross. Wherefore God hath also highly exalted him, and given him a name which is above every name: That at the name of Jesus every knee should bow, of things in heaven, and things in earth, and things under the earth; And that every tongue should confess that Jesus Christ is Lord, to the glory of God the Father" (Phil. 2:5–11).

Topical Index

Scripture Index

Photo & Art Credits
(All Rights Reserved)

Photographers

Corel: 28, bottom; 51, top left; 62; 86, top; 97; 187, left; 227; 230, top; 230, bottom.

Illustrator Photos/James McLemore: 6, bottom; 19 (IAM); 28, top left; 33; 72, top left; 77; 78, top left; 84, bottom left; 86; 89; 90, bottom right; 106-107; 116; 119; 121; 122, top left (NGM); 123, top; 126; 129; 130, top; 135; 137, bottom; 139; 143; 145; 148; 153, left; 160-161; 162-163; 178, top; 185; 189; 190; 198; 200; 203; 206; 223; 236; 248-249; 255; 270-271; 274; 278, bottom right; 280; 282; 283; 287; 288; 289, top right.

Illustrator Photos/David Rogers: 24; 32; 35 (WRN); 46, top left (JMN); 102; top left (TAM); 125; 178, bottom right; 182 (MMA); 191 (JMN); 194 (MPM); 195 (MPM); 242 (JAC); 232 (JAC); 238, bottom (JAC); 240 (TLP); 242 (JAC); 243 (JAC); 244 (JAC); 256 (MPM); 278; top left.

Illustrator Photos/Bob Schatz: 4; 5; 6, center; 7; 11, top left; 11, bottom; 12; 14; 20; 26, top left; 26, bottom; 27; 32; 34; 36; 37; 38; 39; 40; 45 (MSS); 47 (GRM); 50, top left; 51, center; 60-61; 64; 65; 66-67; 70; 72, center; 72, bottom left; 76, bottom; 78, bottom left; 79 (AMP); 81; 83; 84; top right; 85; 87; 90; bottom left; 91; 93; top 95; bottom 95; 96 (AMU); 98 (HAM); 99, top (NMD); 99, bottom (HAM);100; 102-103; 103; top right; 105; 108; 109; 110-111; 117; 118 (NGM); 122; 130 (AMP); 131; 134, top; 134, bottom; 136; 137, top right; 138; 142; 149; 150; 151; 152;153, right; 156; 158, top; 158, bottom; 159, bottom (IAM); 170; 173; 174 (GRM); 175; 188; 209; 211; 212; 213; 217; 221; 231(CME); 233; 235 (JAM); 237; 238, top (HAM); 239 (HMI); 250; 258, bottom left; 264; 267; 268; 279 (CMC); 285; 286; 289, bottom; 295-295; 298-299; 300-301; 302 (CMR).

Illustrator Photos/Ken Touchton: 6, top left; 10 (VMR); 13 (VMR); 25; 29; 30; 46, bottom right (MRC); 50; 52; 53; 54; 55, top center; 55, bottom left; 56, bottom; 63; 101; 123; bottom, 159; top, 164; 177, right; 177, bottom (IMJ); 180; 186; 187, right; 199, top; 199, bottom; 201; 204; 205; 206, center; 207; 219; 220 (RMJ); 222 (KAM); 229; 241; 257; 258, top right; 263; 277.

Illustrators

Charles Cox: 273.
Bill Latta: 157; 172; 273; 281.

Museum Abbreviations

AMP = Archaeological Museum at Pella, Greece
AMU = Archaeological Museum of Um Qeis at Gadara
CMC = Coptic Museum, Cairo, Egypt
CME = Cairo Museum, Egypt
CMR = Capitoline Museum, Rome
GRM = Greco-Roman Museum, Alexandria, Egypt
HAM = Hatay Archaeological Museum, Turkey
HMI = Hazor Museum, Israel
IAM = Istanbul Archaeological Museum
IMJ = Israel Museum, Jerusalem
JAC = Joseph A. Callaway Archaeological Museum, The Southern Baptist Theological Seminary, Louisville, Kentucy
JAM = Jordan Archaeological Museum, Amman, Jordan
JMN = Jewish Museum, New York
KAM = Konya Archaeological Museum, Turkey
MMA = Metropolitan Museum of Art, New York
MPM = Milwaukee Public Museum, Milwaukee, Wisconsin
MRC = Museum of Roman Civilization, Rome
MSS = Museum of Sweda, Syria
NGM = Nof Ginnosar Museum, Israel
NMD = National Museum of Damascus, Syria
RMJ = Rockefeller Museum, Jersulam
TAM = The Archaeological Museum, Ankara, Turkey
TLP = The Louvre, Paris, France
VMR = Vatican Museum, Rome
WRN = William Rockwell Nelson Gallery of Art, Kansas City, Missouri